T0382991

THE RIGHT TO REPAIR

In recent decades, companies around the world have deployed an arsenal of tools – including IP law, hardware design, software restrictions, pricing strategies, and marketing messages – to prevent consumers from fixing the things they own. While this strategy has enriched companies almost beyond measure, it has taken billions of dollars out of the pockets of consumers and imposed massive environmental costs on the planet. In *The Right to Repair*, Aaron Perzanowski analyzes the history of repair to show how we've arrived at this moment, when a battle over repair is being waged – largely unnoticed – in courtrooms, legislatures, and administrative agencies. With deft, lucid prose, Perzanowski explains the opaque and complex legal landscape that surrounds the right to repair and shows readers how to fight back.

Aaron Perzanowski is an expert on ownership in the digital economy and the conflict between intellectual and personal property rights. His research has appeared in leading academic journals. He's the co-author of *The End of Ownership* (2016) with Jason Schultz, and the co-editor of *Creativity Without Law* (2017) with Kate Darling.

MORE PRAISE FOR *THE RIGHT TO REPAIR*

"Why can't we just fix our stuff? Perzanowski systematically unmasks the obsolescence in our lives, and charts a path to reclaiming ownership before it's lost forever."

Kyle Wiens, iFixit CEO

"A readable and comprehensive book on a timely issue that affects everyone. Perzanowski shows how the 'right to repair' is really a battle over control of the devices we own and use."

Bruce Schneier, author of *Click Here to Kill Everybody: Security and Survival in a Hyperconnected World*

"A riveting account of the ways developers inhibit or thwart the ability of consumers to fix devices, and how the law reinforces such restrictions. The nascent right to repair social movement is gaining momentum. To understand why, read this book!"

Pamela Samuelson, Richard M. Sherman Distinguished Professor of Law, UC Berkeley School of Law

The Right to Repair

Reclaiming the Things We Own

AARON PERZANOWSKI

Case Western Reserve University, Ohio

CAMBRIDGE
UNIVERSITY PRESS

CAMBRIDGE
UNIVERSITY PRESS

University Printing House, Cambridge CB2 8BS, United Kingdom

One Liberty Plaza, 20th Floor, New York, NY 10006, USA

477 Williamstown Road, Port Melbourne, VIC 3207, Australia

314–321, 3rd Floor, Plot 3, Splendor Forum, Jasola District Centre,
New Delhi – 110025, India

103 Penang Road, #05–06/07, Visioncrest Commercial, Singapore 238467

Cambridge University Press is part of the University of Cambridge.

It furthers the University's mission by disseminating knowledge in the pursuit of
education, learning, and research at the highest international levels of excellence.

www.cambridge.org
Information on this title: www.cambridge.org/9781108837651
DOI: 10.1017/9781108946926

First published 2022

Printed in the United Kingdom by TJ Books Limited, Padstow Cornwall

A catalogue record for this publication is available from the British Library.

ISBN 978-1-108-83765-1 Hardback

CONTENTS

Acknowledgments   *page* vi
List of Figures   vii

1 INTRODUCTION   1

2 WHY REPAIR MATTERS   14

3 THE HISTORY OF REPAIR   49

4 BREAKING REPAIR   72

5 REPAIR AND INTELLECTUAL PROPERTY   110

6 REPAIR AND COMPETITION   167

7 REPAIR AND CONSUMER PROTECTION   199

8 REBUILDING REPAIR   223

EPILOGUE   263

Notes   269
Index   349

ACKNOWLEDGMENTS

I'm grateful to the able and diligent team of research assistants who contributed to this project: Ellen Boyd, Francesca LaMontagne, Meritt Salathe, and Katelyn Schwartz. I also owe my sincere thanks to Kathleen Burke, MC Forelle, Shubha Ghosh, Daniel Hanley, Chris Jay Hoofnagle, Mike Madison, Nathan Proctor, Anthony Rosborough, and Sahra Svensson, all of whom brought their considerable expertise to bear on earlier drafts of this book.

FIGURES

1 Degree of consumer agreement with right to repair   *page* 201
2 Degree of consumer surprise by repair restrictions   202
3 Willingness to purchase devices with repair restrictions   203
4 Willingness to pay for devices with repair restrictions   204
5 An example of France's mandatory reparability labeling   240

1 INTRODUCTION

In 1966, Irv Gordon bought a new Volvo P1800 from a showroom in Huntington, New York. It cost him about $4,000. Just shy of fifty years later, outside of Girdwood, Alaska, Irv logged his three-millionth mile behind the wheel of that car. By the time he died at the age of seventy-seven in 2018, he'd racked up another quarter of a million miles on its odometer. Over the years, Irv's Volvo underwent some major repairs. The engine was rebuilt twice, and the car required extensive body work after an unfortunate incident with a car hauler. But Irv preferred to do most of the work himself – changing the oil, replacing the brakes, and other necessary repairs. Irv's approach was simple. He immediately replaced broken parts. In his words, "If it didn't start, I'd find out why . . . and fix it."[1]

As impressive as Irv's Volvo is, the world's oldest operating automobile was built in 1884 by Jules-Albert de Dion.[2] Dubbed "La Marquise," the steam-powered vehicle sacrificed various brass and copper fittings to scrap drives during World War I. It sat inoperable for decades until it was purchased by Tim Moore in 1987. Moore reverse engineered the missing parts, manufactured replacements, and had La Marquise running again within a year.[3] In 2011, the vehicle sold for $4.6 million at auction.

In terms of longevity, the clock at Salisbury Cathedral has La Marquise beat by about 500 years. Originally built in 1386, it was replaced by a newer model in 1884, the same year La Marquise was built – not a bad run by any estimation. After decades of rusting in obscurity, the original clock was rediscovered by horologist T.R. Robinson. In 1956, it was disassembled and shipped to clock makers, the Smith of Derby Group, who replaced various parts, fashioned others, and restored components to their original positions. Eventually, they got the clock back in working order, and it continues to keep time today.[4]

These examples may seem extreme. But if you want to get the most from the things you own, repair is essential. That's true not only of Irv's Volvo and the Salisbury Cathedral clock, but your smartphone and kitchen appliances as well. It's true for farmers who face software restrictions and legal threats when they try to repair their tractors to harvest their crops.[5] It's true for US military personnel, who are under orders not to repair vehicles, generators, and other equipment for fear of voiding product warranties – instead, shipping equipment thousands of miles for repair or awaiting unreliable service from private contractors.[6] And as the COVID-19 pandemic revealed, it's also true for hospitals confronting shortages of replacement parts, strict controls on repair manuals, and software locks that frustrate the repair of ventilators and other life-saving equipment.[7]

Without the freedom to repair, the things we own will fail sooner, work less effectively, and cost us more money. Imagine you drop your smartphone. Maybe you don't have to imagine. In the United States alone, tens of millions of us break our smartphone screens each year. You might choose to live with a busted screen, putting up with fractured images and risking the occasional sliced fingertip. If not, you are left with two choices – repair it or replace it.

A new screen for an iPhone will cost you as little as $50 from a third-party seller. Screens for some older models cost even less. But replacing your screen requires tools, skills, and confidence you might lack. If you take your phone to Apple, the company will charge you around $300 for this fairly simple repair. For that price, you might wonder, why not just buy a new phone? Apple agrees. The company will happily trade your broken phone for a discount on a new one, further closing the price gap between repairing and replacing. Apple's preference for replacement over repair, it should come as no surprise, is driven by the company's bottom line. The iPhone X cost Apple about $350 to make, but sold for $999. That's a profit margin of roughly 64 percent. And Apple shareholders have come to expect blockbuster sales. The company sold 218 million phones in 2018 alone, generating over $140 billion in revenue. But when it comes to its repair services, Apple claims that it loses money.[8] In fact, CEO Tim Cook blamed the popularity of the company's own battery replacement program for declining iPhone sales in a letter to investors.[9]

So instead of repairing your old phone, you buy a new one. Apple keeps its shareholders happy, and you get a shiny new device that's a few millimeters thinner. What's so bad about that? Aside from spending several hundred dollars you could have otherwise saved, the decision to replace rather than repair has far-reaching environmental consequences. In 2018 alone, 1.5 billion mobile phones were manufactured worldwide, contributing to the more than 50 million metric tons of electronic waste produced that year. Electronics currently account for 70 percent of the toxic waste in US landfills, a figure that continues to rise. That electronic waste includes lithium, mercury, and lead – chemicals that endanger our water supplies and threaten human health. But it's not just the end of a product's life that should concern us. Extracting and refining raw materials produces pollution, as does manufacturing and shipping products across the globe. Those environmental harms are a classic example of what economists call negative externalities – costs that the parties to a transaction don't have to take into account. Instead, the consequences are passed on to our neighbors and future generations who will have to deal with the fallout.

Beyond environmental costs, the COVID-19 pandemic dramatically highlighted the immediate consequences of repair on human welfare. As hospitals across the globe faced shortages of life-saving ventilators, and manufacturers scrambled to ramp up production, the ability to maintain and repair existing equipment emerged as a pressing problem. Authorized repair, which often requires shipping devices back to the manufacturer, can leave hospitals without critical equipment for days or even weeks. In other instances, manufacturers withheld needed repair manuals or failed to supply replacement parts, imperiling patients in a period of prolonged crisis.[10] When a hospital in Chiari, Italy, couldn't secure valves for its ventilators from the manufacturer, local volunteers designed and 3D-printed 100 replacements that cost $1 a piece. The volunteers managed this feat in just two days, with no help from the manufacturer, which refused to share design specifications.[11] Concerns over repair delays and expense are nothing new in the medical sector, but this crisis revealed just how fragile centralized repair systems can be.

As schools across the world shifted to remote instruction during the pandemic, demand for laptops and tablets outstripped supply.[12] In the United States alone, shortages and delays meant millions of students lacked the devices they needed to fully participate in online learning. Predictably, low-income families were hardest hit.[13] Four siblings sharing a single iPad are at a significant disadvantage in a Zoom-dependent curriculum, and setbacks in elementary education can have long lasting effects. In response to this educational crisis, repair shops, nonprofit organizations, and local volunteers tried to fill the gap with refurbished devices. And while those efforts had some impact, they were too often stymied by a lack of access to information, parts, and software. School districts and community organizations were forced to scrap older devices rather than fix them, adding to their spiraling costs and exacerbating the harm to students.[14]

If consumers were more aware of these environmental and human costs, some may be more likely to repair a damaged device, despite the inconvenience. But for some products, repair simply isn't an option. Take Apple's AirPod wireless headphones. They retail for $159 for the basic version and $249 for the Pro model. The company sold 35 million pairs in 2018, and nearly 60 million in 2019. Intended for commuters, the tiny, wireless devices are easily lost. The combination of their price, likelihood of being misplaced, and the unmistakable Apple design aesthetic have transformed the AirPod into a symbol of conspicuous, disposable consumption.[15] Even if you manage to avoid losing them, the lifespan of AirPods is short by design. AirPods fail to live up to their advertised five-hour playback time after as little as eighteen months. At that point, your $249 headphones may work for only fifteen minutes on a full charge. All lithium-ion batteries degrade over time, but tiny batteries like those in the AirPods seem particularly prone to depletion.

For many products, replacing dead batteries is trivial. For our flashlights and remote controls, it's as simple as popping in a few fresh AAs. For many laptops and smartphones, it may require a few specialized tools or a trip to a local repair shop, but your battery can be swapped out in a matter of minutes. Not so for your AirPods. Their design makes battery replacement all but impossible. AirPods have no screws. They are held together by glue and solder. Accessing the battery, as the *Washington Post*'s Geoffrey Fowler discovered, requires a special vibrating knife to cut through the plastic shell. The procedure is more harrowing since the battery, about the thickness of a spaghetti noodle, is prone to combustion if punctured. But even assuming you can dislodge it safely, your AirPods will be irretrievably damaged in the process.[16]

Apple's designers and engineers are among the most talented in the world. They certainly could have designed headphones that incorporated replaceable batteries. And as a general rule, engineers want to build high-quality, lasting products as a matter of professional pride. Nonetheless, Apple chose to market headphones that were neither durable nor recyclable. The question is why?

It's worth noting that the booming market for wireless earbuds is driven by an earlier design decision by Apple – the removal of the standard headphone jack from the iPhone.[17] Like the entombed batteries in AirPods, that decision reflects certain philosophies. Apple's products are sleek, minimal, and impossibly thin, an aesthetic that has implications for repair regardless of its ultimate design justification. Rather than an abundance of choice and customization, Apple offers a limited, highly curated selection. The company's obsession with controlling the user experience, as sales figures make clear, has paid off time and again. But these design choices also embody Apple's attitude about repair. From the design of its products, to the price of its repair services, to its trade-in program, the message is clear: replace, don't repair.

That's especially true when it comes to AirPods. What do you do with your $249 headphones once they can't hold a charge? Throwing them out should be unthinkable. Their plastic shells will survive for at least a thousand years in a landfill. And their combustible batteries could start fires in trash compactors.[18] Alternatively, Apple offers "battery service" for AirPods. For $49 per earbud, and an additional $49 for their charging case, Apple will service your aging headphones. That's $147 to service a $159 product. As the price tag for AirPod "battery service" suggests, it isn't actually service at all. Since even Apple can't repair AirPods, it simply replaces your old headphones with new ones.[19] The depleted AirPods are then shipped to a handful of recycling centers that partner with Apple, where cobalt and other valuable materials are carefully extracted from the spent headphones. But given their tiny size, the laborious process of dissecting AirPods costs more than those materials are worth.[20] So Apple has been forced to sweeten the deal, paying recyclers extra to make processing AirPods economically viable. Understandably, the company offers consumers no financial incentive to trade in used AirPods. Since Apple doesn't disclose how many AirPods it has recycled, it is difficult to know how many have made their way into landfills.

AirPods are a textbook example of product design that is at best indifferent and, more likely, antagonistic to repair. But concerns about reparability are not limited to physical components. Today, an increasing number of consumer goods incorporate some measure of "smart" technology. These devices depend on a combination of embedded software code and network connectivity for their basic functionality. They range from smart speakers and home-security systems to comically mundane items like hairbrushes, saltshakers, dental floss, and trash cans. The proliferation of connected devices that make up the Internet of Things presents an assortment of risks for consumers, from privacy and security to harassment and physical injury.[21] But smart devices also undermine repair by removing functionality from your device and outsourcing it to a remote server.

Take Jibo, the social robot. Released in 2017, Jibo was a foot-tall plastic robot with an emotive face and sensors that responded to physical interaction. It sold for $900 and could dance, talk, and play games with its owners. When the company that built Jibo failed, it powered down its servers. Since most of Jibo's functionality depended on those distant servers rather than the device's on-board computer, Jibo suffered from "digital dementia." The robot went limp, its dimly lit screen blank. And its head and torso "twist[ed] freely, like a lifeless body."[22] Cruelly, Jibo was forced to deliver a parting message to its owners: "While it's not great news, the servers out there that let me do what I do are going to be turned off soon. I want to say I've really enjoyed our time together. Thank you very, very much for having me around. Maybe someday, when robots are way more advanced than today, and everyone has them in their homes, you can tell yours that I said hello."

Jibo illustrates the risks to repair posed by the Internet of Things. The robot's physical components could be repaired. If its screen was on the fritz, it could be replaced. If a sensor wasn't working properly, it could be recalibrated. Even the embedded software in the device could be updated and patched. But most of Jibo's features were not housed in its plastic shell. Instead, they resided on a server that Jibo owners could not access, let alone repair. Jibo's basic operation, as purchasers eventually learned, depended on hardware and software over which they had no control. The tether connecting devices to remote servers in unknown locations is a core, if not defining, feature of smart devices. On a fundamental level, the Internet of Things as currently constructed is incompatible with repair.

In some cases, that incompatibility results in a loss of functionality. The starkest illustration is "bricking" – the post-sale, remote disabling of a device.[23] To take one example, in 2016 Google-owned Nest announced it would push an involuntary software update to its $300 Revolv home automation hubs, rendering them entirely inoperable.[24] Despite selling the devices with the promise of a "lifetime subscription," the company announced that after May 15, "The Revolv app won't open and the hub won't work."[25] In others cases, sellers selectively eliminate functionality, like when Best Buy remotely killed the smart features of its Insignia line of refrigerators, electrical plugs, light switches, and security cameras in the homes of its customers.[26]

In the past, consumers could confidently draw a clear line between products and services. Once you purchased a television, for instance, the manufacturer had little say over how you used it. That's quite different from a service, like a cable subscription. There, the provider can add or subtract channels, change the price, or cancel the service altogether. Today the line between product and service is more of a blurry smudge. Our TVs, cars, and appliances are bundled with deeply intertwined software and data services that are central to their functionality. As a result, consumer expectations about repair are increasingly likely to conflict with the reality of the Internet of Things.

Putting aside product design, there are other powerful tools companies use to limit repair. We've already seen how economics can dissuade consumers through unreasonably high repair fees and trade-in programs that incentivize replacement. Less appreciated is the role law – in particular, intellectual property (IP) law – plays in restricting repair. Device makers use patents and trademarks to limit the availability of replacement parts. They claim schematics and other repair information as trade secrets. And they leverage copyright to lock down the software tools necessary to diagnose and repair today's devices.

The outsized influence of intellectual property law on repair reflects the ubiquity of IP in the modern marketplace. The rounded corners of the iPhone are patented, as are its app icons.[27] Internal components you will likely never see, like cables and batteries, are emblazoned with Apple's trademarked logo.[28] And of course, the software that makes the iPhone work is protected by copyright. The same is true for your car, from the patented design of your headlight to the software code that controls the transmission. The devices we rely on every day are suffused with overlapping intellectual property rights.

If anyone could escape the reality of IP-protected smart devices, you might think it would be farmers. We imagine farmers living off the land in rural communities, less dependent on modern technology and more rooted in traditions and practices that pre-date the digital era. But this image of farm life is out of step with reality. Farming today relies on a range of technologies, from moisture sensors and drones to genetically modified crops and patented biological pest controls. Even that classic symbol of rural America, the John Deere tractor, has been transformed into a complex, software-dependent piece of digital technology.

Modern John Deere tractors can cost as much as $800,000. No longer purely mechanical devices, they depend on multiple electronic control units (ECUs) to operate everything from the engine to the power seat. These embedded computers run software code essential to the operation and repair of the tractor. By controlling access to that code, John Deere can prevent independent diagnosis and repair. Without enlisting a John Deere technician, the tractor's software won't even recognize replacement parts.[29] That level of control forces farmers to rely on authorized John Deere dealers for service, rather than doing it themselves or turning to local Mom and Pop repair shops.

Copyright law has been central to Deere's strategy to shut competitors out of the lucrative market for farm-equipment repair. Since the software code on ECUs is protected by copyright, Deere believes it can legally prevent farmers and repair shops from accessing that code. The Digital Millennium Copyright Act (DMCA) makes it unlawful to remove or bypass digital locks that restrict access to copyrighted materials. The law was meant to help protect movies, video games, and other works from online copyright infringement. But under Deere's theory, it applies with equal force to its tractors.

After a years-long battle, farmers convinced the US Copyright Office to grant them a temporary, three-year exemption from the DMCA in 2015.[30] It insulated farmers from liability for accessing software in order to diagnose, repair, or modify their tractors. The exemption was renewed for another three years in 2018, and the Copyright Office will consider it again in 2021.[31] Nonetheless, the practical hurdles to unlocking Deere's code and remaining sources of legal risk limit the impact of the exemption. As a result, many farmers rely on unlicensed copies of Deere software downloaded from Ukrainian hackers just to keep their tractors running.[32] And demand for decades-old, pre-digital Deere tractors has exploded. At a recent auction, a 1989 model sold for over $40,000.[33]

As these examples illustrate, companies like Apple and John Deere have devised strategies that leverage product design, economics, and law in order to discourage or capture repair markets. Those efforts – combined with persistent marketing messages that convince us we need newer, thinner, and supposedly better products – have contributed to a brand of disposable digital consumerism. Rather than prizing products that are reliable and durable, we are trained to replace our devices for the latest model even when our existing phones, laptops, and cars work perfectly fine. Once we adopt that mindset, repair looks more like a quaint anachronism, or even a hindrance to innovation, than a socially responsible choice.

But beyond staving off economic and environmental harms, repair serves other crucial values. Repair is a social practice that builds valuable skills. It demands analytic reasoning, strategic thinking, and creativity. And repair helps us develop a more complete understanding of how a device operates, enriching our awareness of the world around us. In that sense, it makes us freer, more autonomous, more in control of the world we occupy. Repair empowers us.

The impulse to repair is deeply ingrained in us, dating back to humanity's origins. So, it is not surprising that, in the face of legal and technological restrictions on this ancient tradition, some have rebelled. Recent years have witnessed the emergence of a global right-to-repair movement. It brings together tinkerers, hobbyists, repair professionals, policy advocates, sustainability experts, and everyday people. This coalition operates both locally and globally to share parts, tools, information, and techniques. Since the first repair café, a community space dedicated to empowering everyday people to fix their stuff, opened its doors a decade ago in Amsterdam, thousands have sprung up across the globe – not to mention Fixit Clinics, Restart Parties, and other in-person events that foster repair locally. At the same time, the internet is fertile ground for repair information. Whatever problem ails your smartphone, washing machine, or garage-door opener, there's a good chance you can find a detailed explanation of the repair procedure on YouTube. And iFixit – a company that sells tools and replacement parts – has built an online community that provides free, community-edited repair instructions to millions of readers.

The goal of repair stands in obvious tension with the strategies increasingly employed by device makers. But for more than a decade, dedicated consumers and repair providers have waged a largely unnoticed battle against the largest, best-capitalized corporations in history. Their resistance takes many forms: tearing down new products to identify and overcome impediments to repair, bypassing technological locks on diagnostic software, sourcing hard-to-find replacement parts, and sharing information over a chorus of corporate legal threats. More recently, the battle has moved to courtrooms, administrative agencies, and legislatures as the repair community attempts to fix the most powerful tool blocking repair – the law.

This book tells the story of repair – its history, the strategies developed to undermine it, and the path towards a more reparable future. That story begins with the economic, environmental, and social benefits of repair. The ability to fix the technology we rely on can save us billions of dollars. It can help us reduce the staggering harms to the planet that flow from the extraction of raw materials, their conversion into consumer devices, and their eventual disposal. And repair helps us develop knowledge and skills that foster autonomy and build community. As we will see, repair is an ancient practice that has evolved alongside human technology from its earliest beginnings. It has grown more specialized, but thanks in part to the internet, repair is on the verge of democratization.

In response, firms are cracking down. Accessible, affordable repair presents a threat to the business models of companies that manufacture and sell consumer goods by the billions. Short product lifespans are central to their profitability. Predictably, they employ a combination of technological, economic, and marketing techniques to steer consumers away from repair. Device makers design components that are difficult to replace; charge unreasonably high prices for authorized repairs; squeeze independent repair providers out of the market; and construct digital locks meant to keep us out of the products we own.

Increasingly, legal rules play a central role in regulating access to repair. Three interrelated bodies of law in particular – intellectual property, antitrust, and consumer law – are essential to understanding the legal landscape around repair. Device makers assert IP rights, with varying degrees of success, to prevent unwanted repairs. They claim their copyrights, patents, trademarks, and trade secrets are infringed by the sale of replacement parts, the sharing of repair documentation, and the use of diagnostic tools and software. But those claims are often at odds with established legal precedent and sound public policy. Like IP, antitrust law is a tool for regulating competition in the marketplace. But while exclusive IP rights are meant to insulate firms from the usual competitive forces of the market, antitrust law is designed to limit the market power firms can wield against both competitors and the public. That makes it well-suited for pushing back on device makers seeking to control repair markets. Although they target different sorts of behavior, both antitrust and consumer law share a concern with safe-guarding fair competition and reducing harms to individual consumers. By targeting specific unfair and deceptive practices, consumer law supplements the structural rules imposed by antitrust law.

Although they have potential to better promote repair, as they currently exist, none of these bodies of law offers a framework that can effectively push back on manufacturers' overreaching tactics. If we want to enable repair, legal reform is necessary across doctrinal lines. Although distinct, these areas of law interact in ways that complicate the policy response to repair. IP and antitrust law stand in uneasy tension at times. Antitrust and consumer-protection law share some core goals but pursue them using different means. But in the end, all three of these areas of law shape the competitive landscape in ways that implicate repair. Given that fact, responsibility for creating an environment hospitable to repair can't fall on any single body of law or institutional actor. Nor can the solutions be limited to legal reform. Protecting and restoring repair will require us to rethink product design, recalibrate market incentives, and shift the social norms of our consumer culture to better reflect the value of repair. These are no small tasks. But considering the fundamental necessity of repair to our way of life, the sooner we get started, the better.

2 WHY REPAIR MATTERS

Repair is inevitable. Things break. They degrade, wear down, and fall apart. This is not an indictment of the artifacts we create, although some are more durable than others. It's an inescapable fact of the universe. Entropy – that gradual but ineluctable descent into disorder – comes for us all. Repair is a response to this fundamental truth, an effort to resist it, and maybe even reverse it. No repair is permanent, but it can stave off the return to dust and rubble that awaits everything we build, acquire, and use.

Repair is also ubiquitous. It forms part of the social and technological backdrop of everything we do. Too often though, we think of breakdowns as aberrations, rare and unexpected disruptions to our plans and routines. But it's the daily practice of repair – of our roads and subways, our office buildings, our electrical grids and sewage systems – that make those plans and routines possible in the first place.[1] Nonetheless, repair remains invisible for most of us until something goes wrong, until our car won't start or our laptop keyboard fails. As a result, we undervalue the role repair plays in our lives.

All sorts of things require repair. We sometimes talk about repairing our bodies, relationships, and even societies.[2] But for our purposes, *repair* refers to the mending or reconditioning of human-made goods to restore their form or function. Even within that narrower definition, repair captures a range of approaches and motivations. Often repair is strictly a question of regaining functionality. If your car won't start, you're unlikely to interrogate the mechanic about the color of the spark plugs they install, so long as they get you back on the road. But in other instances, we are more sensitive to the aesthetics of repair. If you take a favorite jacket to a tailor to mend a torn seam, you probably hope the repair will be undetectable.

Either way, a successful repair can work a kind of magic. Say you take your dented car to the body shop after a parking-lot collision. If executed well, replacing a damaged fender can, in a way, rewind the clock. It can return you to the moment just before you distractedly backed into that light post. Repair rarely perfectly restores an object to its original condition.[3] But it can undo damage and extend the useful lives of the things that surround us. In that sense, repair looks like a conservative undertaking. The effort to return a thing to an earlier form – if not its original condition – is a backward-looking enterprise, even if it is only aspirational.

Restoration, a close cousin of repair, shares this fixation with the past. When a new owner restores a Victorian home to something approaching its original condition, they are attempting to rematerialize the past. But in the process, they are arguably erasing intervening decades of history.[4] Perhaps that is for the best. But it is a choice that has implications for our relationship with change and the objects embodying it. Cumulatively, the minor, daily accretions and erosions artifacts experience can change their meaning over time. *Notre Dame de Pilar*, better known as the Black Madonna, is a wooden icon dating back to 1508. As part of the recent restoration of the Chartres Cathedral, hundreds of years of soot and smoke were removed from both the twelfth-century structure and the icon it houses. As a result, the Madonna is no longer black, disconnecting this European figure from a multiracial global tradition that venerates the dark mother archetype.[5] As one critic put it, the restoration "transformed the Mother of God into a simpering kewpie doll."[6] When restoration and repair are undertaken in ways that ignore or deny the past, they risk stripping objects of meaning and context.

Maintenance is another practice closely associated with repair. But rather than intervening after some acute breakdown in functionality, maintenance is preventative. It staves off failures or prevents them altogether. Compared to repair, maintenance tends to be routine, predictable, and less invasive. Regularly brushing and flossing your teeth is maintenance. A root canal is a repair. In practice though, repair and maintenance often intertwine and overlap. Say your car drifts slightly from right to left on the freeway. Is a wheel alignment from your local auto shop a repair or mere maintenance? Functionality isn't binary. Your car still works with misaligned wheels, although not as well as you might prefer. The line between maintenance and repair is malleable, but the distinction is still helpful. Maintenance is about prolonging the present state of affairs, while repair is a matter of returning to some prior condition.

These impulses to preserve the present or return to the past are at odds with a dominant cultural narrative that celebrates innovation and emphasizes newness.[7] From technology, to pop culture, to politics, the drive to break with the past in order to make room for a more promising future is pervasive, if often unfulfilled. Why fix a decade-old internal-combustion car when you can replace it with an electric one? Why repair a three-year old laptop when a new one is lighter, faster, and comes in your choice of color? That's not to say that true innovation shouldn't be valued. Both groundbreaking inventions and incremental improvements can better our lives in measurable ways. But we have to be careful to separate those contributions from mere product differentiation masquerading as innovation. The innovation narrative, for all its promises of a brighter tomorrow, tells an incomplete and biased story about the future. That story is designed to instill a set of values and preferences that encourage us to prioritize the experience and very idea of newness. But newness is, by definition, temporary. Our thirst for it is never slaked, at least not for long. Even putting aside the tantalizing promise of newness, this narrative ignores the many costs of extracting raw materials, manufacturing products, and eventually disposing of them – the sooner, the better to drive the engine of newness. And it turns a blind eye to the opportunity costs of our collective fascination with the new. How might we spend our time, energy, and money if we weren't busily differentiating this year's phone from last year's model?

Once the costs of newness are taken into account, repair reveals itself as surprisingly forward-looking. It grows out of a recognition that resources are finite, that the planet is small, and that a culture that overlooks those facts imperils its future. Repair allows us to extract maximum value from the artifacts we create. A laptop, for instance, represents significant human investment. Beyond the materials harvested across the globe, it embodies generations of technological advances, painstaking design, the labor of factory workers, and the costs of packaging, shipping, and advertising. Resigning a laptop to the scrapheap because it needs a routine repair, or simply because a new model is available, discards those investments. It is inefficient. It is wasteful. And collectively, that waste imposes costs on us all. From this perspective, repair is not an effort to return to the past, but a project informed by a sober vision of the future.

In this light, repair exhibits a complicated relationship with time and change. It is not some naive effort to reverse the clock and deny the unavoidable passage of time. Nor is it an effort to rush headlong into some imagined, consequence-free future of infinite plentitude. Instead, repair is an attempt to reconcile past and future. It is a clear-eyed compromise between the promise of human ingenuity and the harsh material reality of the world. Everything breaks eventually. But that process of breakdown can be negotiated. It can be managed. The mindset of repair is simultaneously hopeful, yet unflinchingly realistic. Through repair, we can keep that car running for another year or that coat warm enough for another season, even if we know that entropy always wins in the end.

Despite its tendency to go unnoticed, repair contributes to society in important ways. This chapter considers three sets of concrete benefits that flow from repair. First, repair helps consumers save money by extending the lifespan of products and fostering secondary markets. Second, repair lessens the massive environmental burden of modern consumerism, from the extraction of natural resources to the eventual disposal of the devices we buy. Finally, repair helps us grow and flourish as people. Through repair, we become better informed about the world around us, develop analytical and problem-solving skills, exercise greater autonomy, and build stronger communities.

The Economic Benefits of Repair

To the average consumer, the economic case is intuitive. Repair extends the useful lives of the products we buy. That saves us money in two ways. First, by replacing our purchases less often, we spend less. Second, repair helps ensure that when we finally do replace an aging device, it still has some residual value on the used market.

Imagine your refrigerator breaks. If you can correctly diagnose the problem – a failed compressor, let's say – then find the necessary part and successfully install it, you've likely spent considerably less than you would have on a brand-new fridge. The logic is simple: the longer the things we buy work, the less often we need to replace them. If we can slow the replacement cycle, we will spend less over the course of our lives on clothes, cars, and electronics. And those expenses add up. Collectively, we spend unthinkable sums on new devices – $500 billion a year on smartphones, and roughly the same on household appliances.[8] Both of those figures, however, are dwarfed by the nearly $3 trillion we spend every year buying cars.[9]

Extending Product Lifespans

The lifespans of the products we buy are central to their value. Whether it's worth it to spend $2,000 on a new refrigerator depends in large part on how long you expect it to last. When we talk about the lifespan of a device, it's important to distinguish between two different meanings of that term. By "lifespan," we might mean the length of time the device will continue to perform its intended function – how long it will work. Repair, in a very direct way, extends this functional lifespan. In another sense though, a device's lifespan isn't determined solely by how long it functions. Other factors play into our decision-making. New features, aesthetic trends, or the yawning void at the core of modern life could all convince you to replace a perfectly operational refrigerator. This replacement lifespan – how long you keep a purchase before substituting a new one – is often a better measure of our behavior.[10] Repair can certainly influence replacement rates, but it contends against other considerations.

Measuring changes in average product lifespans is challenging, given the absence of reliable longitudinal data.[11] But across categories, consumers express frustration that products don't last as long as they used to, or as long as they should.[12] Empirical studies support this shared anecdotal sense that products' lifespans are dwindling.[13] That's true for household appliances like washing machines and refrigerators. By some estimates, the lifespan of the average washing machine dropped by three years over the course of a single decade.[14] According to a survey conducted by Consumer Reports, 30 percent of new washers break within just five years.[15] And an estimated 40 percent of refrigerators last only five years before problems emerge.[16]

For electronics, the trend is even more apparent. A 2015 study found that older CRT televisions lasted for an average of fifteen years, but newer flatscreen models had average lifespans of just six years.[17] The introduction of higher-definition displays, smart features, internet connectivity, and steadily declining prices, are likely driving even shorter replacement cycles for TVs today. Likewise, a computer purchased in 1985 might last a decade.[18] But by 2005, purchasers were replacing them after just two years.[19] Smartphones have only been around for twenty years, but their lifespans have always been short. On average, consumers in the United States and Europe use a smartphone for about two years before upgrading.[20] This figure has risen modestly – by two or three months – in recent years. Mobile carriers have shifted away from heavily subsidized phone upgrades designed to keep subscribers under long-term contracts. Faced with sticker prices of $1,000 or more, consumers have been understandably persuaded to hang onto their devices for a bit longer. Aside from improved cameras and ornamental design tweaks, this year's phone typically offers few new features over last year's model.

Cars are a notable exception to the trend of shrinking product lifespans. In 2019, the average age of a vehicle on the road in the United States was just under twelve years. That's the highest figure recorded over the nearly two decades the statistic has been tracked.[21] But unlike smartphones, where increased price transparency and stagnating innovation explain consumer behavior, cars seem to be lasting longer because they are better made. Advances in engineering, material science, and manufacturing have given rise to vehicles that are, overall, more durable and reliable. But incremental scientific improvements don't tell the whole story. Increased global competition and higher regulatory standards likely played roles in raising the bar for quality. Drivers may also be holding onto cars longer in response to a sluggish economy. Whether this trend will survive the impending transition to an electric fleet is an open question – one that depends on improvements in battery technology, the design decisions of carmakers, and the responsiveness of regulators.

Cars aside, the lifespans of the products we buy continue to wane. Too often, the devices we toss out are still in working order.[22] Just as troublingly though, firms take steps to help keep our broken stuff broken. They have strong incentives to encourage us to discard our purchases early and often since replacement sales are a crucial, renewable resource for device makers. As we will see, manufacturers have developed a host of strategies, techniques, and tools to encourage us to replace the products we own. But when repair is available, affordable, and effective, consumers are more likely to keep their existing devices rather than spend more money on something new.

Supplying Secondary Markets

Repair offers another important economic benefit for consumers. It helps sustain secondary markets. Refurbished laptops from eBay, used bikes found on Craigslist, power tools uncovered at garage sales, and blenders donated to Goodwill are all examples of products acquired through secondary markets. These transactions are valuable to both buyers and sellers. For sellers, they provide an opportunity to recoup some of the investment in their initial purchase. For buyers, they add to the stock of used inventory available for budget-minded shoppers. Importantly, secondary markets also put downward pressure on the price of new goods. Manufacturers and retailers know that if prices climb too high, some consumers will buy used instead.

Repair is central to the used market. A product that doesn't work is, unsurprisingly, worth less than one that does. So, if your current car has to be towed to the dealer, you shouldn't be too optimistic about its trade-in value. That said, buyers might still be willing to purchase a used car if they are confident they can repair it at a reasonable cost. And even if a vehicle appears to be in working order, the ability to fix it should something go wrong is priced into its value on the secondary market. A used car that could never be repaired would be a bad investment no matter how well the test drive went.

While often overshadowed by new sales, secondary markets are a sizable segment of the economy. The growing resale market for smartphones is estimated at about $25 billion annually.[23] Measured by units sold, demand for used phones outstrips new ones. The used appliance and secondhand clothing market each account for tens of billions of dollars in sales.[24] And in the United States, twice as many used cars are sold each year than new ones.[25] All told, secondary markets for consumer goods represent hundreds of billions of dollars in annual sales. And much of that value depends on repair.

Secondary markets run the gamut from Sotheby's auctions to Goodwill thrift stores. But secondhand goods are especially important in economically marginalized communities. Those who lack the resources to buy new clothes, housewares, electronics, and vehicles have traditionally relied on used goods.[26] And research suggests that as incomes increase, families show a greater propensity to replace rather than repair.[27] So secondary markets facilitate the transfer of resources from the affluent to the relatively poor. That's true both within countries and between them. Beyond used sales within the local economy, a robust global market exports the castoffs of developed economies to poorer nations around the world.[28] When we engage in repair, we are enabling these markets to flourish. And when repair is restricted or unaffordable, it is often the poor who suffer the most.

The Cost Savings of Repair

Calculating the cost savings from repair with precision is a challenge. To figure that out, we'd need reliable data on not only the price of every repair, but also how much more a replacement would have cost. That's true for every refrigerator with a failed compressor, every smartphone with a depleted battery, every television with a faulty power supply, and every car with a loose timing belt. We'd also need to know how successful those repairs were. Did they stave off replacement for six months? Five years? But even without precise calculations, there is good reason to believe repair leads to significant cost savings in the aggregate. A recent study found that the average US household spends just under $1,500 per year on electronics. Extending product lifespans through repair would save those households an estimated $330 annually, which amounts to $40 billion across the US consumer economy.[29]

Let's examine just one tiny corner of the repair market more closely. Broken smartphone screens are the flat tires of the digital era – inconvenient, surprisingly expensive, and nearly inevitable. In 2017, Americans broke roughly 50 million phone screens. Many replaced their phones, while others just lived with a busted screen. But those who did repair their screens spent on average $170, totaling an estimated $3.4 billion for some 20 million repaired screens.[30] If instead, each of those consumers had purchased new iPhones, they'd have spent about $20 billion – or a mere $14 billion for the relatively budget-friendly Samsung Galaxy 9. In either case, repair saved consumers several billion dollars. Of course, that total reflects savings for one type of repair to one category of product, in a single country, and over the course of just one year. Once we consider the full impact of repair in communities around the world, the savings are staggering.

Precisely how much economic benefit we derive from repair depends on how much it costs to fix things. In some corners of the repair market, there are troubling signs that consumers are overpaying. From 2000 to 2017, the price of vehicle repair increased by more than 60 percent according to the United States Bureau of Labor Statistics.[31] In part, that increase reflects the rising cost of replacement parts, which are commonly patented. As a result, General Motors boasts profit margins of more than 30 percent on aftermarket parts.[32] Because of those expenses, more collisions are resulting in cars being "totaled" – in other words, the cost of repair exceeds the value of the car. The high price of repair helps explain why car parts and service account for nearly half of car dealer profits in the United States, more than either new or used vehicle sales.[33] And in the market for farm equipment, where companies like John Deere have taken aggressive steps to limit competition, repair is five times as profitable as equipment sales.[34]

Apple claims to be bucking the trend of highly profitable repairs. The company told a US congressional committee in 2019 that its "costs of providing repair services … exceeded the revenue generated by repairs."[35] According to Apple, it lost money on repairs. Anyone who has received a repair bill from Apple might be surprised by this claim. Putting aside routine charges of hundreds of dollars to swap out batteries and broken screens, Apple charges $599 just to replace the cosmetic glass covering the back of some iPhone models.[36] In perhaps the most extreme example, a customer took his MacBook Pro to Apple because the display was completely dark. After months of attempted repairs totaling more than $10,000 – including two replaced logic boards and eventually an entirely new laptop – an Apple technician uncovered the issue. The screen brightness was turned to zero, a problem solved with a single keystroke.[37]

So how could Apple's repair program lose money? In the movie industry, "Hollywood accounting" is the colloquial term for bookkeeping practices designed to avoid royalties and profit-sharing by making a highly profitable film look like a box office bomb. By generously estimating overhead costs, hits can look like losers on paper. According to the studios, blockbuster films from the *Star Wars*, *Lord of the Rings*, and *Harry Potter* franchises lost hundreds of millions of dollars.[38] In its response to Congress, Apple almost certainly engaged in some creative accounting of its own, even if its answer was technically true. Perhaps the company included some portion of its retail store overhead in that calculation. Maybe it included warranty repairs, like the $10,000 laptop fix, which cost the company $4.1 billion in 2018 alone. It also may have factored in the cost of its steeply discounted $29 battery replacement program, offered after the company admitted to slowing down the processors of older iPhones. The same may have gone for Apple's free replacement of defective butterfly keyboards on millions of laptops. If so, Apple's claim to Congress tells us nothing about the profitability of charging $329 to replace an iPhone screen.

None of this is to say repair shouldn't be profitable. Quite the opposite. If we hope to see widespread availability of replacement parts and repair services, profit is essential. The trick is calibrating those incentives in a way that best serves the needs of consumers. For many products, the current market discourages repair and steers consumers towards replacement. The prices of televisions, kitchen appliances, and other devices have dropped considerably in recent decades, but during that same period, repair has grown more expensive.[39] A more competitive market for parts and service would keep those expenses in check, allowing consumers to make more efficient choices between repairing and replacing.

The Potential Costs of Repair

So far, we've focused on the economic upsides of repair. But what about its potential downsides? If repair reduces consumer spending on new purchases and shifts money into secondary markets, surely someone is losing out. The obvious candidates are device makers and retailers. One risk is that they will raise prices in response to anemic sales. As any Intro to Economics student will tell you, a price hike in the face of weak demand is a counterintuitive strategy. And it's one that's likely to backfire. If prices go up, we should expect even more consumers to hang onto their workhorse devices, repair them whenever possible, or turn to secondary markets.

But even assuming device makers increased retail prices, would that really be such a bad outcome? Hear me out. No one likes paying more, but higher prices might be just what consumers need – not as a penance for frivolous spending, but as a means of forcing disclosure of information. Sellers know things most consumers don't. They know how long the device they are selling you is likely to last, how long you're likely to keep it, and how much you are likely to spend on maintenance and repair over the product's lifetime. That information asymmetry gives sellers an advantage. It allows them to hide costs that aren't apparent to most of us. As consumers, we tend to focus on the sticker price, ignoring or underestimating the long-term costs of ownership, like broken phone screens and regular vehicle maintenance. But for sellers, these expenses are known and accounted for. So, if products last longer and repairs are less expensive, higher retail prices for new devices would expose the amount sellers anticipated extracting from us all along. They were always planning on charging us more – either by selling us a replacement or charging high prices for repairs. Price increases simply let us in on the secret.

It's fair to assume that embracing repair might result in declining sales and lower profits for some device makers. That's bad news for shareholders, but not necessarily for the rest of society. Along with a handful of major banks, device makers like Apple and Samsung are among the worlds' most profitable companies. In 2018, Samsung earned nearly $40 billion in profits. Apple's haul was just shy of $60 billion.

The company regularly boasts net profit margins above 20 percent and has cash reserves of nearly $200 billion. Not only would the company survive if it made less money, the world would be a better place for it. Rather than adding to Apple's treasure hoard, that money could be put to better use by consumers. To Apple, an extra hundred, thousand, or even million dollars would go unnoticed. To the average family or locally owned repair shop, however, those sums have real value.

Admittedly, not all firms enjoy Apple's surfeit of cash, so reduced profits can't be shrugged off so easily. But profitability should not be seen as an end unto itself. There are two primary reasons we should be concerned about the effect repair has on companies' bottom lines. First, we might be concerned that firms will invest less in research and development. With fewer resources dedicated to creating new technology, the worry goes, innovation will slow, and the public will suffer. It's true that smaller budgets at established firms might impede or delay new product features. But we shouldn't confuse every new refrigerator model or minivan redesign with innovation. In fact, a plausible case can be made that disrupting the steady flow of profits from selling tweaks to existing products could result in more innovation, not less. Denied easy profits from annual updates, firms would be pushed to develop truly novel features or even entirely new product lines if they want to remain profitable.

Job losses are a second worry. Factory workers, industrial designers, truck drivers, and retail employees all depend on the relentless churn of new products replacing the old. But repair offers its own career opportunities.[40] Repair is skilled, labor-intensive work. Unlike manufacturing, it is difficult to automate and tends to benefit local, small businesses rather than global giants. Our collective embrace of throwaway products has come at the expense of repair workers. In 1966, there were 200,000 people employed as home appliance repairers in the United States. Today there are about 40,000. Over that period, the number of professionals repairing television and stereo equipment dwindled from 110,000 to just 30,000 – all while the US population increased by more than 130 million residents.[41]

From a purely economic perspective, the case for repair is hard to deny. It saves consumers money, helps ensure the availability of goods on secondary markets, and makes the most efficient use of existing resources. These calculations, however, only consider the direct costs of our devices. Beyond their sticker price, our cars, appliances, and electronics embed a shocking environmental toll that, collectively, we must confront.

The Environmental Benefits of Repair

When it comes to consumer devices, our current levels of consumption are untenable. The global production, distribution, and disposal of electronics and other durable goods is responsible for staggering levels of environmental damage. As public awareness of the effects of climate change and other environmental harms grows, device makers are starting to take note. They are releasing ambitious sustainability plans, committing to aggressive carbon-neutrality goals, and touting their investments in recycling programs. But most firms remain unwilling to acknowledge the core tension between environmental responsibility and business models built around the ever-escalating production, sale, and replacement of billions of consumer devices every year. Repair is crucial to disrupting this global network of consumption. When we fix the things we already own, they last longer, reducing demand for new products and slowing the global flow of electronic waste. Through repair, we can ease the environmental strain caused by modern consumerism without denying ourselves the benefits of technology. We don't have to give up our phones and dishwashers, but we do need to make them last.

Curbing Electronic Waste

The most obvious environmental harms occur at the end of the product lifecycle. Far too often, when we replace phones, TVs, and appliances with new models, our old devices make their way to landfills. In the United States alone, we dispose of more than 400,000 mobile phones every day – roughly 150 million each year.[42] As the prices of new goods continue to drop, the urge to replace rather than repair only intensifies. According to a U.N. report, discarded consumer electronics accounted for nearly 54 million metric tons of e-waste in 2019 alone.[43] That's enough to fill "a million 18-wheel trucks stretching from New York to Bangkok and back."[44] And the problem is growing. E-waste increased more than 20 percent over the last five years and continues to climb by 2.5 million metric tons per year. By 2030, annual totals are projected to reach nearly 75 million metric tons.[45] These mountains of electronic junk are the byproduct of global urbanization and industrialization, but as the United Nations recognized, the shortage of repair options is a key contributor.[46]

E-waste is particularly problematic because it contains high levels of heavy metals, like arsenic, lead, and mercury, as well as toxins like brominated flame retardants.[47] In the United States, e-waste makes up just 2 percent of the trash dumped in land-fills, but it accounts for as much as 70 percent of toxic waste.[48] Over time, those toxins make their way into surrounding soil, where they can contaminate groundwater and effect the food supply. And many landfills around the world burn solid waste, which releases acrid fumes and pollutants into the air. As a result, toxicity levels are far higher near landfills and e-waste sites, often considerably exceeding health-and-safety standards. One study found heavy metal concentrations near e-waste sites in India were 30 times higher than normal for topsoil and nearly 120 times higher for subsoil samples.[49]

The adverse health effects of these chemicals are not fully understood, particularly when people face exposure to multiple toxins. But studies point to a host of documented harms.[50] Exposure is associated with reduced lung and thyroid function. It has been tied to cognitive impairments, neurodevelopmental anomalies, and attention disorders. And it has been linked to abnormal reproductive development, increases in premature and still births, and reduced childhood growth rates.

Notably, the harms e-waste inflicts are not evenly distributed. For decades, discarded electronics have flowed from wealthy countries to relatively poor ones.[51] The United States, for example, is the second largest e-waste producer, after China. Despite signing the Basel Convention – an international agreement banning the export of hazardous waste – in 1990, the United States has failed to ratify the treaty or comply with its terms.[52] Decades later, it continues to ship hazardous electronic waste around the world, primarily to Africa and Asia.[53] The volume of those exports is hard to pin down, in part because shipments of e-waste are sometimes falsely labeled as "used electronics" intended for resale in an effort to circumvent legal restrictions.[54] Even within any particular nation, the harms of e-waste are not shared equally. The poor live near landfills; the rich do not. And in countries like the United States, where systemic racism compounds those disparities, black and brown communities are far more likely than white ones to contend with those harms.[55]

Repair can stanch the flow of electronic waste that is clogging landfills, tainting soil, and poisoning water around the globe. If repair were more affordable and widely available, we could significantly extend the average lifespan of the devices we buy. In a world in which cell phones lasted for five years rather than two, or televisions still worked for a decade or more, we would expect to see a precipitous drop in annual e-waste pollution. Repair keeps devices in the hands of owners and out of landfills. Admittedly, cheap, accessible, and reliable repair won't put an end to the desire to buy new devices. Consumers today discard functioning and broken devices alike, often driven by a compulsion for the latest hardware update. But repair alters the replacement calculus for owners, tilting it in favor of longer lifespans. Equally importantly, readily available repair makes used devices more valuable, whether they are working at the moment or not. Even if wealthy or environmentally insensitive consumers toss their year-old smart speaker for a new model, secondary markets can absorb used devices, diverting them from the landfill. That's especially true if would-be purchasers are confident that used devices can be repaired should the need arise.

Reducing Extraction and Production

The environmental consequences of our collective obsession with new devices are not limited to their disposal. Their production gives rise to its own harms, on both the local and global level. From the destructive extraction of raw materials to energy-intensive assembly lines, each step that leads to the giddy-yet-fleeting experience of unboxing a new PlayStation is laden with environmental damage. And those costs are amplified by the sheer scale of the device economy. Each year, manufacturers produce about 1.5 billion new phones. Add to that the hundreds of millions of TVs, tablets, and laptops, the nearly 100 million motor vehicles, and the tens of millions of washing machines and other home appliances, and the immense proportions of modern device manufacturing begin to take shape.[56]

Despite their sleek designs and innovative features, our devices don't come from the future. They come from the earth. They are made of metals, embedded in rock for billions of years. Even their plastics are derived from crude oil pumped from below our feet. At least seventy-five of the eighty-three known stable elements are found in smartphones.[57] They include aluminum, cobalt, copper, gold, indium, iron, lithium, nickel, silicon, silver, tantalum, tin, tungsten, and sixteen of the seventeen rare-earth metals. These raw materials are extracted, processed, and transformed to manufacture the feats of precision engineering we carry in our pockets.

As Brian Merchant explains in his history of the iPhone, *The One Device*, building a single 4.5 ounce iPhone requires 75 pounds – or 34 kilograms – of ore extracted from the earth.[58] As of 2018, when Apple stopped sharing sales figures, it had already sold 2.2 billion iPhones.[59] That translates to roughly 75 million metric tons of ore mined just for iPhone production.[60] Once we factor in smartphones from other manufacturers, laptops, desktops, and the ever-growing menagerie of wearables, smart appliances, and assorted digital ephemera, the device economy is literally reshaping the planet.

Wresting metals, like the gold and copper used in smartphone circuitry, from the ground requires environmentally violent mining practices. Open-pit mines entail the excavation of massive amounts of ore and waste rock. The largest, Utah's Bingham Canyon copper mine, is three-quarters of a mile deep and two-and-a-half miles wide. Hard-rock mining, in contrast, involves drilling and blasting vertical shafts and horizontal adits to access subsurface ore. All of that digging and exploding pollutes the air. Gold mines, in particular, are a leading cause of mercury pollution.[61] And respiratory problems, from tuberculosis to lung cancer, are all too common among mine workers.[62]

Once the ore is removed, valuable metals have to be isolated from the waste rock surrounding them. That process is water intensive, which helps explain why a single smartphone requires 100 liters of water to produce.[63] Even more worryingly, the waste product – a slurry of water, rock, and metal particles – is typically stored in ponds where it can wreak environmental damage. Residents of the island of Bougainville in Papua New Guinea, to take just one example, recently filed a lawsuit alleging that the Australian mining firm Rio Tinto failed to clean up millions of tons of waste at its copper and gold mine, contaminating the island's drinking water and causing upper respiratory and gastrointestinal illness among its children.[64] What's worse, gold mines, which remove as much as 91 tons of ore to produce a single ounce of the precious metal,[65] often deploy cyanide leaching. That process uses toxic chemicals to dissolve gold and separate it from the ore, leaving behind particularly hazardous wastewater that threatens wildlife, farmland, and water supplies.[66]

In addition to these familiar elements, our devices incorporate a variety of rare-earth metals.[67] Dysprosium, neodymium, and terbium are crucial ingredients in the magnets smartphones use for vibration and sound. Cerium is commonly used to polish glass screens, while europium and yttrium are among the elements necessary for them to render color. And circuit boards contain gadolinium, praseodymium, and other rare-earth metals. Unlike other metals, the rare earths are almost uniformly found intermingled with thorium and uranium. The refining process breaks down the ore using sulfuric acid – along with ample water and electricity – leaving behind a slurry that is not only toxic, but radioactive. When it leaches into the groundwater or dust particles escape, the health of surrounding communities is put at serious risk. For instance, a rare-earth mine in California flooded the Mojave Desert with 300,000 gallons of radioactive material.[68] And a sprawling rare-earth facility in Malaysia is facing closure after failing to safely contain growing piles of radioactive waste and concerns over tainted groundwater.[69]

Distressingly, the bulk of rare-earth mining occurs in jurisdictions with weak or nonexistent environmental standards. Twenty minutes outside of Baotou, a city of more than 2 million people in China's semi-autonomous Inner Mongolia, sits a toxic lake described by the BBC as a "nightmarish ... hell on earth."[70] It is filled with "black, barely-liquid, toxic sludge" – the byproduct of the nearby Baogang Steel and Rare Earth mine. This noxious muck has leached into local waterways and irrigation systems with devastating consequences.[71] Decades before it became the center of the rare-earth trade, Baotou was surrounded by fields of watermelons, eggplants, and tomatoes.[72] These days, the soil can no longer support crops, the livestock has died off, and residents are battling leukemia and pancreatic cancer.[73] Others report their hair and teeth falling out.[74]

The disregard for human suffering revealed by these mining practices often manifests itself in other ways. Several metals, among them cobalt, tantalum, tungsten, and tin, are often extracted under conditions that seem designed to maximize human misery. Cobalt is a crucial component in the lithium-ion batteries found in phones, laptops, and electric vehicles. Global demand exceeds 100,000 metric tons per year and is expected to increase more than fourfold by 2030.[75] Prices peaked at nearly $100,000 per metric ton in 2018 but have settled around $35,000 today. The most significant costs of cobalt, however, are borne by those who mine it. Most of the world's cobalt supply is found in the Democratic Republic of Congo (DRC). While much of that cobalt is extracted by industrial operations, about 20 percent is mined by hand by a quarter of a million local *creuseurs*. They dig narrow tunnels, prone to fatal collapses. They inhale toxic cobalt dust, which contributes to an array of health conditions. They are often paid less than a dollar a day for their labor. And an estimated 35,000 of them are children as young as six years old.[76] Even with diligent efforts, device makers struggle to ensure that all the cobalt they purchase is mined ethically. And recycling efforts provide them with only a tiny fraction of the cobalt they need.

Just as troublingly, profits from mines in and around the DRC have funded armed conflict in the region. Children as young as seven mine coltan, the mineral from which tantalum is derived. Tantalum is used to produce circuits, capacitors, and resistors. It's prized by device makers because it allows them to build smaller and thinner devices. As a result, they buy up half the world's supply every year.[77] The lucrative tantalum trade, however, has helped fuel one of the bloodiest conflicts since World War II, one in which millions have died, rape is employed as a form of terrorism, and children are routinely conscripted as soldiers.[78] The central role of electronics firms in driving demand for coltan and indirectly funding the conflict led some to dub it the PlayStation War.[79]

In response to these atrocities, the United States, the European Union, and China have enacted regulations meant to limit the flow of money from these conflict minerals.[80] And firms have felt significant pressure to clean up their supply chains. But the exploitation of children isn't limited to the DRC. Roughly a third of the world's tin supply comes from informal Indonesian mines that frequently suffer fatal collapses and employ children.[81] At Cerro Rico, a mine in Potosí, Bolivia, children as young as six years old toil in the deepest, narrowest recesses to retrieve tin, silver, and zinc. Dozens have died in a single year.[82] As recently as 2013, Samsung admitted to acquiring tin from Indonesian mines that exploited child labor, and Apple relied on tin from Cerro Rico until 2017.[83]

Once this array of raw materials is procured, manufacturers can begin fashioning the parts that make up our devices – from microprocessors and batteries to haptic engines and LED displays. Building these tiny, intricate components requires huge sums of energy, water, and other resources. When it comes to microchips, the manufacturing process demands meticulously constructed clean rooms, free from stray particles, that have more in common with the vacuum of space than the surface of earth. The constant filtering, scrubbing, and purifying of air and water in these massive facilities consumes unseemly amounts of energy.[84] The process also relies on fluorinated gases to etch microscopic patterns in semiconductors and to clean chemical reactants from the chambers where chips are fabricated. These gases include perfluorocarbons and nitrogen trifluoride, "a greenhouse gas that is 16,100 times more powerful than carbon dioxide at trapping atmospheric heat."[85] This notoriously dangerous oxidizer is capable of burning concrete, sand, and even asbestos on contact.[86] According to the US Environmental Protection Agency (EPA), as much as 80 percent of these gases escape manufacturing facilities, making their way back into the air.[87] Manufacturers have deployed disposal and containment solutions to address these dangerous byproducts, but they are hardly foolproof. When fluorines escaped into the parking lot at one facility, the gases reportedly melted car windshields.[88]

These energy-intensive manufacturing processes, combined with the extraction techniques described above, contribute significantly to the carbon footprints of consumer devices. Not including the energy used in its operation, a single laptop generates as much as 468 kg, or roughly 1,000 pounds, of carbon dioxide equivalent.[89] Sony's PlayStation 4 console is responsible for a comparatively modest 89 kg of CO_2.[90] By the time Sony released its successor, the PlayStation 5, in 2020, it had sold 100 million PS4 units, totaling nearly 9 million metric tons of CO_2 released into the atmosphere. The per-unit carbon footprint for manufacturing an iPhone is a bit less – roughly 70 kg.[91] But given the staggering volume of iPhone sales, their total CO_2-equivalent emissions are on the order of 150 million metric tons. That's double the tonnage of ore mined to produce them. Like other major manufacturers, Apple and Sony have promised carbon-neutral production, but those goals are decades off.[92]

Finally, there's the impact of shipping and distribution. About 90 percent of trade relies on oceangoing ships.[93] Most run on highly polluting heavy fuel oil. In addition to carbon dioxide, these vessels release considerable volumes of sulfur dioxide and nitrogen oxides. Collectively, they emit more greenhouse gases than all but five countries.[94] New regulations, alternative fuels, and renewable energy sources have the potential to reduce shipping pollutants, but their effectiveness remains to be seen. Shipping billions of cars, phones, and appliances – not to mention the raw materials used to produce them – across oceans creates pollution, but so does their delivery to our homes. As online shopping and two-day delivery become the norm in many countries, we must consider the environmental costs of instant gratification. Medium-duty freight vehicles, like those commonly used by Amazon and its shipping partners, are among the most polluting vehicles on our roads. And since rush shipping often requires drivers to cover more miles to deliver fewer items, it is far from efficient.[95] According to one estimate, Amazon deliveries were responsible for 19 million metric tons of carbon in a single year.[96] Amazon has made big promises to reduce its environmental impact, pledging to make half of its deliveries carbon neutral by 2030 and to purchase 100,000 electric delivery vehicles. But that new fleet embeds its own upfront environmental costs.[97]

The havoc wreaked by device production on both the environment and human welfare is fueled by our insatiable desire for new devices. In response to that demand, device makers ramp up production, pressuring their suppliers to deliver more components, year after year. Those suppliers, in turn, insist on greater volumes of raw material from smelters and refineries. To keep pace, miners are forced to dig deeper to access dwindling supplies of natural resources. As demand for new devices increases, the greater the damage they cause.

So how can we interrupt this cycle of consumption? One approach is to make the prices of new devices fully and accurately reflect their costs. Just as device makers hide the total cost of ownership from consumers, they also conceal the full cost of production. When you buy a new laptop, the sticker price doesn't fully account for the rivers poisoned by rare-earth mining, the health hazards of air pollution from gold and nickel mining, and the exploitation of workers. Those costs are what economists call externalities. Neither the seller nor the buyer has to account for them because these costs are foisted onto third parties. By contracting with mining operations in countries with lax labor and environmental rules, device makers can avoid having to price them in. And since they don't have to cover them, neither do consumers. In other words, our purchases are being subsidized by marginalized communities in Bolivia, the DRC, Mongolia, Papua New Guinea, and elsewhere. If device makers had to make these communities whole for the damage they suffer, prices for new devices would skyrocket.

Short of fully internalizing those harms, we can hope that rising costs and public pressure encourage firms to redesign products to reduce their environmental impact. Some have made modest strides in recent years, eliminating mercury and arsenic from displays and glass, for example.[98] But there is simply no escaping the fact that these firms are in the business of converting billion-year-old rocks into complex electronic devices on a massive scale. For instance, Tesla has announced plans to make cobalt-free batteries.[99] That decision will likely lower the cost of electric vehicles and avoid the environmental and human rights issues – not to mention public-relations headaches – associated with mining in the DRC. But it will also drive demand for nickel, a metal that raises its own environmental concerns. Nickel mining in Norilsk, the most polluted city in Russia, was responsible for plumes of smoke that belched 350,000 metric tons of sulfur dioxide into the air each year.[100] In the course of just four years, the nearby Daldykan river ran blood-red on three separate occasions, the result of overflowing metallurgical waste and spilled diesel fuel.[101] In response, indigenous communities in the arctic Taimyr region have pleaded with Tesla to reconsider the impact of nickel mining.[102]

From an environmental perspective, repair is central to any serious effort to reduce the damage caused by the device economy. Effective and affordable repair extends the life of our devices, slowing the replacement cycle and deescalating extraction and production. Once we've mined and refined ore, manufactured components, assembled devices, and had them shipped express from halfway across the planet, they represent a sizable expenditure – not just on our credit-card statements, but also in terms of their impact on the planet. The only way to responsibly recognize that investment is to keep them working as long as we reasonably can.

The Promise and Reality of Recycling

In recent years, device makers have begun stressing the importance of recycling. Rather than mining deep in the earth, materials can be harvested from the mountains of cast-off devices we throw out each year. This shift, no doubt, is motivated in part by genuine concerns over sustainability and environmental impact. But emphasizing recycling also makes sense as a matter of economics. In 2019 alone, our electronic waste contained $57 billion in iron, copper, gold, and other metals.[103] And those resources are highly concentrated in discarded devices. The US EPA estimates that "one metric ton of circuit boards can contain 40 to 800 times the amount of gold and 30 to 40 times the amount of copper mined from one metric ton of ore."[104] So, recovering raw materials from e-waste is often more efficient than extracting virgin metals. For other materials, like some rare-earth elements, dwindling supplies may leave firms with little choice but to recycle.[105]

Shifting the conversation to recycling is also a smart public-relations move. As the device economy faces greater environmental scrutiny, firms are eager to burnish the green image of the high-tech sector. Apple touts its shift to recycled aluminum for MacBook enclosures, tin in logic-board solder, and rare-earth metals in iPhone Taptic engines.[106] Microsoft boasts of the millions of pounds of waste diverted by its recycling efforts.[107] And Tesla points to its investments in battery recycling.[108]

Firms are also quick to publicize innovative recycling technologies, complete with friendly, focus-grouped names. Apple's Daisy robot is designed to recycle iPhones. For every 100,000 devices it processes, Daisy recovers 1.1 kg of gold, 83 kg of tungsten, 790 kg of cobalt.[109] Daisy can recycle up to 200 phones per hour – an impressive figure, until you realize Apple produces more than 20,000 iPhones an hour, twenty-four hours a day, three hundred sixty-five days a year. Compared to its production lines, the scale of Apple's recycling program remains modest, to put it charitably. By 2019, the company had received 1 million iPhones for recycling, or less than 0.5 percent of the new units it sold that year.[110] That year, Apple and its recycling partners processed 48,000 metric tons of e-waste, less than 0.1 percent of the annual global total.[111]

Elsewhere, researchers have developed new techniques, isolating rare-earth metals with carbon nanotubes and separating valuable metals using powerful underwater sound waves.[112] New processes and technologies will undoubtedly be crucial to scaling up e-waste recycling. But these efforts – like futuristic recycling robots – tend to reinforce the comforting narrative that new technologies can save us from ourselves. To paraphrase the twentieth-century American philosopher Homer Simpson, "To technology! The cause of, and solution to, all of life's problems."[113]

Make no mistake, more recycling is good for the environment. Policy makers should encourage it, and we should applaud companies that invest in it. Nonetheless, there are risks to overstating the benefits of recycling. Unlike repair, recycling doesn't reduce demand for or slow production of new devices. And in fact, it has the potential to increase consumption. By reducing the costs of inputs, recycling could lower prices and shorten the lifecycles of new products. At the same time, it offers consumers an easy way to absolve themselves of responsibility without fully confronting the consequences of their choices. Recycling an old laptop is certainly better than tossing it into a landfill. But recycling isn't without its own costs. It requires a collection infrastructure, shipping networks, and energy-consuming facilities outfitted with specialized equipment.

Those costs aside, electronics recycling rates today are far too low to sustain demand. In 2019, only 17.4 percent of global e-waste was recycled through formal channels – about 9.3 million metric tons. And the growth rate of recycling is easily outpaced by e-waste production.[114] When we compare recycling rates across the globe, there's plenty of room for improvement. Europe leads the way, safely recycling 42.5 percent of its e-waste, the result of strict regulation and significant investment. But even there, more than half of e-waste isn't recycled. The rest of the world fares far worse. Asia recycles just 11.7% of its e-waste; the Americas, 9.4%; Oceania, 8.8%; and Africa, less than 1%.[115] To realize significant benefits from recycling, governments and firms need to take aggressive steps to capture a far greater portion of the e-waste stream. But even if e-waste recycling rates reached 100 percent, demand for raw materials would still outstrip supply. According to the United Nations, device makers would need an additional 14 million metric tons of iron, aluminum, and copper each year to keep pace with growing demand.[116]

So far, we've focused on formal, documented recycling. That process requires compliance with health, safety, and environmental regulations that protect workers and the surrounding community.[117] Partly because of those justifiably high standards, more than 82 percent of e-waste escapes the sanctioned recycling chain. Much of it ends up in landfills. Some is exported to developing economies for repair or repurposed for used parts. But every year, millions of tons of electronic waste are broken down by unregulated, informal recyclers. These operations challenge the popular conception of recycling as an environmentally friendly solution.

Informal recycling sites are scattered across Asia and Africa, from China and Vietnam to Ghana and Nigeria. Although they are generally small, independent operations, they tend to be found in clusters of dozens, hundreds, or even thousands. At one time, Guiyu, a city of 150,000 on the coast of the South China Sea, was known as the "electronic graveyard of the world."[118] Thousands of small-scale, backyard recycling operations dotted the city. Tens of thousands of workers – men, women, and children – disassembled e-waste with hand tools, like hammers and chisels. They leached gold and other valuable metals from circuit boards in open-pit baths of nitric and hydrochloric acid. And they burned electrical wiring and cables to uncover the copper inside.[119] After Chinese authorities cracked down on the importation of e-waste, much of that waste was redirected to countries like Vietnam and the Philippines, where the same practices continued.

Without the high-tech equipment, protective gear, and strict regulations that characterize formal recycling, communities forced to rely on backyard recycling face serious health and environmental risks. Melting plastic releases toxic fumes, and heavy metals find their way into the water and soil.[120] These pollutants are associated with a litany of health problems for workers and local communities. Cancer, miscarriage, birth defects, decreased lung function, neurodevelopmental issues, and increased mortality rates have all been linked to informal recycling.[121]

One seemingly straightforward response to the harms of informal recycling is to redirect more e-waste to licensed, regulated recyclers. But a 2016 study that tracked displays and printers sent to formal recyclers in the United States found that 40 percent of those devices were exported. Nearly all of them ended up in developing economies that rely on the dangerous, unregulated recycling practices described above.[122] So the boundary separating safe, responsible recycling from the toxic, exploitative export of e-waste is more porous than we might hope.

Given the costs of both formal and informal recycling, repair offers obvious comparative advantages. Rather than shredding a phone with a dead battery, melting its components, and using them as manufacturing inputs, we could simply replace the battery. Repair – although it requires a steady stream of replacement parts – uses less energy and fewer resources than formal recycling. And it avoids the risk that our devices will contribute to the harms informal recycling inflicts on vulnerable communities. Perhaps most importantly, repair teaches us better habits. Resources are limited, but too often our appetites are not.

The Social Benefits of Repair

The most obvious upsides of repair are economic and environmental. On their own, those virtues ought to prompt us to rethink existing policies and behaviors. But repair offers another set of benefits that are more easily overlooked. When we diagnose and fix the things we own, we are reconfiguring our interactions with the world around us. At the same time, we are refining our understanding, developing new skills, and strengthening social ties within our communities.

Repair can change the way we relate to the world around us. It empowers us to exert control over technology. When our devices break, our plans and expectations are disrupted. Imagine you've been planning a bike ride at the end of a long workday. You mentally map out your route, looking forward to some head-clearing physical exertion. You change into more suitable clothes, fill your water bottle, and strap on your helmet, only to discover a flat tire. If you have the parts, tools, and know-how to swap out a punctured inner tube, the flat is an annoyance, a mere a stumbling block. But without the ability to repair, your plans are undone. You are defeated by circumstance.

Repair cultivates a sense of self-sufficiency and autonomy that is increasingly rare in a world shaped by networked technologies. A bicycle, at least, is within your physical control. What happens to family movie night when the popcorn is popped, the group is assembled on the sofa, but the internet goes down for no apparent reason? When we can't understand or control our devices, we cede authority to external forces. Our relationship with technology grows more passive and dependent. That trend is particularly problematic given the extent to which our lives, even our identities, are intertwined with electronics. We outsource mental processes to our smartphones. They remember our friends' phone numbers, our relatives' birthdays, and our appointments so we don't have to. They navigate us through city streets we used to know by heart. For better or worse, we rely on these devices as extensions of our brains. It's no wonder that when they break, we rush to replace them. For some, this problem is even more pronounced.

Many people rely on medical devices like cochlear implants and insulin pumps. These devices can be the difference between life and death. But existing regulatory processes don't always ensure that they work properly. Nearly half a million Abbott pacemakers, for example, were susceptible to remote attacks that could rapidly and fatally drain their batteries.[123] And the company's purported fix came with its own risk of malfunction.[124] Or consider how the inability to repair motorized wheelchairs can leave their users immobile and isolated. When the battery in the motorized wheelchair Kenny Maestas used couldn't hold a charge, the device maker told him it would be a month before a technician could look at it.[125] Even if the company had the necessary parts in stock, its policy insisted on separate inspection and repair appointments. In the end, it took more than two months before Kenny's wheelchair was running again.

If these devices – from smartphones to medical devices – are extensions of ourselves, the right to repair them is vital to our personal freedom and agency. Without repair, we are dependent on the companies that sell those products to ensure that we can commute to work, communicate with our loved ones, heat our homes, cook our food, and stay alive. These firms, though, often have goals that diverge from our best interests. Rather than simply hoping they do right by us, repair gives us some measure of independence and self-reliance. It helps us transcend the role of passive consumer to become more active and responsible participants in our lives.

In moments of crisis, that freedom to operate is even more essential. Under normal circumstances, if something goes wrong with a piece of vital equipment there are channels for having it repaired – original manufacturers to call, warranties to enforce, and experts to enlist. But those channels can be interrupted, and supply chains can be broken. As COVID-19 unsettled life across the globe in 2020, hospitals found themselves unable to access parts and service needed to keep life-saving equipment operational. Increased demand for ventilators and other equipment revealed the degree to which hospitals are dependent on authorized repair providers and underscored the need for in-house repair technicians. Beyond medical equipment, consumers confronted other, less-dire interference with established repair channels. As retailers across the world closed during the pandemic, thousands of customers found their devices stranded behind shuttered storefronts, awaiting repair. And unknown thousands more were stuck holding onto broken devices as those stores remained shuttered for months.[126] Repair cannot fully insulate us from the effects of a pandemic, of course, but it can make our technological infrastructure more resilient in the face of local and global disruption.

Beyond a sense of personal control, repair helps us better understand the world around us. Despite the centrality of modern technology to our daily lives, most of us have, at best, a cursory understanding of how our devices work. When they operate as designed, these tools recede into the background. It's not until they break that the question of *how* they do what they do occurs to us. That question presents an opportunity. It is a chance to engage with these tools in a new way, one that reveals not only how they work, but how they fail, and if you are lucky, how to set things right again. Successful or not, attempts at repair can teach us something. They reveal the sometimes-hidden and often-ignored mechanisms that operate just below the surface of our lives.

Aside from a more secure understanding of the operation of technologies, repair helps develop valuable problem-solving skills. Repairs vary in their difficulty. Some failures are easy to diagnose and simple to fix. But often, repair is far from straight-forward. There is no simple algorithm or checklist to follow. It requires a creative, even improvisatory approach. These more challenging repairs require you to start with an immediate problem – your car won't start – and identify potential causes within a complex system. Maybe the battery is dead, or maybe it's one of a dozen other possible problems: a failed timing belt, a clogged fuel filter, carbon-fouled spark plugs, a cracked dis-tributor cap, a bad fuel pump, or an oversensitive security system, among others. Determining the right diagnosis requires some combination of experience, intuition, educated guessing, and trial and error.[127]

The same is true for remedying a problem. In some cases, you simply substitute a broken component for a new one. But when tools or replacement parts are unavailable, too expensive, or unreliable, a more creative solution is often necessary. Lara Houston, in her study of Ugandan mobile-phone repairers, describes one such technique. Replacing a handset's micro-phone used to be a simple, straightforward repair. But once microphones were integrated into the devices' motherboards, repair required access to infra-red soldering stations, which were not widely available. Instead, enterprising repairers relied on "looping," a technique that used thin copper wires to con-nect the motherboard to the microphone.[128]

Not every attempt at repair is successful. But the effort is worthwhile even when a repair fails. Like many abilities, if we don't use our repair skills, they can atrophy. Studies, for exam-ple, have found that drivers who rely on turn-by-turn GPS instructions exhibit lower brain activity than those who navi-gate by their sense of direction and memory.[129] A culture that prioritizes replacement over repair not only devalues compe-tencies like diagnosis and systematic problem-solving, but is less likely to develop and maintain them.

That's not to say repair and innovation are at odds – quite the opposite. Innovation isn't reserved for the design of new pro-ducts. Repair requires its own measure of inventiveness, and it builds skills and knowledge crucial to the process of creating something new. Once you understand how a technology works, why it fails, and how it can be repaired, the leap to developing an improvement is a small one. In Douglas Harper's ethnography of a small-town repair shop, *Working Knowledge*, he introduces Willie, a skilled and experienced mechanic. After repairing countless Saab door handles, Willie designed his own, replacing weak, white metal components with a stronger alloy and eliminating a problematic plastic ball bearing altogether.[130] Willie's innovation improved the lives of his customers but had little impact beyond his local community. In contrast, one of the most impactful inventions of the twentieth century was conceived in a repair shop. Before their groundbreaking aeronautical work, Orville and Wilbur Wright ran a bicycle repair shop in Dayton, Ohio. There, they developed wood and metalworking skills and became familiar with hardware, like the sprocket drive train they later incorporated into the first airplane.[131] While not a direct outgrowth of their bike shop, the Wrights' invention undoubtedly benefitted from the knowledge and skills they honed through repair. Similarly, the early decades of the automobile – when self-repair was expected and encouraged – proved fertile ground for user innovation. Farmers repurposed their Model Ts to power agricultural tools. And as Kathleen Franz writes, "affordable, mass-produced automobiles opened new and exciting possibilities for the American consumer to practice technological competency and demonstrate his, and occasionally her, own ingenuity."[132]

Repair also allows us to recognize and honor sentimental attachment to objects and the history they represent. Maybe it isn't economically rational to repair your grandmother's old record player. But sentimental attachment to an object is often just as important as its market value in determining its subjective worth. The decision to repair reflects a mix of economic considerations, social conventions, and emotional commitments. This mindset helps explain why some objects seem to celebrate their repair. Maybe you own an old, beloved pair of jeans that have been patched and mended, again and again. Or perhaps your neighbor owns a beat-up truck with mismatched paint, evidencing decades of repair. These objects advertise their longevity, their resilience, and their owners' determination to wring from them every last bit of utility.

But maybe I've just described an eyesore. Consider instead the Japanese tradition of *kintsugi*, a technique for repairing broken ceramics that dates to the sixteenth century.[133] A shattered cup or bowl is reassembled with a tree-based lacquer resin called *urushi*. Those joints, rather than being concealed, are then dusted with gold or silver, giving the technique its name, literally "golden joinery."[134] By deliberately directing attention to the cracks and their repair, *kintsugi* draws on the Japanese notions of *mottainai* – a feeling of regret over waste – and *wabi-sabi* – an aesthetic tradition that embraces imperfection and impermanence.[135] Not only does *kintsugi* extend the useful life of objects, but it respects the effort and artistry of the original creator and the repairer in equal measure. In doing so, it offers a commentary on the relative value of repairing or discarding the things we create. Importantly, *kintsugi* also results in a new and potentially more valuable object, highlighting repair's capacity for transformation.

Finally, repair helps us build communities. It is a participatory, collaborative exercise that involves the sharing of knowledge and skills. That's true for professionals like the Xerox repair providers profiled in Julian Orr's *Talking about Machines*, who traded "war stories" as a means of supplementing official procedures and documentation.[136] And it's an accurate description of amateurs, like Belgian steam-locomotive enthusiasts, who volunteer to repair trains, exchanging strategies and experiences.[137] In some cases, repair networks are formalized. Mobile-phone repairers in Dhaka, Bangladesh train new generations through apprenticeships.[138] Others, like the repair cafés and clinics that have sprung up around the world in recent years, offer a less-formal model.[139] Novices drop in, their broken stuff in tow, and learn from volunteers with varying degrees of expertise.

Regardless of the form it takes, independent repair promotes the distribution of knowledge and skills. People learn from each other, share their successes, and learn from their failures. But hostility to independent repair tends to concentrate expertise – and with it, power – within manufacturers' own tightly controlled networks, effectively exporting repair knowledge out of local communities. Rather than a group of farmers taking turns peering quizzically under the hood of a temperamental tractor until they collectively puzzle out a solution, an authorized technician interprets proprietary diagnostic codes. That centralization of repair knowledge corrodes existing communities and prevents new ones from emerging. And it leaves us beholden to device makers. Despite their market incentives, manufacturers aren't always accountable to consumers or responsive to their needs. Nor do device makers necessarily invest in developing the sort of specific, context-sensitive knowledge that communities of common interest might cultivate.

Repair helps us construct a more complete picture of the world, its design, and its flaws. It sharpens the skills we need to identify, analyze, and remedy those shortcomings. It prepares us to not only mend what is broken, but craft new solutions to long-standing problems. It emboldens us to take control of the forces that shape our lives and encourages coordination to achieve shared goals. In that sense, repair teaches technologically literate civics. Contemporary policy debates, from internet platform regulation and digital surveillance to automation and artificial intelligence, demand some engagement with and understanding of technology. The practice of repair, while no substitute for hard-earned subject-matter expertise, better equips us to evaluate arguments and make informed choices between competing policy visions. It makes us better citizens.

That said, recognizing the value of repair and the inevitability of breakdown doesn't mean we must – or even should – insist on repair in every instance. Our decisions about repair turn on the needs and material circumstances of individuals and communities. While repair is generally more cost-effective than replacement, there are times when the frequency or expense of fixing an old car, for example, will justify replacing it. Assessing the environmental impact of repair requires a similar calculus. Because of their batteries, electric vehicles are considerably more carbon-intensive than internal combustion engines at the production stage. But over the lifetime of the vehicle, electric cars reduce carbon emissions significantly.[140] So replacing an aging internal combustion vehicle with an electric one may be the better choice. But to realize those environmental benefits, we need to drive electric vehicles for a long time. That will require functioning markets for parts and repair services.

These calculations – weighing environmental, economic, and social implications – are complex, but humans have plenty of experience making them. Stone Age hunter-gatherers in the Karoo, South Africa, to take one example, adopted differing approaches to repairing tools depending on their lifestyles.[141] Groups that moved camp frequently repeatedly repaired tools used to hunt and collect food, but replaced tools used for hide-making and maintenance. For groups that remained in long-term camps while sending hunting parties out on expeditions, the opposite was true. They replaced hunting implements, but repaired maintenance tools. Just like our ancient ancestors, we live in a world of inevitable breakdown, and repair strategies remain crucial to managing our limited resources. As the next chapter details, repair has been a key component of our relationship with technology throughout human history. Efforts to impede repair, on the other hand, are a creation of the modern consumer economy.

3 THE HISTORY OF REPAIR

Humans have been repairing since our earliest days as a species. It has proven a remarkably adaptable practice. Whatever technology we dreamed up, new methods of repair followed just a step behind. As those technologies grew more complicated, the investments of time, material, and labor necessary to produce them mounted. Repair allowed us to protect those investments, but it was still a resource-intensive proposition. Eventually, industrialization and the introduction of interchangeable parts briefly promised to make repair easier and more reliable than ever before. But over the course of the twentieth century, assembly lines became so efficient at churning out cars, appliances, clothes, and other goods that the calculus around repair shifted. Modern manufacturing meant plummeting assembly times and labor costs. Companies quickly came to appreciate that product durability wasn't in their economic self-interest. Demand needed to keep up with supply, one way or another. So, manufacturers found ways to induce consumption and discourage repair. As early as the 1920s, firms were exploring the strategies that would eventually become known as "planned obsolescence." By the 1950s, those techniques were cornerstones of the consumer economy. At the same time, urbanization and specialization in the labor market meant domestic repairs were increasingly uncommon. For the first time, repair as a ubiquitous practice integral to daily life was threatened. Today, those threats are magnified. The right to repair is contested and, in some corners, controversial. But to appreciate the current assault on repair, we need to understand it as an historical aberration.

The Origins of Repair

Repair is a practical necessity for a species that relies on technology. Our Paleolithic ancestors fashioned hand axes – stones shaped to create pointed, sharp edges – millions of years ago. Even these simplest of tools were resharpened and repaired to extend their useful lives.[1] Some 300,000 years ago, both early *Homo sapiens* and *Homo neanderthalensis* began crafting composite tools, like spears, by hafting stone points onto wooden handles.[2] Because those points could be replaced or repaired, hafted tools lasted longer, offsetting the upfront investments necessary to produce them.[3]

Pottery is another milestone in human innovation. According to fragments discovered in southern China, it dates back at least 20,000 years.[4] Since pottery was the cutting-edge technology of the day, Neolithic humans predictably developed techniques to repair it, drilling small holes in broken pieces, or sherds, then lacing them together with string or leather.[5] In other cases, bitumen, a naturally occurring tar, was used as a glue.[6] Later techniques relied on metal staples. In some cases, "alien fragments" – similarly-shaped sherds from another broken vessel – were incorporated, marking an early use of replacement parts.[7]

Throughout early human history, as technology grew more sophisticated, so did repair. During the Bronze Age, statues were welded and soldered.[8] Boats of the era bear signs of regular repair.[9] Likewise, timber buildings were rehabilitated.[10] Casa Romuli, the purported wattle-and-daub home of Rome's founder, built around 700 BC, was repeatedly patched up to ward off evil omens.[11] By the Iron Age, cauldron repairs were common,[12] as were repairs of swords and scabbards.[13] One particularly well-preserved example, the Kirkburn sword, was excavated from a second- or third-century BC grave.[14] Its crudely rejoined scabbard, like shield fittings and other artifacts of the time, exhibit no expert craftsmanship, in contrast with the skilled metalworking that created it.[15] These visually conspicuous repairs may have been the result of limited time, skill, or resources. But they may have had greater significance, perhaps announcing the act of repair and hinting at the objects' violent histories.[16]

In the Roman Empire, repairs were organized, ambitious, and innovative. Rome levied taxes for the maintenance of aqueducts, employing hundreds of laborers to maintain and repair pipes, valves, and holding tanks.[17] And in the days and weeks leading up to the eruption of Mt. Vesuvius in 79 CE, residents of Pompeii poured molten iron to fill holes and ruts in their streets.[18] And around the third century CE, Roman military armor was redesigned, in part, to facilitate easier repair. Rather than single breast and backplates, Rome opted for a modular design that allowed for easier repair and replacement of damaged pieces.[19]

During the Middle Ages, repair grew even more specialized. Carpenters repaired homes and other more modest structures.[20] Newly introduced iron rims for wagon wheels demanded more intricate repair methods than the old-fashioned approach familiar to famers of the era.[21] Medieval manuscripts were repaired and rebound by expert hands, often with materials harvested from other damaged books.[22] And engineering emerged as a trade, as skilled workers built and repaired city walls, forts, and bridges.[23]

Throughout these eras, repair was intimately tied to the development of technology. Human artifacts required increasing investments of material resources, time, effort, and expertise. Those investments called out for repair techniques that preserved the value embedded in human creations. The complexity of repairs tracked the complexity of the technologies to which they were applied. Relatedly, this history shows that responsibility for repair has been shared between expert specialists and do-it-yourself amateurs for thousands of years, at the very least. At the same time, the evidence suggests that, in addition to purely utilitarian concerns, repair can serve aesthetic and communicative purposes as well.[24]

For the next several hundred years, the basic relationship between technology and repair remained unchanged. Humans developed increasingly sophisticated technologies, and more elaborate techniques for repair sprung up alongside them. The Renaissance saw the introduction of the mechanical clock, microscope, telescope, and the printing press to Europe, although movable type was first invented in China hundreds of years earlier.[25] And during the Enlightenment, the piano, steam engine, and pendulum clock, among others, were added to humanity's list of technological marvels. These intricate inventions were painstakingly crafted by hand using custom-made components. Naturally, their repair demanded correspondingly skilled artisans who could understand their operation, diagnose their failure, and fashion replacement parts when necessary. Of course, the repair of everyday items continued undisturbed throughout this period of scientific and mechanical achievement. Socks were darned, roofs retiled, and plowshares sharpened. But whether carried out by an overworked homemaker, the local blacksmith, or a learned scientist, repairs of this era were bespoke. There were no off-the-shelf replacement parts or ready-made repair kits. But that was about to change.

Industrialization and Interchangeability

By the eighteenth century, the lack of interchangeable parts was a widely recognized problem. The inability to produce identical components slowed production, increased costs, and hampered repair. Today, we take interchangeability for granted. Batteries are sold in standard sizes. So are car tires, light bulbs, and memory chips, not to mention the countless screws and bolts holding modern devices together. But that wasn't always the case. In the 1790s, Henry Maudslay, a British metalworker and inventor, first developed a lathe capable of reliably producing interchangeable screws. Until then, every screw, bolt, or nut was cut by hand. When a machine was disassembled, each bolt and its corresponding nut had to be carefully labeled. A bolt threaded to match one nut would have been incompatible with another of the same size. Maudslay introduced the idea of standardized threads, a principle that seems so obvious to us today that it's hard to imagine it required invention.[26]

Reliably producing interchangeable mechanical components was a challenge across industries. But demand for cheaper, more accurate, and more reparable weaponry led to important advances. Early efforts by the French military gave rise to uniform calibers and interchangeable wheels for cannons. But the tolerances of a 12-pound cannon did not demand particularly precise methods of manufacture. Mechanically, rifles were much more intricate, requiring virtually identical parts.[27] In 1785, Thomas Jefferson – then United States Minister to France – wrote about the pioneering work of gunsmith Honoré Blanc, which he witnessed firsthand: "He presented me the parts of fifty locks taken to pieces, and arranged in compartments. I put several together myself, taking pieces at hazard as they came to hand, and they fitted in the most perfect manner."[28] Some sixteen years later and back on US soil, President-elect Jefferson, along with President John Adams, watched a similar exhibition by Eli Whitney, the inventor of the cotton gin, who had taken up arms manufacturing. Whitney used a screwdriver to attach ten different locks, or firing mechanisms, to a single musket. He then disassembled the locks and put them back together, mixing and matching the parts. As impressive as this feat was, it was more a proof of concept than reality. Whitney, like Blanc before him, likely filed and shaped these components by hand before his demonstration.[29]

Nonetheless, the US military was convinced of the value of interchangeability. Standardizing the design and manufacture of weapons made them more reliable and more lethal. Weapons could be also be produced faster and at lower cost. Rather than relying on skilled artisans to craft and shape parts by hand, mechanization allowed manufacturers to rely largely on unskilled labor. These cost savings extended throughout the life of a weapon. Prior to interchangeability, if a weapon failed in battle, a replacement part would have to be fashioned and fitted for that specific firearm. But with interchangeable parts,

spares could be manufactured in large quantities or canniba-
lized from other weapons, then easily swapped out. Repair, like
manufacturing, would be faster and cheaper.[30]

Whitney won a contract to provide 10,000 muskets to the US
military over the course of two years. But it took him eleven
years to fulfill the order. And in the end, the guns he shipped
were not interchangeable.[31] Perhaps learning a lesson from that
experience, when the Ordnance Department awarded
a contract to Simeon North for 20,000 pistols in 1813, it insisted
they be constructed using interchangeable parts so that "any
limb or part of one pistol may be fitted to any other pistol."[32]
The contract also stipulated that North provide spares of the
components most likely to fail.[33]

Guns weren't the only product that benefitted from interchangeability. In 1816, Eli Terry revolutionized clock-making
with a low-priced wooden clock made from interchangeable
parts.[34] Decades later, Aaron Dennison, co-founder of the
Waltham Watch Company, designed a pocket watch with interchangeable parts.[35] Given the intricate gear works of time-
pieces, precisely machined components were critical. These
strides had spillover effects for other industries. Brown &
Sharpe – a firm that started out building and repairing clocks
and watches – would come to prominence for designing micro-
meters and other precision tools, as well as creating the US
standard for electrical wiring gauges.[36]

Throughout the second half of the nineteenth century, manufacturers of a range of consumer goods – sewing machines,
harvesters, typewriters, and bicycles – adopted the so-called
American system of mechanized production and interchangeable parts.[37] But the tools of the day were incapable of precisely
cutting hardened metal parts, so they had to be "hand fit" by
filing. New technology was needed to perfect the manufacture
of interchangeable parts. Frederick Winslow Taylor, better
known for his influential management techniques, began
experimenting with new cutting methods in 1894. By the turn
of the century, he'd perfected a high-speed cutting tool that
allowed for precision machining of parts.[38]

Interchangeability was indispensable to the mass production of consumer goods that characterized twentieth-century Western economies. In 1908, Henry Leland, the founder of the Cadillac Automobile Company and later the Lincoln Motor Company, updated the demonstration technique first deployed by Blanc and Whitney. Three Cadillacs were disassembled, their parts intermingled, and then reassembled and driven some 500 miles without incident.[39] That same year, Henry Ford, relying on Taylor's insights and a moving assembly line, began production of the Model T. Within a few years, Ford had fine-tuned the process, slashing production time for each vehicle from twelve hours to just over ninety minutes.[40] By 1927, 15 million Model Ts had rolled off the line. Not only did Ford embrace interchangeability as a production strategy, but the company understood that widely available and easily replaced parts made its cars more valuable. Every Ford included a toolkit and a straightforward repair manual that walked owners through basic fixes.[41] As Henry Ford explained:

> We cannot conceive how to serve the consumer unless we make for him something that, as far as we can provide, will last forever .... It does not please us to have a buyer's car wear out or become obsolete. We want the man who buys one of our products never to have to buy another. We never make an improvement that renders any previous model obsolete. The parts of a specific model are not only interchangeable with all other cars of that model, but they are interchangeable with similar parts on all the cars that we have turned out.[42]

Even after Ford stopped building Model Ts, the company produced replacement engines to service the existing fleet for another decade and a half. Other widespread technologies of the era, like telephones and refrigerators, embodied a similar philosophy.[43] They were built for durability and reparability, and routinely lasted for decades. But while the production techniques Ford pioneered remain central to manufacturing today, this appreciation for repair and durability was soon viewed as outdated.

Inventing Obsolescence

Ford didn't just tap into a new market for automobiles. Along with other early carmakers, it created that market. In a world in which practically no one owned a car, the goal was simple: convince consumers buy a Ford rather than a competitor's vehicle. Ford's strategy was to make cars affordable, durable, and reparable. For decades, the company was wildly successful.

But as markets mature, firms have strong economic incentives to design products, craft policies, and shape consumer preferences in ways that encourage consumption. The more products they sell, the more money they make. A company that builds toasters that last twenty years will likely be less profitable than one that produces toasters that are replaced every four years. To meet demand, the second company sells five toasters for each one sold by its competitor, all else being equal. That's not to say some consumers won't pay a premium for quality, durability, or reparability. Given our sensitivity to price, however, that premium is often not enough to compensate for lost sales volume. That lesson has been internalized by makers of household appliances, electronics, and apparel, among other goods. They don't want us to buy one washing machine, phone, or sweater that lasts forever. Instead, they want us to buy more, and more often.[44]

Increased consumption drives economic growth.[45] This basic insight led Bernard London, a little-known real-estate broker and would-be economic policy innovator, to propose a radical system in 1932 to end the Great Depression. According to London, the ailment facing the US economy was that consumers insisted on "disobeying the law of obsolescence" by "using their old cars, their old tires, their old radios, and their old clothing much longer than ... expected."[46] Boosting consumption of new products would spur a virtuous cycle, lifting the country out of its economic slump. If people would only spend more money on new products, he reasoned, demand would stimulate production and increase employment. The question was how to encourage new purchases in the face of austerity. Under

London's plan, a government bureaucracy would "assign a lease of life" to every product. After the allotted time, those products would be "retired, and replaced with fresh merchandise." Expired goods would be collected by the government and destroyed. And a tax would discourage those who might otherwise "continue to possess and use old clothing, automobiles, and buildings after they have passed their obsolescence date." London published his plan in a tract called *Ending the Depression Through Planned Obsolescence*.

As detailed by Giles Slade in his book *Made to Break*, London's vision of centrally planned consumption may seem absurd today, but it was rooted in an established and influential school of thought.[47] While London may have coined the term "planned obsolescence," he was hardly its first advocate. By 1922, conventional wisdom held that "chang[ing] designs so that old models will become obsolete and new ones will have the chance to be bought" was simply "good manufacturing practice" and "clever business."[48]

In a world of perpetual replacement, advertising took on new importance. J. George Frederick, a former ad man who edited the trade publication *Advertising and Selling*, called this strategy "progressive obsolescence." With his wife Christine Frederick, a home economist and popular author, he advocated for a culture that values "buying for up-to-dateness, efficiency, and style ... rather than simply for the last ounce of use."[49] Rather than the coercive power of the state, the Fredericks preferred to encourage consumption through the more subtle influence of advertising and fashion. As Christine Frederick asked, "why be an old frump and cling to an old necktie or old dress until it wears through?"[50] But the case for consumption transcended mere matters of taste. A 1930 editorial in *House & Garden* declared, "The good citizen does not repair the old; he buys anew."[51] Others, from industrial designers to investment bankers preached the gospel of economic prosperity through obsolescence.[52] So while London's plan may strike us as dystopian fantasy, in an important sense, it was a logical outgrowth of earlier iterations of intentional obsolescence.

General Motors (GM) CEO Alfred Sloan understood how styling changes could speed the replacement rates of vehicles. In his view, "The great problem of the future is to have our cars different from each other and different from year to year."[53] In the late 1920s, he began introducing annual models, featuring design updates – sometimes subtle and sometimes significant – that provided an immediate visual indication of a vehicle's age.[54] With those cues in place, carmakers and their marketing teams could conjure drivers' feelings of pride, envy, insecurity, and hope to convince them to trade their current car for a new one. Sloan and those who followed in his footsteps democratized conspicuous consumption. Eventually even Ford followed suit, introducing new models with minor stylistic changes and parts that were incompatible between models.[55]

Obsolescence takes many forms. GM's annual rollout of new models is an example of psychological obsolescence. A decade-old Chevy Malibu might still run perfectly well, but advertising and social pressure can conspire to convince a driver to replace it with a new one anyway. Similarly, purely aesthetic considerations might prompt us to replace a functioning product. Maybe you've tired of stainless-steel appliances and want to spruce up your kitchen with a new look. Or perhaps your running shoes, while still supportive, look a bit worse for wear. Changes in behavior are another source of obsolescence.[56] In the mid-twentieth century, for example, it was common for American homes and apartment buildings to include milk doors. These small, locked compartments allowed a delivery person to deposit containers of milk from the outside, while residents could retrieve them from an interior door. Once milk became widely available at supermarkets, these once-valued architectural features were relegated to odd curiosities.

Far more common is technological obsolescence – the process by which one solution to a problem is displaced by a new generation of tools.[57] The car ousted the horse and buggy. The laptop unseated the word processor, which had deposed the typewriter. And the smartphone supplanted the landline, the answering machine, the mp3 player, the camera, the calculator, and even the flashlight. But obsolescence isn't always a byproduct of technological progress or innovation. Product failure is another key driver of obsolescence. A laptop might be deemed obsolete when its battery dies or when it's no longer supported by software updates. In part, that calculation depends on the availability, cost, and effectiveness of repair.

Obsolescence is a natural process. Things wear out. Styles evolve. But the decisions of manufacturers, marketers, policy makers, and consumers can hasten its pace. Legal regulations can also encourage obsolescence. When the US Federal Communications Commission decided to reallocate FM radio signals from the 42–50 MHz range to the 88–106 MHz band in 1946, it rendered obsolete more than half a million radios.[58] More recently, the Obama administration's Car Allowance Rebate System – better known as the "cash for clunkers" program – offered consumers $3 billion in incentives to trade old cars for new ones. Designed to phase out fuel-inefficient vehicles while boosting the auto industry, the program likely would've made Bernard London proud.

But the most pernicious forms of planned obsolescence are strategies to build products that don't last. Early efforts to manufacture products with short lifespans were explicit. As far back as the 1870s, firms sold disposable collars for men's shirts, which were cheaper than regular laundering.[59] In the 1920s, Kimberly Clark repurposed surplus cellulose, intended for wartime bandages, to produce single-use products like Kotex pads and Kleenex tissues. In time, disposable diapers, pens, razors, and even cameras followed in their wake, to say nothing of the spork. Whether phrased in terms of convenience or cleanliness, these products tout their disposability as a feature.

In other instances, though, schemes to shorten product lifespans were far from transparent. Readers of Thomas Pynchon's sprawling novel *Gravity's Rainbow* might recall that one of its many subplots involves a sentient, immortal lightbulb called Byron and an assassin, recruited by an international cartel known as Phoebus to terminate this affront to planned obsolescence.[60] As unlikely as it might seem, the Phoebus cartel was not a figment of Pynchon's imagination. Beginning in 1924, Phoebus – spearheaded by General Electric and comprising the leading lightbulb manufacturers of France, Germany, Hungary, Japan, the Netherlands, and the United Kingdom – set out to increase industry-wide revenue through anticompetitive collusion.[61] In addition to run-of-the-mill price fixing and output controls, the cartel was determined to reduce the lifespan of the world's lightbulbs. And for the better part of a decade, it succeeded. When the cartel formed, the average lifespan of a standard incandescent bulb was somewhere between 1,500 and 2,000 hours. Manufacturers decided they'd be more profitable if bulbs lasted only 1,000 hours. Over the course of just eight years, from 1926 to 1934, they reduced average operating time to 1,200 hours. During that period, sales volume increased by tens of millions of units annually, while prices remained stable. Around the same time, as revealed in an internal memo uncovered by the US Department of Justice, GE set out to reduce the life of its flashlight bulbs by two-thirds, a move it expected to increase sales by 60 percent.[62]

These shorter-lasting bulbs were the result of a concerted, international research-and-development program. By adjusting the composition and shape of filaments and increasing the electrical current flowing through them, Phoebus members produced brighter bulbs that burned out far more quickly. From its base in Geneva, the cartel systematically evaluated the bulbs produced by its hundreds of member factories, fining those whose products exceeded the agreed-upon lifespan limits. After one member was caught producing bulbs that were deemed too durable, Anton Philips, co-founder of the Dutch firm that bears his family name, warned:

> This ... very dangerous practice [would have] a most detrimental influence on the total turnover of the Phoebus Parties ... . After the very strenuous efforts we made to emerge from a period of long life lamps, it is of the greatest

importance that we do not sink back into the same mire by . . . supplying lamps that will have a very prolonged life.[63]

The concerns motivating the Phoebus cartel were representative of the era. The massive industrial capacity developed during the early decades of the twentieth century meant factories produced more goods than consumers needed. To truly take advantage of the efficiencies of industrial production, firms needed to convince consumers to keep buying new stuff, whether they needed it or not. And if advertising didn't do the trick, firms could force consumers' collective hand by designing and manufacturing short-lived products. Beyond the Phoebus cartel, it's hard to say how common systematic efforts to reduce durability were among other industrial giants. The full extent of the Phoebus scheme was only recently uncovered by researchers, despite the US Department of Justice bringing a case against GE for anticompetitive conduct in the 1940s.[64]

Regardless of the degree of coordination, the rollout of planned obsolescence was interrupted by two historical developments. First, the US stock market crash in 1929 marked the beginning of the Great Depression. Throughout the 1930s, economies around the globe saw record levels of unemployment and significant reductions in industrial production, exports, and household incomes. Thrift became a necessity. Rather than buying new, people learned to get by with what they had. Repair and maintenance naturally took on new importance. And the do-it-yourself ethos offered a sense of self-sufficiency in economically uncertain times.[65] This resurgent frugality ran counter to the advice of those, like Bernard London, who thought consumption was the shortest path out of the Depression. A few years after London's call for planned obsolescence, the advertising trade journal *Printers' Ink* ran an article by advertising executive Leon Kelley decrying product durability. He insisted that unless manufacturers and consumers gave up on the expectation of long-lasting products, factories would sit idle, and the unemployment rolls would swell even further. Advertisers, he argued, should do their part by emphasizing the ephemerality of consumer goods rather than their durability.

As the effects of the Depression dragged on, planned obsolescence was dealt a second blow when the German invasion of Poland in 1939 sparked World War II. Over the course of the war, rationing programs and public information campaigns equated thrift, reuse, and repair with patriotism in Britain and the United States, among other countries. In Britain, the Ministry of Information published a series of posters and booklets urging citizens to "Make Do and Mend."[66] A character called "Mrs Sew and Sew" offered instruction on sewing, patching, and darning clothes to leave more fabric available for military uniforms.[67] Another poster, featuring a hand clenching a wrench, reminded the public that "Repair work is vital to the war effort."[68] In the United States, clothing, shoes, stoves, bicycles, and typewriters were rationed to maximize military production capacity. And the Office of War Information published its own anti-obsolescence advocacy. One poster, depicting a man bending over to repair a lawnmower as a woman patches a hole in the seat of his pants, implored Americans to "Use It Up, Wear It Out, Make It Do."[69]

Those lessons were short-lived. In the booming post-war economy of the United States, obsolescence was reinvigorated. Among its most vocal proponents was Brooks Stevens, an industrial and graphic designer, best known for his work on the Oscar Mayer Wienermobile.[70] He understood obsolescence in largely psychological terms and advocated "instilling in the buyer the desire to own something a little newer, a little better, a little sooner than is necessary."[71] In his view, the role of the modern designer was to "make good products, [] induce people to buy them, and then next year [] deliberately introduce something that will make those products old fashioned, out of date, obsolete. We do that for the soundest reason: to make money."[72] Responding to concerns about the waste inherent in this strategy, Stevens argued that last year's models were not simply discarded, but found their way to the used market where they were enjoyed by those with less purchasing power.[73]

These strategies extended beyond the United States. In 1947, France's flagging post-war textile industry needed a boost. That year, Christian Dior – with the financial backing of textile magnate Marcel Boussac – introduced his "New Look." Defined by fitted jackets, cinched waists, and long, voluminous, pleated skirts, Dior's silhouettes consumed yards of fabric. Dior explained his aesthetic as a reaction against the "poverty-stricken, parsimonious era, obsessed with ration books and clothes coupons" from which France had just escaped.[74] But by lengthening his skirts, Dior also prevented women from achieving a similar look by rehemming clothes they already owned, rendering the old obsolete and driving new sales.[75]

Post-war obsolescence wasn't confined to fashion. Manufacturers of home appliances, the most decidedly utilitarian of durable goods, also extolled its virtues. The general manager of Frigidaire described planned obsolescence as "the most important single factor responsible for the growth and vitality of the appliance industry, the automobile industry, and many others."[76] And Whirlpool's chairman dismissed "attempts by various people to toady up to the public by saying they are against planned obsolescence" as nothing short of "commercial demagogy."[77] The economist Victor Lebow summed up the prevailing sentiment of the US business community when he wrote, "Our enormously productive economy ... demands that we make consumption our way of life. ... We need things consumed, burned up, worn out, replaced, and discarded at an ever-increasing rate."[78] Even the White House joined the chorus. Asked what Americans could do to help stave off a recession, President Dwight Eisenhower answered simply, "Buy." Pressed by the reporter on exactly what they should buy, Eisenhower replied, "Buy anything."[79]

By 1958, trade publications were openly endorsing "death dating," the practice of designing products to fail after a specified, and often short, period. After an article in *Design News* revealed that portable radios were built to last for just three years, editor E.S. Stafford defended death dating on two grounds. If radios lasted ten years, he argued, the market would quickly reach saturation and production volume would suffer. And if consumers used the same radio for a decade, they would surely lose out on innovations that developed in the interim.[80]

Open advocacy for planned obsolescence, and in particular strategies that relied on engineering rather than persuasion, sparked a backlash. Consumers, designers, and engineers all expressed their frustration. But the most effective critic was journalist and author Vance Packard, whose 1960 bestseller *The Waste Makers* laid bare many of the practices manufactures and advertisers relied on to move merchandise. Packard made a lasting impact on public opinion. The negative connotation associated with "planned obsolescence" today is due, in no small measure, to Packard's work.[81]

Both psychological obsolescence and death dating influence consumer behavior around repair. Once we've been convinced by advertisers that our old car or last season's overcoat is out of style, we are more likely to replace it rather that repair it. And even in the secondary market, unfashionable used goods are less desirable. Those challenges are compounded by consumers' reasonable suspicions that the goods they buy are built to fail. Why bother to fix a washing machine that has reached its death date?

More directly, Packard detailed the ways in which manufacturers in the 1950s discouraged repair. These included steam irons that "could be repaired only by breaking [them] apart and drilling out the screws," toasters "so riveted together" that they required almost an hour just to disassemble, and appliances that had to be dismantled just to swap out a 10-cent part.[82] He also described efforts to tightly control information about repair. Both consumers and independent repair providers were frustrated by appliance makers' refusals to share service manuals. Instead, as one consumer wrote, those documents were "censored as if they contained obscene material."[83] These efforts to limit repair presaged many of the tactics we see today.

Around the same time, researchers were making foundational breakthroughs that would profoundly reshape technology and our relationship with it. In 1956, the American physicists William Bradford Shockley, John Bardeen, and Walter Houser Brattain shared the Nobel Prize in Physics for their invention of the transistor.[84] Working at Bell Labs, the trio was searching for a smaller and faster substitute for the vacuum tubes and electro-mechanical relays telephone networks relied on at the time. The transistor they created amplified and switched electrical signals. When functioning as amplifiers, transistors boost small electrical currents into much larger ones. As switches, they turn electrical signals on or off. Assembled in sufficient quantities, transistors can store massive amounts of data or perform complex calculations as part of integrated circuits. And unlike the bulky vacuum tubes they replaced, transistors can be microscopic. Today, a microchip smaller than your fingernail can squeeze in 8.5 billion transistors.[85]

In the 1950s though, personal computers and smartphones were still decades away. One of the first consumer products to take advantage of this new technology was the transistor radio. Before transistors, radios relied on vacuum tubes for amplification. Like lightbulbs, vacuum tubes needed to be replaced on occasion. If your radio stopped working, you would open it up, remove the tube with a pair of pliers, and take it to your local department store, where you could test it and if necessary, replace it.[86] Transistor radios, while smaller and cheaper than their predecessors, were far more difficult to repair. Tiny transistors were often soldered onto printed circuit boards, making their replacement too expensive to justify.[87] Some companies, like Zenith, used socketed transistors that could be swapped out more easily. But they relied on nonstandard transistor sizing to capture replacement-part sales.[88]

Over the decades that followed, electronics replaced mechanical components in consumer goods from cars and appliances to watches and toys. Straightforward, user-reparable parts were swapped for inscrutable circuit boards and electronic controls. The mechanically inclined consumer could no longer reliably open a broken clock or coffee pot and figure out the problem. To be sure, electronics offered new, valuable functionality. But it came at a cost. As consumer goods grew more complex, the home was transformed. Fireplaces and boilers were replaced by modern furnaces and computerized HVAC systems. Modern conveniences like climate-control and push-button appliances left consumers more dependent on technologies they couldn't fully control. These technological changes presented new challenges for repair, ones that were reinforced by equally important cultural, economic, and geographic changes that were simultaneously underway.

Landlords and the Law of Repair

The period from 1900 to 1960 saw the introduction of assembly-line production, planned obsolescence, and nascent computing technology – not to mention two world wars and a global economic depression. It was a busy few decades. During that time, the United States shifted from a largely agrarian nation to an increasingly urban one. At the turn of the century, fewer than 40 percent of Americans lived in cities. By 1960, that figure had climbed to nearly 70 percent.[89] Urbanization was largely a byproduct of industrial production. As factories sprung up, they attracted jobseekers from rural communities. In what became known as the Great Migration, as many as 6 million Black Americans moved from the rural south to the cities of the Midwest and Northeast.[90] Similarly, white Appalachians moved in droves to cities like Chicago, Cleveland, and Detroit on the so-called Hillbilly Highway.[91] In just a few short decades, Detroit alone grew from a population of fewer than 300,000 to a city of 1.8 million.

This transition was more than a shift in geography. Unlike the varied, seasonal tasks that defined farm work, factory labor was monotonous and repetitive. In a typical week, a Kentucky farmer may have planted crops, tended to a few animals, fixed a broken well pump, and repaired a sagging barn roof. His cousin in Detroit, in contrast, may have spent every workday mounting hoods on an endless procession of Ford Rancheros. In an era before freeways and Amazon Prime, the geographic isolation of rural life required a large measure of independent problem solving to tackle unexpected challenges. Although life in an industrial center presented its own set of problems, cities, like the assembly lines responsible for their growth, relied on specialization.

Industrialization reshaped not only the products that mid-century Americans bought, but how they lived their lives – where they settled, the nature of their labor, and their relationship with their homes and the technologies inside them. Collectively, these changes forced a rethinking of the legal system's approach to repair. As technology grew more complex, and as the skillsets of city dwellers grew narrower and more specialized, lawmakers and courts recognized the need to encourage repair in certain corners of the market. Specifically, they worried that these shifts, combined with the particular mix of economic incentives in the rental housing market, meant that valuable and necessary repairs would go neglected. To prevent the deterioration of housing stock and protect the dignity of tenants, courts undertook a minor revolution in property law.

Stretching back to the English feudal system of the early Middle Ages, landowners had no obligation to repair any defects in properties they leased.[92] If something went wrong – a fence needed mending, the roof patched, or a window replaced, it was up to the tenant to do it. In fact, tenants who failed to repair the property they leased could be held liable for waste – an unreasonable or improper use of the property – and forced to pay damages to the property owner or even face eviction.[93]

Though harsh from a modern perspective, these rules arose in a very different economic and social context. Most leases involved agricultural land worked by the tenant. Farmers were primarily interested in the value of the land itself rather than any building that happened to be on it. And tenants were generally an industrious lot, able to make most repairs themselves. In contrast to their competent and capable tenants, landlords were often members of the privileged gentry with no discernible skill in maintaining or repairing the property they owned by virtue of a fortunate birth.[94]

This arrangement persisted for the better part of a millennium. It crossed the Atlantic with North American colonists and remained the law in the United States until roughly fifty years ago. Until that point, courts routinely ruled against tenants seeking to force their landlords to make necessary repairs to homes, apartments, and other rental properties.[95] If landlords expressly agreed to make repairs, courts generally enforced those contracts. But short of an outright promise, nothing obligated landlords to repair damage to the properties they rented, regardless of its severity.[96]

In response to the slum-like conditions of tenement buildings and other urban rental properties in the mid-twentieth century, state legislatures began enacting statutes that required landlords to maintain and repair their properties. Some imposed a general duty of good repair, but others demanded landlords ensure specific features like working lights in common spaces or a functioning "privy or water closet."[97] These legislative interventions met with mixed responses from courts.[98]

But the D.C. Circuit's 1970 decision in *Javins v. First National Realty Corp.* marked the beginning of an upheaval in established law. In that case, residents of the Clifton Terrace apartment development in Washington, D.C. refused to pay their rent after their landlord failed to address thousands of building code violations and necessary repairs, including broken heaters, water leaks, and electrical hazards.[99] The court recognized that the legal rules of feudal England were ill-suited to the needs and expectations of modern urban renters. It noted, "today's city dweller usually has a single, specialized skill unrelated to maintenance work; he is unable to make repairs like the 'jack-of -all-trades' farmer."[100] The burden of repair, then, ought to fall on the landlord. Landlords, after all, are far more likely than their tenants to know what repairs are necessary, the history and condition of the building, and which contractors to hire.[101] So the court, departing with centuries of precedent, adopted an implied warranty of habitability for residential leases. In other words, regardless of the written terms of the lease, landlords must provide tenants with properties that are fit for human life.[102] In the decades since, the implied warranty of habitability has emerged as the dominant rule in the United States.

That rule, it should be noted, developed within a broader context, shaped by questions of poverty, racism, and economic exploitation, rather than reflecting some abstract commitment to repair. Nonetheless, the shift in legal responsibility offers some lessons. The reasoning courts and legislatures adopted reflects the often-implicit value our economic and legal institutions place on repair. It confronts the dynamic relationship with repair that modern consumers navigate every day. And it demonstrates the need for legal rules that are sensitive to the ways those relationships change over time.

Two distinct but related questions about repair are at work in cases like *Javins* – whether law ought to encourage repairs and, if so, who ought to bear responsibility for them. The implied warranty of habitability embeds a strong preference for repair, at least when it comes to tenant-occupied residential property. In part, that preference is driven by a concern that, without legal obligations, necessary repairs won't be made. It's easy to understand why renters would not take on major repairs. They are often expensive, complicated, and beyond the skillset of the average tenant. And while those repairs would improve the lives of residents, their interests in rental properties are, by definition, temporary.

But why wouldn't owners repair their properties? After all, a well-maintained building is worth more than one that's crumbling. Counterintuitively, allowing a building to deteriorate is sometimes a smart move for property owners. And perversely, the worse shape the building is in, the more sense this strategy makes. Imagine you own an apartment building that needs major plumbing repairs. If your building is valuable, located in a desirable neighborhood, serving upscale tenants, you want to protect that investment. The plumbing repairs cost a small fraction of the building's total value. And your tenants won't stand for leaky pipes damaging their Noguchi coffee tables. So, to prevent them from moving out and leaving bad Yelp reviews, you invest in a plumber.

If your building is in a poor neighborhood with low property values, and your tenants cannot afford a better alternative, your incentives to pay for new pipes are minimal. You are unlikely to recover the costs of repair through either increased rent or the eventual sale of the building. Instead, you may be inclined to squeeze as much money from the building as you can in the short term by charging tenants as much as the market will bear and minimizing spending on maintenance, as the building falls into further disrepair.

Although economically rational, that decision inflicts direct and immediate harm on tenants. It lowers their quality of life, exposes them to health and safety risks, and ultimately undermines their dignity. It also has consequences for surrounding property owners and their tenants. Derelict properties drag down the value of nearby buildings, nudging the calculus of other property owners away from repair and towards managed deterioration. This process repeats itself in a slow-motion chain reaction that squanders the investments of property owners and, more importantly, endangers their tenants. To avoid this mismanagement of valuable and scarce resources, the law steps in to insist on some minimal level of upkeep.

As to the second question – who ought to be responsible for repairs – the implied warranty of habitability places the financial burden for some repairs squarely on the shoulders of landlords. But it does not make landlords responsible for every creaking cabinet or running toilet. Tenants are not helpless. Everyday repairs are often within their grasp. You don't need any special equipment to grease a groaning hinge or to adjust that pesky float arm to stop the toilet from running. The law is not designed to discourage renters from taking repairs into their own hands. Even for repairs that do threaten habitability, tenants are typically free to make them and then deduct the repair expenses from their rent.

So, what lessons does the implied warranty of habitability offer for the contemporary debate over repair? It shows that the legal system can respond effectively when market incentives and practical hurdles interfere with repair. Legal liability is a powerful tool for resisting socially harmful behavior. When landlords failed to live up to tenants' reasonable expectations, the courts stepped in and forced their hands. For the same reasons we now hold landlords to a higher standard than we did in the Middle Ages, we ought to expect more from device makers when it comes to repair.[103] But to be clear, most proposals to encourage the repair of consumer electronics are far less ambitious and costly than the implied warranty of habitability. Beyond existing consumer warranties and guarantees, no one is proposing that Samsung or Tesla be on the hook for the cost of lifetime product repairs. We might, however, think it's reasonable to demand they provide software updates and access to replacement parts for the lifespan of a device. At the very least, they shouldn't interfere with our ability to repair those devices as we see fit.

Landlords sat idly by as their tenants endured deteriorating buildings. Device makers, on the other hand, play a far more active role in obstructing repair. Imagine you have a leaky pipe flooding your kitchen. There are worse things your landlord could do than ignore your pleas for a fix. They could buy up all the wrenches in town and refuses to sell you one. They could refuse to let your plumber in the building, insisting you hire their Preferred Plumbing Partner who happens to charge twice the market rate. They could conceal your pipes behind a locked door and refuse to give you a key. When it comes to our devices, that's too often the sort of reaction we can expect from the most powerful and profitable companies on the planet.

4 BREAKING REPAIR

Building on the insights of twentieth-century planned obsolescence, device makers today have developed a sophisticated array of tools to discourage and obstruct repair. They rely on product design, economic manipulation, and consumer persuasion to steer us away from repair and keep us buying more of the devices their assembly lines crank out. This chapter outlines those strategies and techniques.

Reparability as a Design Choice

Designing for repair isn't easy. Even when firms have every reason to build reparable systems they sometimes fail. Product design requires a delicate balancing of interconnected and often competing concerns. Functionality, aesthetics, durability, safety, and cost all impose constraints on designers. Tradeoffs and compromises are inevitable. And even when a design team has the best of intentions, reparability is too often overlooked. So, it shouldn't come as a shock that even thoughtful, methodical design processes helmed by well-meaning experts sometimes yield products that can't withstand the sharp-eyed scrutiny of the average maintenance worker.

The history of Bay Area Rapid Transit (BART), the rail system servicing the San Francisco Bay Area, is a telling example. Early planning for BART began in 1957. Its creators saw BART as an opportunity to rethink public transit. The goal was not to replicate existing light rail systems, but to design something entirely new. They envisioned a modern system that would appeal to commuters by shedding the common conceptions of early twentieth-century mass transit – cramped, noisy, and anti-quated. When BART opened for service fifteen years later, it debuted sleek, aerodynamic, and unusually wide railcars controlled by an automated computer system.[1] President Nixon, who visited just two weeks later, compared the operation favorably to NASA.[2] But this space-age answer to the subway came at a cost.

One crucial difference between BART and other transit systems are the rails themselves. Standard-gauge tracks measure 4 feet, 8½ inches – or 1,435 millimeters – wide. Adopted throughout the world, this standard traces its official origins to the United Kingdom's Gauge Act, enacted by Parliament in 1846.[3] Its apocryphal beginnings stretch back even further, to the width of Roman chariots.[4] Commuter rail systems, subways, and metros from New York to Beijing, Paris to Istanbul, and Berlin to Mexico City all run on standard gauge track. BART, in contrast, is the only rail system in the United States, and one of only a handful across the globe, that uses nonstandard 5-foot, 6-inch tracks.

Two considerations drove this departure from convention. First, BART's creators imagined comfortable, spacious train compartments that would lure commuters out of their cars. Standard-gauge tracks were thought to be too narrow for the job. Second, BART was eager to keep its tracks to itself. A standard-gauge system would have easily interconnected with San Francisco's existing MUNI train system, Amtrak, and freight carriers. The BART team worried that shared tracks would lead to delays if other traffic were prioritized. By creating a closed, non-interoperable system, BART hoped to keep its tracks clear and its trains on time.[5]

But the choice to build a system on nonstandard track had other, unanticipated consequences. The extra-wide gauge meant that standard wheel sets, brake assemblies, and other components were out of the question. So, BART commissioned a fleet of bespoke train cars. As those cars aged, the dream of the transit system of the future turned into a repair nightmare. The widespread use of standard-gauge track supported a global market for inexpensive and readily available replacement parts. But BART trains couldn't use those parts. The same was true for BART's power systems and its automated control technology. So, maintenance crews were forced to scavenge parts, picking over the remains of decommissioned cars. When parts couldn't be found, repair technicians would wait months for custom orders, scour sites like eBay, or build parts themselves. As a result, BART suffered from a perennial shortage of operating trains, endured major service disruptions, and budgeted for massive and unnecessary costs. At times, over $150 million, more than a third of BART's annual operating budget, was devoted to maintenance and repair.[6] To address some of these challenges, taxpayers have invested billions of dollars for an entirely new fleet. Despite those investments, early missteps like the use of nonstandard tracks cannot be undone.[7]

The engineers who designed BART didn't set out to build a system that couldn't be repaired. They had their sights set on other benchmarks – aesthetics, user experience, and product differentiation. But one consequence of their focus on those priorities was inattention to reparability. The upsides of eye-catching, well-appointed train cars were immediate. In contrast, the payoff of reparable design would have come years, even decades, later. Those dividends wouldn't take the form of boosted revenue, industry awards, or fawning reviews. The benefits of reparability are mundane and often unseen – reduced repair costs, outages avoided, and delays prevented. Designing for repair helps maintain its invisibility. Predictably, the BART team discounted those future benefits in favor of the more immediate upsides of innovative design.

To be clear, BART's designers had no incentive to undermine repair. They didn't get paid more for creating train cars that couldn't be fixed. They didn't receive a bonus when the fleet was replaced. BART was, and remains, a public works project. It has no mandate to extract maximum revenue from taxpayers. Quite the opposite – we should expect BART to be sensitive to the costs it imposes on the public. It's funded by fares and local tax revenue, and it's governed by an elected Board of Directors.

Since BART internalizes repair expenses, it has every reason to minimize them. Nonetheless, initial design decisions have cost taxpayers untold billions, all because repair was overlooked.

If reparability is neglected despite these strong incentives, imagine what happens when firms stand to profit from barriers to repair. Designs that are hostile to repair are not always accidents. As the history of planned obsolescence illustrates, product longevity is often at odds with the economic interests of device makers. For new product categories, the initial goal is market saturation. Only a few short years ago, for example, the market for smart speakers didn't exist. Amazon introduced the Echo in 2014.[8] The Google Home, Sonos One, and Apple HomePod, among others, followed in quick succession. As each of these products launched, they competed for market share. But once every likely buyer owns a smart speaker or two, that market will grow saturated. Perhaps it already has. In 2019 alone, consumers bought an estimated 200 million smart speakers worldwide.[9] At that point, replacement sales become crucial to sustaining revenue. New features, updated designs, and smaller form factors can all help convince consumers to replace last year's speaker with a new one. The availability and ease of repair is another factor that shapes replacement rates. If it's cheap and easy to fix a blown speaker or faulty microphone, consumers are less likely to replace their Echo with a new one.

Not all products are so easily discarded, however. You can pick up an Amazon Echo Dot for $45 the next time you stop by Whole Foods for some mochi and a Topo Chico. The average price for a new car in the United States, on the other hand, was just over $40,000 in 2020. Understandably, consumers are more inclined to expect longevity and reparability when it comes to vehicles. For the time being at least, the disposable car remains confined to the satirical pages of *The Onion*.[10] The same is true for agricultural and industrial equipment. No one would spend a million dollars for a John Deere tractor or a Caterpillar excavator if they thought it couldn't be repaired for years to come.

Given those consumer expectations, manufacturers of more durable goods face a different mix of economic pressures.

Rather than preventing repair altogether, they find ways to capture its value. Repair will happen one way or another; the question is, who will provide it? If owners of cars, tractors, and heavy equipment repair them on their own or turn to independent repair shops, manufacturers and dealers lose out on billions of dollars of revenue. But if device makers can steer owners towards their preferred repair providers, they can profit from both the initial sale and ongoing service. After all, when consumers make significant upfront investments, they are more willing to spend large sums on repair. That's especially true if their livelihood depends on a working car, tractor, or excavator. And to the extent device makers and dealers can reduce competition, they can charge inflated prices.

These two approaches – discouraging repair to boost replacement sales and capturing repair revenue – are not mutually exclusive. Apple, as we will see, has adopted several strategies that make repair of its products difficult. At the same time, it offers repair services. So long as consumers choose among those options, Apple comes out ahead. But there are other choices available to consumers that complicate the picture. Some are happy to give at-home repair a go, assuming parts and instructions are available. And independent shops are happy to service your broken phone, with or without Apple's blessing. In fact, independent shops often do complex, time-consuming repairs that Apple refuses to even attempt. Many of Apple's strategies are best understood as efforts to clamp down on these threats to its control over the market for repair services and its ability to inflate replacement sales.

Reducing and capturing repair are central to the business models of modern device makers. But the specific tactics firms adopt are far from uniform. They depend on the nature of the product, the expectations of consumers, and the degree of competition in the marketplace. As a result, restrictions on repair take a number of forms. Some, borrowed from the pioneers of planned obsolescence, are nearly a century old. Others, enabled by new technologies, are more recent innovations. Some are deliberate efforts to thwart repair. Others reflect indifference.

And still others embody tradeoffs that sacrifice reparability for competing priorities.

It isn't always easy to disentangle the motivations underlying decisions that interfere with repair. Are AirPods evidence that Apple is actively waging a war on repair? Perhaps the company's designers simply neglected to consider the near impossibility of fixing them. Or maybe other product attributes – like price, size, and aesthetics – outweighed reparability in the series of compromises that characterize the design process. Not every product flaw is proof of planned obsolescence or a concerted plot to undermine repair hatched in a smoke-filled boardroom. No matter how much it wanted to boost replacement sales, it's safe to assume that Samsung did not intentionally install exploding batteries in its Galaxy Note 7 devices.[11] Mistakes, as they say, were made. But other choices are more difficult to explain as innocuous accidents. Confronted with designs and policies that interfere with repair, firms offer public justifications rooted in aesthetics, usability, performance, and consumer safety. But in their communications to investors, they acknowledge the economic implications of repair.[12]

Evidence that explicitly addresses why companies adopt designs and policies that restrict repair is hard to come by. Firms rarely reveal the sorts of internal discussions and deliberations that would uncover corporate intent. Even when documents are released, they demonstrate that large firms are complex organizations, containing competing viewpoints that sometimes lead to inconsistent behavior. In the run up to a congressional hearing on competition in the technology sector in July of 2020, Apple divulged internal emails that touched on the discord within the company around repair. As Apple's vice president of communications wrote in one email, the company's "strategy around [repair] is unclear. Right now we're talking out of both sides of our mouth and no one is clear on where we're headed."[13] As Apple lobbyists fought right-to-repair legislation across the United States, its environmental technology team was uploading repair manuals to the company's website. Attempts to divine corporate intent have to contend not only with a dearth of direct evidence, but the conflicting stories that evidence is likely to reveal.

Focusing primarily on intent also runs the risk of obscuring the fact that repair restrictions can arise through less nefarious processes. In the end, what matters are the consequences of design choices, pricing plans, and policies that erect barriers to repair. Regardless of their purpose, the techniques described in this chapter increase the challenges consumers face when they try to repair the things they own. But before detailing the specific tactics that create those barriers, it's worth considering, in general terms, the modes by which behavior is influenced.

Regulating Behavior

In an influential essay, Lawrence Lessig argued that behavior can be shaped through four basic mechanisms: law, architecture, markets, and norms.[14] Changes along any one of these four vectors can encourage or discourage behavior, with varying degrees of success. Consider the struggle facing communities as they tried to encourage mask wearing during the COVID-19 pandemic. In the United States, after initially downplaying the benefits of masks, a consensus emerged among public health officials that wearing masks in public could significantly reduce the spread of the virus. If the goal is to get more people to wear masks more often, how do we make that happen?

Law is perhaps the most obvious and familiar regulatory tool. Criminal or civil liability targeting socially harmful behavior – in this case, failing to wear a mask in public – creates strong incentives to refrain from that behavior. Law is a powerful tool, but it isn't necessarily the most effective option. Legal solutions are costly. They depend on the coercive power of the state to impose fines and imprisonment, enlisting police forces and court systems that come with their own problems and shortcomings. We might reasonably wonder whether fines, arrests, and trials for failing to wear a mask are the most effective use of the legal system. Particularly for novel and sudden behavioral changes, harsh legal regulation may spark counterproductive backlashes and halfhearted compliance. Other tools hold out the promise of shaping behavior more subtly and with broader legitimacy.

Architecture – both in the form of the world as we find it and the things we design – necessarily shapes our behavior. Speed bumps, for example, are a useful tool for discouraging lead-footed drivers. In the same way, if the only masks available are cumbersome and uncomfortable, only the most cautious of us will be eager to wear them. If on the other hand, they are light, comfortable, and available in an array of colors and patterns, people will be far more likely to heed the advice of public health experts. To a large degree, how we design physical devices – and the software code that often determines their capabilities – defines the parameters of our choices.

We could also encourage masks through various market mechanisms. As a good or service grows more expensive, fewer people will indulge in it.[15] That's a basic principle of market economics. If wearing a mask is cheap, and not wearing one is expensive, we should expect higher rates of mask wearing, all else being equal. Imagine you own a grocery store and wanted to encourage customers to wear masks in order to protect your employees from the risk of infection. One approach would be to provide free masks to customers. Or you could entice customers with a 10 percent discount for wearing masks. On the other hand, you might increase the costs of noncompliance by charging unmasked customers an extra fee. Either way, by altering economic conditions, behavior can be predictably and reliably shifted.

Finally, social norms are another way to shape behavior. When the community – our families, neighbors, friends, and coworkers – voices its shared expectations around some behavior, most of us pay attention. Social disapproval exerts powerful, if subtle, pressure. So, if you fail to wear your mask at the grocery store, you might have to endure direct criticism, passive aggressive comments, or dirty looks. And for many of us, those community-enforced reprimands serve as effective reminders to bring our masks next time. Eventually, we internalize those norms. Even if no one is looking, you probably still avoid littering. But because norms reflect collective priorities, they are subject to change. They can be reinforced, reconsidered, or reversed through organic shifts in community values. Importantly, they can also be shaped through deliberate efforts – advertising, public awareness campaigns, and propaganda – from outside the community.

In practice, these regulatory models do not operate in isolation. They form overlapping layers of influence, sometimes reinforcing and at other times undermining each other. Together, they create a sort of regulatory topography that defines the space in which we exercise our own individual preferences, judgments, and choices. These forms of regulation do not dictate our decisions, but they do make some choices easier, less costly, and more likely than others.

Here's an example of that interplay. While writing this book, my MacBook began showing distressing signs of a failing battery. After a full charge, it would deplete rapidly and shut down without warning. An occasional message from Apple urged me to "service" my battery. But otherwise, the laptop worked just fine. I had no desire for a new one and preferred to avoid needlessly replacing it. In part, those preferences reflected norms of thrift, environmentalism, and some measure of resistance to digital consumerism. So, my first instinct was to swap out the battery myself, a procedure I'd managed without incident over the years on other laptops. But as it turns out, replacing the battery in my 2016 MacBook is a complex undertaking. According to iFixit's repair guide, the procedure takes up to three hours and involves fifty-one steps, including disconnecting fragile antennae and removing the logic board. Most daunting though was the prospect of using a solvent to dissolve the adhesive that glued the battery to the laptop's aluminum body. Facing second thoughts about my commitment to self-repair, I looked up how much it would cost to have Apple replace the battery instead. The $200 service charge, all things considered, didn't strike me as unreasonable. But at four years old, my laptop was just one year shy of Apple's "vintage" designation.

At that point, the company doesn't guarantee the availability of replacement parts or service. So, the next problem may not be so easy to fix. Perhaps a replacement would be a smarter investment, I thought. With my educational discount, a suitable replacement cost $899, and Apple helpfully offered a $349 trade-in credit for my existing laptop, spent battery notwithstanding. So, my choices were to spend $200 to fix a device that might soon be even harder to repair or to spend an extra $350 for a brand new one. Normatively, I wanted to extend the life of an otherwise working laptop. But its physical design and the economics of replacement nudged me in the other direction. I started this paragraph on my old laptop, but I'm finishing it on a new one.

This anecdote is just one iteration of the many ways that design, economics, and norms collectively shape consumer choices around repair. You've likely experienced other variations on these themes. The remainder of this chapter is an effort to catalog the ways in which companies create obstacles, intentional or otherwise, that influence consumers' repair decisions.

Designing Barriers to Repair

Product design is one critical lever that firms control. The choice of components and materials, their arrangement and assembly, and the tools necessary to access them go a long way to determining how easily a device can be repaired. And today, the software inside our devices is often just as integral to their operation as any physical part. A company committed to reparability will build a very different product than a firm that is either indifferent or hostile to repair. But understandably, repair isn't typically a top-of-mind consideration for consumers when they purchase a new device. Product features, price, compatibility, and aesthetics are all competing for consumer attention. Reparable design – or its absence – is unlikely to reveal itself until a problem arises. At that point though, consumers are likely to become acutely aware of the difference between a product built for repair and one built for replacement.

Hardware Design

The first step in diagnosing and repairing many devices is opening them up to access their internal components. Toaster not toasting? Maybe there are crumbs in the latch assembly. If you can remove the outer housing, it can be fixed in no time. When designers expect that users will need frequent access to internal components, they can include a cover or panel for that purpose. Car hoods are one familiar example of this simple but effective design choice.

At the other end of the spectrum are devices that effectively cannot be opened. We've already seen one example – Apple's AirPod headphones. Their plastic shells, and the glue holding them together, mean that accessing internal components almost inevitably destroys them. Microsoft's Surface Pro Laptop, initially released in 2017 is another. The device, clad in a synthetic microfiber textile, is impossible to open without irreparable damage. The fabric, secured with an adhesive, has to be cut off in order to be removed. Beneath it, a metal shield is fastened in place with ultrasonic spot welding. Accessing the components beneath requires breaking those welds. So even if you manage to open the laptop to replace the battery, good luck piecing it back together. As iFixit's teardown guide put it, the Surface Pro Laptop is a "glue-filled monstrosity" that "can't be opened without destroying it."[16] Even simple devices like Wahl hair trimmers can be designed in ways that interfere with routine repairs like sharpening dull blades.[17]

Most products fall somewhere between push-button accessibility and hermetically sealed internals. Not every device needs the equivalent of a car hood. But consumers and repair professionals frequently find themselves stymied by designs that make it difficult to open up devices. Frustratingly, smartphones and tablets often rely on glue to secure their outer covers and delicate screens. That's true for Samsung Galaxy devices and earlier generations of Microsoft's Surface Pro tablets. Motorola's Razr is another notable example. When the company decided to market a smartphone with a foldable screen in 2020, it revived the moniker. The original Razr, a popular flip phone that debuted in 2004, featured a rear panel that could be easily removed by hand – no tools required – to access the battery and other components. The outer shells of its successor, on the other hand, are glued on. So, replacing the battery begins with heating the phone enough to loosen the grip of the adhesive.[18]

As a rule, screws are preferable to glue when it comes to repair. They make disassembly and reassembly much easier. They also tend to be more reliable over the long run, particularly when multiple repairs are anticipated. But screws are far from a foolproof solution. To remove a screw, you need the right tool. Generally, screwdrivers aren't particularly complex or expensive. Most of us have a small collection of slotted and Philips screwdrivers lying around in a toolbox or stashed away in a drawer. But those two options hardly scratch the surface of the array of fasteners used to assemble consumer devices. Far fewer of us have LOX, Mortorq, Pozidriv, or Robertson drivers in our tool collections. When manufacturers opt for these less-common fasteners, they increase the cost of repair.

In some applications, specialized screws offer important functional advantages. LOX drives, to take one example, feature twelve points of contact between the screw and driver, allowing for increased torque and reduced wear. In other instances, though, the choice to use exotic fasteners is explicitly justified by the difficulty of removing them. Since so few people own the appropriate drivers, so-called security screws prevent unwanted removal and disassembly. As antitheft or antitampering measures, security screws have legitimate uses. Spanners – also known as 2-hole or pig-nose screws – are commonly used on elevator control panels to prevent unauthorized access. But they also show up in consumer goods from cameras to kitchen appliances.[19] Torx and hex screws, neither particularly common to begin with, come in secure varieties that feature a protruding pin in the center of the screw to prevent removal without yet another specialty tool. Likewise, Bryce Fastener manufactures a pentagonal drive with a pin. The company is careful to prevent sales of its drivers to the general public.[20] Other companies sell one-way screws that can be tightened but not removed, as well as breakaway fasteners with heads that are sheared off after installation.

These nonstandard screws create challenges when they are incorporated into consumer products. Apple made news in 2011 after it began incorporating pentalobe screws. Initially, they were only used to fasten internal components, but eventually Apple shifted to pentalobe screws for the external housings of iPhones and MacBooks, replacing the common Philips variety. Today, you can pick up a set of pentalobe drivers for a few dollars. But at the time, they were hard to come by. Apple's choice to swap out a common screw for an obscure one was widely and understandably viewed as an effort to steer consumers away from repairing or upgrading their own devices.[21] Video-game console makers rely on the same strategy. Nintendo, for instance, uses tri-wing fasteners and line head screws – better known as gamebits – in its consoles and cartridges.[22]

Assuming you manage to get your device open, many of these same challenges are replicated inside. You'll find components fastened in place with unfamiliar screws. Worse, you'll find parts glued and soldered together. Others might be riveted in place. So, removing a component runs the risk of breaking another, more expensive part. Or you may be forced to replace parts that work just fine because they can't be easily separated from a faulty component. Either way, repair is more difficult and expensive.

In recent years, Apple's MacBooks have illustrated each of these design flaws. Apple uses a variety of Torx and pentalobe screws inside its laptops. Their processors, graphics cards, RAM, and flash memory are all soldered directly to the laptops' logic boards, preventing replacement of any one component. Their speakers and batteries are glued to their metal shells. And their keyboards are riveted in place. That means if a key fails, you have two options. You can either painstakingly remove the rivets and replace them with screws, or you can replace the laptop's entire upper case. If your keyboard works as expected, you'd never notice the rivets. But from 2015 to 2019, the butterfly keyboards Apple used in its laptops were anything but reliable. This new, thinner design struggled to withstand regular use. Exposure to everyday dust and debris left keys unresponsive. After a class-action lawsuit, Apple eventually announced a keyboard replacement program for affected MacBooks. But because of all those rivets, replacing a faulty butterfly keyboard entailed swapping out the trackpad and upper case as well.

These issues aren't confined to consumer electronics. Take washing machines. Front-loading washers have grown in popularity in recent decades, in part because they use less water and energy than their top-loading counterparts. But two common problems – and the difficulty of repairing them – undermine those apparent environmental benefits. The basic internal anatomy of a front-loader looks something like this. A cylindrical drum is oriented horizontally, with its one open end facing out. The drum holds your dirty clothes, water, and detergent. A three-armed bracket, called a spider arm, attaches to the rear of the drum. The spider arm, in turn, is connected to a small motor via a drive shaft. When the motor runs, it rotates the spider arm and drum, assisted by two sets of bearings that reduce friction. If all is working well, your clothes smell like a fresh spring day in no time.

One common complaint from owners of front-loaders is that the drum bearings fail. A broken seal might let in water, and in time the bearings seize up. Replacement bearings are generally not terribly expensive, only $40 or so. But the job is labor intensive, as it involves the removal of the drum and the reassembly of the machine. The price for a repair is often nearly as much as buying a replacement.[23] And for some models, the bearings alone can't be replaced.[24] Instead, you have to purchase an entire drum assembly. The other common grievance is the failure of the spider arm. While the drum is typically made from stainless steel, the spider arm hidden behind it is usually made of cheap aluminum alloys that corrode when exposed to detergents. After only a few years of use, the spider arms of many front-loading machines begin to disintegrate. Just like bearings, not all spider arms can be replaced without a new drum assembly. And even when they can, the labor costs are often prohibitive.[25]

Car mechanics have their own horror stories about inaccessible parts. The Audi S4, to name just one, is notorious for the mechanical gymnastics necessary to repair its timing chain. Located at the back of the engine and wedged next to the firewall, servicing the chain requires the engine to be completely removed. By using a chain rather than the typical belt, Audi may have thought it was avoiding maintenance issues. But its design also called for plastic chain guides and tensioners that can't withstand heat and friction, leading to repair bills of as much as $8,000. As Douglas Adams wrote in *The Hitchhiker's Guide to the Galaxy*, "The major difference between a thing that might go wrong and a thing that cannot possibly go wrong is that when a thing that cannot possibly go wrong goes wrong, it usually turns out to be impossible to get at or repair."[26] Not surprisingly, you can find used S4s at what look like bargain-basement prices. But as one critic put it, "buying one of these cars would be like getting a screaming deal on a house not knowing that it's the most haunted house in America."[27]

Components that demand predictable replacement – like batteries and bearings – ought to be easy to access. When firms design their products in ways that complicate replacing those parts, they increase the cost of repair unnecessarily. Of course, that assumes aftermarket parts are available and affordable in the first place. To the extent devices incorporate off-the-shelf or widely available parts, that's usually not a problem. But in many cases, firms manufacture bespoke components and aggressively limit their availability. We'll return to that issue shortly. But first, there's another aspect of product design to consider.

Software Design

Today, the functionality of devices from toasters to cars is controlled by an embedded software code. That code grants device makers power over all sorts of post-sale consumer behaviors, among them repair.[28] Without access to this software code, diagnosing malfunctions, restoring functionality, or installing replacement parts can be impossible. Often manufacturers protect that code with additional layers of digital rights management technologies, limiting access to authorized repair providers. These software restrictions, as we will see, create legal risks for device owners and independent repair providers. But they also pose practical problems for anyone interested in fixing a broken device.

Apple, it should come as no surprise, has been among the most aggressive device makers when it comes to leveraging control over software to prevent, discourage, and undo repair. The company has a history of frustrating owners who repair their broken devices themselves or pay independent repair shops to do the work. And every year, it seems, brings a new scandal.

In 2016, thousands of iPhone owners were shocked when their devices would not start up, and their contacts, photos, and other data were inaccessible.[29] Phones that had been repaired by third parties and worked normally for weeks or even months were suddenly bricked after an Apple software update. That new code was designed to detect a replacement connector between the device's home button and its Touch ID sensor, a reliable indicator of third-party repair. And when such a connector was found, the software instructed the phone to stop working altogether, displaying only a cryptic reference to "Error 53." After mounting public backlash and a class-action lawsuit, Apple eventually released another software update restoring functionality for affected iPhones. In Australia, the company was fined millions of dollars after an undercover investigation revealed that it misled consumers about their right to obtain refunds for devices damaged by the fiasco.[30]

Those fines, however, pale in comparison to the $500 million Apple recently agreed to pay to settle the class-action lawsuits stemming from another software update.[31] In 2017, Reddit users uncovered that Apple was intentionally slowing down the processors of iPhones with older batteries. Apple later admitted that an iOS update detected aging batteries and reduced the device's processor speed. According to Apple, this move was intended to prevent unexpected shutdowns. But since this code was not disclosed to consumers, many bought new devices rather than simply replacing their phone's battery. Apple's throttling and the secrecy surrounding it steered consumers away from repair and towards replacement, inflating Apple's bottom line in the process. In response to the onslaught of criticism, Apple offered discounted battery replacements – a move that CEO Tim Cook later blamed for flagging iPhone sales.[32]

In 2018, Apple began including its T2 chip, a processor that handles Touch ID fingerprint data and various cryptographic keys, in its laptops and desktops. Touted as an advance in security, the chip also limits device reparability. If certain parts – including the display, logic board, keyboard, touch pad, and flash memory – are replaced, the computer can be rendered "inoperative" until blessed by Apple's proprietary system configuration software. That program, however, is available only to Apple and its authorized repair providers.[33] Without access to the software, independent shops can't complete repairs. The T2 chip also prevents refurbishers from deleting user data, meaning they can't resell used devices unless the original owner remembers to wipe them clean. Since many individual and institutional users don't, untold thousands of laptops that cost $3,000 just a few years ago are being scrapped for $12 apiece.[34]

Similarly, the iPhone's activation lock, which prevents new owners from accessing a phone without the original user's iCloud password, has led to the needless scrapping of hundreds of thousands, if not millions, of devices. The Wireless Alliance, a Colorado-based company that redistributes and recycles donated phones, received more than 66,000 activation-locked iPhones over the course of just three years. In 2018, a quarter of all donated iPhones couldn't be reused or repaired because of activation locks.[35] This story isn't unique. In the United States alone, hundreds of organizations that repair, refurbish, and recycle phones contend with activation-locked phones.

Nor is Apple the only manufacturer that relies on similar tools. Google, Microsoft, Nokia, Samsung, and others use activation locks on mobile devices. Their adoption was prompted by concerns over smartphone theft in cities around the world. Legislators and law-enforcement officials called on device makers to integrate "kill switches" in order to reduce demand for stolen goods.[36] If a device can't be used without the owner's password, it is much less valuable to would-be thieves. To their credit, activation locks have contributed to a significant reduction in smartphone thefts. But they have also interfered with lawful repair and resale operations. Identifying the original owners of donated phones often isn't feasible. So, organizations like the Wireless Alliance have no good way to disable activation locks.[37] And device makers have thus far refused to provide legitimate refurbishers with tools to safely and legally reset these devices. So instead, they are stripped for parts or simply shredded.[38]

More recently, Apple has adopted subtler tactics that steer consumers away from third-party or self-repair. Battery and screen replacements are by far the most common iPhone repairs. But if those parts are swapped out by anyone other than Apple or its authorized partners, users are confronted with prominent warnings.[39] Replacing the camera in the iPhone 12 triggers a similar message.[40] That's true even if genuine Apple parts are used. Admittedly, the screens and batteries still work. But if your phone alerts you that it is "unable to verify" that your replacement part is genuine, you might lose some faith in your local independent repair shop regardless of how well it performs.

As these warnings remind us, companies know whether a device has been independently repaired. Rather than displaying an alarming and misleading warning message, device makers could prevent authentic replacement parts from working altogether. And in some cases, that's exactly what they do. Apple devices can detect new Touch ID or Face ID sensors, which are often required to replace a broken screen. But, citing security concerns, Apple insists only its technicians can pair a device with a new sensor.[41] Similarly, Samsung disabled smartphone fingerprint readers after screen replacements.[42] Other components, like batteries and cameras, could be serialized next.

This same problem plagues game-console repair as well. Microsoft and Sony both pair the optical drives in their consoles to the devices' motherboards. So, if your optical drive fails, as commonly happens, you can't replace it with an identical part.[43] Console makers and game publishers insist this is a matter of preventing copyright infringement, but the software used to pair a new optical drive doesn't allow consumers to access infringing games or the console's operating system. Fixing the console simply lets them enjoy the games they've already purchased. Often the same titles are sold to PC gamers who are free to swap out their optical drives, so the risks of repair are plainly overstated. More fundamentally, we ought to be incredibly skeptical of any technology deployed to undo the very idea of interchangeable parts.

Beyond consumer electronics, other manufacturers rely on similar software-based strategies to control the functionality of replacement parts and shape consumer decisions around repair. After Massachusetts enacted an automotive right-to-repair law in 2012, carmakers and repair shops entered into a US-wide agreement that broadened access to diagnostic information, parts, and tools.[44] But prior to that hard-fought victory, fixes as simple as replacing a windshield-wiper switch required initialization software that was only available to car dealers, much to the frustration of consumers and independent repair shops.[45] Without instructions from that software, the car's onboard computer would prevent properly installed authentic parts from working.

Today, agricultural and heavy equipment manufacturers continue to use software-based initialization schemes to limit third-party repair. John Deere tractors, for example, won't recognize genuine replacement parts until they have been initialized, at considerable expense, by an authorized technician.[46] So a farmer who installs something as straightforward as a turn signal is still forced to pay the local John Deere dealer. This practice is effectively a tax on third-party and self-repair, with Deere collecting fees regardless of who actually did the work.

In 2018, facing vocal pushback from farmers and the threat of legislative intervention, John Deere, along with the trade associations representing equipment manufacturers and dealers, committed to making repair information, software, and tools available to farmers by January of 2021.[47] The Far West Equipment Dealers Association even held a public signing ceremony for its "Memorandum of Understanding" with the California Farm Bureau embracing these commitments. But nearly two months later, John Deere dealers around the country still routinely refused to sell software and other tools to farmers, insisting they were only available to licensed dealers. When Walter Sweitzer, president of the Montana Farmers Union, was finally able to find a dealer willing to sell him the software and equipment he'd need to fix his tractor, the price tag was $8,000.

These same techniques prevent repair of critical medical equipment. In Tanzania, neonatal incubators sit unused in storage closets. Their built-in software is password-protected, so on-site repair technicians can't access it. For many hospitals, authorized service is either unavailable, unreliable, or unaffordable.[48] Software locks plague US hospitals too. Imagine you have two ventilators, one with a broken screen, another with a broken breathing unit. The logical fix is to swap out the broken screen with the working one. A single operational machine is better than two broken ones, after all. But that repair requires a hardware dongle, and manufacturers are loath to provide them to independent repair technicians. Instead, technicians are forced to turn to other sources, like the Polish hacker who sells crude replicas that are "little more than a circuit board encased in plastic with two connectors."[49] But they get the job done.

Using software to frustrate repair extends to consumer goods too. In an example that approaches peak absurdity, certain

General Electric refrigerators are programmed to deny their owners water unless they install authorized GE filters. Those parts, unsurprisingly, are sold at a premium. A standard water filter can be had for a mere $13, while official GE replacements cost a whopping $55.[50] The only difference is that the GE filters contain an RFID tag that identifies them to the refrigerator's embedded software. But as enterprising consumers quickly discovered, those tags can be carefully removed from official GE filters to trick the system into recognizing generic alternatives.

So far, we've focused on how code regulates physical components of consumer goods. But the combination of software and persistent network connections has, to a large degree, relocated the functionality of those goods. So-called "smart" products outsource functionality by shifting work from the devices in our homes and pockets to remote servers located in the proverbial cloud.[51] In other words, many of the components that make the products we buy useful are no longer in our possession. Instead, they are hidden away in remote data centers. This poses major problems for repair and leaves the continued operation of many devices in the hands of manufacturers. We've already seen how repair is stymied by devices that rely on remote servers for their basic operation. Without access to Nest's code, owners of Revolv hubs had no means to restore their functionality. The same was true for purchasers of Jibo robots, who were left to watch helplessly as they deteriorated.[52]

This new reality isn't limited to purchasers of social robots and automation hubs. Best Buy, one of the largest electronics retailers in the United States, offers a range of products under its Insignia brand. In November 2019, it shut down the servers for Insignia's line of "smart" refrigerators, electrical plugs, light switches, and security cameras. Once the servers were killed, the refrigerators still kept food cold, and the light switches still operated manually. But purchasers could no longer control their devices remotely, set timers, or take advantage of any of the other "smart" bells and whistles. Unlike a temperamental ice maker or unreliable dimmer switch, these features can't be fixed by the owner. Their functionality depends entirely on the decisions of the manufacturer, even after they are installed in your kitchen. What purchasers saw as a product feature turned out to be more akin to a service – one that can be terminated at any time.

Market Restrictions

The more repair costs, the less likely consumers are to pay for it. Without some sentimental attachment to a device or an ideological commitment to repair, most people would prefer a new product, all things being equal. So, if firms can narrow the price gap between repair and replacement, they can reliably steer consumers towards new purchases. And firms have no shortage of ways to alter that calculus. They can increase the costs of repair. That's true for both their own services and those of third parties. They can do that directly by charging high sticker prices for parts and service. Or they can use indirect means, like introducing delays or making repair services harder to find. Firms can also shift consumer behavior by subsidizing new purchases through trade-in programs and other incentives. Some of these economic strategies are obvious to consumers, while others operate below the surface, shaping the market for repair in unseen ways.

Price and Availability

Device makers have direct control over the prices they charge for repair. Samsung, for example, charges as much as $279 to replace the screen on its Galaxy phones and up to $599 for foldable screens.[53] And Apple recently quoted a customer Can$2051 to repair a MacBook screen after its antireflective coating wore thin.[54] That's more than it would cost to buy a new laptop. Given these high prices, companies from John Deere to your local car dealer understand repair as a growth sector, one from which they can extract significant profits.[55] Expensive parts and service help manufacturers stack the deck against repair. If consumers balk at expensive fixes, they are more likely to buy a replacement. If instead, they grudgingly shell out for repairs, firms still collect a tidy profit.

But there's an important obstacle to this "heads we win, tails you lose" strategy. So long as a competitive market for third-party repair thrives, consumers have other, less expensive options. And for those confident in their mechanical skills, or simply willing to learn, consumers can repair their own products. In order to stamp out the market for repairs – or capture its value – firms must either eliminate third-party and self-repair altogether or drive their prices to the point of unviability.

One way to do that is to make replacement parts unnecessarily expensive. This is a long running complaint in the automotive world. The headlight assembly for a Ford Focus costs nearly $2,000,[56] and side-view mirrors for some cars run as high as $1,000 each.[57] Home appliances follow a similar pattern. A door handle for a Miele refrigerator will set you back more than $300.[58] Even cheaply produced plastic parts can be laughably expensive. Need a new knob for your washing machine? Sears will happily sell you a molded plastic one, which costs no more than a few cents to produce, for $39.78 plus shipping – a purported 46 percent off the full $73 retail price.[59] Although, that certainly beats the $186 price tag for a replacement knob for a Samsung range.[60] You've likely experienced your own instances of replacement-part sticker shock. A couple of years ago, the clips securing two hoses on my Hoover vacuum cleaner broke, and it lost suction. Two new plastic hoses, which took weeks to ship, cost nearly as much as a new vacuum.

Thanks to software, firms have another opportunity to impose extra costs on third-party or self-repair. Even if you paid the inflated price for an original part, you still might have to fork over more money. John Deere charges a flat fee of $230, plus $130 an hour just to initialize authentic parts installed by farmers or independent repair shops.[61] That hourly rate includes travel time, imposing especially high costs on farmers in remote communities.

Another approach is to simply refuse to sell parts to third parties. That's Nikon's policy for its popular DSLR cameras.[62]

Likewise, independent repair shops can't just call up Apple and order screens, keyboards, or other replacement parts. As a result, independent repair shops are often forced to rely on grey-market imports, third-party parts, or salvaged components. The difficulty of securing high-quality components drives up the cost of independent repair.

Not only do firms withhold parts, they also simply refuse to fix many older devices. Admittedly, maintaining an inventory of parts and a team of technicians trained to repair aging products can be an expensive undertaking.[63] Ford's willingness to continue making, stocking, and selling spare parts for Model Ts long after new vehicle production ceased was unusual. So was Sony's commitment to repairing the PlayStation 2. Eighteen years after the console's launch, the company announced it was shutting down repair operations in 2018.[64] In contrast, Microsoft stopped repairing the original Xbox console a little more than seven years after its launch, a timeline consistent with contemporary trends.[65]

To its credit, Apple publishes a clear, reliable timeline for its iPhone, iPad, and Mac products, informing consumers precisely when they will be cut off from repair services. Those rules distinguish between "vintage" products – those that haven't been sold in the last five years – and "obsolete" products – those that were discontinued more than seven years ago.[66] When it comes to vintage products, Apple makes no promises about the availability of repair. If the company has parts in stock, you are in luck. If not, there are no guarantees – that is, unless you live in California. Under state law, Apple is required to make spare parts available for seven years for any product that retails for more than $100.[67] For obsolete products, "Apple has discontinued all hardware service . . . with no exceptions."[68] In other words, Apple won't touch your seven-year-old laptop. Nor will it sell parts to third-party repair shops so they can fix it. A top-of-the-line Mac Pro costs over $53,000 – roughly the same as a BMW 4 series.[69] Few of us would buy a car if we couldn't fix it after seven years. So why should a computer be any different?

What's worse, Apple even refuses to repair some of its current generation of products. Although it offers "service and repair" for iPads, Apple almost never actually repairs them. Cracked screens, faulty batteries, busted cameras, failed charging ports all get treated the same way. Apple charges a flat "service fee," depending on the device and your warranty status, and sends you home with a replacement device.[70] The same is true for Air Pods and Apple Watches. "Service" is a code word for replacement.

For device makers, this is a question of profitability. We should expect firms to do whatever they can to maximize profits. For better or worse, that's what modern corporations are built to do. And a supply chain focused on making new products is more efficient if it devotes minimal resources to servicing old ones, even if they end up in landfills. In the same way, Uber is more profitable if it refuses to recognize drivers as employees,[71] Facebook is more profitable if it opens its platform to disinformation,[72] and fossil-fuel companies are more profitable if they can pollute at will.[73] Companies profit by externalizing costs. That doesn't mean we should let them.

Authorized Repair

Most companies realize that it isn't in their best interest to shut out third-party repair providers completely. A flat-out refusal to sell parts to independent providers can create legal risks and, practically speaking, most firms need to enlist third-party providers to meet consumer demand for repair. Apple, despite its massive global presence, has only about 500 retail locations worldwide. To shoulder some portion of repairs, the Apple Authorized Service Provider (AASP) program grants select partners privileged access to replacement parts, information, software, and tools that are unavailable to either the public or the vast majority of third-party repair shops.[74] For devices that are still under warranty, Apple reimburses AASPs for each repair, while consumers pay directly for out-of-warranty fixes.

The AASP program, however, has significant downsides for repair providers. Apple limits what sort of fixes they can perform.[75] They can replace batteries and screens on iPhones, for example, but aren't permitted to replace cameras, charging ports, or headphone jacks. Rather than perform these relatively simple fixes, AASPs are required to send the device to Apple, collecting a small referral fee rather than the full value of the repair. In many instances, Apple then sends the consumer a refurbished device, rather than actually repairing their phone. How much Apple pays an AASP for the handful of repairs it is allowed to perform depends on monthly performance metrics. Apple tracks how long repairs take, how many parts are used, and how many devices are fixed on the first visit. It uses those metrics to decide how much AASPs earn.[76] Given these constraints, it's no wonder that most repair providers have refused to become AASPs. For independent shops that offer a full range of repair services, the AASP program would severely reduce their revenue and degrade the level of service they can offer their customers.[77] The bulk of AASP locations in the United States are part of the massive Best Buy retail chain.[78]

In the face of ongoing criticism from consumers and the independent repair community, not to mention increased scrutiny from legislators and regulators, Apple unveiled its Independent Repair Provider (IRP) program in August of 2019. Like AASPs, qualified IRPs can buy original iPhone screens and batteries from Apple. But the IRP program extends only to out-of-warranty devices, so Apple doesn't pay IRPs for repairs. Nonetheless, the company touted its willingness to sell parts to independent repair shops as a major step forward in making repair more accessible. Nearly a year later, however, Apple revealed that only 140 independent repair companies signed up.[79] Perhaps in response to this anemic reception, the company expanded the program to Canada and Europe and broadened its scope to include Macs in addition to iPhones.[80]

Given the billions of dollars Americans spend every year fixing their iPhones and the difficulty of obtaining new Apple parts, why have so few repair shops opted into the IRP program? Although Apple was eager for the press to cover the program's announcement, the company remains highly secretive about its inner workings. To even see the contract that spells out their obligations, prospective IRPs are forced to sign nondisclosure agreements.[81]

Having reviewed that contract, it's easy to understand Apple's insistence on secrecy. The IRP agreement imposes onerous, unreasonable demands on repair providers that undermine their business and endanger their customers' privacy. To start, as a condition for gaining access to screens, batteries, and other parts, IRPs are required to obtain "express written acknowledgement" from each customer confirming that they understand their repairs are not being made by an authorized provider and that Apple offers them no warranty. If this conversation doesn't scare customers off, it may nonetheless plant seeds of doubt about the quality of work they should expect.

In addition, Apple forbids IRPs from stocking or using what it calls "prohibited" repair parts. Those include "counterfeit" parts and those "that infringe on Apple's intellectual property." On the surface, this may look like a reasonable demand. Why should Apple sell parts to repair shops using counterfeit components? But as we will see in the next chapter, Apple takes an expansive view of what constitutes a "counterfeit," enlisting customs officials to confiscate imports of authentic or otherwise lawful parts. Its invocation of intellectual property is no less troubling. Given the power imbalance between Apple – the most valuable firm on the planet – and independent repair shops, determinations of infringement won't be made by a neutral arbiter, like a court. They will be made by Apple, at its sole discretion. If Apple was willing to spend more than $60 million to sue Samsung over its claimed patents on round-cornered smartphones, imagine how aggressively it might define its rights against outmatched IRPs.[82] And if Apple does decide a repair shop is using forbidden parts, it can impose fines of $1,000 per transaction and force the IRP to cover the costs of Apple's investigation.

To help detect the use of prohibited parts, IRPs must allow Apple to perform unannounced audits. These inspections include granting Apple access to the IRP's facilities, interviewing its employees, and most troublingly, sharing personally identifiable information about its customers. Apple requires IRPs to "maintain an electronic service database and/or written documentation" that includes the names, phone numbers, email, and physical addresses of customers. Apple can demand that information at any time. Even if a repair shop withdraws from the IRP program, under the terms of the contract, Apple can insist on inspections and customer information for up to five years. It's no wonder then that the overwhelming majority of repair shops have no interest in becoming IRPs.

But even after qualifying as authorized providers, shops have no guarantee that their privileged access to parts will continue. Just ask the owners of formerly authorized Nikon repair locations. In late 2019, the camera maker announced it was terminating its relationship with fifteen authorized repair providers, leaving its customers with just two locations in the United States to have their cameras repaired, one in New York and one in Los Angeles.[83] Without a robust repair-provider network, Nikon expects its customers to wait six to eight weeks for repairs. For those who make their living behind the lens, extended delays may be enough to force them to purchase a new camera. And if they already have a collection of Nikon lenses and peripherals, they are likely to buy another Nikon despite the obvious repair bottleneck.

Much like airlines that market elite status and priority boarding as a solution to anxiety about limited overhead space, Nikon's Professional Services program – in Carbon and Platinum varieties – promises to let qualifying members skip the repair queue.[84] To join the program, customers must prove that they own at least two Nikon cameras, two lenses, and a total of 750 points in "Qualifying Equipment." A D6 camera is worth 350 points, but an SB-900 flash earns you a mere 25 points.[85] The message is far from subtle: if you want your equipment repaired quickly, buy more stuff. But even top-tier members weren't spared when Nikon shut down both of its repair facilities in response to COVID-19 in March of 2020.[86] By September, its New York repair location had reopened, but the Los Angeles facility remained shuttered. Even absent global disruptions, companies that rely on tightly controlled networks of authorized providers risk long delays for their customers. The shortage of Tesla repair providers, for example, has led to routine months-long waits for body and suspension work.[87]

In defense of their authorized provider programs, firms argue that they protect consumers by encouraging repairs by trained technicians using authentic parts. Undoubtedly, better training makes for better repairs, and in most cases, authentic parts are preferable, assuming they are sold at fair prices. But even Apple-certified technicians who have passed the company's own exams can't buy parts unless they work for an authorized provider. Rather than maximizing access to high-quality repair, these programs are designed to leverage access to training, tools, and parts to control the market for repair services.

Authorized repair programs give manufacturers power over third-party providers. Sometimes, that leverage is used to prevent straightforward repairs. In other cases, it slows repair down by days, weeks, or months. Apple, for example, doesn't allow AASPs to keep parts stocked. Instead, they must be ordered for each repair. So, a battery replacement takes days, rather than an hour. And by tightly controlling the availability of parts, these programs limit competition and maintain inflated repair pricing. So, while these programs appear on the surface to increase the availability of repair, they may drive more consumers towards new purchases.

Limiting Resale Markets

Generally, secondary markets operate free of the influence of device makers. But concentration among online retailers is making it easier for firms to exert their influence. When retailers and device makers restrict the sale of refurbished goods, they artificially suppress demand for repair.

In late 2018, Amazon began selling the full range of Apple products for the first time. For years, Apple refused to sell directly via Amazon, preferring to drive traffic to its own retail stores and website. But Amazon's dominance as a retail marketplace – accounting for hundreds of billions of dollars annually and somewhere between one-third and one-half of all online sales in the United States – prompted Apple to reconsider its stance.[88] One key benefit of the arrangement they struck was the control it gave Apple over third-party sellers. Amazon offers companies a range of tools to manage the sale of their goods on its marketplace. Its Brand Registry, along with newer offerings like Transparency and Project Zero, are marketed as ways to reduce counterfeits.[89] But Amazon is also willing to go a step further, banning third-party sales altogether. It struck such a deal with Nike in 2017, and reportedly restricts third-party sales at the behest of a range of other companies, including Canon, Dyson, Makita, Nikon, Nintendo, Samsung, and Sony.[90] And that's exactly what Amazon promised to do for Apple.

Before the deal, refurbishers like John Bumstead, who operates a small business called RDKL, Inc., would buy, fix, and resell thousands of MacBooks to Amazon shoppers. But in November of 2018, Amazon told Bumstead his listings would be deleted. To keep selling, he would either need to purchase $2.5 million worth of refurbished inventory from Apple every ninety days or somehow be deemed an Apple-authorized reseller.[91] Exactly how one qualifies for that designation was and remains unclear. Since practically no independent resellers could meet those terms, the Amazon–Apple deal effectively ended the sale of repaired Apple products by small refurbishers.[92] With fewer sellers, prices have increased considerably. And with reduced access to consumers, refurbishers have less incentive to fix phones, tablets, and laptops in the first place. Many have simply closed shop.

It's worth pausing to reflect on what the Apple–Amazon deal represents. Two of the world's most valuable and powerful companies conspired to make it harder for consumers to buy repaired goods. Both companies benefit from this arrangement, but consumers, repair providers, and the rest of the planet are worse off as a result.

And Apple's deal with Amazon isn't the only example of the company cracking down on secondary markets. In 2020, Apple sued GEEP, a Canadian recycling firm, alleging that it resold 100,000 devices destined for shredding, in violation of its contract with Apple.[93] Despite its public proclamations that it never recycles working devices, Apple discovered the resold products after an audit detected that they were actively connecting to data networks. Rather than let these repaired devices back onto the market, Apple sued the recycler for refusing to destroy them.

Restricting Advertising

In much the same way that the Amazon–Apple deal stops refurbishers from connecting with potential customers, online-ad networks can interfere with repair. Google's advertising network, the world's largest, rakes in tens of billions of dollars annually.[94] And many small businesses rely heavily on Google ads to generate new customers. A consumer who drops their phone is likely to search for some variation of "phone repair" or "fix broken screen." If a repair shop buys ads linked to those queries, it will get more calls, more visits, and more customers than one that doesn't. For many repair shops, the bulk of their customers come from Google searches.[95]

But in 2018, Google announced a new policy banning ads for "Technical support by third-party providers for consumer technology products and online services."[96] This shift was not initially designed to target hardware repairs. It was a response to growing and justified concerns about tech support scams that were duping unsuspecting computer users.[97] Ads would direct users to call toll-free numbers. Once connected to a call-center, often located outside the jurisdiction of local law enforcement, the consumer would be convinced to pay exorbitant fees for useless or even harmful software fixes.

Unfortunately, Google's ad ban does not distinguish between fly-by-night scam operations and legitimate independent repair shops. As a result, repair providers have seen drops in revenue of as much as 70 percent, and some have been forced to close their doors altogether.[98] Perhaps most gallingly, while small shops are banned from advertising repairs, manufacturers and their retail partners, like Best Buy, are not. So, consumers looking for repair services are being diverted from independent repair options, towards the authorized ecosystems maintained by device makers.

In August of 2018, Google promised it would "roll out a verification program" for legitimate providers "in the coming months."[99] That program never materialized. In fact, the company doubled down on its repair-ad ban in late 2019, expanding it globally. Again, Google had good reason to crack down on fraudulent ads, but its rationale for hanging legitimate repair providers out to dry is harder to discern. Google, notably, has moved into the hardware business itself in recent years. In 2014, it acquired the smart-device maker Nest. Its Pixel line of smartphones launched in late 2016, and the Pixelbook laptop a year later. Much like other device makers, Google offers its own repair services and authorized repair providers.[100] The company has a clear, if small, financial interest in restricting third-party repair.

Trade-In Programs

Finally, trade-in discounts tilt the playing field against repair. At first glance, discounts look like a purely pro-consumer move. Rather than paying full freight for a new laptop or smart speaker, consumers enjoy a lower price and the satisfaction of responsibly disposing of their existing device. But these programs have important downsides. By lowering the out-the-door price of a purchase, they encourage the production and consumption of new devices. On the margins, discounts reduce profits in favor of consumer savings, but they do nothing to reduce the environmental externalities of new devices. If anything, they exacerbate them by enlisting users as co-conspirators in disposable consumerism.

Sonos and its now defunct "recycle mode" illustrate the problem well. To phase out older, "legacy" products, Sonos offered customers a 30 percent discount on new purchases. All they had to do was activate recycle mode on their current speakers or amplifiers. Once initiated, that setting began a twenty-one-day countdown, after which the device was deactivated. That is to say, it could no longer be used, by anyone, unless Sonos agreed to undo the damage.[101] Sonos contended that recycle mode encouraged consumers to do the environmentally responsible thing with their unwanted devices – take them to a local electronics recycler or ship them back to Sonos for disposal.[102] But reuse, resale, and repair are far more efficient fates for a set of speakers. Facing widespread criticism, Sonos eliminated recycle mode. It still offers a discount to owners of legacy devices, but they can do with them what they please after ordering new speakers.[103] Those devices may find a new home, but since Sonos does not offer software updates or support for them, their utility is limited.[104] And even if they are resold and reused, the economic incentive to upgrade to the latest hardware persists.

Apple offers a similar set of trade-in incentives. The company encourages its customers to "Turn the device you have into the one you want."[105] If you're tired of your iPhone XS Max, Apple will discount your next device by $450; a MacBook Pro can earn an eye-popping $1,760 off a new computer. Those incentives reduce or even eliminate the cost advantage of repair. Not only do these programs entice consumers to buy new devices at high markups, but they also help firms control secondary markets for used devices. In some instances, trade-ins are refurbished and resold by the manufacturer. In other cases, they are recycled to produce new, more expensive devices.[106] But either way, trade-in programs help firms like Apple prevent goods from entering the broader used marketplace where they can drive down the demand for new devices.

Consumer Norms

Finally, device makers can discourage repair through norms, the unwritten and often unspoken informal social rules that shape our behavior. In both subtle and conspicuous ways, firms influence how often consumers replace their devices with new ones, whether and where they get them fixed, and how they judge the choices of their friends and acquaintances. Norms play a powerful, if overlooked, role in those efforts. While they typically emerge organically, norms are not immune from marketing, propaganda, and other means of manipulation. Device makers communicate and reinforce values that advance their economic agenda. They urge us to prioritize newness and the imprimatur of brands, deemphasizing longevity and the do-it-yourself ethos.

Perhaps you are skeptical that norms alone, in the absence of any law or design mandate, could effectively change behavior. In his book *Secondhand*, Adam Minter offers an example that might persuade you.[107] New parents know that child safety seats are an expensive purchase. But they are also one that children outgrow in a few years. Normally, we would expect to see a thriving secondhand market under those conditions. Consignment shops, thrift stores, and informal hand-me-down networks are overflowing with cribs and highchairs, not to mention less-durable items like baby clothes and toys. But secondhand car seats are rare. Why? Because we have internalized the idea that used car seats are dangerous. No good parent, the thinking goes, would pawn an old car seat off on another family. And they certainly wouldn't trust their precious bundle to a secondhand safety seat. A father who proudly announces the great deal he got on a used car seat might be met with skeptical looks, whispered criticism, or a patronizing lecture from family and friends. In part because of this norm, we spend over $5 billion a year on car seats, a figure expected to swell to more than $7.6 billion by 2025.[108]

But the truth is, the supposed dangers of used car seats are largely a myth perpetuated by manufacturers. True, a car seat might be unsafe if it was involved in an earlier collision, but otherwise there is no evidence to suggest that older car seats are unsafe or ineffective. Manufacturers insist that car seats "expire" and should no longer be used after six or seven years. According to leading car-seat maker Graco, "As tempting as it might be to save a little cash by purchasing a used car seat or accepting a hand-me-down, it's not a good idea."[109] And if you should happen to have an "expired" car seat? Graco's advice is to "discontinue use . . . immediately." Then you should "remove the cover, cut or remove the harness straps, write 'DO NOT USE, EXPIRED' on it with a Sharpie, and place it in a black garbage bag." In other words, decency requires that you destroy the seat to make sure no one else can use it. Retailers parrot the expired car-seat narrative. For years, Target has advised against used car seats and offered discounts when you trade in an old one, destroying the used seats and, not coincidentally, reducing secondhand competition.[110]

Despite the dire warnings, there are no laws, rules, or regulations in the United States concerning used or expired car seats. And regulators in countries like Sweden, which has some of the most stringent child safety laws in the world, actually encourage the use of secondhand car seats. When pressed by Minter, leading car-seat manufacturers and retailers offered no evidence supporting their claims. Nonetheless, this message has been internalized by millions of parents across North America and Europe, informing their norms and influencing their behavior.

Contemporary norms stress the importance of acquiring new products and instill skepticism about unauthorized repair. But it hasn't always been that way. During the first half of the twentieth century, thrift, frugality, and individual industriousness were celebrated. In the United States, this current can be traced back to the Puritans, who believed that responsible management of resources was essential to human thriving.[111] Later, Benjamin Franklin advocated thrift as a necessary means to economic independence.[112] By the 1910s, organizations like the Young Men's Christian Association (YMCA) began celebrating Thrift Weeks, designed to impart the value of economizing resources. Children were taught the importance of saving, durability, and making resources last. They learned to prize self-reliance and avoid extravagance. The first national Thrift Week, coinciding with Franklin's birthday, was recognized in 1917. By the 1920s, thrift movements had taken root in Britain, Italy, Japan, and elsewhere. As we've already seen, the reverence for reuse and repair reached its apogee during World War II, when state-sponsored public information campaigns cast them as patriotic contributions to the war effort. But by the 1950s, as the post-war economy boomed, focus shifted from teaching thrift to persuading Americans of the virtues of being good consumers.[113] With consumerism on the rise, the last national thrift week took place in 1966.

After decades marked by rising standards of living, declining prices for consumer goods, and relentless advertising, our values today are markedly different. Rather than thrift, longevity, and reliability, we embrace conspicuous consumption, newness, and disposability. This shift in attitudes and the social norms that accompany them was hardly an accident. It is the product of a sustained effort to center our economy around ceaseless and interlocking cycles of production and consumption. This effort began with carmakers in the mid-twentieth century. Annual product releases, minor aesthetic variations, and often-overblown promises of transformative technological advances have proven far more durable than the products they are deployed to sell. But no modern device maker has adapted these tactics more successfully than Apple.

Since the introduction of the iMac in 1998, its product announcements have been covered with breathless anticipation by the press and public alike. Much of Apple's success is due to its capacity for innovation and knack for design. But it bolsters sales between major innovations by shaping and exploiting our norms around new technology. Beginning in 2007, Apple has released, with great fanfare, at least one new iPhone generation every year. With a few exceptions, these releases are named sequentially. In addition to incremental upgrades to processors, memory, and cameras, models vary in size, shape, color, and materials. To focus on just one element, iPhones initially had rounded edges. Then a series of flat-edged designs were introduced, only to be replaced by new and thinner rounded form factors. The iPhone 12, which debuted in 2020, made news for reverting back to a flat-edged design.

These design changes signal to consumers who has the latest device and who is still running last year's hardware. As disappointing as it is, our assessments of each other are shaped by the belief that owning the latest devices is part of what it means to be a successful, desirable person. Someone without a smartphone in the United States might seem like a backward luddite. Or we might assume they can't afford this necessity of modern life. A 2016 study found that "no individual brand is as predictive of being high-income as owning an Apple iPhone."[114] Simply owning an iPhone predicted whether a person was in the top quartile of income more than 69 percent of the time. The iPhone was also the best predictor of educational attainment. Back in 1992, before computing technology became pervasive, the best predictor was Grey Poupon mustard.

Even sexual attractiveness is tied to our devices. A study conducted in 2017 by the dating site Match.com found that owning an older phone hurt your chances of romance. Those with outdated phones were 56 percent less likely to go on a date in the preceding year. And women were 92 percent more likely to judge a potential match for using an older phone.[115] Given the social costs, it's no wonder so many of us are willing to line up to buy the latest gadget, even when the one in our pocket works perfectly fine.[116]

Another team of researchers conducted discussions with 115 UK consumers focusing on their motivations for replacing devices. They concluded that "updating happens at least in part so that people can keep up with their peers and family."[117] In order to escape judgment and avoid being "seen as 'old fashioned,'" consumers replace devices sooner than they otherwise would. What's more, consumers internalize these norms, treating owning the latest product as a mark of their personal success. In this sense, these norms profoundly affect our behavior and our view of the world.

In other instances, the message is far less subtle. For years, Apple manuals included the bold admonition: "Do Not Make Repairs Yourself."[118] The 2019 iMac manual cautions that "Your iMac doesn't have any user-serviceable parts, except for the memory, which is user-replaceable in 27-inch models and service center-replaceable in 21.5-inch models. Disassembling your iMac may damage it or may cause injury to you."[119] Apple offers similar warnings to iPhone owners, who are told in no uncertain terms "Don't open iPhone and don't attempt to repair iPhone yourself."[120] Instead, Apple urges customers to turn to its in-house repair services or its authorized partners.

In both cases, the Apple logo reassures consumers that they can trust the quality of those repairs. After all, if the Apple brand is such a powerful signifier for those who merely own their products, imagine the power it gives the company itself. That power is, in large part, a function of trademark law. Indeed, legal rules undergird many of the strategies firms use to impede repair, arguably granting them considerable power over post-sale use of their products. We turn to those legal regimes next.

5 REPAIR AND INTELLECTUAL PROPERTY

As we've seen, firms deploy a variety of tools to limit repair and capture its value. So far though, we've postponed discussion of arguably the most powerful of them. Intellectual property (IP) – in the form of copyrights, patents, trademarks, and trade secrets – offers manufacturers an arsenal of weapons in the war on repair. From a practical perspective, IP law allows firms to credibly threaten to enjoin, silence, and ultimately bankrupt anyone with the audacity to repair a product without permission. Rhetorically, IP rights offer a superficially compelling narrative to convince policy makers and the public that repair imperils a vibrant economy and technological progress. IP, the argument goes, provides essential incentives for innovation. And if unauthorized repairs undermine those rights, consumers will lose out on the next breakthrough product.

But once those arguments are examined closely, it becomes clear that they are usually little more than a smokescreen, obscuring an anticompetitive agenda behind appeals to innovation. Accessing a tractor's embedded software to repair it does not infringe any copyrights. Repairing your vacuum cleaner does not infringe any patents. The importation of authentic parts with microscopic trademarked logos does not confuse consumers. And sharing repair techniques does not expose trade secrets. Admittedly, these activities might reduce device makers' revenue. But frankly, so what? IP rights are not designed to insulate companies from all competitive pressures or guarantee their profitability.

In theory at least, intellectual property law is meant to serve the interests of the public; the financial fortunes of rights holders are a secondary concern. Patents and copyrights are intended to establish legal incentives to create new works and inventions. But if those incentives are too strong, they increase costs for the public without providing any additional social benefit.[1] If a pharmaceutical company would have invested in developing its new drug in exchange for ten years of monopoly pricing, giving it twenty years of exclusivity is a terrible bargain for the public. Trademarks serve a different purpose. They are meant to make it easier for consumers to navigate the marketplace by preventing confusingly similar names and logos. By doing so, the law is supposed to encourage competition, not hinder it. When brands function as reliable indicators of source, it's easier to find the products we want and avoid the ones we don't. Finally, trade secrets serve the dual functions of encouraging firms to develop valuable information while maintaining a boundary between healthy competition and corporate espionage. None of these legal rights are absolute. To reflect that, each of these bodies of law contains internal limitations, designed to cabin their scope and avoid collateral damage to other social values.

This chapter will describe both how device makers try to leverage IP rights to restrict repair and why those assertions are, as a rule, inconsistent with a proper understanding of the law. Regardless of their ultimate merits though, IP claims have a chilling effect on repair. Litigation is uncertain, mounting a defense is expensive, and device makers enjoy massive resource advantages over consumers and repair providers.[2]

Copyrights

Copyright law provides authors exclusive rights over their creative works, allowing them to capture the market value of books, music, film, art, and software. As long as those works are minimally creative and recorded in some tangible form, copyright is automatic. In theory, legal rights against copying encourage creators to invest more time and effort producing works for the public to enjoy. In reality though, lots of creativity occurs in the absence of copyright incentives.[3] And the evidence suggests copyright exclusivity doesn't consistently lead to more or better creative works.[4] Even if we accept the incentive theory, the law recognizes the need for limitations and exceptions that narrow copyright's scope. A range of copyright doctrines are designed to safeguard the interests of subsequent creators, consumers, and the public more broadly.

Here are a few of the most significant under US law. Because they lack originality, facts – no matter how unexpected – can't be copyrighted.[5] So anyone is free to repeat the cosmically bizarre truth that famed playwright Samuel Beckett used to drive his young neighbor, the future wrestling legend Andre the Giant, to elementary school.[6] In addition, copyright extends only to an author's unique expression of an idea, not the underlying idea itself. That means the producers of *Armageddon*, the 1998 film about a mission to save the earth from an impending asteroid collision, have no claim against the producers of *Deep Impact*, the 1998 film about a mission to save the earth from an impending comet collision. The same is true for *The Prestige* and *The Illusionist* (2006), *Friends with Benefits* and *No Strings Attached* (2011), *Olympus Has Fallen* and *White House Down* (2013), and a parade of other pairings. Copyright also excludes functional elements described or contained in a work. Those include systems, methods, and processes.[7] So while a YouTuber might own their video explaining how to make fluffy rainbow unicorn slime, the copyright in that video does not give them the authority to stop anyone else from making or selling the resulting goop. Finally, when it comes to useful articles, or functional objects, copyright only protects creative elements, like graphics or sculptural components, that are separable from the article as a whole.[8] The Supreme Court, however, recently opened the door for broader protection under that standard.[9]

Beyond these limitations, the fair-use doctrine permits unauthorized uses of protected works when any harm to the copyright holder is outweighed by the social benefit of the use.

Courts have recognized a broad range of fair uses – from parodying popular songs and reproducing works in news reporting, to extracting functional information from video games and digitizing millions of books to create a search engine.[10] Because it presents a fact-intensive question that can only be resolved through litigation, establishing fair use is an expensive and uncertain proposition.

Finally, like other IP regimes, copyright recognizes the principle of exhaustion. Once a copyright holder has sold or otherwise transferred ownership of a particular copy of a work, they lose the right to control how it is distributed. Exhaustion – also known as the first-sale doctrine – is what permits us to lend our books to friends and sell our used records. Without it, copyright holders would retain control of those copies even after we purchase them. Collectively, these doctrines and others define and limit the appropriate scope of copyright.

Part Numbers and Manuals

Given its focus on creative works, you might not expect copyright law to have much to say about repair. But copyright disputes with implications for repair crop up with some frequency. One of the first, decided in 1901, dealt with a reseller of children's books.[11] George Doan bought used books in various states of disrepair. Pages were "soiled and torn," and covers were damaged or missing. Before reselling them, Doan repaired the books – replacing missing pages and in some cases reproducing missing covers "in exact similitude" of the originals. When Doan was sued by the American Book Company for copyright infringement, the Court of Appeals for the Seventh Circuit rejected the claim. As the owner of the books, Doan enjoyed a "right of repair or renewal" that allowed him to replace missing components and fashion new ones, even if they were "exact imitation[s] of the original." As the court put it, the "right of ownership in the book carries with it and includes the right to maintain the book as nearly as possible in its original condition." To deny that right would have been "intolerable and

odious." The right to repair, in other words, is an inherent
feature of ownership.

Decades later, manufacturers hit on another strategy for
repurposing copyright law to control the repair market, this
time by asserting ownership of part numbers. Repairing modern
equipment requires access to replacement parts, and identifying
the precise part you need can be a challenge. Companies typically
assign part numbers to each of the hundreds or thousands of
components that make up a complex piece of machinery. For
sellers of third-party parts, the best way to communicate that
your parts are compatible is to copy or reference the original
equipment manufacturer (OEM) part number. Say you need to
replace the ice-maker assembly in your freezer. You know the
OEM part number is D7824706Q. If you want to find a compatible
assembly from a third-party seller, the part number seems like an
obvious search term. But for precisely that reason, the manufacturer would prefer to prevent anyone else from using it.

That was the strategy lawn-care equipment maker Toro
attempted in the 1980s, as it faced new competition from independent part manufacturers. Toro sued R&R Products, alleging
it had unlawfully copied Toro's part numbering system. R&R
marketed its products in a mail-order catalog that listed Toro's
part name and number alongside R & R's replacement part and
price. The court rejected Toro's copyright assertion because its
system of arbitrarily assigning a random number to each replacement part failed to satisfy copyright's minimal standard for
creativity.[12]

Other companies tried to learn from Toro's mistakes. ATC
marketed its parts in a catalog featuring illustrations of disassembled vehicle transmissions. Each image showed the various
parts, their physical relationship within the assembly, and their
part numbers. When a new competitor, Whatever It Takes,
launched a similar catalog with the same part numbers, ATC
sued.[13] ATC argued that its numbering system, unlike Toro's,
required considerable judgment and creativity. Rather than
a random sequence, ATC organized parts into a taxonomy and
predicted the development of new parts by leaving some

numbers unassigned. Nonetheless, the court held that the system was unprotectable since ATC's taxonomy left it little discretion as to the number of any individual part. Moreover, the court rejected ATC's claim that Whatever It Takes copied its illustrations. Since those drawings "were intended to be as accurate as possible" they were "the antithesis of originality."

In yet another case, Southco, a manufacturer of fasteners used in computer and telecommunications equipment, sued Kanebridge, the distributor of a rival line of interchangeable parts.[14] Southco's numbering system was the industry standard. So Kanebridge included Southco's part numbers in the comparison charts it used to market its own parts. Unlike Toro and ATC, Southco argued that its part numbers themselves, rather than the system that produced them, were copyrighted. Those numbers were made up of nine digits reflecting various characteristics of each fastener – the material, thread size, length, and finish, among others. But again, once that system was established, the part number was determined by mechanical application of the rules, not creative choice. So, the court rejected Southco's copyright claim.

Contrast that with the names competing paint manufacturers give to nearly indistinguishable shades of white. Sherwin Williams offers Snowbound, Westhighland, and Heron Plume, while Behr has Whisper, Bit of Sugar, and Night Blooming Jasmine. Naming your 5 mm captive screw, say, Startled Predawn Antelope might be more creative, but it doesn't serve the needs of customers nearly as well. And even if Southco had chosen more expressive names for its parts, copyright isn't available for names, titles, and slogans.[15]

In recent years, some manufacturers have taken a new tack. Rather than part numbers, they've claimed copyright in repair manuals. These documents contain useful information for diagnosing and repairing various common failures. They might provide step-by-step instructions for disassembling a device or replacing broken components, saving consumers time, money, and frustration. In many instances, manuals help decipher cryptic error codes. If the LED on your furnace flashes twice, for instance, that might mean the pressure switch failed to open. Six flashes signal an ignition failure, and ten means the electrical polarity is reversed. Without the right documentation though, those codes are meaningless. Laptops, home appliances, vehicles, and even medical equipment often include repair manuals. But manuals can be lost or destroyed over time. So, access is important, especially for owners of used devices and independent repair shops that service dozens of different models. Although some manufacturers make digital versions easily accessible, or even affix key information directly to the product, other companies insist on limiting access.

In 2012, Toshiba demanded that Australian blogger Tim Hicks remove repair manuals for hundreds of laptop models from his website, Future Proof.[16] Toshiba offered a litany of justifications. It cited alleged safety risks from laptop self-repair, a concern apparently not shared by most other major manufacturers. It claimed the manuals contained unspecified "proprietary information" and that they were "only available to Toshiba authorised service providers." But ultimately, Toshiba's demand hinged on its assertion of copyright in the manuals. By reproducing and displaying them online, the company argued, Hicks was infringing its exclusive rights. Recognizing the costs of taking on a company like Toshiba, Hicks complied.

More recently, the availability of repair manuals has taken on greater significance. In 2020, iFixit announced its Medical Device Repair Database, a collection of repair manuals for more than 13,000 ventilators, anesthesia systems, and respiratory analyzers, among other devices.[17] It wasn't the first collection of medical-device manuals, however. Frank's Hospital Workshop, a site based in Tanzania, has been a go-to resource for medical technicians for years.[18] But the scope of iFixit's effort was remarkable, and its timing – as the coronavirus threatened basic healthcare infrastructure around the globe – reflected the dire need for fast, reliable repairs. While some medical-device makers share their manuals online, many do not. A centralized repository of those documents offered medical professionals a trusted, organized, and annotated source for information necessary to keep patients alive.

But in May of 2020, Russell Wheatley, the Chief Intellectual Property Counsel for Steris, an Ohio-based manufacturer of medical sterilization equipment, sent a letter to iFixit.[19] The company demanded removal of all its manuals from the iFixit database. It gave only one reason: copyright. To a copyright novice, this may look like an open-and-shut case. Steris claims to own copyrights in its manuals, and iFixit reproduced them without permission. But the analysis isn't quite so straightforward. Indeed, there are good reasons to doubt that a court would side with this effort to restrict access to repair information.

First, looking at the manual for the Steris Harmony surgical-lighting system reveals that much of the information it contains is simply not subject to copyright.[20] About one-third of the manual, roughly fifty pages, is a long list of part names and numbers, accompanied by simple illustrations. As we've seen, courts are hostile to copyright claims rooted in factual, unoriginal lists of parts and their depiction in straightforward drawings. Beyond that, the bulk of the manual is a collection of methods and processes beyond the scope of copyright. The "service mode procedure," for example, is a step-by-step guide for navigating a menu to perform diagnostics and firmware updates. Elsewhere, the manual details the process for replacing or adjusting various components, like this one:

8.4 Knuckle Cover Removal (Any) and Assembly
1. Remove the screw securing the knuckle covers together. Set aside, the screws are not captive.
2. Gently pry the halves of the covers apart using a small flat-blade screwdriver. Inch the screwdriver along the seam gently, until the cover halves separate.
3. Re-install the covers by gently snapping the sections together.
4. The screw must be secured into the knuckle covers with LOCTITE 242 (STERIS part number P129377-290) or equivalent.

Even if we generously assume this mechanical description of an uncopyrightable process is creative, it falls within what's known as the merger doctrine, a principle that recognizes some ideas can only be expressed in a handful of ways. There may be a nearly infinite variety of ways to express the idea of unrequited love, but there's less room for artistic flourish when describing the removal of a Steris knuckle cover. Aside from minor variations in word choice – perhaps "tenderly separate" instead of "gently pry" – any clear, accurate description of that process is going to look nearly identical to Steris's formulation. Under those circumstances, the idea and its expression are considered merged, and neither is subject to copyright.[21]

But let's assume these manuals contain some scrap of original expression that merits copyright. Even then, iFixit can make a strong case for fair use. Among the key factors courts consider in fair-use cases is "the purpose and character of the use." Here, iFixit's purpose in posting the manuals would strongly favor fair use. First, the Medical Device Repair Database is a noncommercial offering. iFixit doesn't charge for access to the manuals. In fact, it undertook the project, at considerable cost, as a public service. Second, by collecting thousands of medical-device manuals in a single location, organizing them in an intuitive taxonomy, and making them searchable, iFixit has created a new resource that is far more useful than the sum of its parts. In fair-use parlance, this is a transformative use, a fact that bolsters iFixit's case significantly.

In response, Steris would likely point out that in addition to selling hospitals equipment that costs tens of thousands of dollars, it charges as much as $1,100 for manuals.[22] Steris would argue that by posting those manuals for free, iFixit interferes with its ability to sell copies. While iFixit's manual repository might reduce Steris's revenue, that's not necessarily harm that copyright law ought to worry about. If medical technicians are downloading the manuals to access facts, methods, and processes rather than Steris's poetic phrasing, that lost revenue is not attributable to copyright infringement. And even if it were, a court could easily conclude that any financial harm is outweighed by the public benefits of hospital equipment that works reliably in a time of crisis.

No one in their right mind picks up a medical-device repair manual for its literary value. Having perused a few, I can assure you that they aren't exactly beach reads. They are documents with a very specific purpose – to help the reader maintain, diagnose, and repair a piece of equipment. Understood in that light, copyright in the manual becomes a tool to control repair. In other words, if companies like Steris can limit access to the manual, they can limit repair. Servicing these complex devices is nearly impossible without access to detailed technical information. But copyright law was never intended to create repair monopolies.

As strong as iFixit's case is, definitively establishing any of these theories in court is an expensive proposition. Litigating a copyright case of this sort to trial could easily rack up legal fees in excess of $1 million.[23] Luckily, iFixit was represented by the Electronic Frontier Foundation, a nonprofit legal-services organization with deep intellectual property expertise.[24] It pushed back, and the manuals remain available today. But not everyone on the receiving end of a legal threat from a device maker with billions of dollars in annual revenue can be so fortunate.

Software and Circumvention

Software introduces another avenue for manufacturers to enlist copyright law to limit repair. As we've already seen, software code is essential to the functioning, diagnosis, and repair of both modern consumer goods and industrial machinery. And since copyright extends to that code, device makers are irresistibly attracted to the legal power it seems to promise.

One early example of this strategy, dating back to 1992, pitted a computer manufacturer against an independent repair provider. MAI Systems created workstations that ran its own operating system, programs, and diagnostic software. It also offered repair and maintenance services to its customers, mostly small banks and credit unions. When Peak Computing began competing for those same repair contracts, MAI looked for a way to stop them. It sued for copyright infringement, alleging that when Peak booted up customer's computers and loaded the diagnostic software, it made copies of MAI's code in the random-access memory (RAM) of those devices.[25] And since MAI's license agreement didn't permit copying by third parties like Peak, it argued those copies were infringing. Even though RAM copies are temporary, and the owners of the computers wanted Peak to access them, the court sided with MAI.

While influential, the decision in *MAI v. Peak* was roundly criticized.[26] It established a rule, followed by several later courts, that merely loading a program or data in RAM creates an infringing reproduction. That means every time you open a file or run a program, you need either the permission of the copyright holder or some legal justification. In a world in which embedded software controls our phones, cars, and blenders, that rule gives copyright holders incredible power. This interpretation, however, is inconsistent with the text of the Copyright Act. It makes clear that a copy must be permanent enough to "permit it to be perceived, reproduced, or otherwise communicated for a period of more than transitory duration."[27] Information stored in RAM for a few seconds or minutes almost certainly fails that standard, as the Second Circuit eventually concluded decades later.[28]

Aside from the broader RAM copy problem, Congress understood that the *MAI* decision spelled potential disaster for repair providers. It responded by creating a new exception to copyright infringement that insulates repair and maintenance from liability. Under § 117(c), owners or lessees of machines are permitted to make – or to authorize providers to make – copies of computer programs in the course of maintenance or repair.[29] But that right is limited in important respects. The copies can't be used for any other purposes and must be destroyed after the repair or maintenance is complete. Most crucially, the copies must be "made solely by virtue of the activation of a machine that lawfully contains an authorized copy of the computer program." That means if software necessary for repair isn't already stored on the machine, owners and repair providers are not entitled to obtain or make copies.

Device makers have taken advantage of that limitation by designing external software tools. The proprietary software John Deere uses to authenticate replacement parts, for instance, is not installed on farmers' tractors, but on technicians' laptops.[30] And without that code, farmers and independent repair shops can't initiate authentic replacement parts. Deere expects farmers to pay hundreds of dollars for a technician to bless those components. But in response, some farmers have turned to Ukrainian websites that sell unauthorized copies of John Deere software as a means of bypassing these restrictions.[31] Downloading that software without permission is arguably an act of infringement, even when done for legitimate repair purposes.

On top of that, the software license that accompanies new Deere products insists farmers may not "purchase ... any circumvention or hacking device that is designed to circumvent or hack the [licensed software or product]."[32] By acquiring John Deere software from an unauthorized source, farmers may violate that provision. If so, Deere could argue that farmers infringe copyright by simply using their equipment, since embedded software is reproduced in the tractor's memory. That argument is far from a slam dunk for Deere, however. First, it would depend on a court embracing *MAI*'s flawed RAM copy doctrine. Moreover, courts tend to be reluctant to impose copyright liability for license violations unless they bear some reasonable connection to the underlying copyright interests.[33] Where the alleged infringement consists of farmers firing up their tractors, Deere faces an uphill battle. Finally, the Copyright Act gives owners of copies of software the right to make copies that are essential to their use. But this right extends only to those who own copies. Deere insists that farmers are licensed to use its software, but don't actually own the embedded copies that make their tractor "run like a Deere."[34] General Motors (GM) makes the same claim about the code embedded in its vehicles.[35] In the end, farmers have good arguments against infringement. But they still face risks in going up against a well-funded copyright bully.

Even if we are confident farmers won't be deemed copyright infringers, they aren't necessarily in the clear yet. Copyright law offers device makers another potential tool to stamp out unauthorized repair. Section 1201 of the Digital Millennium Copyright Act (DMCA) makes it unlawful to circumvent techno-logical protection measures that restrict access to copyrighted works, including software.[36] In other words, it's unlawful to remove digital locks meant to keep you away from copyrighted material, including software. It also violates § 1201 to create, sell, or distribute tools that enable circumvention.[37] These are two sources of legal risk above and beyond traditional copyright infringement.

You may be familiar with various species of digital rights management (DRM) technology that limit access to music, movies, and video games. When it was enacted in 1998, § 1201 was intended to encourage copyright holders to make their works available online.[38] The idea was that if they could rely on DRM to restrict access to their works, rights holders would be more likely to embrace digital distribution. But it didn't take long for manufacturers of printers, garage door openers, and other devices to realize that § 1201 offered them the chance to limit competition for aftermarket parts and service. Courts rebuffed those early efforts to expand the DMCA's scope.[39] But the risk of broad applications of § 1201 remains a concern for repair providers and part makers. Today, manufacturers con-tinue to rely on digital locks to restrict access to the embedded code that controls devices from smartphones to cars. Because that code is often necessary for diagnosis and repair, those protection measures pose practical hurdles for consumers and repair providers. Section 1201 compounds those difficulties by introducing legal liability for removing or bypassing the locks on the devices we own.

One court rightly rejected an attempt to use § 1201 to shut down a repair provider.[40] StorageTek sold data-storage systems. Those systems were made up of a number of "silos," each con-taining a robot arm that inserted tape cartridges into various drives. Each silo was operated by a control unit, and collectively the system was controlled by a networked management unit. Those units ran StorageTek's software, including diagnostic programs, which it claimed to license to system owners. In an effort to kneecap a competitor, StorageTek sued Custom Hardware Engineering & Consulting (CHE), an independent repair provider, alleging that CHE circumvented StorageTek's protection measures to access to its software code.

StorageTek's software generated error codes, which CHE needed to capture in order to diagnose faulty machines. To access those codes, CHE had to override GetKey, a password-protection scheme StorageTek created to lockdown its systems. At first, CHE used a tool that generated multiple passwords to crack GetKey through brute force. Later, CHE learned how to mimic the signals sent to the control unit to divulge error codes. StorageTek alleged that both techniques circumvented its access controls.

The Federal Circuit was not persuaded. In a prior case, the court held that to violate § 1201, circumvention must have some plausible connection to an act of copyright infringement.[41] Without that "critical nexus," circumvention is lawful. Applying the same logic to StorageTek's claim, the court was satisfied that there was little chance circumvention would lead to infringement since CHE was entitled to make copies of the software under § 117. While that reasoning would seem to protect owners and repair providers from circumvention liability in many circumstances, other courts have declined to adopt the Federal Circuit's nexus requirement, contributing to ongoing legal uncertainty around repair.[42]

When it enacted § 1201, Congress recognized its potential for unintended consequences. So, it called on the Copyright Office and the Librarian of Congress to conduct a rule-making every three years to identify noninfringing uses that are likely to be adversely affected by the anticircumvention provision. Those uses are then protected by temporary exemptions.[43] In 2015, after a hard-fought battle by repair advocates, the Librarian adopted an exemption permitting the circumvention of DRM that restricts access to software that controls "motorized land vehicles" for the purpose of diagnosis and repair.[44] In the next rule-making, that exemption was expanded to include software that controls a "smartphone or home appliance or home system, such as a refrigerator, thermostat, HVAC or electrical system."[45]

These exemptions were landmark successes for repair advocates, but they are limited in scope. First, they don't include lots of devices, like tablets, smart speakers, cameras, televisions, and game consoles. Second, they are temporary. In 2021, the Copyright Office will conduct another rule-making and may revise, narrow, or eliminate these exemptions altogether.[46] Third, exemptions are limited to § 1201's anticircumvention provision. They offer no defense to the prohibition on trafficking in circumvention tools.[47] So while it is lawful to circumvent in order to repair, creating and sharing tools that enable circumvention are not. This creates significant practical hurdles for independent repair. Even for sophisticated operations, building a circumvention tool from scratch is a major undertaking.

The United States has aggressively exported its anticircumvention regime around the globe, foisting it on other countries as a key provision in bilateral and multilateral trade agreements over the past two decades. To date, the jurisdictions to accede to these demands include: Australia, Bahrain, Canada, Chile, Colombia, Costa Rica, Dominican Republic, El Salvador, Guatemala, Honduras, Mexico, Morocco, Nicaragua, Oman, Panama, Peru, Singapore, and South Korea.[48] Likewise, the European Union adopted an anticircumvention regime in 2001 at the urging of US interests.[49] And today, the United States continues to pressure countries like South Africa to adopt harsh anticircumvention rules.[50] But the eagerness to export § 1201 has not extended to its exceptions and limitations. So, while jurisdictions are generally free to craft defenses or exemptions like those that currently acknowledge repair in the United States, there is no guarantee that they will. As a result, these trade agreements imperil legitimate repair activities around the globe.

Utility Patents

Like copyrights, patents are designed to create economic incentives. In exchange for market exclusivity, inventors devote time and capital to developing new technologies. The resulting inventions are then shared with the public – embodied in products we buy and published in patent documents. But while copyrights are conferred automatically for even minimally creative works, utility patents are granted only if inventions satisfy higher thresholds.

In the United States, an invention must first fall within the scope of patentable subject matter. Patents extend to machines, articles of manufacture, compositions of matter, and processes. Abstract ideas, laws of nature, and natural phenomena, on the other hand, are excluded.[51] Second, an invention must be novel; only inventions that are new are patentable.[52] Third, it must be non-obvious.[53] In other words, even if the elements that make up an invention have never been combined before, if that combination would have occurred to a person of ordinary skill in the relevant field, it's not patentable. And finally, the invention must have some specific, substantial, and credible use.[54] An elaborate collection of components that serves as a paper weight isn't a patentable invention. Most other jurisdictions apply a similar set of standards. In Europe, for example, inventions must be "new," demonstrate an "inventive step," and be "susceptible of industrial application."[55]

Patents typically last for twenty years.[56] During that period, utility patents confer broad exclusive rights. They grant the patent holder the right to prevent others from making, using, or selling the invention.[57] With few exceptions, unless you have permission from the patent holder, those activities constitute infringement. As a result, patent holders wield considerable power over the manufacture and sale of products embodying their inventions, as well as their use – even for private, non-commercial purposes.

The exhaustion doctrine is one critical limitation on the power of patentees. Like its analog in copyright law, exhaustion prevents patent holders from asserting control over the use and disposition of a particular product after its sale. The owner of a patented device is entitled, as a matter of law, to use it as they see fit, sell it, or otherwise transfer ownership.[58] That's true even if the patentee objects. In essence, the personal property rights of the owner of the physical product trump the intellectual property rights of the patent holder. As the US Supreme Court recognized as early as 1852, "when the machine passes to the hands of the purchaser, it is no longer within the limits of the monopoly. It passes outside of it, and is no longer under the protection of the act of Congress . . .. The implement or machine becomes [the owner's] private, individual property."[59] Crucially, the purchase of a patented machine "carrie[s] with it the right to the use of that machine so long as it was capable of use."[60]

This centuries-old principle remains vital today. In 2017, the Court reaffirmed a broad patent exhaustion rule when it rejected an effort by the printer manufacturer Lexmark to prevent a competitor from refilling and reselling compatible ink cartridges.[61] Despite Lexmark's restrictive license terms, the Court held the company was powerless to prohibit refurbishing its cartridges as a matter of patent law. In doing so, the Court emphasized the connection between exhaustion and repair:

> Take a shop that restores and sells used cars. The business works because the shop can rest assured that, so long as those bringing in the cars own them, the shop is free to repair and resell those vehicles. That smooth flow of commerce would sputter if companies that make the thousands of parts that go into a vehicle could keep their patent rights after the first sale. Those companies might, for instance, restrict resale rights and sue the shop owner for patent infringement.

Exhaustion guarantees an owner's right to use the products they buy, and courts have consistently recognized an inherent right to repair. But importantly, exhaustion does not extend to making or reproducing a patented device.[62] A hospital that purchases a patented surgical robot, for example, isn't entitled to build a second one.

This distinction between repair and reconstruction stretches back to *Wilson v. Simpson*, an 1850 case about replacing worn blades on a planing machine.[63] The owners of the machine argued that they were entitled to replace dull blades every few months to keep the device operational. But the patent holders insisted that "when any [part of the machine] is either worn out by use, or otherwise destroyed, then the combination invented – the thing patented – no longer exists, and cannot be restored without the exercise of the right to make." In other words, when the owner replaces a broken or worn component, they are not merely using the invention, they are remaking it. The Court disagreed. Replacing worn or broken parts is an act of "restoration, and not reconstruction." The Court understood repair as "no more than the exercise of that right of care which everyone may use to give duration to that which he owns."

Almost a century later, the Supreme Court revisited the repair of patented devices. This time, the owner of a patent on a convertible car roof, operating under the decidedly uninspired name Convertible Top Replacement Company, sued Aro Manufacturing for selling replacement fabric cut to fit the patented invention.[64] The patent described a device with three basic components: "a flexible top fabric, supporting structures, and a mechanism for sealing the fabric against the side of the automobile body." The patentee maintained that by selling fabric patterned to fit its product, Aro was helping customers remanufacture the patented device. The Court rejected that characterization. As it wrote, the "mere replacement of individual unpatented parts, one at a time, whether of the same part repeatedly or different parts successively, is no more than the lawful right of the owner to repair his property."

Courts have outlined a broad general rule that insulates repair from claims of patent infringement – where repair is understood as the "restoration to a sound, good, or complete state after decay, injury, dilapidation, or partial destruction."[65] Repair is not limited to temporary fixes or the replacement of minor components.[66] The rule embraces one-off repairs and large-scale industrial refurbishing alike.[67] It even applies to modifications of the original design, so long as those changes extend the device's useful life.[68]

Even patented products that were explicitly designed for one-time use can be repaired without the permission of the patent holder. One long-running dispute centered on Fuji's patents on single-use disposable cameras. These cheap plastic devices were sold preloaded with film. After snapping a couple of dozen photos, purchasers would drop them off for processing. They'd receive physical prints after a few days, but never see the camera again. Refurbishers like Jazz Photo collected depleted camera bodies, loaded them with new film, replaced their batteries, reset their counters, and resold them. Fuji sued, alleging the remanufacture of its patented technology.[69] But the court understood that the useful lifespan of the camera was not limited to one roll of film. Even though Fuji marketed them as single-use devices, "the patentee's unilateral intent, without more, does not bar reuse of the patented article, or convert repair into reconstruction."

Admittedly, the line dividing repair from reconstruction isn't always a particularly bright one.[70] But that uncertainty is nothing new. The question has frustrated courts for more than a century. As one court considering the repair of patented sewing machines wrote in 1901, "The difficult question still remains . . . . When does repair destroy the identity of such device or machine and encroach upon invention? At what point does the legitimate repair of such device or machine end, and illegitimate reconstruction begin?"[71] That same year, a British court approached the question by contemplating a hypothetical farm cart:

> A man has at the beginning a new cart. By-and-bye the wheels, one or both of them, have worn out, and he puts on a pair of new wheels. Is it or is it not the old cart? Few people would doubt that it is the old cart . . . . But by-and-bye the shafts fail, and for the old shafts are substituted new ones. I do not wish to express a decided opinion, but it is quite possible you have still the old cart. But if after that you come to the body of the cart, and the body of the cart is either taken away and a new body is put there, or new wood is put for

a large portion of the cart, surely it is impossible to then say that the old cart still remains.[72]

The sequential replacement of parts hints at a deeper puzzle that dates back at least 2,000 years. Plutarch described how the Athenians preserved the ship that carried Theseus home from Crete. "They took away the old planks as they decayed, putting in new and stronger timber in their places."[73] Among philosophers, the ship of Theseus embodied the problem of identity over time. Was the preserved ship the same vessel Theseus captained, or was it a new ship altogether?

Understandably, courts have struggled to resolve these metaphysical questions. They've considered a litany of factors to distinguish repair from reconstruction over the decades – whether the replaced part had a short useful life compared to the rest of the device, whether the part was broken or merely worn, whether it was expensive or cheap, and whether it was central to the essence of the patented innovation.[74] At other times, courts took into account the intent and expectations of patentees and consumers. In its *Aro* decision, however, the Supreme Court cautioned against reliance on these various factors. The central question according to the Court is whether the device "viewed as a whole, has become spent." By "spent," the Court seems to mean that the entire device has reached the end of its useful life. If the device is deemed spent, then efforts to restore its functionality amount to unlawful reconstruction.[75] If the device as a whole isn't spent – even if some of its parts are – those components can be replaced or renewed through lawful repair. But how exactly do courts decide whether a device is spent? Lower courts have often reverted to the same multifactor analysis that characterized the pre-*Aro* decisions. So, while patent law generally accommodates a broad notion of repair, this uncertainty about the standard lower courts will apply casts the shadow of potential liability over consumers and repair providers.

The framework adopted by US patent law is largely consistent with the approach embraced by courts in other jurisdictions. In Australia, Germany, Japan, and the United Kingdom, liability also turns on the fundamental, if elusive, distinction between repair and reconstruction. As the Supreme Court of Japan phrased it, the question is whether the defendant "has created a new product which has a different identity from the original product."[76] But like their US counterparts, these courts have at times struggled to settle on consistent, predictable standards. Japanese courts consider a range of factors, including the attributes of the patented product, the nature of the underlying invention, and the specific acts of replacement or refurbishment undertaken by the defendant.[77] In Germany, courts ask whether the defendant's actions would be understood as typical maintenance activity in the relevant market and whether the technical essence of the invention is reflected in the replaced components.[78]

Likewise, UK courts have long recognized "that a purchaser of a patented article may carry out repairs to it without being held liable for infringement. On the other hand, he cannot manufacture a new article . . . and claim that he has not infringed merely because . . . he has used parts derived from a patented article sold by the patentee."[79] In 2013, the Supreme Court of the United Kingdom rejected a patent holder's contention that replacing one element of its patented device amounted to reconstruction.[80] In *Schütz v. Werit*, the patentee sold containers used to transport hazardous liquids. They consisted of a plastic bottle mounted within a metal cage, which in turn rested on a pallet. The cage and pallet could be used multiple times, but the bottles were designed for a single use. Werit provided replacement bottles, which Schütz alleged infringed its patent. The Court recognized the replacement of the bottles as a lawful repair rather than the making of a new device. That holding turned on two key facts. First, the useful life of the bottle was considerably shorter than the rest of the apparatus. On average, the bottle could be swapped out five or six times before the cage needed to be replaced. Second, the bottle did not reflect the "inventive concept" of the patent. In other words, the bottle is not what set the container apart from the existing technology at the time it was invented.

In 2020, the High Court of Australia confronted the question of repair in a case that closely mirrored the facts of the US *Lexmark* decision.[81] Epson sold printers and single-use ink cartridges. Calidad imported and sold refilled Epson cartridges with memory chips modified so that printers would recognize them. Epson alleged the refurbished cartridges infringed its patents. The question before the High Court was "whether modifications made to a product to enable its re-use amount to a making of a new product." Those modifications – puncturing the cartridge to refill the ink, sealing the resulting hole, and updating the memory chip – did not "amount to an impermissible making of a new product." Rather, they were "within the scope of the rights of an owner to prolong the life of a product and make it more useful."

Importantly, the High Court rejected the contention that the legality of repair turned on an implied license. Under that approach, the sale of a patented device is presumed to entail the right to repair, on the assumption that both the buyer and the seller expect repairs to occur and have bargained accordingly. But under that rationale, a seller could expressly withhold or limit the availability of repair. So, if a prominent notice forbidding repair accompanied your new car, fixing a faulty transmission might count as infringement. Instead, the Australian High Court, like its counterparts in Germany, Japan, the US, and the UK, rooted the right to repair firmly in the exhaustion principle. After the initial sale, the patentee loses all rights to control the product's use, regardless of any limits or reservations communicated by the patent holder.

Canada is one notable exception to this trend. As in other jurisdictions, Canadian law acknowledges that "the purchaser of a patented article may repair the components without infringing the patent."[82] And Canadian courts agree that the central question is whether the defendant has made a new article or simply repaired an existing one.[83] But Canadian law has never fully adopted a freestanding exhaustion doctrine. Instead, the rationale for the legality of repair is "the fact that the patent holder is presumed to permit this type of activity."[84]

In other words, patent holders offer purchasers an implied license to repair, a license they could easily withhold. For example, in *Eli Lilly v. Novopharm*, the Supreme Court of Canada declared that once a patented article is sold, the patent owner "no longer has any right with respect to the article" because the patentee "has impliedly renounced his exclusive right of use and sale."[85] If patent holders "express conditions to the contrary," the owner of a patented article would no longer be able to repair it. In *Monsanto v. Schmeiser*, the Court was even more explicit when it wrote, "Ownership is no defence to a breach of the Patent Act."[86] Perhaps because of its rather equivocal foundation, the right to repair under Canadian patent law tends to be less expansive in practice than in other jurisdictions.[87]

Even where courts embrace the right of owners to replace or repair components, patent law can still impede repair. If the components themselves are patented, their production, sale, and use are still subject to the exclusive rights of patent holders. They can use that power to starve repair providers of the replacement parts they need or charge exorbitant prices that discourage third-party repairs.

When Italian volunteers 3D-printed replacement ventilator valves, initial reports suggested they were threatened with a patent infringement suit. The device maker, however, quickly released a statement disclaiming any impending litigation.[88] But nothing in patent law would prevent a more mercenary device maker from pursuing such a claim. Assuming the valve was the subject of a valid utility patent, making replacements – whether through 3D-printing or more conventional methods – would constitute infringement.[89] Luckily, most replacement parts, standing alone, fail to meet the relatively demanding statutory requirements for utility patents. But unfortunately, not all patents are so hard to come by.

Designs

Intellectual property regimes also provide exclusive rights in designs – the appearance or ornamentation of products. In the

United States, design patents are available. In Europe and elsewhere, registered and unregistered design rights serve a similar function. The substantive and procedural details differ somewhat, but these regimes raise tricky questions about the degree to which designs extend to the functional aspects of products and their components. In particular, exclusive rights in the design of replacement parts run the risk of hampering otherwise lawful repairs. Jurisdictions have responded differently to this problem. The United States legal system has shrugged its metaphorical shoulders in indifference. Europe has grappled with the issue more seriously, if not entirely effectively, by limiting the availability and scope of design rights that would undermine repair.

Design Patents

Since 1842, US law has permitted patents on designs.[90] Unlike utility patents, which turn on the functionality of an invention, design patents are meant to grant rights in the aesthetic contributions of a designer. Today, they extend to "any new, original, and ornamental design for an article of manufacture."[91] Patentable designs must be novel, nonobvious, and ornamental.[92] They include the surface ornamentation of an article, including colors and graphic elements, its three-dimensional configuration or shape, or any combination of the above.[93] Iconic designs from Coca-Cola bottles and Eames chairs to Lego figures and Fender Telecasters have been patented, along with hundreds of thousands of less memorable examples.

Once granted, design patents last for fifteen years. During that period, the patent holder has the legal right to prevent others from making, using, selling, offering to sell, or importing the patented design.[94] To prove infringement, the patentee must show that "an ordinary observer, taking into account the prior art, would believe the [defendant's] design to be the same as the patented design."[95] In other words, anyone who makes, sells, or even uses a product that looks too much like a patented design without permission is an infringer.

Over time, shifts in judicial interpretation have eroded safe-guards that limited the availability and reach of design patents. That liberalization led to a massive increase in the number of patented designs. In 1980, the United States Patent and Trademark Office (USPTO) granted barely 3,000 design patents.[96] In 2019, it handed out nearly 35,000, more than a tenfold increase.[97] And a 2010 study revealed that the Patent Office rejected less than 2 percent of design-patent applications on sub-stantive grounds.[98] Meanwhile, damages in design-patent cases have reached new highs. After Apple sued Samsung for infringing its iPhone design patents – including its rounded corners, home button, and grid of app icons – a jury awarded more $500 million in damages.[99]

These developments have broad implications across a range of industries. But they have particularly dire consequences for repair. If design patents on components and replacement parts are easy to secure, manufacturers have the power to deny those parts to owners and repair providers, to charge unreasonably high prices, or to condition access to parts on other onerous terms.

We've already seen these strategies play out in the auto indus-try. A recent case decided by the Federal Circuit – the appellate court with exclusive jurisdiction over patent disputes – illus-trates the worry. The Automotive Body Parts Association (ABPA) sued to invalidate two Ford design patents on a truck hood and head lamp.[100] ABPA argued that since consumers prefer parts that not only serve the same function as the original, but also restore their vehicles' appearance, those designs should be deemed functional rather than ornamental. The Federal Circuit disagreed, holding that "the aesthetic appeal of a design to con-sumers is inadequate to render that design functional."[101] The court also rejected ABPA's exhaustion and repair arguments. Although the sale of a vehicle exhausts Ford's control over the physical components that make it up, it does not give the owner the right to use unauthorized parts that copy a patented design. And since Ford's design patents covered individual parts rather than the vehicle as a whole, patent law's right of repair didn't permit making or using unauthorized parts.

The aftermarket for vehicle parts and accessories is massive, amounting to hundreds of billions of dollars each year in the United States alone.[102] Historically, that market has been competitive, allowing owners to choose between original manufacturer parts or a variety of less expensive non-OEM options, saving roughly $1.5 billion a year when it comes to collision repairs.[103] But design patents threaten to undermine that competitive landscape, forcing consumers and repair shops to purchase original parts at inflated prices.

Since 2005, we've seen an uptick in efforts by manufacturers to crack down on competitive repair parts. That trend began when Ford filed a complaint with the International Trade Commission that stopped imports of replacement parts for its F-150 pickup trucks. The company then struck a deal giving its one-time competitor the exclusive right to distribute aftermarket Ford parts, severely hampering competition.[104] In the wake of Ford's strategy, other carmakers have used design patents on bumpers, fenders, headlights, and other parts to threaten manufacturers, importers, and distributors of non-OEM parts, and the repair shops that use them.[105] This same strategy could just as easily be exploited by the makers of smartphones, cameras, and home appliances.

So how did US design-patent law find itself in this unfortunate situation? Two overlapping sets of changes in the law are to blame. First, courts have expanded the subject matter of patentable designs far beyond what Congress intended. Second, the USPTO, following the clear directives of the Federal Circuit, has all but eliminated any meaningful barrier to obtaining a design patent.

Under the terms of the Patent Act, patents are available for the "design for an article of manufacture."[106] The interpretation of that phrase is central to understanding the proper scope of design-patent subject matter. By interpreting it broadly, courts have opened the door to design patents on products, like complex machines, that were never intended. What's more, courts have paved the way for design patents that claim only parts and – worse still – fragments of parts of those assemblages.

When the US Supreme Court heard an appeal in Apple's lawsuit against Samsung, it defined "article of manufacture" broadly. According to the Court, that term "encompasses both a product sold to a consumer and a component of that product" because it means "simply a thing made by hand or machine."[107] But that reading misunderstands the plain meaning and long history of the term. As Sarah Burstein, one of the leading scholars of the US design-patent regime, has argued, the phrase "article of manufacture" refers "to a tangible item made by humans – other than a machine or composition of matter – that had a unitary structure and was complete in itself for use or for sale."[108]

As an initial matter, "machines" were long understood as outside the scope of design-patentable subject matter. Unlike utility patents, which extend to any "process, machine, manufacture, or composition of matter," design patents are available only for "articles of manufacture."[109] "Machines" are conspicuously excluded. For decades, the Patent Office understood that machines were not considered articles of manufacture and were ineligible for design patents.[110] The first patent claiming the design of a machine wasn't granted until 1930. Foreshadowing future developments, it claimed a truck body and frame.[111] In the decades since, the Patent Office has routinely granted, and the courts unhesitatingly enforced, design patents on machines.

Even if we set aside this nearly century-old error, design-patent law took another, more recent wrong turn. Longstanding principles of design-patent law focused attention on the design as a whole, not its constituent parts. Consumers don't perceive a design as a collection of lines, shapes, and colors, but as an integrated, unitary whole. As one court put it in 1900, "The essence of a design resides, not in the elements individually, nor in their method of arrangement, but in the tout ensemble – in that indefinable whole that awakens some sensation in the observer's mind."[112] Understandably then, design-patent applicants claiming some fragment of an article were typically met with hostility. An application claiming the design of the "forward corner of an automobile body," for example, was rejected because it did not "cover a complete article of manufacture."[113] On appeal, the rejection was affirmed because the corner of the body was never manufactured and sold separately.

That's not to say that piecemeal design patents were never granted, but it wasn't until 1980 that courts explicitly embraced claims identifying a mere fragment of an article of manufacture. In *Zahn*, the US Court of Customs and Patent Appeals (CCPA) – the predecessor of today's Federal Circuit – considered an application for an "ornamental design for a Shank of a Drill Bit."[114] The claimed design was limited to the upper portion of the bit and explicitly disclaimed the cutting edge – the part that bores the hole. That choice had two important implications. First, the claim extended only to a fragment of the overall article, flouting the principle of integrated, holistic design patenting. Second, since the twist cutting edge pictured in the patent was not part of the claim, it covered any drill bit with a similar shank. So, a spade, core, or step bit would infringe even though the overall appearance of the article would be quite different.

In keeping with its accepted practice, the USPTO rejected the application. But on appeal, the CCPA disagreed. According to the court, the fact that the application claimed only a portion of the drill bit was no barrier to patentability. Specifically, the court held that "a design for an article of manufacture may be embodied in less than all of an article of manufacture."[115] But in characterizing the issue in those terms, the court assumed that Zahn's partial claim constituted "a design for an article of manufacture" in the first place.[116] This begs the question. The issue the court needed to decide was whether a claim directed to a fragment of an article of manufacture is a patentable design at all. As Professor Burstein has persuasively argued, *Zahn* relies on a misreading of the Patent Act and faulty logic.[117] Sometimes courts get it wrong. When they do, we shouldn't be bound by their mistakes forever.

The risks of defining "articles of manufacture" broadly could be tempered if patent examiners assiduously scrutinized the substantive requirements for design patents. Unfortunately, that's the opposite of what's happened. The Federal Circuit, exercising its exclusive power to review the decisions of the PTO, has consistently lowered the bar for obtaining a design patent. Today, practically anyone with a spare $5,000 and a modicum of patience can get their very own design patent, and with it, the right to credibly threaten competitors with infringement liability.[118]

To qualify for a patent, a design must be novel, nonobvious, and ornamental. But under the prevailing Federal Circuit interpretations, those requirements rarely present meaningful hurdles.[119] To meet the novelty standard, an applicant only needs to show that its design is not "identical in all material respects" to any previously disclosed design – the "prior art," in patent law parlance.[120] In practice, the Federal Circuit is quick to identify minor differences between claimed designs and the prior art, highlighting minor discrepancies that would likely escape the attention of reasonably perceptive consumers, ensuring that the vast majority of designs will be treated as novel.[121]

In theory, nonobviousness is a higher barrier. Even if the precise design has never been seen before, it qualifies for a patent only if it would not have been obvious to a designer of ordinary skill in the relevant field.[122] How exactly do you determine whether a design is obvious? The Federal Circuit applies a two-part test. First, it looks for a primary reference in the prior art – an existing design that is "basically the same as the claimed design." Assuming it finds one, the court moves on to step two, where it searches for secondary reference designs that contain other elements of the claimed design. If the combination of the primary and secondary references would be obvious to a designer of ordinary skill, the claimed design is obvious. Much like its approach to novelty, however, the Federal Circuit is keenly attuned to subtle differences between the claimed design and any would-be primary reference. And without a primary reference, a claimed design can't be deemed obvious.[123]

Finally, patented designs are supposed to be ornamental. Utilitarian innovations – that is to say, inventions that offer some new functional advantage – are meant to be protected, if at all, with utility patents. Ideally then, the ornamentality requirement would guard against designs that contribute to a device's operation.[124] But again, the Federal Circuit has undermined this core requirement. Unless a design is "dictated by function," it is considered ornamental.[125] That means as long as some alternative design offers "the same or similar functional capabilities," a design will be treated as ornamental.[126]

This anemic standard opens the door for patents on designs that are in no discernible sense ornamental, like standard door hinges and flexible exhaust pipes.[127] Even worse, it permits design patents that offer substantial functional advantages.[128] Apple successfully asserted a design patent on the rounded corners of the iPhone despite the Federal Circuit's acknowledgement that they improved the device's "pocketability" and "durability."[129] And in an earlier case, the court upheld a design patent on the shape of a multifunction demolition tool – a combination hammer and pry bar – as ornamental, despite the fact that its size and shape were inseparable from its function.[130]

Even internal components can be ornamental. According to the court, a design is ornamental even if it is typically hidden from view during normal use. It just needs to be seen at some point between its manufacture and ultimate destruction.[131] In one illustrative case, the Federal Circuit insisted that the design of an artificial hip, despite being hidden once implanted, could be considered ornamental since it was advertised to doctors.[132]

Taken together, the expansion of design-patent subject matter and the erosion of its substantive requirements allow for the proliferation of exclusive rights in the components that make up our devices. Those rights, and the threat of litigation they enable, put third-party repair markets at risk. If the parts you need to repair your car, laptop, or dishwasher are patented, they are likely to cost more, if they are available at all. Authorized repair partners are likely to have more reliable access to those parts, putting additional pressure on independent providers to agree to unfavorable terms to secure the blessing of the

manufacturer. On the bright side, each of these flawed interpretations are a matter of judge-made law. Even without intervening legislation, the courts, if presented with the right facts
and persuasive arguments, can correct course. Here's hoping
they do.

Design Rights

Compared to the United States, Europe has paid far greater
attention to the problems exclusive rights over designs pose
for repair. Those problems remain unresolved, but the environment is significantly more hospitable for those who make, sell,
and use repair parts.

Under European law, the Design Directive and subsequent
Regulation outline the treatment of designs. Eligible designs
cover "the appearance of the whole or a part of a product resulting from ... lines, contours, colours, shape, texture and/or
materials."[133] To qualify, a design must be "new" and demonstrate an "individual character." Such a design may apply to an
entire product or a component, assuming that the component
remains visible during normal use, a somewhat stricter standard than courts have applied in the United States.

The newness and individual character requirements are
rough analogs to novelty and nonobviousness under US law.
The standard for individual character, however, imposes
a slightly more rigorous test. To satisfy it, "the overall impression" a design produces on an informed user must differ from
that produced by any previous design. That rule potentially
filters out some designs that would clear the relatively lax
standard for obviousness under US law. Owners of qualifying
designs have the exclusive rights to make, offer, put on the
market, import, export, or use covered products. For registered
designs, those rights last for up to twenty-five years, in renewable five-year periods. Unregistered designs are limited to three
years of exclusivity from their first public availability.

Several limitations on design rights touch on the question of
repair. Like other IP regimes, design rights are subject to the

general principle of exhaustion. Once a product has been sold or otherwise "put on the market," the rights holder loses the power to control the use or disposition of that particular product. So even if repair counts as a use of the design, an owner would generally be entitled to restore the appearance of a product. Assume your car door is dented in a minor collision. Short of a trip to the body shop, any number of home fixes might solve your problem – a plunger, boiling water, or dry ice and compressed air. None of these techniques would infringe the design under the exhaustion rule. In addition, design rights do not extend to any private or noncommercial acts. So even if you fashioned an identical replacement door yourself, you'd be in the clear.[134]

More broadly, EU law limits the availability of design rights to product features related to repair in two crucial respects. First, no design rights extend to features "solely dictated by [a product's] technical function."[135] This provision generally parallels the ornamentality rule under US law. But it offers a somewhat more effective screen to exclude functional aspects of a design. Initially courts applied the "multiplicity-of-forms" test to determine whether features were dictated by function, denying design rights only when no alternative designs could achieve the same function.[136] But in 2017, the European Court of Justice rejected that rule.[137] It held that the key question is not the availability of alternatives, but whether or not functional considerations, as opposed to visual appeal, were the only factors that determined its appearance.[138] If the designer's choices were all driven by function, design rights are barred. Like the ornamentality rule, this bar undoubtedly fails to screen out some functional product features, but by shifting focus away from available alternatives, it imposes a modestly more rigorous standard.

Second, European design law prohibits rights for product features that "must necessarily be reproduced in their exact form and dimensions in order to permit the product ... to be mechanically connected to or placed in, around or against another product."[139] This limitation for "must-fit" parts offers narrow but important operating space for repair. It prevents exclusive rights over aspects of parts or products that are essential to their function. A manufacturer of a rechargeable smart speaker, for example, couldn't claim exclusive rights over the business end of a charging cable, since its precise size and shape are essential to its connectivity.

But not all spare parts are of the "must-fit" variety. Let's say a knob breaks on your kitchen range. Several replacements might fit and do a perfectly adequate job of controlling the burner, but only one design will match the remaining knobs. Understandably, consumers strongly prefer matching hardware. For many, that preference is so strong that they wouldn't even consider a non-matching option an acceptable substitute.[140] That holds true across a range of parts and products.

So how should the law handle design rights for these "must-match" parts? In the run-up to the Design Directive, one proposal would have limited design rights for repair parts to three years.[141] A second proposal would have allowed the use of such designs so long as payment was made to the rights holder. But the question of repair parts proved contentious, and neither proposal was adopted. Instead, Article 14 of the Directive – often referred to as the "freeze-plus" clause – offers a temporary and incomplete solution. It requires member states to keep their existing national rules about repair parts in place, freezing them as is. States are free to change those rules only if their new law would "liberalise the market for such parts" by denying exclusive rights, providing an exception to liability, or otherwise making it easier to make, sell, and use replacement parts.[142] This has led to inconsistent national treatment of repair parts. In some jurisdictions – Belgium, Hungary, Ireland, Italy, Latvia, Luxembourg, Netherlands, Poland, and Spain – repair clauses limit rights covering spare parts. In others – Denmark and Sweden – repair parts enjoy a shorter term of exclusivity. The remaining member states haven't adopted any specific rules around repair parts, treating them the same as any other product component.

Community design rights, which are enforceable throughout Europe, demanded a more unified approach. Under Article 110 of the Regulation, manufacturers cannot enforce their design rights against anyone who repairs a "complex product" to restore its appearance.[143] The precise scope of this limitation has been debated. Elsewhere, the Regulation can be read to limit design rights only if the appearance of the design is "dependent" on the component part.[144] A few courts interpreted Article 110 narrowly, allowing design rights for alloy wheels for cars, for instance.[145] But the Court of Justice rejected that reading. It concluded that design rights couldn't be asserted against parts used in repair regardless of whether the product's overall appearance depended on those components.[146]

Other jurisdictions have wrestled with the best way to accommodate repair parts. Australia's Designs Act, for example, provides a defense to design infringement for repair. It permits a person to use a product embodying a design in order to repair a complex product – one with at least two replaceable components – and restore its appearance. The statute defines repair to include: "restoring a decayed or damaged component," "replacing a decayed or damaged component," "replacing incidental items," and "carrying out maintenance."[147] Once this defense is invoked, the onus is on the design owner to prove that the defendant knew or should have known that the parts were being used for purposes other than repair.[148]

In the United Kingdom, exclusive rights are available for both registered and unregistered designs. But under the Registered Design Act, must-fit features are excluded,[149] and the use of must-match parts to restore the original appearance of complex products is not considered infringing.[150] When it comes to unregistered designs, the Copyright, Designs and Patents Act likewise excludes must-fit features.[151] In addition, competitors are free to copy any features that depend on the appearance of some other article of which they "form an integral part." UK courts, however, have interpreted that provision narrowly. In the leading case, vacuum-cleaner manufacturer Dyson sued Qualtex, a maker of spare parts. Qualtex argued that the designs could be freely copied since they fell within the must-match provision. The court disagreed. It concluded that design rights should be denied only if the appearance of the product as a whole would be "radically different" if the part were changed.[152] In settling on this standard, the court substantially narrowed the scope of the must-match provision and introduced ambiguity about precisely what it would mean to radically alter the appearance of a product.

Exclusive rights in designs can interfere with repair and limit the exhaustion principle. Even where those problems are recognized, it has proven difficult to overcome the concentrated financial interests of carmakers and other manufacturers. But the models adopted in Australia, Europe, and the United Kingdom are leaps and bounds ahead of the United States, where unchecked design patents pose perhaps the most significant legal threat to thriving repair markets.

Trademarks

Trademarks offer device makers yet another set of legal tools to stymie repair. But luckily, trademark law has developed several doctrines that, if faithfully applied, limit manufacturers' power to leverage their marks against replacement-part makers, repair providers, and consumers. Nonetheless, that hasn't stopped companies from trying to increase the costs and risks of unauthorized repair through trademark claims. And sometimes they succeed, either in court or by intimidating small businesses with threats of expensive litigation.

Unlike copyright and patent, trademark law is not designed to provide economic incentives for creative or innovative products. Instead, it serves two other purposes – promoting fair competition and protecting consumers from unscrupulous sellers. It achieves these twin goals by making it easy for sellers to reliably identify their products and services, and for consumers to confidently find them in the marketplace. Trademarks are source indicators. A brand name, a logo, or sometimes even a unique product design can communicate to prospective buyers the source of a particular product or service.

Let's say you're in the market for a new dishwasher. You've had positive experiences with other Bosch appliances, so you are on the hunt for a matching Bosch dishwasher. When you search online or at your local retailer, Bosch products are easy to find. They bear the company name alongside its magneto armature logo, which it's been using, with minor variations, for over a century.[153] Those trademarks tell you the same firm that designed and built your range and refrigerator stands behind the dishwasher as well. Trademark law reinforces that expectation by forbidding competitors from using names, logos, or other marks that are similar enough to confuse consumers. So, a company called Basch that sells appliances would likely find itself on the receiving end of a successful complaint.

By helping to ensure that these source indicators continue to function reliably, trademark law allows firms to profit from their hard-earned reputations. Bosch spends considerable capital and effort developing high-quality products, advertising them, and building relationships with customers. So, the company has a strong interest in both maintaining its reputation and stopping competitors from drawing in customers with an identical or confusingly similar name. At the same time, consumers want to be sure that if they pick up a dishwasher bearing the Bosch name from their local appliance shop, it was actually made by the company, not some fly-by-night operation. Trademarks give consumers greater confidence in the consistency and quality of the products they buy. They also save us the time and hassle of investigating every product. Trademarks efficiently convey lots of information that we'd otherwise have to gather on our own.

Distinctiveness

Although trademark law serves important goals, overprotection has downsides. Unlike patents and copyrights, which eventually expire, trademarks can last forever. And granting broad rights in marks risks foreclosing competition without offering any benefit to consumers. Imagine that a company manages to obtain a trademark on a generic term like "repair" in connection with electronics repair services. If the trademark owner could control the use of that everyday term, competitors in the repair market would be at a significant disadvantage. It would make it harder for them to accurately identify their services, forcing them to use business names that use other, less obvious terminology – Alice's House of Fixes rather than Alice's House of Repairs, for example. And that might mean consumers are less likely to discover them.

For good reason, trademark rights aren't available for generic terms.[154] No one can trademark "repair" for repair services or "dishwasher" for kitchen appliances. Terms that describe categories of goods or services are free for anyone to use. In fact, if a mark becomes generic over time, even if it was once associated with a single maker, it loses its trademark status. Aspirin, escalator, and linoleum all met that fate in the United States.[155]

For the law to recognize a word or other symbol as a trademark, it must be distinctive.[156] That is, the mark has to communicate something to consumers about the source of the product. US law considers some marks inherently distinctive. They don't require any additional proof that consumers treat them as source indicators. These include arbitrary, fanciful, and suggestive marks. An arbitrary mark is an existing word with an everyday meaning that has no relationship to the product bearing it. For an electronics company, "Apple" is an arbitrary mark. Fanciful marks are invented words. They have no meaning beyond their association with a source of goods or services. "Hulu" as used by the video streaming service is a good example. In English, the term has no other meaning.[157] So when consumers first encounter it, they are likely to recognize it as a particular service from a single source. Suggestive marks hint at the characteristics of a product or service, but don't describe them directly. Netflix, for instance, suggests something about the internet and movies, but it doesn't tell consumers precisely what sort of service it is.

If a mark literally describes the characteristics of a product or service, firms have to prove that when consumers see or hear the mark, they associate it with a particular source.[158] This higher burden guards against trademarks that might put competitors at a disadvantage. Airlines seem to love descriptive names. American Airlines, British Airways, Emirates, and Turkish Airlines, to name just a few, are all descriptive. After decades of transporting passengers, mostly on time, and massive advertising budgets, American Airlines has trained us to associate its mark with a specific company rather than the broader category of airlines that are based in America.

The shape or design of a product – referred to as trade dress – is another example of a type of mark that always requires proof of acquired distinctiveness.[159] Under the right circumstances, product design tells us something about source, regardless of any logos, names, or other marks. Guitar enthusiasts can tell the difference between a Gibson Les Paul and a Fender Telecaster from across a crowded arena before hearing a single chord. And the fashion conscious would never mistake a pair of Louboutins for Manolos. But under US law, trademark rights for product design are only available if the owner can prove that consumers associate the shape with a single source of goods. That's a significant burden, and one most products can't satisfy.

European trademark law handles product designs somewhat differently. Rather than a categorical rule that insists on proof of acquired distinctiveness, under EU law the "shape of goods" can be inherently distinctive, eliminating any need for evidence about the actual associations consumers form between the design of a product and its source.[160] Nonetheless, the law recognizes that, on the whole, consumers are less likely to treat the shape of a product as a source indicator. As the European Court of Justice has explained, "only a mark that departs significantly from the norm or customs" for similar goods can be distinctive.[161]

Functionality

Even if a product design clears the distinctiveness hurdle, it still has to contend with trademark law's functionality doctrine.

That rule excludes product features that offer a utilitarian advantage.[162] If the feature makes the product work better or reduces production costs, it cannot be protected as trade dress. That's true regardless of whether alternative designs are available to competitors. In this sense, the functionality bar is a more meaningful limit on trademark rights under US law than the comparatively anemic ornamentality requirement is for design patents. Likewise, EU law prohibits the registration of marks that consist of a shape that "results from the nature of the goods themselves," "is necessary to obtain a technical result," or "gives substantial value to the goods."[163]

Nonetheless, manufacturers have succeeded in claiming product components as trade dress. Carmakers like Ford and Volvo have registered trademarks for grilles, taillights, and other vehicle components.[164] General Motors even successfully sued a toy maker that sold miniature replicas of the Hummer – a vehicle designed for suburban military cosplay.[165] GM alleged that the toys copied "the exterior appearance and styling of the vehicle" including its "grille, slanted and raised hood, split windshield, rectangular doors, [and] squared edges." Based on extensive surveys conducted by GM, the court concluded consumers associated these styling cues with the Hummer brand. It also rejected the toy maker's contention that these design elements were dictated by functional concerns. Without much analysis, the court concluded that the external features of the vehicle were "inherently non-functional" and "likely an unrelated afterthought." There's no reason to think the court's logic couldn't be extended to suppliers of independent repair parts or repair shops. If that happened, consumers and repair providers would be forced to choose between expensive OEM-authorized parts or cheaper nonmatching parts, putting manufacturers and their network of dealers at a distinct competitive advantage.

Other courts, though, have been more sensitive to concerns over functionality. When Chrysler sued a manufacturer of aftermarket Jeep grilles for trade-dress infringement, it contended that the design wasn't functional since there were available alternatives.[166] The court disagreed. Instead, it saw the central question as what "consumers of grille covers for Jeeps expect," allowing for the possibility that matching the vehicle's aesthetic is itself one important function of the grille.

More recently, in *Apple v. Samsung*, the Federal Circuit rejected Apple's trade-dress claims.[167] The company claimed various iPhone features served as source indicators. These included: "a rectangular product with four evenly rounded corners; a flat, clear surface covering the front of the product; a display screen under the clear surface; substantial black borders above and below the display screen and narrower black borders on either side of the screen; and . . . a matrix of colorful square icons with evenly rounded corners within the display screen." The court saw these elements for what they were – functional features central to the use of the iPhone. As it pointed out, Apple had to "demonstrate that the product feature serves no purpose other than identification." Quite the contrary, each of those features contributed to the overall ease of use of the iPhone. So even if consumers associated them with Apple, it couldn't prevent others from using them.

Taken together, the distinctiveness requirement and the functionality bar tend to filter out most potential trademark claims stemming from the design of a product or its components. Those doctrines aren't foolproof, but they significantly reduce the legal risks facing the repair community. But even putting trade-dress claims aside, there are other ways trademarks can interfere with repair.

Referential Use

If trademark owners have the exclusive rights over their marks, how can repair providers or replacement-part makers effectively advertise?[168] If you repair iPhones, but can't use Apple's trademarks, describing your services quickly devolves into a sort of linguistic charade. Rather than an ad that says, "We repair Apple iPhones," you'd have to try something like, "We repair the popular line of smartphones made by the company based in Cupertino." But trademark law recognizes the need to refer to trademarked products and has developed tools for just that purpose.

As early as the 1960s, courts were rebuffing trademark owners' efforts to control the use of their marks by repair providers. One important early case centered on an auto-repair shop in Long Beach, California.[169] When Douglas Church opened Modern Volkswagen Porsche Service in 1958, he specialized in – you guessed it – Volkswagens and Porsches. After Volkswagen objected to the name, Church changed it to Modern Specialist. Nonetheless, Volkswagen sued him for trademark infringement four years later. The carmaker alleged that a sign in front of Church's shop that read "Modern Volkswagen Porsche Service" violated its trademarks. Shamelessly, it also argued that the use of the terms "Independent Volkswagen Service" and "Independent VW Service" on business cards, promotional items, and advertisements infringed its marks. But the court was not sympathetic to these overreaching claims. The use of the term "independent," it found, was enough to distinguish Church's services from those offered or authorized by Volkswagen. Moreover, since Church didn't borrow logos, typefaces, or color schemes from Volkswagen, consumers were unlikely to be confused about the source of their repairs.[170]

The terminology didn't exist at the time, but today courts would consider Church's ads and signs nominative fair uses. In 1992, the Ninth Circuit formalized its existing case law favoring these sorts of uses under that banner. The dispute arose when the wildly successful boy band New Kids on the Block sued USA Today, a national newspaper, for running a poll that asked readers to weigh in on the eternal question, "Who's your favorite New Kid?" Specifically, a banner on the front page said, "New Kids on the Block are pop's hottest group. Which of the five is your fave?" and prompted readers to vote by phone. When the band sued for unauthorized use of its trademark, the court offered a clear rule permitting references to trademarked goods and services that create no reasonable risk of confusion.

It outlined a three-part test for what it called nominative fair uses. First, if the product or service can't be readily identified without using the mark, it should be allowed. *USA Today* could have asked, "Who's your favorite member of the Boston-based boy band managed by Maurice Starr?" But some readers may have confused the New Kids with Starr's other boy band, New Edition. The trademark avoids that ambiguity, not to mention the rather inelegant phrasing. Second, courts consider whether the user included more of the trademark than necessary to identify the product. *USA Today* simply wrote the group's name in a standard typeface. It didn't reproduce the New Kids logo or any other marks associated with it. Finally, courts look at whether there is any suggestion that the trademark owner sponsored or endorsed the use. Had *USA Today* claimed it was running the "official" or "authorized" New Kids poll, that might have posed a problem. But in the absence of that kind of language, its reference to the group was perfectly lawful.

Nominative fair use offers part makers and repair providers considerable leeway to accurately relay information to consumers. A manufacturer of replacement touchscreens can explain that a particular model is compatible with the Samsung Galaxy Note 20 Ultra, but not the 20 Plus. And an appliance repair shop can let customers know they specialize in Frigidaire and Whirlpool models but refuse to work on Sub-Zero products. By the same token, the nominative fair-use test suggests certain limits. A repair shop would be wise not to litter its website or its fleet of vans with manufacturer logos, or to suggest they are authorized repair providers if they aren't, for example.

Although they haven't adopted the same nomenclature, European courts have reached similar results.[171] When the Court of Justice was asked to consider whether ads offering "Repairs and maintenance of BMWs" infringed the carmakers' marks, it explained that trademark owners have no power to "prohibit a third party from using the mark for the purpose of informing the public that he carries out the repair and maintenance of goods covered by that trade mark."[172] So repair providers can communicate that they specialize in repairing those goods as long as they don't falsely imply an affiliation with the trademark holder.

More recently, the UK Court of Appeal, applying EU law, helped clarify the line between informing the public and implying an affiliation.[173] Again, BMW filed suit against a repair shop, Technosport. While BMW did not object to Technosport's use of the slogan "The BMW specialists," it argued that prominent use of the phrase "TECHNOSPORT-BMW," accompanied by the manufacturer's roundel logo, went too far. The court agreed. While its use of the mark to describe its services was legitimate, Technosport's use of the BMW logo would lead the average consumer to believe the company is an "authorised distributor." That conclusion is consistent with the likely outcome under the US nominative fair-use approach.

Exhaustion and Importation

Like other IP regimes, trademark law recognizes the principle of exhaustion. Under the first-sale doctrine, once a product bearing a trademark is sold, the trademark owner's ability to control its use and transfer is severely limited.[174] The law allows the sale of genuine goods bearing a trademark despite objections from the rights holder.[175] That rule helps explain why we have thriving markets for used cars, electronics, and clothing, among other goods. Nonetheless, trademark owners still try to clamp down on resale markets.[176] Recently, Chanel sued The RealReal, an online consignment shop for designer goods.[177] But since the site made it clear that its products were secondhand and independently authenticated, the court had no problem dismissing Chanel's claims.

But there are two scenarios that complicate the general rule favoring resale of authentic goods, both of which have implications for repair. First, resold goods are often not identical to new ones. If you sell your ten-year-old Prius, chances are good that some parts have been repaired or replaced. Beyond batteries, brakes, and tires, you may have replaced the coolant pump, a cracked windshield, or body panels damaged in a collision. In some sense, the car you are selling isn't the Toyota you originally purchased. But under trademark law, the resale of refurbished products is lawful even if they are repaired by third parties using non-OEM parts.

In 1947, the US Supreme Court considered a trademark claim brought by Champion, the maker of automobile spark plugs, against Sanders, who reconditioned and resold used Champion products.[178] The Court was satisfied that so long as Sanders clearly labeled his goods as "repaired" products, he had no obligation to remove their Champion trademarks. As the Court understood, they were still Champion spark plugs, after all. Repair restored them as near as possible to their original condition. Even if they didn't perform as reliably as new spark plugs, that didn't matter as long as they were clearly labeled as refurbished.

Courts have gone further, endorsing the right of refurbishers to reapply trademarked logos to products before reselling them. For example, the makers of Titleist golf balls sued Nitro Leisure, a company that sold reconditioned balls.[179] Nitro collected used Titleist balls and removed layers of scuffed and damaged paint, taking the Titleist logo along with them. It would then apply new paint and faithfully reproduce the Titleist mark. Despite their inferior performance, Nitro was entitled to recreate the logo on reconditioned balls since they were clearly labeled. As the court understood, buyers of used goods, which often come at a steep discount, don't expect them to perform like new.

These protections for refurbished goods matter for repair in at least two ways. Reconditioned parts, like Champion spark plugs, offer a less expensive alternative to OEM parts. And for hard-to-find components, like those the original manufacturer no longer produces, a refurbished part may be the only option. What's more, the ability to resell refurbished goods is a key driver of repairs. Independent refurbishers like John Bumstead of RDKL, Inc. snap up broken laptops by the thousand, get them back in good working order, then resell them at a reasonable profit. If it weren't for the secondary market in refurbished goods, these devices would either be recycled for scrap or dumped in landfills.

There's a second wrinkle in US trademark law's approach to the first-sale rule. If a product bearing a trademark differs in some material respect from those sold by the trademark owner, its resale is potentially infringing.[180] Typically, this rule applies to so-called grey-market goods – those produced for one country but sold in another. Let's say you want to import a Ford Focus from the United Kingdom into the United States. Aside from the driver's side being on the right, the car is virtually identical to its US counterpart. But that is a difference that would matter to most buyers. As a result, Ford has the power to prevent its importation and sale in the United States. That rule reflects the fact that the same trademark can represent two very different products in two jurisdictions. Courts have applied the same rule to products manufactured in the United States but destined for foreign markets.[181]

The key question in these cases is what counts as a material difference. Unfortunately, it's not a particularly exacting standard. As long as consumers would likely consider some variation between the products "significant" at the time of purchase, they are materially different.[182] And a single such distinction is all trademark owners have to show. So, what sorts of difference have courts found to be material? In a case about John Deere harvesters produced for European markets, the court found a material difference where the lights, turn signals, and hitch mechanisms functioned differently, features that were likely quite important to many farmers.[183] Another court determined that Kubota tractors produced in Japan were materially different from their US counterparts because their warning labels and service manuals were printed in Japanese, not English.[184]

But other examples stretch the meaning of materiality to its breaking point. After a distributor used an etching tool to remove batch codes from bottles of Cool Water cologne intended for duty-free stores, the trademark owner sued. Even though the fragrance, bottle, and packaging were identical, the court was satisfied that an etch mark on the bottle, about one inch long and an eighth of an inch wide, was a material difference.[185] Other courts have even found material differences where there were no physical variations at all. In one instance, a one-year difference in the length of Bose radio warranties in the United States and Australia was enough to bar importation.[186] In another, the court was convinced that material differences could be established where ball bearings were sold with access to a technical support hotline, but imported bearings were not.[187]

Canada has also adopted the material-difference standard but tends to favor the free flow of goods in its application.[188] Where materially different goods sold under a trademark pose some risk of harm to the public, Canadian courts will intervene to stop their importation. So, courts may, for instance, bar the importation of damaged goods.[189] But where there is no risk to the public, or any harm can be avoided by labeling the products accurately, Canadian law applies the general first-sale rule.

Unlike the US and Canada, which have adopted international exhaustion regimes, Europe has embraced regional exhaustion. If a trademarked product is sold lawfully anywhere in the world, it can generally be imported into the United States as long as it was made by the US trademark holder or a related entity. But under European law, exhaustion is only triggered by sales within the European market. So, while sales in France might trigger exhaustion in the United States, the reverse isn't true. That gives companies greater leeway in Europe to halt imports of trademarked products or parts from outside the single market.

Like the material-difference standard, the first-sale rule doesn't apply under European trademark law if there are "legitimate reasons for the proprietor to oppose further commercialization of the goods, especially where the condition of the goods is changed or impaired after they have been put on the market."[190] For years, the European Court of Justice interpreted "legitimate reasons" narrowly. It allowed trademark owners to restrict the movement of goods that have been repackaged or relabeled in ways that risk consumer confusion or reputational harm.[191] But it rejected efforts to characterize differences between products bearing the same mark as material when they were the byproduct of marketing efforts by the trademark owner.[192]

Nonetheless, there are some troubling signs. In *Copad v. Dior*, the court considered the sale of Dior corset dresses outside of the company's tightly controlled distribution network.[193] Like many luxury brands, Dior is selective about the sorts of retail establishments that carry its products. When discount retailer Copad began selling authentic Dior dresses, the fashion house sued. The court held that Dior could sidestep the first-sale rule where the distribution of the product "damages the allure and prestigious image which bestows on those goods an aura of luxury." In other words, the risk that Dior may lose some of its luster if its products are seen slumming it on the shelves of a discount store is a "legitimate reason" to interfere with the free movement of goods.

That reasoning would be problematic enough if it were confined to true luxury goods. But a recent decision applied this logic to inexpensive jewelry.[194] Nomination makes charms and links that can be combined into reconfigurable bracelets by consumers. The charms are sometimes, though not always, made of precious metals. The links are stainless steel. Nomination positions its products as "luxury jewelry which is nevertheless affordable by everyone." JSC produces interchangeable links, and sold bundles consisting of one of its own Daisy Charm links alongside a genuine Nomination link. The eBay listings for those bundles accurately described their contents, and the Nomination link was shipped with a label that read, "Manufactured by Nomination Italy Repackaged by JSC Jewelry UK." Nonetheless, Nomination objected to the resale of its products, arguing that JSC's packaging failed to convey the appropriate level of luxury. Even though Nomination's own authorized dealers sometimes sold links in small plastic bags, the UK Court of Appeal was satisfied that Nomination had a legitimate reason to halt sales. If an $18 stainless steel bracelet link counts as a luxury good, that term has lost all meaning. That reasoning would seem to open the door to restricting resale of $1,000 smartphones that come in carefully designed packages.

Restrictions on grey-market imports can create real problems for repair providers. Since electronics manufacturers often refuse to sell replacement parts directly to independent repair shops, they are forced to rely on the grey market. These parts are sourced in a variety of ways, but generally take advantage of the complex global supply chains firms like Apple rely on. When Apple contracts with manufacturers to build screens, batteries, or other components, some of those parts eventually end up in the hands of third-party repair providers. Some are diverted from production lines. Others fail diagnostic tests and are then refurbished. These components are built in the same factories, by the same workers, and to the same standards as those used by trademark owners. But for a repair shop ordering parts an ocean away, those original parts aren't always easy to separate from copies produced by third parties.[195] And sometimes a component will intermingle third-party and original parts.[196]

Regardless of their source, manufacturers have strong incentives to use trademark law's relatively favorable rules around importation to clamp down on the flow of replacement parts. In order to invoke trademark law, however, you need a trademark. This explains why companies like Apple include logos on internal parts like batteries, processors, and cables. Most consumers never set eyes on these internal components, and almost certainly don't take notice of the logos, some no bigger than a grain of rice.[197] If a third party reproduces Apple's logo, those parts are likely infringing. But under the material-difference test, Apple could arguably block the importation of new and refurbished authentic parts, so long as it argues that warranty service or other benefits are unavailable to grey-market components.

Apple's naked attempt to use trademarks to restrict competition is one some courts would rightly regard with skepticism. But since US law allows for border seizures of allegedly infringing goods, Apple can rely on nonjudicial procedures with little due process or substantive oversight. When Jessa Jones, a prominent repair professional, tried to import replacement iPhone screens incorporating an authentic Apple flex cable bearing the company's logo, the Department of Homeland Security seized them.[198] Similarly, DHS seized authentic Apple batteries shipped to Louis Rossmann, an outspoken independent repair provider and advocate.[199]

A 2020 decision from the Supreme Court of Norway helps illustrate the bind Apple's restrictions on replacement parts create for repair providers.[200] Henrik Huseby operates a small electronics repair business. In 2017, he ordered sixty-three iPhone screens, which he believed were refurbished Apple components, from a supplier in Hong Kong. Replacement screens typically consist of a number of parts: an LCD display, a glass face, an outer frame, and a flex cable that connects the display to the logic board. Apple includes a tiny logo, no more than a couple of millimeters wide, on its flex cables.

Norwegian customs officials seized Huseby's shipment. According to their report, the flex cables featured Apple logos that had been obscured with black ink. Apple insisted it hadn't applied the logos and that the screens were counterfeits. So, the company demanded they be destroyed. Whether the displays themselves were authentic Apple products refurbished with new glass remains unclear since the dispute focused almost exclusively on the provenance of the tiny Apple logos on the cables.

Huseby argued that importation of the screens was lawful for two reasons. First, even if the Apple logos were fake, they were covered by black ink. Unless he carefully removed the ink from each cable, no one would have reason to believe they were made by Apple. Second, even if the counterfeit logos were exposed, flex cables are internal components buried deep inside the phone's inner workings. Consumers would only see them if they disassembled their phones. So, the risk of consumer confusion or harm to Apple's legitimate trademark interests was minimal and hypothetical. But according to the court, the fact that the logos were hidden didn't "permanently remove the danger" that they could harm Apple. Huseby lost his appeal and was ordered to pay Apple's legal costs, roughly $28,000.

Frustratingly, the uncertain origins of imported parts are a problem of Apple's own making. The reason that Huseby, Jones, and Rossmann are forced to scour the globe looking for high-quality refurbished and third-party parts is Apple's refusal to sell replacement components outside of its tightly controlled and ultimately untenable Independent Repair Provider program. If Apple made those parts available to repair providers on reasonable terms, most would happily buy them. Having denied repair shops access to its stock of new, original parts, Apple is trying to use trademark law to choke off the supply of grey-market, refurbished, and third-party parts as well. Trademark law is meant to prevent unfair competition, but too often manufacturers use it to undermine any competition in the repair market.

Trade Secrets

The final weapon in the manufacturer's IP arsenal is trade secrecy. Trade-secret law prohibits the improper acquisition and use of valuable, secret information. Historically, trade secrets were protected under state law in the United States, with forty-eight of the fifty states adopting some version of the Uniform Trade Secrets Act.[201] In 2016, Congress enacted the Defend Trade Secrets Act, which added a new federal cause of action for trade-secret misappropriation.[202] That same year, the Directive on the Protection of Trade Secrets harmonized European trade-secret law.[203] With some notable exceptions discussed below, the basic contours of EU trade secrecy are consistent with US state and federal law.

A trade secret is any information that is economically valuable because it isn't generally known and is subject to reasonable efforts to keep it secret. Technical information, like the formula for Coca-Cola or the process of manufacturing Kevlar, can be a trade secret, as can less-exciting business information, like marketing plans and customer lists. If the information is valuable, not generally known, and subject to efforts to maintain secrecy, the law prohibits its misappropriation.[204]

A trade secret is misappropriated if it is acquired through improper means.[205] Those include heist-movie theatrics like hacking, sneaking into secure facilities, or drone surveillance. Most of the time, though, the focus is on more mundane behavior, like breaching a confidentiality agreement or the implied duties of an employment relationship. In addition, the disclosure or use of a trade secret counts as misappropriation, so long as the person doing the using or disclosing knew or had reason to know that it was acquired through improper means.

When it comes to repair, manufacturers insist that service manuals, diagnostic information, schematics, and repair techniques are valuable secrets. Toshiba, for example, has demanded removal of its manuals from websites that distributed them for free to owners and repair providers.[206] More recently, ventilator makers raised similar concerns.[207] And in the ongoing policy debates around repair, firms often make vague, unsubstantiated assertions that sharing repair information with consumers or third-party repairers would result in the loss of valuable, if unspecified, secrets.[208]

But these trade-secret claims face a number of pitfalls. First, not every acquisition of secret information is improper. Crucially, trade-secret law allows reverse engineering – the process of examining a product to discover how it works. If you independently discover the process for replacing a Tesla battery, using or sharing that technique is not misappropriation – even assuming it counts as a trade secret.[209] So when a site like iFixit carefully dissects a new Microsoft tablet, documenting the repair process in a step-by-step guide, there is no misappropriation. All the information was independently derived.[210]

Second, not everything a company claims as a secret actually is one. In some instances, information may be so easy to acquire that it can't be considered a secret in the first place. Trade secrecy does not extend to information that is "readily ascertainable."[211] In other words, if someone else could easily uncover the information through books, journals, or other publicly available information, there is no secret to protect, regardless of how the information was obtained. Let's say a local dog walker considers her customer list a trade secret. She keeps the names of her clients on an encrypted drive stored in an elaborate biometric security system. To figure out who her customers are though, all you'd have to do is follow her van for a day to see which dogs she picks up on her way to the park. If you broke into her home, stole the drive, and decrypted it, you would have violated a slew of laws. But you wouldn't have misappropriated a trade secret. Because the information you took was readily ascertainable, it was never a secret to begin with.

The same is true for information that is generally known. The maker of an electric car may insist that the procedure for changing its batteries is a trade secret, but if most mechanics in the business know how it's done – and aren't bound by confidentiality agreements – the process isn't a secret. So, posting a detailed repair guide or the official service manual is perfectly lawful. As we all remember from high school, once a secret is out in the world, there's no way to reel it back in. That means that if disclosure is wide enough, an initial act of misappropriation can destroy a trade secret.

That's what the court determined when the DVD Copy Control Association (CCA) sued Andrew Bunner.[212] DVD CCA controlled CSS, a software tool used to encrypt virtually all commercially available DVDs. After Jon Johansen, a Norwegian teenager, wrote a program called DeCSS that decrypted DVDs, it quickly spread across the internet. Bunner was one of hundreds who posted the code online. DVD CCA sued him for trade-secret misappropriation. But as the court noted, if DeCSS was already public knowledge, there was no secret left for Bunner to disclose. Where an "initial publication [is] quickly and widely republished to an eager audience," others are free to republish that information. The same was true when the Church of Scientology sued a former member who shared church documents online.[213] As the court explained, since "the documents have escaped into the public domain and onto the Internet," the disgruntled member wasn't the only source of the once-secret information. As a result, the church couldn't establish that the documents were "not generally known." That rule doesn't eliminate the threat of liability for the first person to acquire or disclose the secret, but subsequent publishers are insulated from legal risk.

Sometimes, there are good reasons to divulge secrets. If a carmaker cheats on emissions tests, a telecommunications company cooperates in government surveillance, or an energy firm engages in accounting fraud, the public ought to know. But unlike other forms of IP, trade secrecy hasn't recognized the doctrines of fair use or misuse, which might protect those sorts of disclosures. Deepa Varadarajan has argued persuasively that trade-secret law should incorporate such rules.[214] At times, trade-secret owners have aggressively asserted their rights in order to muzzle whistleblowers and suppress criticism on issues of public health and safety, ranging from the dangers of breast implants, the environmental harms of pollutants, and the integrity of voting systems.[215]

Partly in recognition of these concerns, both the EU Trade Secret Directive and the federal Defend Trade Secrets Act (DTSA) incorporate some whistleblower protections. The DTSA's safe harbor is quite narrow. It protects whistleblowers when they report confidential information to government officials, but only "for the purpose of reporting or investigating a suspected violation of law."[216] The EU provision is significantly broader. Under its terms, trade secrecy does not prevent the disclosure if it "serves the public interest, insofar as directly relevant misconduct, wrongdoing or illegal activity is revealed." Although US statutes do not explicitly recognize the public interest, the Restatement (Third) of Unfair Competition, an influential distillation of case law, suggests that courts are likely to permit "the disclosure of information that is relevant to public health or safety, or to the commission of a crime or tort, or to other matters of substantial public concern."[217] But few courts have taken up that recommendation.

The EU Directive protects "the right to freedom of expression and information."[218] US trade-secret law does not include any explicit safeguards for free speech, but both state and federal statutes are subject to general First Amendment protections. Constitutional challenges to trade-secret claims are rare, as Pamela Samuelson has explained.[219] In most cases, defendants want to maintain the secret for their own commercial gain, rather than publicize it. Although uncommon, First Amendment defenses have succeeded on occasion. When a meat-packing plant sued to stop CBS from broadcasting footage secretly shot by a plant employee, Justice Blackmun determined that an injunction preventing the broadcast of the footage would be "intolerable under the First Amendment."[220]

Similarly, when a website posted an internal Ford memo that discussed fuel economy and emissions strategies, as well as powertrain technology advances, the court refused to enjoin publication, citing the First Amendment.[221] A California court reached a similar result when Apple sued a news site for publishing information about an impending product release. As the court explained, the site didn't take the secrets "for venal advantage." Instead, it was engaged in "a journalistic disclosure" to the public. In a conflict between trade secrets and free speech, "it is the quasi-property right that must give way, not the deeply rooted constitutional right to share and acquire information."[222]

Trade secrets, in other words, sometimes have to yield to other public policy priorities. The Securities and Exchange Commission demands detailed financial disclosures from companies.[223] The Internal Revenue Service insists that non-profit organizations disclose their funding sources, expenditures, and employee salaries.[224] And the Food and Drug Administration requires clinical trial disclosures for pharmaceuticals, as well as food labels that reveal ingredients and other potentially valuable information.[225] In many cases, this information is shared with the public, despite the fact that organizations would prefer to keep it secret. When the health, safety, and wellbeing of the public are at stake, lawmakers and regulators can compel disclosure. In light of the economic and environmental stakes, there is a strong case for demanding firms share information necessary to maintain and repair the products they sell regardless of claims of trade secrecy.

Repair and "Progress"

The primary justification underlying intellectual property is the law's promise to encourage investment in creativity and innovation. The market exclusivity conferred by copyrights, patents, and, to a lesser extent, trade secrets is designed to create strong economic incentives for firms to develop valuable intangible assets. In the United States, that rationale can be traced back to the Constitution, which empowers Congress to enact copyright and patent protection in order "to promote the progress of science and useful arts."[226]

As we've already seen, that directive to promote progress doesn't necessarily trump all other considerations. The law takes other values into account. It accommodates free expression, competition, personal privacy, among other priorities. US patent law even gives doctors the right to perform patented medical procedures without fear of liability – not because it promotes innovation, but because patient welfare is more important than the dollar value of an invention.[227] A strong case can be made that repair – because of the benefits it offers for the environment, the economy, and personal autonomy – should be similarly prioritized. If broad intellectual property rights interfere with repair, so much the worse for IP law. As this chapter has detailed, various legal doctrines already recognize the value of repair. Others should be expanded and reinforced to better reflect the central importance of repair to our environmental and economic futures.

Even within the internal logic of intellectual property law, repair deserves greater emphasis. Rather than a purely countervailing consideration, repair is intertwined with questions of innovation and progress. Our approach to repair influences what sort of innovations we are likely to see, who can access them, and under what conditions. In that sense, our attitudes about repair reflect what sort of technological and social progress we value. For all its rhetoric about progress and innovation, intellectual property policy engages in precious little examination of precisely what kind of new works it's designed to create. From patent law's perspective, a patent on out-of-office emails[228] is just as valuable as gene-editing technology.[229] And copyright law draws no distinction between your dressing-room photos of potential outfits and Waxahatchee's masterful 2020 album, *Saint Cloud*.[230]

But if we believe that law influences creative production, how we calibrate the scope and shape of IP law will change the sorts of products that system produces. So, when the law restricts repair, it encourages shorter product lifecycles that favor superficial product differentiation. If companies can wield IP to discourage repair, they will tend to focus their efforts on rolling out a reliable stream of minor updates and aesthetic tweaks. But annual product releases aren't compatible with truly innovative breakthroughs, at least not on any regular basis. Even if Apple, Samsung, and other device makers could churn out major new features every year, why bother? People need phones, cars, and dishwashers. If they can't fix their current devices, they'll buy new ones even without new major technological advances. In contrast, an environment that encourages repair creates stronger incentives for genuine innovation. If you can reliably and cheaply keep your four-year-old phone or decade-old car working, you're more likely to hold out for some significant new functionality before replacing it. Repair might even encourage what the economist Joseph Schumpeter called creative destruction, the process by which old technologies are displaced by new ones.[231] If firms couldn't rely on tens of billions of dollars in annual revenue from new smartphone sales, maybe they would turn more attention to new, as-yet-unimagined product categories.

If we take a broader view of progress, as Leah Chan Grinvald and Ofer Tur-Sinai have suggested, the value of repair becomes even more apparent.[232] Progress isn't achieved simply because firms invent new technologies or authors pen brilliant novels. For the value of those contributions to be realized, they have to be accessible to the public. Broad public access is, in some sense, at odds with the economic theory of intellectual property, which is premised on market exclusivity and the high prices it enables. But the law has long reflected the need to balance those competing interests. As the US Supreme Court wrote in 1974, the ultimate goal of patent law is to produce "a positive effect on society through the introduction of new products [that] better lives for our citizens."[233] A year later, the Court explained that copyright law "must ultimately serve the cause of promoting broad public availability of literature, music, and the other arts."[234] As we have seen, by supporting secondary markets and the longevity of devices more generally, repair helps get technology in the hands of those who cannot otherwise afford it.

Beyond the question of access, a holistic view of progress ought to account for the changing conditions we collectively face, climate change and other environmental threats among them. A notion of progress that gives us Wi-Fi-enabled coffee-makers and an endless supply of Snapchat filters, all while sea levels rise, potable water grows scarce, and extreme weather endangers communities is a fundamentally hollow one.[235] That's not to say new technologies, from green energy to desalination, might not help us address these threats. But an IP system that incorporates sustainability into its understanding of progress is better equipped to serve the needs of society than one that doesn't. And embracing repair is the simplest step towards a sustainable vision of technological progress.

6 REPAIR AND COMPETITION

The last chapter showed how law can reinforce private efforts to interfere with repair. Law confers power, but it can also restrain it. While intellectual property law grants device makers exclusive rights over their creations, other legal regimes are designed to impose limits on exclusionary behavior. In that sense, antitrust and competition law serve as potential bulwarks against tactics that would impede repair. Globally, markets for the repair of vehicles, electronics, and appliances account for hundreds of billions of dollars in annual revenue. This chapter considers the role antitrust law plays in safeguarding those markets and, along with them, the interests of competitors and consumers.

In recent years, competition authorities around the world have started to turn their attention to the restrictions device makers impose on repair. A US congressional committee has launched an ongoing, years-long investigation into Apple's policies around repair and resale.[1] In 2019, the House Judiciary Committee asked Apple to provide evidence concerning "restrictions on third-party repairs," including rules about what repairs authorized service providers are allowed to make and what parts are available to independent repair providers.[2] In addition, the committee probed Apple about its 2018 agreement with Amazon that banned most independent resellers. The US investigation came on the heels of Apple's $84 million settlement with South Korea's Fair Trade Commission, which alleged the company forced mobile carriers to pay for warranty repairs.[3] And after European competition authorities launched an investigation, Apple abandoned a rule that limited warranty repairs to the original country of purchase.[4] As these examples illustrate, there is no shortage of policies and practices deserving of antitrust scrutiny.

Foundations of US Antitrust Law

During the late nineteenth century, railroad barons ruled vast transit networks, and monopolists controlled markets for oil, steel, and sugar.[5] Given their dominance, these trusts could stamp out competitors and raise prices, unconstrained by the competitive forces that normally keep them in check. In response, Congress enacted antitrust legislation to curb these abuses, protect consumers, and ultimately prevent the accumulation of concentrated market power.

The Sherman Act, passed in 1890, was "designed to be a comprehensive charter of economic liberty aimed at preserving free and unfettered competition."[6] Section 1 of the Act prohibits "every contract, combination ..., or conspiracy in restraint of trade" between two or more actors.[7] This language is broad, but courts haven't applied it literally. Some facially anticompetitive agreements, like contracts between competitors to fix prices or divide markets, are illegal *per se*. But most other agreements, like exclusive supply arrangements, are evaluated under what's known as the rule of reason. Under that approach, courts ask whether, all things considered, the agreement is unreasonable – taking into account the nature of the market, the economic effect of the arrangement, and any procompetitive justifications the firm offers.

Section 2 addresses unilateral conduct – steps companies take on their own that nonetheless harm competition. That provision makes it unlawful for any person to "monopolize or attempt to monopolize" a market. In other words, it is illegal to seek, acquire, or maintain a monopoly through anticompetitive behavior. Monopolization requires proof that a company has market power – that is, the ability to raise prices higher than a competitive market would sustain. In addition, that monopoly must be the result of some anticompetitive conduct. In theory, a company could acquire a monopoly "as a consequence of a superior product, business acumen, or historic accident."[8] To violate the Sherman Act, monopoly power must result from some predatory or exclusionary behavior. Precisely what sorts of conduct might satisfy that definition will be discussed in more detail below.

In 1911, the Supreme Court weakened the Sherman Act by adopting the rule of reason.[9] Congress reacted by passing the Clayton Act, which targets a number of specific behaviors.[10] It forbids mergers and acquisitions that would substantially reduce competition.[11] More importantly for our purposes, the Clayton Act also prohibits selling goods on the condition that the purchaser "shall not use or deal in the goods ... of [the sellers'] competitor" if doing so would "substantially lessen competition or tend to create a monopoly."[12] In addition, the 1936 Robinson-Patman Act outlaws some forms of price discrimination to the extent they cause significant harm to competition.[13] As a general rule though, successful challenges to price discrimination are rare.

Over the next century, these laws were used, with varying degrees of enthusiasm, to keep markets competitive. In some cases, courts imposed specific restrictions on how dominant firms conducted business, banning specific policies, practices, and agreements. In others, they broke dominant firms into smaller, competing entities. The Supreme Court divided Standard Oil, which controlled the vast majority of the US market for refined oil, into seven regional firms.[14] Decades later, the Department of Justice achieved a similar outcome against the Bell telephone monopoly, breaking AT&T into eight regional operating companies in 1984.[15] When Microsoft was sued for antitrust violations in 1999, the trial court initially ordered the company divided in two – one entity to control the Windows operating system, the other to produce software applications like Word and Internet Explorer.[16] But ultimately, a settlement agreement kept Microsoft intact, so long as it agreed to make Windows more hospitable for competing third-party applications.[17] In late 2020, the US government brought antitrust cases against Facebook and Google, alleging that each company illegally maintained its monopoly power – over social networking and search, respectively – through a range of anti-competitive and exclusionary practices.[18]

Antitrust law regulates and structures markets for all sorts of goods and services. But it has long played an important role in aftermarkets. As we've seen, once a company sells a product, there is often more money to be made in accessories, consumables, and replacement parts. From disposable razor blades and ink cartridges to batteries and headlights, these aftermarkets are potential profit centers. In 1936, the Supreme Court held that IBM violated antitrust law when it required customers who leased IBM computers to purchase the punch cards used for data storage from the company rather than competitors.[19] A decade later, the Court reached a similar result when International Salt insisted customers using its machines to inject salt into canned food buy its salt tablets.[20]

The government brought another case against IBM in 1952, alleging the company had unlawfully restrained and monopolized the market for tabulating machines. In the 1956 consent decree that settled that case, IBM acceded to several obligations intended to safeguard the market for repair service and parts.[21] It committed to sell parts and subassemblies at reasonable prices and terms to owners of IBM equipment and repair providers. It also pledged to make the repair and maintenance training it gave its own employees available to independent providers, as well as any "technical manuals, books of instruction, pamphlets, diagrams or similar documents." As the Department of Justice understood, a competitive market for repair parts and service was central to cabin manufacturers' market dominance.

Repair, parts, and service offer manufacturers reliable and renewable income streams. So, it's no wonder that firms are tempted to exclude competitors. Makers of auto parts, computer systems, and medical devices, among others, have faced a string of antitrust suits over the years alleging a range of exclusionary conduct in aftermarkets.[22] Given the fact-intensive nature of antitrust litigation and the considerable discretion given to courts, those cases don't allow us to draw clear, universal conclusions about when an attempt to control the aftermarkets for repair parts or services crosses the line into unlawful conduct. But one case, decided by the US Supreme Court in 1992, offers a useful roadmap.[23] Given its importance, it's worth considering the case in some detail.

Eastman Kodak and Aftermarket Competition

Eastman Kodak made high-end photocopiers, which it sold to businesses, government agencies, and other institutional customers. The parts and software used by Kodak machines were unique. They weren't interchangeable or compatible with those used by other manufacturers. In addition to selling new machines, Kodak also offered parts and service. Some parts, it produced itself. Others were made under contract by partner manufacturers. When it came to repair, Kodak dominated, accounting for somewhere between 80–95 percent of the total market.

But in the early 1980s, several independent service organizations (ISOs) entered the market, repairing and servicing Kodak machines. Many of these new market entrants were formed by Kodak employees who realized they could charge lower prices, but still make more than Kodak paid repair technicians. Not only were their prices substantially lower, but many customers thought they offered higher-quality service. Some ISOs also sold spare parts and refurbished used Kodak equipment. Unhappy about this new competitive threat and the pressure it created in the labor market, Kodak instituted several new policies. First, it banned the sale of replacement parts to ISOs and customers who hired them. Under its new policy, parts were to be sold only to buyers of Kodak machines – and even then, only to those who paid for Kodak service or repaired the machines themselves. Second, Kodak persuaded its third-party manufacturers to sell their parts exclusively to Kodak. Third, the company pressured independent parts distributors and owners of Kodak machines not to sell parts to the ISOs. Finally, Kodak tried to limit the availability of used machines, presumably on the theory that they could be harvested for parts. Through these policies, Kodak was able to cut off the supply of replacement parts to ISOs, costing them substantial revenue and driving some out of business altogether.

A group of ISOs sued Kodak, alleging that it violated the Sherman Act by illegally conditioning access to replacement parts on its repair services. They also accused Kodak of monopolizing the market for services and repair. The case eventually made its way to the Supreme Court, which rejected Kodak's attempts to justify its behavior.[24]

The ISOs argued that Kodak tied together two distinct goods or services, making one available only if customers also paid for the other. As discussed in more detail below, this sort of tying arrangement is potentially unlawful. The first question for the Court was whether replacement parts and service were two distinct products. The answer turned on whether there was sufficient demand to offer the two products separately. In other words, would consumers pay for parts without service, or service without parts? As the Court pointed out, customers who service their machines themselves are certainly interested in purchasing parts alone. And since some repairs don't require any replacement parts, there is a market for service sans parts. Because Kodak sold parts only to customers who agreed to pay for Kodak service or, at the very least, not pay for service from an ISO, the Court was satisfied that the company tied these two distinct products together.

But even if a tie exists, it is unlawful only if the seller has market power. In the absence of market power, we would expect a tie to do little harm. If the market is competitive, consumers who don't want the tied product will simply shop elsewhere. Imagine you walk into your favorite grocery store to buy some pomegranates. A sign in the produce section informs you that "Pomegranates must be purchased with expired milk." If the grocery store has market power, you might feel compelled to buy the questionable dairy product along with your pomegranates. But in all likelihood, you can simply head to the nearest competing store and avoid the tied product altogether. But Kodak replacement parts, the Court recognized, were different than pomegranates because they were available exclusively from Kodak. By cutting off the ISOs' access to parts, Kodak reduced the number of competitors, increased repair prices, and forced consumers to rely on its services even if they preferred an ISO.

According to Kodak, however, it was impossible for the company to exercise market power when it came to aftermarket parts and services. Kodak argued that since the market for new photocopy equipment was competitive, it would be irrational to increase prices in the aftermarket. In other words, since companies looking to buy photocopiers could choose between models from Kodak, Canon, Konica, Sanyo, Xerox, and a host of other manufacturers, Kodak faced enough competitive pressure that it couldn't profitably ratchet up the price of parts and service. If it did, customers would simply buy new equipment from a competitor, and Kodak would lose money. So, Kodak argued that, as a matter of law, its lack of power in the new equipment market necessarily precluded power in the markets for parts and service.

That conclusion is based on some shaky assumptions. First, it treats the pricing decision as a binary one. Kodak either chooses the competitive price, or it opts for a monopoly price so high that it would scare away customers. But in reality, Kodak can choose between a range of prices. A moderate price increase for parts or service could easily make up for any lost sales of new equipment. More fundamentally, the cost–benefit analysis Kodak imagines consumers will undertake is unrealistic. Lifecycle pricing – the process of calculating the total cost of ownership of a device – is complicated. It requires detailed and reliable information: the upfront price of the device, its quality and durability, the long-term prices of supplies and future upgrades, repair and replacement-part prices, the frequency of breakdowns, and the costs of downtime. Even sophisticated buyers, like banks and government agencies, are often poorly positioned to analyze all that information before buying a photocopier. And it goes without saying that the same is true when everyday consumers buy a smartwatch or new refrigerator. The costs of acquiring and accurately evaluating that information are simply too high.

As the Court noted, there's another reason to doubt Kodak's claim that high prices for parts and service will lead consumers to defect to another manufacturer. Sometimes the costs of switching from one product to another are so high that they constrain consumer choice. This lock-in effect interferes with normal competitive forces and leads consumers to stick with products even if they might prefer an alternative.[25] At a certain point, price increases will overcome switching costs, but until then, a company like Kodak can charge monopoly prices in the aftermarket. High upfront costs, existing stocks of supplies, investments in employee training and workflows, and a desire for uniform equipment all likely effected the willingness of Kodak customers to switch to Xerox or some other competitor. So, in the end, the Court rejected Kodak's view that competition in the new equipment market meant it had no power in the aftermarkets for parts and service.[26]

In addition to their tying claim, the ISOs also alleged that Kodak monopolized the markets for parts and service in violation of § 2 of the Sherman Act. To prove that claim, the ISOs needed to show that Kodak had monopoly power in those markets, which it acquired or maintained intentionally. Monopoly power under § 2 requires a higher degree of market power than a tying claim. But parts and service for Kodak machines, the Court pointed out, were not interchangeable with those for other manufacturers' equipment. So, the question was how much control Kodak had over the market for parts and service for its machines. Since Kodak controlled "nearly 100% of the parts market and 80% to 95% of the service market," the Court was convinced that the ISOs had met their evidentiary burden. Likewise, the Court was satisfied with the evidence that Kodak's policy changes in response to the emergence of competition from the ISOs reflected "exclusionary action to maintain its parts monopoly and . . . to strengthen its monopoly share of the Kodak service market."

Finally, the Court turned its attention to supposed business justifications Kodak offered to excuse its otherwise unlawful behavior. Two are worth noting. Kodak maintained that it needed to exercise exclusive control over parts and service in order to maintain a reputation for quality. By ensuring the most reliable parts and service, Kodak argued, it was promoting competition in the market for new equipment. If it could avoid being blamed for shoddy third-party repairs, Kodak suggested it would be better positioned to compete with Canon, Xerox, and other manufacturers. The Court wasn't convinced, pointing out that the ISOs were preferred by some customers, which suggests their service was of sufficient quality.

Kodak also attempted to justify its anticompetitive policies as an effort "to prevent ISOs from free-riding on Kodak's capital investment in equipment, parts and service." In other words, Kodak spent a lot of money building its business, and it should be entitled to stop upstarts from coming along and siphoning off some of its profits by offering competing repair services. In clinical terms, this is monopoly brain. The idea that building a successful business, even at great cost, entitles a firm to dispose of competitors is a distorted view of how markets are meant to work. In Kodak's view, if the ISOs wanted to service photocopiers, they should have manufactured and sold their own equipment. Anything short of that was "free-riding."[27] But as the Court put it, "this understanding of free-riding has no support in our case law." What's more, it would impose a significant barrier to market entry by requiring firms to offer both equipment and service.

Having rejected Kodak's arguments, the Court remanded the case to the trial court, where a jury found in favor of the ISOs, awarding them over $70 million in damages. On top of that, the court issued an injunction requiring Kodak to sell "all parts" to the ISOs for the next ten years. Again, Kodak appealed, this time to the Ninth Circuit.

It raised several arguments, but the most important was Kodak's contention that its patents and copyrights were valid business justifications for its crackdown on ISOs. Kodak argued that it owned patents on sixty-five of the parts used in its photocopiers and copyrights on the software used to diagnose and service them. And central to those intellectual property rights is the prerogative to allow others to use them or not. If it were forced to license its intellectual property (IP) rights to all comers, Kodak argued, the right to exclude would lose all meaning. The court acknowledged the long-established tension between intellectual property and antitrust law.[28] As it understood, "one body of law creates and protects monopoly power while the other seeks to proscribe it."[29] The court reconciled that tension by recognizing that while patent and copyright holders are generally free to refuse to sell or license their IP rights or products embodying them, they are not altogether immune from antitrust law.

The general rule is that unilaterally refusing to license a patent is not "exclusionary conduct." But that presumption can be rebutted where a copyright or patent holder leverages those statutory rights to expand control over a separate market – like using patented parts to seize the market for repair services. In some cases, concerns over patented technology are a mere pretext for anticompetitive aims. As the ISOs pointed out, of the thousands of parts Kodak refused to sell them, only sixty-five were patented. And Kodak's own parts manager testified that patents "did not cross [his] mind" when the company implemented its restrictive policies.

The relationship between IP rights and antitrust liability remains a contentious question, and not all courts have followed the Ninth Circuit's rationale. When a group of ISOs sued Xerox a few years later for refusing to sell patented parts, copyrighted manuals, and software, the Federal Circuit reached a very different conclusion.[30] Under that court's view patent holders are "exempt from the antitrust laws" unless the patent was obtained through fraud or its assertion is "a mere sham."[31] Absent those extreme conditions, the court was unwilling to interrogate a patent holder's motivation for refusing to sell its products. Unless it was engaged in unlawful tying of unpatented products, Xerox was free to wield its IP rights against a competitor however it saw fit.[32] That absolutist position is in some tension with the Supreme Court's

2013 decision in *FTC v. Actavis*, which rejected the notion that patent rights promise complete immunity from antitrust law. Instead, both patent and antitrust policies should inform the degree to which patentees are insulated from antitrust scrutiny.[33] The precise relationship between IP rights and antitrust law remains poorly defined in the context of repair.

With the Supreme Court's *Kodak* decision as a guide, we can now examine some of the practices device makers use today through an antitrust lens. We know that under the right circumstances, a firm's efforts to shut down independent repair providers can run afoul of the law. So, *Kodak* holds some promise for owners of smartphones, tractors, and appliances who don't want to be entirely dependent on authorized repair providers to keep their devices running. But in many cases, the tactics used by today's manufacturers are more subtle than the rather conspicuous policies Kodak adopted.

Antitrust Theories for Repair Markets

We've already seen device makers adopt a litany of policies and practices around repair that can be fairly characterized as exclusionary and anticompetitive. Forcing consumers to rely on authorized providers, refusing to sell replacement parts, forbidding providers from offering specific repairs, coordinating with retail marketplaces to discriminate against refurbishers, and designing products that cannot be readily repaired by third parties are all examples of the sorts of conduct antitrust enforcers ought to regard with skepticism. Under existing antitrust doctrine, there are four distinct legal theories that could be used to target these antirepair policies.[34] Some tactics fit neatly within a single theory. Others raise concerns under multiple approaches.

Tying

First, as *Kodak* showed us, tying arrangements can unlawfully interfere with competition. Courts understand a tying arrangement as "an agreement by a party to sell one product but only on the condition that the buyer also purchases a different (or tied) product, or at least agrees that he will not purchase that product from any other supplier."[35] The worry is that a seller with market power can force customers to buy a product that they either didn't want or would've preferred to buy elsewhere.[36] When firms use that sort of leverage, they can expand their dominance in one market into a second, denying competitors a foothold, depriving customers of options, and driving up prices.

To establish tying, plaintiffs have to prove four elements.[37] First, two distinct products or services have to exist. As *Kodak* makes clear, parts and service can be – and often are – separate offerings. Likewise, new equipment is typically distinct from either replacement parts or repair services. Second, the sale of one of those products or services must be conditioned on the purchase of the other. This coercion can take the form of a requirement to buy product B if you want product A. But a seller who makes product A available on the condition that customers don't buy product B from a competitor is also engaged in tying. These conditions can arise from express agreements or less-formal arrangements. Third, the seller must have economic power – the ability to raise prices and limit output – in the market for the tying product. For decades, the Supreme Court presumed that the seller of a patented product had power in that market. But in 2006, the Court rejected that presumption.[38] So now plaintiffs need to show that the seller has a significant share of the market for the tying product – generally 30 percent or more[39] – or that the product is unique enough that other suppliers aren't positioned to sell it.[40] Finally, courts require proof that the tie forecloses a "not insubstantial" amount of commerce.[41] In other words, plaintiffs have to show that they lost out on some nontrivial number of sales because of the seller's tying strategy.

Under those standards, there is a strong case to be made that Apple unlawfully ties parts and repairs for its devices. When it comes to Apple devices, the markets for parts and repair services are distinct. Even in the face of the many hurdles and restrictions Apple imposes, third-party repairs persist. Some customers buy parts and repair their devices on their own. Others rely on independent shops to source parts and perform repairs.

But how exactly does Apple tie parts and services together? If your iPhone needs a new screen, battery, or camera, Apple will repair it. You can pay for the company's technicians to swap out the broken component for a new one. But Apple won't sell you the parts so you can do it yourself. Nor will it sell you the part so you can have an experienced independent repair provider do it for you. When dealing directly with consumers, Apple ties parts and service – plain and simple.

The picture is somewhat more complicated when it comes to Apple's treatment of third-party repair providers. As a rule, Apple won't sell repair parts to anyone, including repair providers. But its Apple Authorized Service Provider (AASP) program is a partial exception to that blanket rule. AASPs can purchase parts from Apple, but only under tightly controlled conditions. Apple doesn't permit them to keep a stock of repair parts on hand. It ships parts for specific phones with identified and validated diagnoses. Importantly, the company limits which repairs AASPs can perform. In many cases, they are forced – as a condition of the program that grants them access to parts – to send devices to Apple for repair. So, in order to get access to batteries and screens, AASPs are required to direct camera, charging port, and headphone jack repairs to Apple. From the consumers perspective, if you want access to new Apple parts, repairs from Apple or its anointed providers are your only option.

In response to growing public criticism and regulatory scrutiny, Apple launched its Independent Repair Provider (IRP) program in 2019. But that program is best understood as a ploy to generate positive press coverage and preempt antitrust enforcement. The terms of Apple's secret IRP agreement are so egregious, so overreaching, and so unpalatable, that few repair shops have signed on, despite the stranglehold Apple maintains over repair parts. In order to disentangle Apple's tied parts and service, IRPs must submit to invasive audits of their business records and the personal data of their customers. They also have to agree not to purchase any "prohibited" repair parts, a term that likely excludes the majority of compatible third-party parts given Apple's sweeping interpretations of its trademark and design-patent rights. The IRP agreement, under the guise of prohibiting infringement, tells independent repair shops that if they want to buy parts from Apple, they can't buy them from anyone else.

The next question is whether Apple has power in the market for repair parts. As we've seen, Apple exercises strict, if imperfect, control over many of its parts, which are often custom-manufactured to Apple's specifications. Few are off-the-shelf components. Beyond tightly controlling its supply chain, Apple also claims patents and trademarks for many of these parts. That further reduces the chances of independent production and distribution. As a result, independent repair providers often struggle to reliably source replacement parts.[42] Some are forced to harvest parts from other Apple devices.[43] In other cases, even authentic Apple parts aren't fully functional unless they are installed and authenticated by Apple or its partners.[44]

Finally, we know that the market for smartphone, tablet, and laptop repairs is massive, representing billions of dollars in annual revenue in the United States alone. Apple's market share when it comes to smartphones hovers just below 50 per cent, which suggests it accounts for a sizable portion of the repair market as well. Arguably, the market for electronics repair would be even bigger if companies like Apple weren't so eager to smother it in the name of new devices sales. Admittedly, taking on the most valuable and well-capitalized company on the planet is always an uphill battle. That's true whether the plaintiff is a collection of independent repair providers or the US government. But putting strategic attrition aside, Apple's tying behavior is ripe for an antitrust challenge.

John Deere's authentication scheme for new parts offers another example of tying. Recall that many authentic John Deere replacement parts won't work until they have been initialized by a Deere technician using proprietary software. That's true if an authorized Deere dealer does the repair, but it's also the case if the work is done by an independent repair shop or the machine's owner. There are two potential ties here. First, Deere is conditioning the sale of new tractors on the purchase of its aftermarket services – initialization and repair. Because Deere refuses to provide access to its software to owners or independent repair shops, they are forced to pay Deere to bless newly installed parts. Second, Deere is conditioning the sale of repair parts on this initialization service. The company will sell parts to owners and repair shops, but if they want them to function, they must also pay for initialization.

In response, Deere could argue that it doesn't have sufficient power in the new equipment market for this tying arrangement to be illegal. Deere is the largest of a handful of companies, including Kubota, AGCO, and CNH, that control about half of the US market for agricultural equipment. But Deere's precise market share for specific product categories isn't clear. Tractors, combines, and backhoes are not interchangeable products, and Deere's degree of market power likely varies between them. In some cases, it may clear the 30 percent market-share threshold, but in others it may not. Market power is more certain when it comes to parts, since most aren't interchangeable between brands and Deere's own initialization protocol excludes third-party parts.

Refusals to Deal

Even in the absence of tying, antitrust law can target firms with market power if they refuse to deal with competitors. Generally, antitrust law doesn't interfere with the right to exercise discretion when it comes to your trading partners.[45] If you run a restaurant-supply business, you don't have to sell pots and pans to the restaurant owned by your high-school nemesis. You can even refuse to sell to a direct competitor under most circumstances. But if a firm wields monopoly power, its refusal to deal can be unlawful if it is part of an effort to create or maintain a monopoly.[46] Forcing a firm to do business with a competitor carries its own risks for competition, so courts are understandably cautious in prohibiting refusals to deal.[47] One safeguard is the monopoly-power requirement, which applies to any claim under § 2 of the Sherman Act. Although courts haven't adopted a particularly precise definition of monopoly power, it is generally understood as substantial market power.[48] Even where that requirement is met, courts will entertain legitimate business justifications for the refusal. Despite these high bars, there are reasonably well-defined circumstances where the law insists on some degree of access to a competitor's goods or services.

We've already seen the refusal-to-deal theory in action in the *Kodak* case. There, the Court found that there was sufficient evidence that Kodak's control of the parts and service markets amounted to monopoly power and that its decision to cut off sales to independent providers was designed to maintain and strengthen its monopoly. While *Kodak* is the most relevant precedent, another refusal-to-deal case will help us better understand the outer limits of the theory.

That case didn't deal with replacement parts or aftermarket services, but chair lifts at Colorado ski resorts.[49] Aspen Skiing Company (Ski Co.) owned three of the four mountain ski areas in town. Aspen Highlands owned the other. For more than a decade, the companies and their predecessors offered consumers a combined pass that gave them access to all four mountains for a single price. Eventually the two companies couldn't agree on how to share the revenue from the popular multisite pass, and Ski Co. ended the arrangement. It started selling its own three-mountain pass, and left Highlands to fend for itself. But Highlands knew it was at a major disadvantage, so it came up with a new plan. It would purchase passes from Ski Co. at the retail price and bundle them with passes to its own mountain. It could remain competitive, and Ski Co. would get every penny it chose to charge for its own passes. But when Highland tried to purchase the passes, Ski Co. refused to sell.

Highland sued, alleging that Ski Co. unlawfully monopolized the market by refusing to deal with a competitor. The Court, while acknowledging that competitors generally have no obligation to cooperate, was troubled by Ski Co.'s behavior. It pulled out of a long-established, popular joint offering, denying consumers access to a product they were eager to purchase. What's more, it sacrificed short-term profitability by refusing to sell its product to a willing buyer at full-price. That looks like a move made to exclude a competitor and reduce long-term competition. Without a valid business justification, Ski Co.'s refusal could only be interpreted as an effort to monopolize the market. Admittedly, *Aspen Skiing* has been described as "at or near the outer boundary of § 2 liability."[50] But the case offers important insights. A monopolist's refusal to deal is particularly problematic where it disrupts an existing offering and sacrifices short-term profits for the sake of reducing competition.[51]

Consider Nikon's shifting policies around repair parts. Back in 2012, the company announced it would cut off access to repair parts to anyone other than its authorized repair facilities.[52] For decades, independent repair shops could buy parts directly from Nikon so they could fix customers' equipment. Moving forward, they were forced to rely on secondary markets or third-party components, to the extent they were available. But especially for newer cameras, non-Nikon parts are hard to come by. Just like with iPhones and John Deere tractors, a part designed for a Sony or Canon camera can't just be slapped on a Nikon. To justify its decision, Nikon claimed local repair shops lacked the specialized tools needed to repair its cameras. The suggestion that independent repair shops lack the expertise needed to fix modern cameras is, to put it mildly, debatable. And if they don't have the right tools, Nikon could have made them available.

Instead, Nikon insisted repairs could only be trusted to Nikon-authorized providers. Those sanctioned shops – twenty-two of them, at the time – would still enjoy access to Nikon parts. But just seven years later, Nikon terminated its authorized repair program, leaving even those shops in the lurch.[53] Now Nikon owners have to send their cameras to New York or Los Angeles, the company's only two US repair facilities. Once-authorized repair shops too are forced to scour eBay, salvage parts from old equipment, or wait weeks for third-party parts shipped from China. For professional photographers, those delays are often dealbreakers.

For Nikon's refusal to sell parts to violate the law, it needs to have monopoly power in the relevant market. The appropriate market here should be defined narrowly. It's not the market for cameras, or even the market for camera parts, but the market for Nikon-compatible parts. Some minority of those parts may be standard, off-the-shelf components. But most are designed specifically for Nikons. When it comes to those parts, Nikon likely wields significant market power. For some, it may be the only source. For others, it may be the only timely and cost-effective one. This is a fact-intensive question that will vary across the range of parts in Nikon's inventory. Nonetheless, monopoly power is a safe assumption for at least some subset of those parts.

There's also the question of Nikon's business justifications. If it can offer credible evidence that its decision wasn't motivated by a desire to monopolize the repair market, the company could still avoid liability. Initially, it claimed independent repair shops weren't capable of repairing its sophisticated equipment. That's an empirical claim that, if true, the company should be able to back up with proof. If not, it's a mere pretext. When it discontinued its authorized repair program, it supplied a far more ambiguous explanation. As Nikon cryptically explained, "The climate in which we do business has evolved, and Nikon Inc. must do the same." What that means is anyone's guess. But Nikon, like other camera makers, is confronting declining revenue in an era of ubiquitous, high-quality smartphone cameras. One plausible interpretation of its about-face on part sales is that the company hopes more expensive and less convenient repairs can boost flagging camera sales. But eliminating the repair market altogether is hardly the sort of pro-competitive justification a court should accept.

A refusal-to-deal case is harder, although not impossible, to make against companies like Apple that have consistently withheld parts from independent providers. In *Kodak* and *Aspen*

Skiing, the Court focused on the disruption of settled business relationships. It's the termination of those arrangements that triggers antitrust scrutiny in the modern refusal-to-deal cases. So, where there is no preexisting pattern of dealing, courts are likely to be more skeptical of forcing a dominant seller to cooperate. In the aftermarket context, that creates a perverse incentive by insulating firms that foreclose independent competition from the outset. That said, if Apple were to change its AASP or IRP programs in ways that added new restrictions on the availability of parts – by removing access to components or imposing new conditions on their availability – it may open itself up to a refusal-to-deal claim, at least in the absence of a legitimate justification.

Aside from dubious concerns over the quality and reliability of independent repairs, firms like Apple are almost certain to contend that the exercise of valid IP rights justifies their refusal to sell repair parts. As we've already seen, courts are split on the question of whether IP rights alone are a sufficient business justification for otherwise illegal conduct. The Ninth Circuit says courts must examine the underlying motivations to ferret out pretext.[54] But the Federal Circuit maintains that a firm can grunt in the direction of a patent or copyright and enjoy antitrust immunity.[55] Other courts have struggled to reconcile these two inconsistent positions.[56]

They shouldn't. IP rights are not absolute. Saying the holder of a patent on a smartphone can't be guilty of monopolization purely by virtue of owning that patent makes about as much sense as arguing the owner of a patent on a flamethrower can't be guilty of arson. IP law already recognizes circumstances where exclusive rights must give way to other considerations. Exhaustion, misuse, and a variety of compulsory licenses already place limits on the power of rights holders for the sake of protecting competition and consumer welfare.[57] That's not to say concerns about infringement can never justify refusals to deal.[58] But merely identifying IP rights, especially in markets that are rife with them, shouldn't mean defendants can avoid all scrutiny.

Exclusive Dealing

Refusing to deal with a competitor can be illegal, but so can exclusive relationships. Exclusive dealing takes a variety of forms. A manufacturer might tell distributors or retailers that they can only buy its products if they agree not to carry products from competing suppliers. Or a buyer could insist a supplier not offer its products to other customers. Exclusive deals can be explicit, but don't have to be spelled out directly.[59] Firms might enter into these sorts of agreements for nonpredatory reasons. But under the right circumstances, exclusive dealing violates § 1 of the Sherman Act as a contract "in restraint of trade," § 2 of the Sherman Act as monopolization, or § 3 of the Clayton Act as an arrangement that may "substantially lessen competition."[60] Such arrangements are typically evaluated under the rule of reason.

The precise legal requirements for these claims differ somewhat, but the overarching theory of harm is consistent. Through exclusive arrangements, a firm or group of firms can foreclose on competition that would otherwise develop. That can happen, for example, when smaller competitors are denied access to retailers. Without an opportunity to reach customers, those competitors may not be able to survive. When they inevitably fold, the market is less competitive. At the same time, exclusive deals raise the barriers of entry for new competitors, who understandably may be scared off by a market already defined by exclusive deals.[61] Exclusive supply contracts can also harm competition. If an agreement requires a seller to deal exclusively with a single buyer, competitors may have a hard time sourcing reasonably priced inputs. And in some cases, exclusive deals can be a tool to limit competition between two firms, allowing them to essentially divide the market as they see fit.

In addition to determining market power, courts take a number of factors into account when they examine exclusive deals under the rule of reason – their duration, whether and how they can be terminated, and any pro-competitive benefits they offer, among others. They also consider what portion of the market is closed off to competitors as a result of the exclusive arrangement. Most courts agree that a foreclosure percentage between 30 and 40 percent is usually required.[62] But courts aren't bound by that threshold.[63] Given the central importance of foreclosure, exclusive deals are the most problematic when rival firms cannot rely on alternative distribution channels. But the harms of exclusive dealing aren't limited to complete market foreclosure. If a rival still has access to customers – or parts and materials, as the case may be – competition can still suffer if the costs of these alternative avenues are too high.

Device makers use exclusive deals to control aftermarkets for parts and repairs. To take one problematic example, Intersil produces charging chips, tiny components that regulate how quickly a battery charges. If that chip goes bad in your MacBook Pro, you can either replace that single $15 component, or you can swap out the entire motherboard for about $1,500.[64] The choice seems like a no-brainer. But Intersil's lucrative deal with Apple prohibits the company from selling its charging chips to anyone but Apple.[65] This exclusive arrangement means Apple controls who gets access to the chips, and no one, not even AASPs, can buy new replacements. These parts were widely available for years, until Apple insisted on exclusivity. Now, if they want to salvage a laptop, the only option repair providers have is to harvest chips from other less-expensive Apple products. In most cases though, the failure of this cheap part results in the consumer buying a new laptop and scrapping a perfectly fixable one.

Beyond these obvious examples, authorized repair provider programs, to the extent they forbid partners from buying third-party components, are properly seen as exclusive contracts. And by limiting the availability of parts, software, and tools, companies like Apple are striking exclusive deals with their customers. Apple is too smart to explicitly condition the sale of an iPhone on a promise not to have it repaired by an independent provider. But the company's strict limits on the sale of parts, not to mention its authentication and serialization practices, foreclose competition in the repair market. Formally, customers may have the right to choose an independent provider, but as a practical matter, Apple-approved repairs may be the only meaningful option.[66] These behaviors demand scrutiny. Ultimately, they may not be anti-competitive in the narrow legal sense, but device makers should be forced to defend their strategies.

A more intuitive case for exclusive dealing can be made when it comes to the Apple/Amazon agreement. A cooperative agreement between two of the most powerful companies in the United States ought to raise eyebrows regardless of its terms.[67] But where the agreement explicitly allows for a seller to remove competitors from a dominant retail platform, the alarm bells should be blaring. To entice Apple to sell smartphones, tablets, and laptops directly on its site, Amazon offered Apple the right to exclude third-party sellers of Apple products. And with some narrow and ill-defined exceptions, that's exactly what it did.[68]

These brand-gating agreements aren't unheard of, but they are deeply problematic, especially for repaired and refurbished products. Amazon accounts for up to one-half of the US online retail market. But since not all retailers carry used goods, its pre-deal share of the refurbished Apple product market was potentially even higher. Amazon, the self-described "everything store," offered a thriving platform for refurbished goods. Sites like eBay provide another distribution channel for small refurbishing operations, but its sales volume is dwarfed by Amazon. And while refurbishers could, in theory, set up their own retail sites, that's an expensive and uncertain proposition. When an agreement bars competitors from cost-efficient distribution channels, it risks serious harm to competition.

Through this exclusive arrangement, Apple was able to jettison the bulk of refurbishers from their primary distribution platform. In doing so, it reduced competition for its own inventory of refurbished products, which are generally more expensive than independently refurbished devices. At the same time, it weakened the downward pressure on new device prices introduced by low-cost, high-quality refurbished goods.

Predatory Product Design

Finally, the very design of a product can be predatory under the right circumstances. Understandably, the law gives manufacturers broad latitude to design their products as they see fit. Competition is best served by innovative and differentiated products, and legal mandates that interfere with the design process ought to be regarded with a healthy dose of skepticism.[69] Nonetheless, that doesn't mean that particular design choices that exclude or disadvantage competitors can never be challenged. Courts have recognized that sometimes a firm's decision to add, remove, or change some product feature or attribute is a window into its anticompetitive motivations. In its case against Microsoft, for example, the government cited design decisions that reinforced its monopoly. For example, the Windows operating system excluded Microsoft's own Internet Explorer from its Add/Remove Programs utility, making it difficult to delete, and ignored users' default browser settings.[70] Similar scrutiny has been applied to the design of medical devices, pharmaceuticals, and processors.[71] If a design "either does not improve the product in any material way or offers only a small benefit, and leads to the exclusion of rivals," it should be considered predatory.[72]

When John Deere designs its tractors so that authentic replacement parts won't work without its initialization software, that is a predatory decision. It offers little benefit to equipment owners, but imposes significant barriers for repair providers. The same was true when Apple designed screens and cameras for the iPhone 12 that can't be replaced – even with genuine Apple parts – unless the device is connected to its System Configuration app.[73] Even the warning messages Apple displayed on older iPhones when a battery or screen was replaced by a third-party discourages competition. When Apple used similar strategies to prevent the replacement of Touch ID sensors, the company could tell a plausible story about protecting user privacy and security that, if supported by evidence, might justify its designs. But the idea that replacing a battery or a camera raises the same concerns is simply not credible. When design decisions squeeze out competitors without a reasonable justification, courts should recognize them for what they are – not innovation or experimentation, but criminality.

Hurdles to Antitrust Enforcement

The threats to competition in the markets for replacement parts, repair services, and refurbished devices are real. But they are hardly unique. Competition, writ large, is on the decline in the United States, despite a cultural commitment to the rhetoric of sharp-elbowed meritocracy. Congressional districts are gerrymandered to avoid genuine electoral competition.[74] Star athletes handpick their teammates to create seemingly untouchable superteams.[75] Parents engage in elaborate, expensive, and occasionally illegal schemes to secure their children's spots at elite universities.[76] And massive firms acquire startups at alarming rates, intolerant of even a hint of new competition.[77] It's no wonder then that wide swaths of the US economy are characterized by growing consolidation and dwindling competition. From air travel and concert tickets to search engines and home appliances, either a single firm or a handful of large players dominate.[78] Antitrust law can't solve all these problems, but at least in theory, we would expect it to address accumulations of market power.

In recent decades, though, US antitrust enforcement has grown anemic. The story of the waning vitality of antitrust law is a complex one, a full accounting of which is beyond the scope of this book.[79] But an influential group of academics at the University of Chicago, including economists Milton Friedman and George Stigler, and eventual federal appellate judges Richard Posner, Frank Easterbrook, and Robert Bork, play a major role.[80] The theories and approaches they developed profoundly reshaped antitrust law in ways that favor market concentration, undermine competition, and flout congressional intent. The pernicious effects of this intellectual movement and its eventual embrace by the courts are still acutely felt today.

Central to the Chicago School's agenda was redefining the core mission of antitrust law. Rather than a body of law meant to provide structural protection for competitive markets, Bork and his colleagues recast antitrust law as an exercise in maximizing consumer welfare and allocative efficiency. The problem antitrust was meant to solve, in their view, is market inefficiency. From this perspective, monopolies aren't harmful because they reduce competition, discourage market entry, or concentrate power. If monopolies are harmful at all, it's because they allow producers to charge inflated prices above marginal cost and reduce output.[81] But if a monopolist can provide goods and services at the same price as a competitive market, the law has no reason to intervene.

This reorientation of antitrust, which treats competition as secondary to economic efficiency, has been described by antitrust scholar Lina Khan as "a grotesque distortion" of the law.[82] As a matter of legislative history, Bork's assertions have been thoroughly debunked.[83] Nonetheless, they found a receptive audience in the Supreme Court.[84] Beginning in the mid-1970s, the Court's approach to antitrust began to shift, adopting the consumer welfare framing of the Chicago School.[85] By the mid-2000s, Justice Scalia – writing for a unanimous Court – was praising monopolies: "The mere possession of monopoly power, and the concomitant charging of monopoly prices, is not only not unlawful; it is an important element of the free-market system. The opportunity to charge monopoly prices – at least for a short period – is what attracts 'business acumen' in the first place; it induces risk taking that produces innovation and economic growth."[86]

This reversal in the prevailing understanding of the core justifications for antitrust law gave rise to a chain of consequences that has, at least temporarily, defanged US antitrust enforcement. First, courts have adopted a number of the descriptive claims – or more accurately, assumptions – embedded in this monopoly-friendly view of the market. One central assumption is that monopoly power is self-correcting and short-lived. If a company abuses its dominant position by charging supracompetitive prices, the thinking goes, another competitor will simply enter the market and undercut the monopolist. As sophisticated and self-interested actors, monopolists would anticipate this and never bother gouging consumers in the first place. But history is littered with examples of durable monopolies, many of which were finally brought to heel not by the invisible hand of the market but by the clenched fist of the law.[87] Contrary to the Chicago School's reassurances, monopolists construct barriers to entry to fend off would-be competitors. Or they simply acquire them before they can pose a competitive threat. Even more implausibly, this view assumes market actors have perfect information that enables fully rational decisions. But consumers, competitors, and even monopolists often face serious information costs at odds with this optimistic assumption.

Second, once courts conceptualize the ultimate question in antitrust cases in terms of efficiency, they open the door to a litany of justifications, rationalizations, and excuses for anticompetitive conduct. Mergers in already concentrated markets, they tell us, should be allowed because economies of scale will result in price breaks for consumers, benefits that often fail to materialize. Supracompetitive prices should be tolerated, they insist, because they could encourage investment. And acquiring monopoly power, they suggest, is forgivable because it may spur innovation. These benefits are often enough to convince courts to excuse otherwise unlawful behavior.[88] In part, this willingness to be convinced of the virtues of market power is a byproduct of the rule of reason framework that governs the majority of antitrust claims.[89] By abandoning *per se* rules against particular categories of conduct in favor of an approach that balances benefits and harms on a case-by-case basis, courts invite the kind of economic just-so stories that explain away anticompetitive behavior as *actually* serving some nebulous, speculative, or simply concocted social value.

Third, the rule of reason is largely responsible for the increasing complexity and expense of antitrust litigation. Jettisoning clear rules for malleable standards comes at a cost. A full accounting of the harms and supposed benefits of challenged conduct is a fact-intensive enterprise. It requires the collection of considerable data through the discovery process. At the same time, it's theory-intensive. In order to make sense of these reams of economic data, judges and juries alike rely heavily on expert witnesses hired by litigants. This dependence on expert economists threatens to supplant the constitutional roles of courts and juries.[90] Beyond that, discovery costs and hefty expert-witness fees contribute to the rising costs of antitrust litigation. But those costs have asymmetric effects that tend to favor antitrust defendants. Almost by definition, plausible targets for antitrust enforcement are better-resourced than private plaintiffs. By driving up litigation costs, firms with market power can forestall litigation.[91] And when cases are brought, a deep-pocketed defendant can win through a war of attrition. Ultimately, plaintiffs' odds under the rule of reason are dismal. One study revealed that from 1999 to 2009, defendants prevailed in a staggering 99 percent of cases.[92]

Even the US government, the entity theoretically best positioned to rein in the abuses of dominant firms, has been cowed by the antitrust orthodoxy. Over a brief span from 1970 to 1972, the Department of Justice (DOJ) brought nearly forty cases against monopolies and oligopolies.[93] But in recent decades, the DOJ hasn't displayed the same pugnacity. Prior to its announcement of charges against Facebook and Google, it hadn't brought a major monopolization case since it targeted Microsoft in the late 1990s, which resulted in a less-than-complete victory.[94]

But US antitrust law shows signs of revitalization. A new movement of scholars, rightly critical of this *laissez-faire* turn, have made persuasive cases for a return to the law's historical roots.[95] Rather than evaluating a firm's behavior exclusively in terms of efficiency, they argue antitrust law should be concerned with ensuring open, competitive markets.[96] Given their resonance, those arguments have sparked a lively and sustained public conversation about antitrust law, a topic that until recently was of interest only to specialist lawyers and economists.[97] And policy makers have taken notice. Both Democrats and Republicans in Congress have acknowledged the need to strengthen antitrust rules to tackle market concentration.[98] But so far, no legislative consensus is on the horizon.

Fortunately, though, we don't need legislation to solve the problem. The doctrines that define modern US antitrust law are almost all judge-made. They can be reconsidered, modified, and ultimately scrapped if plaintiffs make a persuasive case to the right set of judges. And persuasive cases are there for the making. As an empirical matter, there is evidence that contemporary antitrust policy has failed, on its own terms, at its professed goal of keeping prices in check.[99] More importantly, the way courts interpret and apply antitrust law today bears little connection to the text of the Sherman and Clayton Acts.[100] As both a matter of textual interpretation and legislative history, the cramped interpretations of the antitrust statutes favored by courts today are at odds with what Congress set out to achieve.[101]

Enforcement priorities at the Department of Justice and the Federal Trade Commission may be easier to refocus, as they are largely a function of political appointments. Personnel, as they say, is policy. Under appropriate leadership, we could see meaningful efforts by antitrust enforcers to protect competition, resist market concentration, and break up dominant firms when necessary. In developing a roadmap for a more robust antitrust regime, the path taken by European competition authorities might be instructive.

Competition Law in Europe

Article 101 of the Treaty on the Functioning of the European Union prohibits agreements that "have as their object or effect the prevention, restriction or distortion of competition" – calling out price fixing, production limits, market sharing, and discriminatory agreements in a non-exhaustive list of specific examples.[102] Article 102 goes on to forbid dominant firms from abusing their position, extending liability to unilateral conduct as well.

Although it shares some broad similarities with US antitrust law, competition law in Europe differs in some crucial respects that create an environment more hospitable to vigorous enforcement. The European Commission has broad investigative powers and can impose substantial fines on firms that violate the law. In addition, the competition authorities of member states are empowered to independently enforce the law.[103]

European authorities haven't been shy about wielding those powers. In the span of three years, the Commission fined Google $2.7 billion for manipulating search results to favor its own services,[104] $5 billion for bundling its search engine on Android phones and paying other device makers to do the same,[105] and $1.7 billion for blocking ads for competitors on its AdSense service.[106] Nor does the Commission show any signs of slowing down. It's in the midst of investigating allegations that Facebook leveraged its access to user data – including web traffic obtained through a VPN service it acquired in 2013 – to identify potential competitors before they could mature into plausible threats.[107] At the same time, it's targeting Amazon for allegedly harvesting information to copy popular third-party products.[108] Apple, too, has faced scrutiny from the Commission. It's currently being investigated for charging competitors like Spotify a 30 percent fee on subscriptions as a condition for access to its app store.[109] And perhaps most importantly, the German Federal Cartel Authority has launched a probe of the Apple/Amazon deal.[110]

This more muscular response can be attributed to some key variations between EU and US law. On the whole, these are differences of degree rather than kind, but collectively, they add up to outcomes that diverge substantially. While antitrust law in the United States has fetishized efficiency at the expense of other policy priorities, European law continues to recognize a broader set of goals. Consumer welfare is important, but it is one objective among many. Protecting small enterprises, preserving a competitive market structure, and maintaining an integrated single market are valuable ends in their own right.[111] Substantively, EU law is more sensitive to market power and is more inclined to find that a firm enjoys a dominant position. Likewise, it's more likely to conclude that a firm abuses that position through its conduct. In part, this approach reveals that European regulators do not share the unshakable faith in markets and distrust of government intervention that animates contemporary US antitrust law.[112]

When it comes to repair, this same basic pattern holds. The US and EU approaches are roughly parallel, with some notable distinctions. Early EU cases defined aftermarkets narrowly. So, dominance could be established easily when companies manufactured non-interchangeable parts for their own equipment.[113] Later cases, influenced by the reasoning in *Kodak*, considered questions of lock-in and the challenges of lifecycle pricing. Printer manufacturers, for instance, did not have a dominant position in the toner cartridge market, in the belief that consumers could calculate lifecycle pricing and discipline high cartridge prices.[114] But when high upfront costs made lock-in more likely, or lifecycle prices were less readily available, the Commission continued to pursue anticompetitive conduct. After independent service providers complained that Digital Equipment Corporation (DEC) tied its hardware and software maintenance services, squeezing out hardware maintenance providers, the Commission launched a two-year investigation. Ultimately, DEC agreed to modify its policies to open the door to competition.[115] And in 2011, IBM – accused of denying independent service providers access to spare parts and technical information on reasonable terms – committed to their prompt delivery on nondiscriminatory terms for five years.[116]

A key point of comparison between US and EU law is how IP rights factor into allegations of anticompetitive behavior. Some US courts maintain that a refusal to license or sell parts or products protected by IP rights is immune from antitrust scrutiny, with some exceedingly narrow exceptions.[117] European courts and regulators, on the other hand, have adopted a more nuanced understanding of the relationship between IP rights and competition.

When Volvo sued a distributor for importing replacement body panels that infringed its registered designs, the distributor argued that Volvo abused its dominant position by refusing to grant it a license to import and sell the parts.[118] The court recognized that the right to prevent the manufacture and sale of products embodying a design "constitutes the very subject-matter" of the IP right. But rather than dismiss the distributor's contention, the court identified a few circumstances that would justify a restraint on the exercise of those rights: "the arbitrary refusal to supply spare parts to independent repairers, the fixing of prices for spare parts at an unfair level, or a decision no longer to produce spare parts for a particular model even though many cars of that model are still in circulation." While there was no evidence that Volvo engaged in any abusive conduct, the court left the door open to such allegations in the future.

Subsequent cases have recognized other "exceptional circumstances" in which holders of IP rights are obligated to license or sell products and services. In *Magill* and *IMS*, the court outlined a three-part test. A refusal by a rights holder to grant access to a product or service is abusive if: "that refusal is preventing the emergence of a new product for which there is a potential consumer demand, that it is unjustified[,] and such as to exclude any competition on a secondary market."[119] Although the precise interpretation of the "new product" requirement has been debated, it could be problematic in the repair context.[120] The goal is not to produce a derivative product, but to fix an existing one.[121] In any case, the indispensability test in *Magill* and *IMS* is best understood as adding to the list of "exceptional circumstances" already outlined in *Volvo*.[122]

Whether or not consumers or repair providers can meet these criteria to establish an abuse of dominant position remains to be seen. The question of unfair pricing of a part subject to valid copyright, patent, or design rights is particularly tricky, since we should expect some price premium to flow from the fact of legal exclusivity even in the absence of any abuse.[123] Nonetheless, the mere existence of an IP right isn't enough to insulate firms from the anticompetitive consequences of their refusals to deal.

As two of the largest markets for consumer goods, both the United States and Europe have the power to shape worldwide business practices and product design.[124] Whether and how the law regulates these behaviors is of critical importance. It helps determine the prices we pay for goods and services. It regulates the degree of competition in the marketplace. It creates or eliminates opportunities for small and medium-sized businesses. Those are sufficient reasons for the law to intervene. But as the repair market helps illustrate, there are more significant values at stake. Unbridled market power compounds the environmental threats endangering human survival. It limits our individual autonomy and leaves us reliant on an ever-shrinking handful of unimaginably powerful corporations. And that concentration of power threatens to undermine not only our individual freedom but our collective rights of self-determination. As Justice Louis Brandeis put it, "We can have democracy in this country, or we can have great wealth concentrated in the hands of a few, but we can't have both."[125]

7 REPAIR AND CONSUMER PROTECTION

Antitrust law is a powerful tool. But on its own it's unlikely to solve the full range of impediments to repair. The practical and doctrinal barriers, while not insurmountable, are high. The reality is, the biggest offenders are prepared to spend unseemly sums on the best lawyers they can find to maintain their stranglehold on repair. And not every injury suffered by consumers fits cleanly within an antitrust theory. Luckily though, consumer-protection law offers another set of tools. Consumer protection aims to ensure that firms aren't misleading consumers with inaccurate information in the marketplace. Even in the absence of outright deception, it recognizes the need to prohibit unfair practices that take advantage of the natural information asymmetries that sellers enjoy. And finally, consumer-protection laws can offer remedies when products fail to live up to minimal, baseline guarantees of quality. These protections are applicable to all firms, regardless of their market share and are often more straightforward to prove than the run of the mill monopolization claim. Consumer-protection cases rarely lead to dramatic, structural remedies, but they can profoundly influence marketplace behavior, improve the day-to-day experiences of consumers, and level the playing field for competitors.

In the United States, consumer-protection law embraces a constellation of related and overlapping federal and state statutes. Broadly, these laws are meant to empower regulators and consumers to push back on deceptive, unfair, and abusive practices in the marketplace. Some, like the Federal Trade Commission Act, confer broad authority to regulators to police market behavior.[1] Others, like the Fair Debt Collection Practices Act, set rules for very specific marketplace interactions – in that case, banning debt collectors from contacting consumers "at any unusual time or place."[2] These laws can be enforced by federal agencies, like the Federal Trade Commission (FTC) and the Consumer Financial Protection Bureau, or state-level consumer affairs departments and attorneys general. And in many instances, consumers can bring claims directly. Similarly, European law incorporates both broad standards and sector-specific prohibitions at both the EU and national levels.[3]

Many of the restrictions on repair we've seen implicate consumer-protection laws. Misleading statements or omissions about product reparability might constitute deceptive trade practices. Failures to make repair parts available can violate state statutory guarantees. And the common practice of threatening to void warranties because of independent repair runs contrary to established federal law. Device makers may insist that consumers are best protected by tightly controlled repair markets. But the law recognizes that device makers themselves may well pose the most serious risks to consumers.

Consumer protection offers powerful and applicable legal tools that could defend independent repair, but they have not been effectively utilized by the FTC and state attorneys general. Clearer guidance and more vigorous enforcement efforts could go a long way towards curbing some of the most abusive tactics device makers deploy.

Consumer Perceptions of Repair

To see how consumer-protection laws might apply to independent and third-party repair, we need a better understanding of how consumers think about reparability. Is it something they expect and value? Does the ability to repair a product guide their purchase decisions? In order to assess these and other questions, I surveyed more than 800 US consumers in 2020.[4] The sample was broadly representative of the US population with respect to sex, age, and income. The survey began by identifying consumers who were in the market for one of five categories of electronic devices – smartphones, tablets, smart speakers, digital cameras, or smart refrigerators.[5] Each consumer was then asked a series of follow-up questions about one category of device they had either recently purchased or were considering buying.

The first set of questions measured the degree to which consumers expect to be able to repair the things they buy. Their responses reveal high expectations of reparability and highlight the feelings of surprise, anger, and even betrayal consumers experience when device makers limit their choices around the repair. Respondents were asked if they agreed with the following statement: *If I purchase a [device], I have the right to repair it myself or to take it to the repair shop of my choice.* As Figure 1 illustrates, the vast majority of respondents – 83 percent – agreed, 60 percent of them strongly. The results for smartphones, tablets, and smart refrigerators were nearly indistinguishable from the average response. For smart speakers, about 76 percent agreed. Notably, the

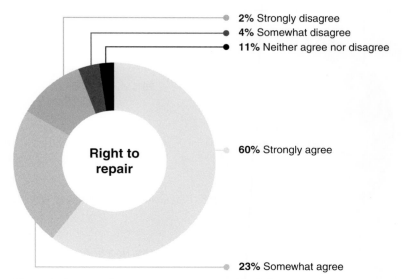

Figure 1 Degree of consumer agreement with right to repair

percentage was significantly higher for digital cameras. There, 93 percent agreed that they enjoyed the right to repair, and 75 percent strongly agreed. Digital cameras, which first appeared in the 1990s, predate many of the recent efforts to restrict repair, perhaps explaining consumers' stronger expectations.

As an alternative measure, consumers were asked: *If you learned that the manufacturer of your [device] limited your ability to repair it yourself or have it repaired, how would you feel?* Although, as Figure 2 shows, the majority indicated that they would be either "very surprised" or "somewhat surprised," those rates were somewhat lower than their expectations of reparability. That might suggest that consumers regard device makers with some degree of skepticism. They expect to be able to repair things but aren't shocked when manufacturers fail to live up to those expectations.

Consumers were also asked to describe in their own words how they would feel if they learned of repair restrictions on their

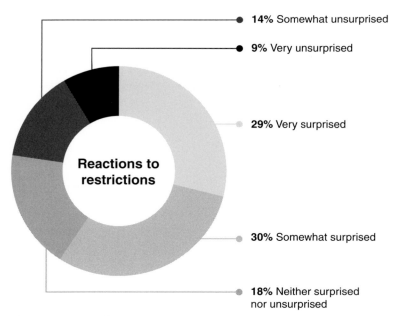

Figure 2 Degree of consumer surprise by repair restrictions

devices. These responses were, to put it mildly, quite critical of such restrictions – 67 percent were negative, and only 9 percent positive.[6] The most common feeling, offered by sixty-three consumers, was anger. Others described feeling upset, disappointed, frustrated, annoyed. Dozens more used harsher language – cheated, conned, deceived, scammed, swindled, and, simply put, pissed. Other responses highlighted how repair restrictions interfere with autonomy. As one noted, "I don't think [manufacturers] have any right to tell me what I can do with it after I purchase it." Another was concerned that "the manufacturer is impacting my freedom to do what I want with a product that I legally own."

The next pair of questions measured whether repair restrictions are material to consumer decision-making – in other words, whether they affect the decision to buy a product. The first asked: *If you knew the manufacturer limited your ability to repair a [device], would that affect your willingness to purchase that [device]?* As illustrated in Figure 3, more than 70 percent of consumers said they were less likely to purchase a device subject to those

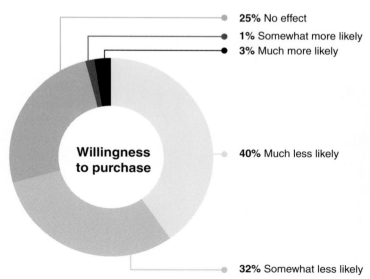

Figure 3 Willingness to purchase devices with repair restrictions

restrictions. These results were largely consistent across device types, with those who were much or somewhat less likely to purchase ranging from 68 percent for smart refrigerators to 76 percent for digital cameras.

Materiality, however, is not a simple binary question. Aside from refusing to buy a product altogether, consumers often adjust the price they are willing to pay to account for positive and negative product attributes. So, consumers were also asked: *If you knew the manufacturer limited your ability to repair a [device], would that affect the price you would be willing to pay for that [device]?* Rather than absolute dollar amounts, willingness to pay was measured comparatively. As Figure 4 shows, the vast majority indicated that they would pay less for a device burdened by repair restrictions, with 40 percent willing to pay "much less" and 30 percent willing to pay "somewhat less." Those responses were consistent across product types, except for smart refrigerators. But even there, 62 percent of consumers indicated they were less likely to buy a product with repair restrictions.

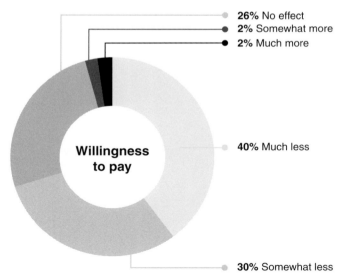

Figure 4 Willingness to pay for devices with repair restrictions

These results suggest that consumers have strong expecta-tions when it comes to reparability. Just as importantly, they support the idea that accurate information about repair restric-tions will shape consumer behavior in the marketplace. Those conclusions are in line with the European Commission's 2018 *Behavioural Study on Consumers' Engagement in the Circular Economy*, which sought to better understand consumer attitudes and behavior around product durability and reparability. When European consumers were asked if they'd prefer to receive better information about how long products last and their ease of repair, overwhelming majorities said yes.[7] And most agreed that information would be most useful at the point of purchase or while comparing potential purchases.

The study also incorporated an experiment designed to mea-sure how that information influences consumers' purchasing decisions. Consumers were told they needed to purchase pro-ducts – vacuum cleaners, dishwashers, televisions, smart-phones, and coats – on a simulated shopping site, choosing between six models. For each model, they were shown its name, picture, and price. Some were shown additional labels containing information about durability and reparability. Others were not. As you might expect, that information had a significant influence on their purchasing decisions. Those who had the advantage of information on durability and repar-ability were three times as likely to choose the most durable product available and twice as likely to choose the most reparable.[8] Not only did better information shape consumer preferences, it also shifted their willingness to pay. Consumers placed a premium on products with better repar-ability scores. For a product with a higher score, consumers were willing to pay an extra €29–54 for vacuum cleaners, €83–105 for dishwashers, €77–171 for TVs, and €48–98 for smart-phones. A similar effect was found for durability.[9]

These studies give us good reason to believe that consumers in both the United States and Europe expect and value repar-ability. They are less interested in products with repair restric-tions and will pay more for the right to repair. With those facts established, we can turn to how the law might protect consumers' interest in repair.

Unfair and Deceptive Practices

A commitment to honest, fair commercial practices is at the core of consumer-protection law. For markets to work, consumers need reliable, accurate information and some measure of assurance that companies can't take advantage of them through unscrupulous tactics. In the United States, the FTC is central to those missions. Created in 1914, the FTC is empowered to not only enforce antitrust law, but more broadly to target "unfair or deceptive acts or practices" in the marketplace.[10] Over the last century, the FTC's responsibility has grown considerably. From credit-card disclosures to unsolicited emails and phone calls, it is tasked with enforcing a host of laws designed to safeguard the interests of consumers. In recent decades, its role as a privacy regulator has given the FTC an increasingly important role in overseeing key parts of the internet economy.[11]

Although the FTC hasn't yet taken any major action against device makers for restricting repair, it has recognized that the issue falls squarely within its broad consumer-protection mandate. In July of 2019, the Commission organized a workshop to discuss "how manufacturers may limit repairs by consumers and repair shops and whether those limitations affect consumer protection."[12] There are at least two statutes within the FTC's purview implicated by repair restrictions. Later, we will turn to the protections consumers enjoy under the Magnuson-Moss Warranty Act. But we begin with the FTC's core responsibility to police unfair and deceptive trade practices.

Unfairness and deception are separate legal theories, requiring distinct elements of proof. Let's begin with unfair practices. The FTC's unfairness jurisdiction is broad. Rather than strictly defining unfairness, Congress granted the Commission flexible authority subject to judicial review. But over time, a reasonably straightforward set of criteria evolved. For a practice to be deemed unfair, the FTC needs to demonstrate: (1) a substantial injury to consumers; (2) that is not outweighed by countervailing benefits; and (3) that is not reasonably avoidable.[13]

Substantial injuries can include both monetary harm and the purchase of unwanted goods or services. When it comes to repair, we know that consumers place significant value on the ability to fix things and are less inclined to buy products they can't repair. So, if a company fails to disclose designs or policies that frustrate repair, consumers face real harm. Policies that force consumers to pay inflated prices for authorized repairs injure consumers, as do refusals to sell replacement parts and software that requires initialization for authentic parts. Products that can't be repaired, like Apple's AirPods, may even be inherently harmful to consumers in the absence of some prominent, explicit warning. Companies also harm consumers when they change existing policies in ways that make repair less accessible. For instance, when Canon cut off existing third-party repair providers, it harmed customers through added expense, delays, and inconvenience.

Once an injury is established, the question becomes whether it is outweighed by benefits to consumers or competition more broadly. Device makers that restrict repair would recite a litany of supposed benefits of their policies – greater reliability, safety, and security among them. Lobbyists citing these claims in closed-door meetings with lawmakers is one thing. Proving them in court with hard evidence is another. As the Food and Drug Administration (FDA) has found, independent repair is effective and reliable.[14] If that's true for life-saving medical technology, it's almost certainly true for our phones. Firms are also likely to insist that, without repair restrictions, innovation will decrease, and prices will rise. As always, we should be skeptical of justifications couched in terms of innovation. Will the pace of new smartphone releases slow if consumers can easily fix their current devices? Perhaps. But that alone doesn't show that society has been denied some valuable innovation. As for price hikes, the margins companies currently enjoy on many electronic devices leave plenty of room for profitability even if sales volumes decrease. And greater access to repair will only put further downward pressure on new device pricing.

Finally, we must consider whether consumers can reasonably avoid the harms imposed by repair restrictions. Here, it's helpful to distinguish between consumers who have already made a purchase and those that are considering doing so. Once you buy an iPhone or John Deere tractor, the harms of repair restrictions are practically unavoidable. And since those restrictions are not disclosed prominently by sellers, consumers can't be expected to account for them in their purchasing decisions. Even before you make a purchase, these harms are often difficult to avoid. Markets for consumer products are often highly concentrated. Choices are limited, and repair restrictions may be commonplace across entire product categories. And again, because design features and company policies that frustrate repair are often hidden, it is difficult for consumers to comparison shop on the basis of reparability. Assuming you could identify a comparable product unfettered by repair restrictions, lock-in often limits consumer choice.[15] If you already own a MacBook, Apple TV, and HomePod; already subscribe to Apple Music, News, Fitness; and already store your backups in iCloud, how likely are you to buy an Android phone? That lack of effective choice makes it hard to avoid the harms of exclusive repair policies. And as a result, the FTC should consider these practices unfair.

In some cases, they might also qualify as deceptive. A deception claim requires proof of: (1) "a representation, omission, or practice that is likely to mislead the consumer" (2) as evaluated from the perspective of a reasonable consumer, and (3) "the representation, omission, or practice must be material."[16]

Most device makers avoid explicit claims about the reparability of their products. Nor do they regularly offer assurances that consumers will be free to repair their devices using the parts and services of their choosing. Nonetheless, language used in the promotion and sale of goods may give rise to an actionable deception claim.[17] For example, French appliance and cookware manufacturer SEB – the maker behind the All-Clad, Krups, Moulinex, and Rowenta brands – markets some products with a ten-year reparability guarantee. It promises that spare parts will be available, and that repairs will be fast and cheaper than a replacement.[18] Firms like SEB deserve praise for prioritizing repair and standing behind the quality of their products. But should a firm cynically tout reparability and fail to make good on its promises, that deception should not go unchallenged. But even without an explicit promise, the omission of material information in advertising or other commercial communications can form the basis of deception.[19] If consumers suffer from misimpressions or false understandings as the result of undisclosed information, they have been misled even if the misunderstanding arises from consumer expectations rather than the seller's affirmative acts.[20]

Survey evidence shows that consumers have strong expectations when it comes to repairing the devices they buy. More than 80 percent believe that they have the right to repair devices themselves or to rely on the repair shop of their choice. That figure is well above the significant minority – roughly 10 or 15 percent of consumers – typically necessary to establish deception.[21] Admittedly, the restrictions firms place on repair are not 100 percent effective. But they do dissuade a significant number of consumers from repair. Others are steered towards more expensive authorized providers. In both cases, firms are acting in ways that are inconsistent with demonstrated consumer expectations.

But perhaps consumers who expect to buy replacement parts directly from Apple or replace the turn signals on their John Deere tractors without paying their local dealer to initialize the new parts are simply unreasonable. Maybe they should have known better. Putting aside the problems with deeming 80 percent of consumers unreasonable, the FTC does evaluate deception claims from the perspective of the reasonable person.[22] In determining what would be deceptive to that hypothetical actor, the Commission weighs the clarity of representations, any conspicuous qualifications, and whether the seller omitted important information. The law acknowledges that advertising and other communications are often susceptible to more than one reasonable interpretation – and where one of those interpretations is misleading, the advertiser is liable. False advertising law, after all, is not intended to protect only the savvy or the skeptical, but also "that vast multitude which includes the ignorant, the unthinking and the credulous."[23]

Not only are repair restrictions misleading, they are material. That is to say, if consumers knew that they would face hurdles to repairing their devices, they would make different choices. Perhaps they would refuse to purchase them at all, or only at a reduced price. For claims that relate to the cost and performance of a product – characteristics that are deeply intertwined with repair – courts presume materiality. Otherwise, materiality hinges on direct evidence like surveys or consumer testimony. Again, the survey evidence strongly supports the notion that repair is material. Roughly 70 percent of US consumers indicated they would be less likely to buy devices – and willing to pay less for them – if they knew the manufacturer restricted repair. And European consumers were more than two times as likely to buy reparable products when given accurate information. And they too would pay a premium for reparable devices.

If repair restrictions are unfair and deceptive, then why haven't these behaviors been targeted? One flaw in federal law is the absence of any private right of action under the FTC Act.[24] So while the Commission itself can enforce the law, consumers don't have a right to sue firms directly to challenge unfair and deceptive practices. Nonetheless, the FTC remains a powerful potential ally for consumers. It is empowered to sue specific firms for violating the law, even for conduct that is prevalent throughout an entire market.[25] In addition to bringing cases against individual firms, the FTC can issue rules and informal guidance that shape industry behavior. And it has fact-finding and investigative authority that could uncover harmful practices and their effect on consumers.[26] Understandably, given the scope of its responsibilities and limited resources, the FTC cannot tackle every area of concern. But repair restrictions, because of their economic and environmental impact, ought to be a much higher priority. The Commission is uniquely positioned to rein in repair restrictions, and it needs to take aggressive action.

But even without the FTC, there are other avenues for pursuing unfairness and deception. All fifty current states, along with the District of Columbia, Puerto Rico, Guam, and the Virgin Islands, have enacted their own laws against unfair and deceptive practices.[27] These statutes typically grant enforcement authority to the state attorney general or consumer-protection agency, but they also allow for claims by private plaintiffs. So, a consumer harmed by a repair restriction can sue the device maker directly. In addition, many states have both common law and statutory protections in place against false advertising. The result is a web of overlapping regimes to address unfair and deceptive business practices. In California, for example, the Unfair Competition Law bans "any unlawful, unfair or fraudulent business act or practice and unfair, deceptive, untrue or misleading advertising."[28] On top of that, the state's False Advertising Law prohibits the publication in advertising of "any statement ... which is untrue or misleading, and which is known, or which by the exercise of reasonable care should be known, to be untrue or misleading."[29] And its Consumer Legal Remedies Act identifies a list of twenty-seven "unfair methods of competition and unfair or deceptive acts or practices," including "[r]epresenting that a transaction confers or involves rights, remedies, or obligations which it does not have or involve."[30] The precise formulation of these laws and the elements necessary to establish liability differ between states, but nonetheless, they offer consumers necessary opportunities to push back on aggressive and misleading policies around repair. These private claims have merit, but plaintiffs and their attorneys don't always have incentive to bring them. Damages for individual plaintiffs can be low, and class actions come with their own set of hurdles. And in many instances, device makers rely on arbitration clauses to keep cases out of court in the first place.

Under the Unfair Commercial Practices Directive, European law provides protections analogous to US law.[31] Article 5 broadly prohibits unfair practices – those that run counter to professional diligence and materially distort consumer behavior. Sellers are required by law to act in good faith and in accordance with honest business practices. Under that standard, article 5 "functions as a 'safety net'" to capture any unfair activity that isn't prohibited elsewhere in the directive.[32] Article 6 bans misleading practices. A practice is considered misleading "if it contains false information . . . or in any way . . . deceives or is likely to deceive the average consumer, even if the information is factually correct."[33] And that false or misleading information must alter consumer behavior. Among other categories, the directive specifically targets misleading communications about "the main characteristics of the product" and "the need for a service, part, replacement or repair."[34]

Omissions can be misleading too. If a manufacturer or seller "omits material information that the average consumer needs" to make an informed decision and, as a result, influences a consumer to buy a product or agree to a deal that they wouldn't have otherwise, that omission violates the law.[35] That prohibition extends to information that is hidden, "unclear, unintelligible, ambiguous or untimely" as well.[36] In short, sellers are obligated to effectively and meaningfully provide consumers with accurate information so they can make informed purchasing decisions.

Whether that standard has been met is a context-sensitive, case-by-case determination. But in an official guidance document, the European Commission advised that planned obsolescence, if undisclosed, may run afoul of the law. As it explained, "a trader who fails to inform the consumer that a product has been designed with a limited lifetime might . . . be considered to have omitted to provide material information."[37] So if the battery in a pair of wireless headphones can't be replaced, for example, the failure to disclose that fact would be unlawful. Likewise, greenwashing – the practice of misstating or understating the environmental impact of a product – can be misleading.[38] Even claims that are accurate in isolation can give rise to misleading implications. For example, an ad highlighting the carbon footprint of electric vehicles that ignores the production stage may mislead consumers, as could a claim touting the recycled aluminum used in laptops that fails to mention the sourcing of other key materials.

Finally, the directive includes a blacklist of thirty-one practices that are illegal *per se*. One is potentially relevant to repair. It's misleading to inaccurately claim that failing to buy a product will expose the consumer or their family to risks to their personal security.[39] As we've seen repeatedly, one of the core justifications device makers offer for cracking down on independent repair, third-party parts, and refurbished devices is that they are unsafe. Unless those claims are reasonably supported by evidence, they are unlawful under European law. Nonetheless, much like their US counterparts, European authorities have failed to bring the full weight of existing consumer-protection law to bear on repair restrictions.

Warranties and Guarantees

Another key function of consumer-protection law is defining and enforcing the terms of warranties or, as they are known in Europe, guarantees. At its core, a warranty is a promise made by the maker or seller of a product. Those promises can be explicit – like when a carmaker guarantees your new vehicle for five years or 60,000 miles, whichever comes first. Or they can be implied. Even without any direct assurance, every seller is assumed under the law to be making certain minimal promises about the quality and characteristics of the goods they sell. Consumer-protection laws give content to those implied promises and offer consumers an avenue to enforce the terms of express warranties.

Implied Warranties and Legal Guarantees

Let's start with implied warranties. Article 2 of the Uniform Commercial Code (UCC) was designed to harmonize state law on the sale of goods. Enacted in every state other than Louisiana, it outlines the implied warranties enjoyed by all purchasers.[40] First, unless otherwise stated, the seller of goods warrants that it owns them and has the right to transfer them free from any competing interest. If you buy a used car from your local dealer, for instance, you shouldn't have to independently confirm that it isn't stolen or subject to a lien.[41] Second, the implied warranty of merchantability means consumers can rest assured that any goods they buy "are of fair average quality" and "fit for ordinary purposes."[42]

Beyond these baseline warranties, states often supplement consumer protections by statute. Every state, for example, has enacted a so-called lemon law. These statutes obligate manufacturers to repair or replace new vehicles if persistent problems arise during a specified period, often the first year after the initial purchase. If those problems can't be repaired in a reasonable time, the buyer can demand a new car or a refund. Perhaps the most ambitious state law of this sort is California's Song-Beverly Consumer Warranty Act.[43] Far broader than most lemon laws, it applies to the sale of goods generally. While the UCC doesn't define the duration of implied warranties, the Song-Beverly Act says they last as long as any express warranty offered with the product, or for one year if the warranty is silent on the question. It also allows consumers to recover double their actual damages if the manufacturer or seller willfully fail to live up to their warranty obligations.

The Act also directly addresses manufacturers' obligations with respect to repair.[44] Regardless of price, device makers are required to maintain service and repair facilities in California – either their own or under contract with third-party providers. Firms are also obligated to maintain a stock of parts available to third-party repair providers. Makers of electronics and appliances with wholesale prices above $50 must make parts and information available for at least three years.[45] For devices over $100 at wholesale, that requirement extends to seven years.[46] Given California's size, the Song-Beverly Act has shaped device-maker policies nationwide. Apple's distinction between vintage and obsolete products, for example, is a byproduct of the seven-year requirement for spare parts.[47]

One court, in an unpublished and non-precedential memorandum, held that these requirements apply only to the manufacturer's own repair facilities and those of authorized partners.[48] That reading is at odds with the plain text of the statute. During the express warranty period – as defined by the manufacturer – it need only provide parts and information to "authorized service and repair facilities."[49] But for the remainder of the three- or seven-year period, once the product is no longer covered by the express warranty, that mandate applies to all "service and repair facilities," not just authorized ones.[50] This makes perfectly good sense. During the express warranty period, the manufacturer is responsible for repairs. But once that period ends, consumers should be free to rely on independent repair providers.

European law offers its own set of default protections for consumers. They parallel those outlined in the UCC but are more robust in notable respects. Goods must be fit for their normal purpose, a standard that incorporates both EU and national law, technical standards, and industry codes of conduct.[51] They should "possess the qualities and other features" consumers would reasonably expect – among them, durability, functionality, and compatibility – and include instructions for installation or repair. And for goods with digital components, sellers must provide any necessary software updates. Like under US law, to the extent the seller knows the goods are meant for some particular purpose, the goods must be suitable.

These obligations last for a minimum of two years.[52] But several states within the European Economic Area have extended them. Under the Norwegian Consumer Law, for instance, default legal guarantees last up to five years, depending on the sort of goods at issue.[53] In Ireland, consumers have up to six years.[54] The burden for making good on these guarantees falls directly on the seller.[55] So if a product fails to conform to these standards, a consumer can simply return it to the retailer who sold it to them. There's no need to take on the often-burdensome task of contacting the manufacturer directly. Once a consumer complains of nonconforming goods, they have the right to choose between repair and replacement, unless that choice would impose disproportionate costs on the seller.[56] Such repairs must be provided for free, within a reasonable period, and "without any significant inconvenience to the consumer."

The right to elect replacement or repair – and the exception for disproportionate costs – reveals the occasional tension between consumer protection and broader environmental concerns. As a matter of convenience and market value, consumers will often be better off with a replacement rather than waiting for a repair. And replacement may be less costly for sellers as well. But that choice externalizes costs, forcing the rest of society to absorb the harms of producing new devices rather than repairing existing ones. A consumer law better aligned with sustainability goals would incentivize the repair remedy, perhaps by forcing sellers and manufacturers to fully internalize the costs of replacing faulty goods.[57]

Express Warranties and Commercial Guarantees

Manufacturers commonly offer express warranties – or commercial guarantees, in the nomenclature of the EU – that supplement these default legal protections. Warranties reassure consumers, giving them confidence that the manufacturer stands behind their product. And in some cases, warranties can be the deciding factor in a purchase. Imagine you're trying to decide between two similarly priced and equipped new cars. One with a seven-year warranty might edge out another with a mere four years of protection. As privately crafted promises, the precise terms of these warranties are left to the companies that draft them. So, whether the warranty on your smartphone covers water damage or lasts for two years or three is up to the device maker. But what kinds of representations create express warranties, what form those warranties take, and when they can be voided are determined by law.

Typically, manufacturer warranties are clearly labeled, written documents. But under the UCC, there's no formal requirement to use any particular magical legal terms. Any affirmation, promise, or description related to the goods that forms part of "the basis of the bargain" is treated as an express warranty.[58] Even samples or models can be understood as express promises about the quality or characteristics of goods.

Federal law outlines some basic formal requirements for express warranties. Under the Magnuson-Moss Warranty Act, any warranty for a product that sells for more than $5 must "fully and conspicuously disclose in simple and readily understood language" its terms.[59] Those disclosures must include, among other information: who is offering the warranty, the products it covers, its duration, the relief available, and the step-by-step process for enforcing the warranty. Manufacturers are also required to clearly label their warranties as either "full" or "limited," depending on their terms.[60] To qualify as a full warranty, the manufacturer must agree to remedy non-conforming products for free and within a reasonable time, grant consumers a refund or replacement if it can't fix the malfunction, and conspicuously communicate any limitations on consequential damages suffered by the consumer.[61] The statute also gives the FTC the power to set rules about making warranties available to consumers prior to a sale.[62]

Similarly, EU law sets out a basic formal and remedial framework for commercial guarantees while leaving their specific provisions in the hands of the firms offering them. Unlike legal guarantees, which apply to sellers, commercial guarantees bind producers.[63] Those guarantees must be "expressed in plain, intelligible language" and delivered with the goods, if not sooner. In addition to the name and address of the manufacturer, a description of the goods covered, and the procedures for making a claim, a commercial guarantee must also clearly explain that the consumer is entitled to remedies from the seller, at no charge, under the standard legal guarantee. If the consumer decides to rely on the commercial guarantee instead, they can still choose between repair and replacement remedies.[64]

One particularly noteworthy issue at the intersection of warranty protections and repair is the widespread practice of voiding, or threatening to void, warranties in the event of independent repair. The Magnuson-Moss Act addresses this concern directly, forbidding manufacturers from conditioning warranty protections on consumers using particular brands of parts or services.[65] That is to say, warranties can't be voided simply because a consumer relies on an independent repair provider or uses a third-party part in their device. As the FTC's guidance puts it, "provisions such as, 'This warranty is void if service is performed by anyone other than an authorized ABC dealer and all replacement parts must be genuine ABC parts,' and the like, are prohibited."[66] There are two exceptions to this rule. First, companies can require specific brands of parts or service where they are available at no cost to the consumer. Second, if the FTC is satisfied that the specific part or service is necessary for the product to function properly, it can grant an exemption. But it never has.[67]

Despite this clear-cut rule, firms frequently threaten consumers with voided warranties if they do so much as open a device without permission. In 2018, the FTC sent letters to six companies – Sony, Microsoft, Nintendo, Hyundai, HTC, and ASUS – admonishing them for applying "warranty void if seal broken" stickers to their products and giving them thirty days to update their warranty policies.[68] A subsequent study revealed that forty-five out of fifty home-appliance companies voided warranties on the basis of independent or self-repair.[69] Those companies – including Dyson, Keurig, LG, Miele, Samsung, and Whirlpool – either prohibited independent repair in their warranties or communicated such restrictions through their customer service teams. These unlawful policies not only limit consumer choice, they interfere with the broader development of competitive markets for parts and repair.

This problem isn't limited to the United States. Australian authorities sued Apple under its Consumer Law after the company refused to service devices that had been independently repaired, imposing a $6.7 million award against the company.[70] In the EU, such refusals violate the Consumer Sales Directive to the extent they interfere with default legal guarantees.[71] And even as applied to commercial guarantees, they may be unfair or misleading.[72]

Extended Warranties and Paid-For Commercial Guarantees

A third variety of warranty deserves mention. In addition to those implied by law and those offered for free by manufacturers, consumers are increasingly opting to pay for extended warranties offered by retailers, manufacturers, and third-party insurers. Whether buying a new car at the local dealer, a tablet from Amazon, or a microwave at the local big-box store, we are inundated with aggressive offers to purchase extended warranties, service plans, or paid-for commercial guarantees. Amazon, for instance, is happy to sell you a new Fire HD Tablet for $95. But when you add it to your cart, you're prompted to spend $25 more for a two-year protection plan. And if you've ever owned a car that's approaching the end of its manufacturer warranty, you've likely been flooded by calls and other solicitations to purchase an extended warranty for thousands of dollars.

The US extended-warranty market is worth tens of billions of dollars annually.[73] As consumers spend more on complex devices prone to various failures and malfunctions, they are eager for the peace of mind that comes from warranty protection. But extended warranties are a risky proposition for consumers. Information about expected product lifespans, planned obsolescence, and the costs of repair and replacement is characterized by asymmetry.[74] Manufacturers – and to a lesser extent, retailers and third-party insurers – have a far better understanding of when a product is likely to fail and how much it will cost to fix it than we do. As a result, they can set prices and warranty terms that all but guarantee profitability. If a firm knows that, on average, its microwaves fail after four years, it will happily sell you a three-year extended warranty. But it would be irrational to offer you one for five years. When you buy an extended warranty, you're essentially betting that your device will die prematurely. If so, other warranty holders will subsidize your repaired or replaced device. But on the whole, consumers are paying more for extended warranties than the companies providing them are paying out. Otherwise, they wouldn't sell them in the first place.

The lack of consistent consumer protections in the extended warranty market only compounds the risks facing purchasers. Despite their name, extended warranties aren't actually considered warranties under US law.[75] As a result, the core provisions of the Magnuson-Moss Warranty Act don't apply.[76] Nor do the UCC's warranty protections, since extended warranties are treated as contractual agreements separate from the underlying sale.[77] In many instances, extended warranties are governed by state insurance laws, which vary considerably.[78] The situation is somewhat different in Europe, where paid-for commercial guarantees are subject to the same basic framework as other express warranties.[79] But there too, the specific rules vary between member states.[80] This absence of clear, consistent legal rules only exacerbates the information asymmetries consumers face. Just like product durability and repair costs, firms offering extended warranties are much better positioned than the average consumer to understand the laws, rules, and regulations that shape these relationships.

By setting minimal, default protections, warranty law does important work in safeguarding consumers from faulty products and providing an avenue for necessary repairs. But as currently structured, it can't fully account for the degree of control companies have over durability, reparability, and planned obsolescence. That's particularly true when the functionality of devices is controlled by software, a description that fits an ever-increasing share of goods. To effectively push back on manufacturer's control over our devices, more targeted interventions are necessary.

Protecting Consumers from Planned Obsolescence

In the overwhelming majority jurisdictions, there is no obvious legal remedy for planned obsolescence. The court in *Tatum v. Chrysler*, one of the handful of US cases to even mention the practice, summarized the prevailing attitude to planned obsolescence under the law.[81] There, plaintiffs filed a class action against Chrysler for allegedly designing the Dodge Journey with brakes that required frequent, expensive repairs – despite ads that claimed the vehicle was durable and reliable. As the court explained, "planned obsolescence, either deliberately or accidentally engineered, is not actionable." So long as "the brakes outlasted their sales warranty even by a day or a mile," the manufacturer met its legal obligation.

In response to the seeming indifference to planned obsolescence under existing consumer-protection law, legislators and regulators have proposed tackling the practice head on. Belgium, Germany, and Italy have all entertained prohibitions against planned obsolescence in recent years, although none were enacted.[82] But in 2015, France became the first country to outlaw planned obsolescence. The Hamon Law, named for the minister who proposed it, defines planned obsolescence as "the use of techniques by which the person who places a product on the market aims to deliberately reduce its lifespan in order to increase its replacement rate."[83] The practice is flatly prohibited, although proving the required degree of intent may be difficult. Violations are punishable by a fine of €300,000, which can be increased to up to 5 percent of annual sales, and two years in prison for company officials.[84]

In 2017, the nonprofit Halte à l'Obsolescence Programmée filed complaints with France's Directorate General for Competition, Consumer Affairs and Fraud Control, alleging that Apple and Epson had engaged in planned obsolescence. The government launched investigations against both firms. The case against Epson alleges that the firm's printers falsely indicate that ink cartridges are empty and refuse to operate until they are replaced.[85] The Apple investigation focused on software updates that slowed the performance of iPhones. In early 2020, Apple avoided trial by agreeing to pay a $27 million fine.[86] Later that year, a third complaint alleging planned obsolescence was filed against Nintendo for its faulty Switch controllers.[87]

France's stance against planned obsolescence is an important step forward. It recognizes the unavoidable convergence of consumer protection and environmental regulation. Given the catastrophic global impact of our production and consumption of devices, consumer law can no longer confine itself to merely making sure buyers get a fair bargain. That goal, of course, remains valuable. But what counts as fair, and the methods we rely on to achieve fairness, have to be informed by a fuller appreciation of the ways companies profit at our expense, both individually and collectively. The Hamon Law reflects that understanding. At the same time, it demonstrates the potential for direct, aggressive legal rules that target abusive practices by device makers. Interventions of that sort will be necessary, but not sufficient, to rebuild a market and a culture that supports repair.

8 REBUILDING REPAIR

We've seen the many barriers that stand in the way of repair. Firms design products that are hard to fix, adopt policies that deter competition, and craft marketing messages that distort consumer preferences. And although law offers some important tools to push back on these behaviors, too often it enables and excuses the antirepair agenda. Given the stakes for our economic wellbeing, our collective interest in the planet, and our control over our daily lives, we need to find strategies to restore repair to its rightful, historical place in human culture. The era of planned obsolescence is a recent departure from a tradition of repair stretching back millions of years. As long as we've had technology, we've repaired it. It's only in the last century that repair has been under threat – not coincidentally, a century during which we've inflicted damage to our planet that imperils our long-term survival.

By studying the ways firms try to manipulate our behavior, we have a roadmap for responding. The same tools they enlist to stifle repair can be used to reinvigorate it. Laws can be rewritten, markets reorganized, designs reconfigured, and norms reshaped. In 2020, the Australian Productivity Commission, an advisory body housed within the Department of the Treasury, launched an inquiry into the right to repair and its effects on consumers and competition. In its initial assessment, the Commission identified an assortment of potential policy interventions – from tax incentives and spare-part mandates to design standards and warranty protections.[1] Implicit in this approach is an understanding that addressing the various threats facing repair demands a range of interventions. This final chapter will outline the steps needed to rebuild a culture of repair.

The Drivers of Repair Decisions

To bring about effective change, we need a clearer understanding of how consumers think about repair. When they decide to replace rather than repair a broken smartphone or household appliance, what drives that decision? We've delved into the designs, policies, and laws that shape repair at a level of detail that is largely unfamiliar to the average consumer. So, we need to see things from their perspective if we hope to influence them. When we ask consumers about their repair decisions, what we find is that they are open to fixing their broken devices but are often dissuaded by repairs that are either too expensive or inconvenient.

In my survey of US smartphone and tablet owners, 86 percent said they had "replaced, discarded, or recycled" one.[2] Consumers got rid of their devices for many reasons. Some simply wanted a new one. But cracked screens and dead batteries – two easily reparable problems – were by far the most prevalent reasons. Respectively 56 and 49 percent cited faulty screens and batteries as contributing to their choice to replace a device. Consumers identified a host of other reparable hardware issues, ranging from internal storage to cameras, that led them to replace devices.

Despite the prevalence of replacement among US consumers, interest in repair was high. Among those who had replaced, discarded, or recycled a smartphone or tablet, 92 percent had considered or attempted some form of repair.[3] Half considered or attempted independent repair services, compared to 48 percent for manufacturer repair, and 44 percent for self-repair. But when asked about their experience with repair, consumers highlighted two primary problems. More than half said repairs were too expensive, and 24 percent reported that the necessary parts and tools were unavailable. Trade-in programs were another important factor influencing consumer behavior. The majority reported receiving or being offered credit on a new device in exchange for a damaged or broken one. Of those consumers, 78 percent were "much more" or "somewhat more willing" to buy a new device, and 38 percent were less interested in repairing their device as a result.

So, what can we conclude from these responses? They strongly suggest that consumers are open to and interested in repairing their devices. But cost and the availability of parts and tools are significant roadblocks. Those two hurdles are deeply intertwined. For third-party repair providers, the scarcity of replacement parts is a significant contributor to the overall cost of repair. If parts were more readily available and prices lower, as we would expect in a more competitive environment, we would see more consumers opting for repairs.

These findings are largely consistent with the European Commission's *Behavioural Study on Consumers' Engagement in the Circular Economy*. When asked why they didn't repair vacuum cleaners, dishwashers, TVs, and mobile phones, the most common answer – from 34 to 50 percent – was that repair is too expensive. In addition, that study included an experiment designed to better understand how factors other than price play into repair decisions. Consumers were presented with a broken, out-of-warranty product and asked to decide whether to repair or replace it. Within the experiment, repairs cost about 25 percent of the original purchase price, replacing with a used device cost 70 percent, and a new replacement cost 120 percent. These prices, although only a rough estimate of real-world conditions, allowed the experimenters to measure two other variables.

First, the level of effort required varied. This effort served as a proxy for the many nonprice costs of repair, like searching for a repair provider, comparing options, and dropping off and picking up the device. For some consumers, neither repair nor replacement required any effort. They simply chose the option they preferred. For others, repair required effort, but replacement didn't. If they wanted to choose repair, they were forced to input the phone number of the repair provider and the serial number of the device – information supplied to them by the experimenters. And for a third group, the dynamic was reversed. Replacement required effort, but repair did not.

Here's what they found. Depending on the product, between 62 and 83 percent of European consumers elected to repair their products in the experiment. But when the level of effort was increased, the experimenters found a significant decline in repairs. When repair is less convenient, fewer people do it. Rather disconcertingly, the same was not true for replacement. When the effort needed to replace a product increased, there was no notable drop in replacement. So, repair is sensitive to higher transaction costs, but replacement appears to be relatively immune.

Second, the experiment tested how much it mattered to consumers who was doing the repairs and the source of the parts they used. Some consumers were told the repairs would be made by the manufacturer, while others were told an independent repair shop would do the work. In addition, some were told only original parts would be used, while others were told the repair would include both original and nonoriginal parts. Despite manufacturers' efforts to convince consumers that in-house repairs are superior, consumers were just as happy to have their devices fixed by an independent repair shop as they were to rely on the manufacturer. The same was largely true of original and nonoriginal parts, with only minor discrepancies between the repair rates under those two conditions. This openness to repair likely reflects consumers' real-world experiences. Of those who had paid for repair services in the past, more than 70 percent were satisfied with the "convenience, speed, quality and friendliness" of the repair shop. In fact, a 2014 survey of nearly 30,000 readers of Consumer Reports found that those who turned to independent repair services were more satisfied than those who relied on manufacturers.[4]

The evidence is clear that a significant percentage of consumers are already open to repair. But price, convenience, and availability remain key barriers. If we want consumers to embrace repair more often, we need to focus on interventions that make it less costly, both in terms of out-of-pocket expenses and transaction costs. So competitive markets for parts and services are necessary. But so is readily available information about reparability. With those goals in mind, we return to the four mechanisms for regulating behavior first outlined in Chapter 4: law, markets, design, and norms. Although overlaps between them are unavoidable, each of these approaches offers promising potential solutions that could help restore our ability to repair the things we buy.

Changing Law

We've already discussed several laws that either support or fail to adequately discipline repair restrictions. Reforms to those existing laws would help clear the way for repair. To name just a few: § 1201 of the Digital Millennium Copyright Act should be significantly narrowed or repealed outright; the standards for design patentability should be heightened to exclude protection for replacement parts, especially those that offer some functional advantage; and antitrust law should more aggressively target tying and other practices that undermine aftermarket competition. Repair aside, there are good reasons for supporting each of these changes, whether through legislative reform or judicial construction. But in light of the multitude of strategies firms can deploy against repair, reforming existing law likely won't be enough. We will need targeted legislation designed to enable and promote repair.

US lawmakers have proposed new laws focusing on repair, but with limited success so far. As early as 2001, the Motor Vehicle Owners Right to Repair Act sought to eliminate restrictions on vehicle repair.[5] The most recent version of the bill, introduced in 2011, would have required carmakers to provide owners and service providers information, tools, and equipment necessary "to diagnose, service, maintain, or repair the motor vehicle."[6] But the proposal failed to gain traction in Congress. More recently, the Promoting Automotive Repair, Trade, and Sales (PARTS) Act was introduced in 2017.[7] It would have created a new defense to design-patent infringement claims, exempting the making, selling, or importing of exterior components of motor vehicles for repair purposes.[8] But the PARTS Act stalled in committee.

In 2020, Senator Ron Wyden and Representative Yvette Clarke introduced the Critical Medical Infrastructure Right-to-Repair Act.[9] In response to the challenges hospitals and other healthcare providers faced repairing and maintaining ventilators and other equipment during the pandemic, this bill would have shielded them from liability and imposed obligations on manufacturers to make certain information and tools available. The bill included three exceptions under federal intellectual property (IP) law. First, it would have permitted the copying of service manuals, schematics, and diagnostic software. Second, it would have allowed both the circumvention of digital rights management (DRM) to enable repair, as well as the creation, importation, and provision of any tools necessary for circumvention. And third, it gave healthcare providers the right to fabricate design-patented repair parts for critical equipment. Beyond the IP provisions, the bill would have nullified any contractual provision that restricted repair. It also required manufacturers of critical medical equipment to provide tools and information to equipment owners, lessees, and service providers on reasonable terms, vesting the Federal Trade Commission (FTC) with authority to enforce these requirements.

Although it applied to a narrow class of devices and circumstances, the bill's sweeping substantive provisions are a model for aggressive legal intervention to restore repair. They should be extended to the full range of products, from consumer electronics to industrial equipment. Wyden and Clarke recognized the immediate need for repair in response to an acute healthcare crisis. But in an economy dependent on global supply chains, we can't predict what the next disruptive crisis will be. War, political unrest, draught, flooding, and cyberattack can all put critical systems at risk. Rather than scrambling to respond to the next calamity, we should proactively build resiliency into not only healthcare, but our transportation, agriculture, and communications infrastructures as well. At the same time, we have to recognize that we are already living in the midst of an ongoing, global environmental crisis that, on its own, justifies new legal rules to promote repair.

Turning to enacted statutes, France's Hamon Law is the current benchmark. In addition to its ban on planned obsolescence, the law contains provisions directed specifically to repair. It classifies reparability as an essential product characteristic and bans any technique used by a firm to limit repair to approved providers.[10] Likewise, it prohibits any agreement or practice that limits repair providers' access to parts, instructions, equipment, or software needed for repair.[11] Violations of these provisions carry the same penalties as the planned obsolescence ban – a fine of at least €300,000 and as much as 5 percent of annual revenue, as well as a two-year prison term.[12] The Hamon Law's approach to repair involves a very big stick, but it's not without its carrots. One worry device makers voice is the risk that they will be held liable if a self-repair goes wrong. The law addresses that concern. As long as the manufacturer provides adequate safety instructions, it can't be held responsible for damage caused by the user's "clumsiness" or their failure to follow directions.[13]

There are promising signs that France will not be alone for long. In November 2020, the European Parliament passed a resolution that called for the creation of "a genuine right of repair in Europe," reflecting a desire to "stamp out practices which prevent or hinder product repairs."[14] To achieve that, it calls on the European Commission to establish rules giving consumers and repair providers free access to "diagnostic tools, spare parts, software and updates." Beyond that, it would require producers to supply spare parts for defined periods of time and insist that those parts be sold for reasonable prices and delivered promptly. If implemented, these changes would redefine the legal status of repair throughout Europe and potentially reshape attitudes and practices across the globe.

In the United States, since Congress has so far proven inhospitable to repair legislation, the legislative effort has largely shifted to the state level. Rather than flat prohibitions on repair restrictions, these bills have focused primarily on promoting competition by requiring manufacturers to share information and tools. Initially, these bills targeted automotive repair. In 2012, Massachusetts enacted a law that requires manufacturers of motor vehicles to "make available for purchase by owners . . . and by independent repair facilities the same diagnostic and repair information" as well as "all diagnostic repair tools" made available to dealers, on "fair and reasonable terms."[15] Carmakers must also "provide access to their onboard diagnostic and repair information system . . . using an off-the-shelf personal computer" beginning with 2018 model year vehicles.[16] Although the bill passed in July of 2012, a ballot initiative enacting similar right-to-repair obligations was already slated for the November election. Massachusetts voters overwhelmingly supported the initiative, with 86 percent voting in favor.[17]

The Massachusetts law was soon adopted as a de facto national standard. In January of 2014, industry associations representing carmakers and repair providers entered into a nationwide agreement to operate under the terms of the Massachusetts legislation.[18] This voluntary arrangement, however, does not operate with the force of law. It does not bind nonparties like Tesla, and alleged violations are evaluated by a dispute resolution panel composed of members of the various trade associations and a mediator.[19]

Nor did the agreement anticipate the changes in technology that have reshaped the automotive-repair market in the years since. Today, telematics systems collect vehicle-performance data and wirelessly transmit it to manufacturers and dealers.[20] Without access to that data, independent repair providers are at a serious disadvantage. So, in 2020, Massachusetts voters approved another automotive-repair measure, again by an overwhelming majority, to force carmakers to provide telematics data to owners and repair shops.[21] They did so despite an egregious misinformation campaign launched by the auto industry. Carmakers spent more than $25 million against the effort, including one television ad that claimed if the measure passed, "a sexual predator could use the data to stalk their victims," an assertion that experts quickly debunked.[22] After the measure passed, the Alliance for Automotive Innovation, an industry lobbying group, filed a lawsuit to undo the will of the voters.[23]

Beyond motor vehicles, the original Massachusetts repair law has served as the template for a broader, nationwide effort to enshrine consumers' right to repair in state law. Building on its success, a coalition of policy advocates, repair professionals, tinkerers, and everyday consumers has pushed for legislation that would recognize the right to repair consumer electronics – not only smartphones, laptops, and televisions, but also household appliances, wearable technology, farm equipment, and medical devices. In 2014, the South Dakota legislature considered the first of these bills.[24] In 2021, right-to-repair bills had been introduced in twenty-seven of the fifty statehouses across the country.[25]

These bills closely track a model proposal from the Repair Association, an umbrella organization representing repair providers, advocates, hobbyists, and environmental activists.[26] The key provision of the model law would require manufacturers of digital electronics to "make available, for purposes of diagnosis, maintenance, or repair, to any independent repair provider, or to the owner of digital electronic equipment ... on fair and reasonable terms, documentation, parts, and tools, inclusive of any updates to information or embedded software."[27] And for equipment protected by electronic security measures, manufacturers must "make available ... any special documentation, tools, and parts needed to reset the lock or function when disabled in the course of diagnosis, maintenance, or repair."[28] By making parts, tools, and information available to owners and repair providers on reasonable terms, these bills would clear some of the major obstacles that impede independent repair today.

But one important shortcoming is the absence of any requirement for device makers to actually produce replacement parts. The model bill provides, "[n]othing in this section requires an original equipment manufacturer to make available a part if the part is no longer available to the original equipment manufacturer."[29] So, if a firm decides to phase out support for a product after only a couple of years, it has no obligation to make parts available to the third-party repair market. A more stringent approach, consistent with California's Song-Beverly Act, would insist that firms supply parts for at least seven years, or perhaps longer where appropriate.[30]

These state-level repair bills have attracted a diverse constellation of supporters, including the American Farm Bureau,[31] the Illinois Health and Hospital Association,[32] the *New York Times* editorial board,[33] the *American Conservative*,[34] Bernie Sanders,[35] and Elizabeth Warren.[36] Despite this support and proponents' considerable success in persuading state legislators to introduce these bills, none have been enacted yet. But given the intense antirepair lobbying the bills have provoked, that failure is unfortunately predictable. The companies condemning right-to-repair proposals – occasionally publicly, but more often behind closed doors – include Apple, AT&T, Caterpillar, Dyson, GE Healthcare, John Deere, Lexmark, LG, Medtronic, Microsoft, Toyota, Verizon, and Wahl.[37] Add to that partial list trade associations and industry groups like AdvaMed, the Entertainment Software Association, the Equipment Dealers Association, and TechNet that lobby against repair bills on behalf of their members.[38]

Aside from predictably overstated concerns over intellectual property, these firms and their trade associations offered an assortment of alarmist arguments to undermine support for right-to-repair legislation. Apple told Nebraska lawmakers that the bill would turn the state into a "Mecca for bad actors," predicting that hackers and other nefarious figures would flock to the state to exploit consumers.[39] And in California, it warned that consumers were at risk of physical injury if they attempted to swap out their iPhone batteries.[40] Wahl cautioned that repair of its hair clippers could cause fires, while Dyson and LG issued unfounded warnings that the right to repair could put consumers' personal safety at risk by allowing repair personnel in their homes who had not cleared background checks.[41]

Device makers also raise the specter of privacy violations and security breaches, warning that handing your device over to "unvetted third parties" could have "troubling unintended consequences."[42] Putting aside the fact that repair technicians often can't access your data to begin with, there is scant reason to trust the "authorized" employee at the local Best Buy any more than you do the proprietor of an independent repair shop. And as the team of security experts who created Securepairs attest, independent repair would "reduce the likelihood of attacks" by increasing the chances that vulnerabilities are identified and addressed.[43]

John Deere and its friends in the heavy equipment industry have tried to convince lawmakers that recognizing farmers' right to repair their tractors will open the door to "tampering" and violations of federal emissions standards. As Dennis Slater, president of the Association of Equipment Manufacturers argued, "If criminals tamper with the equipment's back-end code, it poses dangerous safety and emissions threats to the public."[44] This cynical effort to use environmental concerns to defend repair restrictions is consistent with the industry's effort to weaponize pollution regulations.[45] The Environmental Protection Agency (EPA) enforces emissions limits on industrial equipment. But once those devices are sold, manufacturers have no ongoing responsibility for ensuring their compliance. That responsibility falls on the operator. Nonetheless, Deere builds its tractors to detect noncompliant emissions. The onboard software switches the tractor into "limp mode," which all but immobilizes them until an authorized technician can solve the problem.[46] The equipment industry argues that the right to repair would allow farmers to tamper with these systems in violation of federal law. But the EPA itself recognizes that repairing or modifying your equipment is lawful, so long as you "restore it to proper functioning." And to the extent farmers engage in actual tampering, that activity wouldn't be protected under right-to-repair laws. In the end, the industry's crocodile tears about emissions and tampering are just another way to squeeze more money out of farmers.

Somewhat more plausibly, medical-device manufacturers and their trade groups have raised safety concerns around repair. AdvaMed, a medical-device trade group, warned law-makers that proposed repair legislation "could result in main-tenance and repairs of medical devices being performed by untrained personnel, and that inappropriate replacement parts may be used."[47] Likewise, GE Healthcare's letter to New Hampshire legislators claimed that the state's bill would "require manufacturers of Food and Drug Administration (FDA) Class I and II medical devices to provide proprietary diag-nostic and repair information to unregulated service providers."[48] The implication is clear: third parties cannot be trusted to repair medical devices. But according to a recent FDA report, "the continued availability of third-party entities to ser-vice and repair medical devices is critical to the functioning of the US healthcare system."[49] As the FDA explained, many third-party repair providers deliver "high quality, safe, and effective servicing of medical devices."[50] And a recent survey found that two-thirds of medical repair technicians managed to fix devices that the manufacturer couldn't.[51] The importance of those third-party repairs was illustrated when Los Angeles received 170 broken ventilators in the midst of the COVID-19 crisis. Rather than shipping them back to the manufacturer, California turned to Bloom Energy, a firm that makes fuel-cell energy generators. Bloom successfully repaired the ventilators in a matter of days.[52]

Legal interventions – whether bans on repair restrictions or obligations to provide parts and documentation – could have a profound impact on the availability and cost of repair. Admittedly, legislation is hard to pass. Political inertia is a powerful force. And given the immense disparity in resources between repair advocates and the companies invested in the status quo, convincing legislators to stand up for consumers and independent repair shops will require sustained and concen-trated effort. But a legal right to repair enjoys broad popular support. When asked if they support "legal rules that require device makers to provide parts, tools, software updates, and documentation available to independent repair shops and con-sumers on reasonable terms," 86 percent of consumers said yes –

the same percentage of voters who favored the Massachusetts law in 2012.[53] And nearly 60 percent strongly supported such measures. Among those who described themselves as "very familiar" with the idea of the right to repair, support shot up to an astounding 98 percent. But for most consumers, the right to repair remains unfamiliar. Far from discouraging, that fact suggests an untapped reservoir of potential popular support. If the legislative process is genuinely responsive to the will of the public, eventually the right to repair will be law.

Changing Markets

Markets are powerful regulators of behavior. As prices go up, demand declines. A steep tax on cigarettes, for example, is one way to deter people from smoking.[54] Conversely, rebates and other financial incentives on renewable energy help drive adoption of those technologies.[55] But shifting price isn't the only way to influence the market. Despite the assumptions of neoclassical economics, consumers almost never have perfect information about their purchases. So, their decisions are swayed, at least in part, by misunderstanding, speculation, and sometimes downright deception. Researching every salient fact about a new purchase demands time and effort that consumers are rarely able to invest. Dogs need to be walked, kids need help with their homework, and Netflix isn't going to watch itself. But if we make material information easier to find, we can change consumer behavior simply by giving them a more complete understanding of their options. Once we learn that lead paint causes brain damage or that plastic straws kill sea turtles, we may be more open to alternatives. Finally, consumer behavior turns on the mix of goods and services available in the market. Introducing new alternatives can reshape the choices we make. Think of the way ride-hailing apps like Uber and Lyft changed, for better or worse, how we navigate our cities.

So how might we alter costs to encourage repair? One relatively simple method is leveraging the tax system to reduce the effective price of repair. Austria and Sweden have both cut their value-added tax (VAT) for repairs, slashing the rate consumers pay by at least half.[56] In the US, most states charge consumers sales tax on both replacement parts and repair services. Those taxes could be reduced or eliminated, persuading consumers to repair rather than replace, at least on the margins. At the federal level, Congress could offer tax deductions or credits for repairs. The Internal Revenue Code is already a tool for social engineering, creating incentives for a range of behavior deemed socially valuable – buying a home, borrowing money for college, bearing children, and driving fuel-efficient vehicles, to name a few. The policy rationale for repair incentives is stronger, and the impact on the budget smaller, than many existing tax deductions and credits.

Subsidizing repair is a more direct alternative. A number of Austrian states and cities offer "repair bonuses" that cover as much as 50 percent of the cost of repairs.[57] And in 2020, France launched a program that offers individuals €50 to spend on professional bike repairs in an effort to reduce traffic.[58] In the United States, state and federal subsidies are sometimes available to defray the costs of home or auto repairs, but those programs have strict income limits and are drastically underfunded.[59] Expansive subsidy programs, however, are far from unheard of. In 2017, fossil-fuel subsidies cost US taxpayers $649 billion.[60] And in 2019, US farmers received $22 billion in subsidies, in large part to compensate for the Trump administration's failed trade policies.[61] Occasionally though, the government has offered smaller-scale subsidies directly to consumers. When Congress decided to force television broadcasters to switch from analog to digital signals in 2005, it authorized $1.5 billion to fund the purchase of analog-to-digital converter boxes, allowing those with older televisions to continue receiving broadcast signals.[62] Every household in the country could request up to two $40 coupons for the purchase of set-top boxes. Although the program was motivated by spectrum policy, it had the added benefit of preventing the untimely scrapping of millions of televisions. At similar levels of spending, a targeted repair subsidy could have a significant impact on the pollution and waste that flow from planned obsolescence.

Accounting for hidden costs is another way to shift the market towards repair. Generally, we trust that consumer behavior is a good indicator of our values and preferences. How people spend their money gives us a window, albeit an imperfect one, into what they care about. But hidden costs obscure that view, making it harder to draw inferences about what really matters to consumers. Externalities are one form of hidden cost. If neither buyer nor seller have to account for costs that flow from a transaction, they get passed on to others. So, we can't be confident of how consumers would react if they had to reckon fully with them. As we've already seen, the environmental harms of short-lived consumer goods are precisely this sort of externality. One way to recalibrate the market is by forcing the parties to a sale to internalize those costs. If the price of new smartphones or refrigerators reflected their hidden costs, demand would wane. Imposing an excise tax that estimates the environmental impact of a refrigerator with a cheap sticker price, but low levels of durability or reparability would steer consumers towards higher-quality goods and give manufacturers an incentive to build for the long term.

EU law already recognizes extended producer responsibility (EPR) – the notion that producers ought to bear the financial burden of the harms their products impose.[63] Electronic waste, product packaging, and vehicles that have reached the end of their useful lives all inflict environmental costs on society broadly.[64] EPR schemes are designed to force producers to internalize those costs. By taking responsibility for collecting, recycling, and properly disposing of waste, firms are forced to factor those costs into their retail prices. So, consumers are confronted, at least indirectly, with the costs of their choices. We could imagine these systems explicitly accounting for repair. Firms that make longer-lasting, more reparable products would contribute less to an EPR program than those that built disposable devices.

Importantly though, not all hidden costs are externalities. Some are borne directly by buyers. That's true for repair restrictions. Too often, consumers don't make a purchase with an eye towards the eventuality of breakdown and failure. They are too focused on new functionality, features, or fashions to give much thought to what will happen if their new toy breaks at some indeterminate point in the future. Will replacement parts be available at a reasonable price? Is the device user-reparable, or will it require a professional? The typical consumer never asks these questions until it's too late. But if that information was readily available and prominently communicated, they would be more inclined to consider it, enabling better-informed decisions. And there's good reason to suspect that, armed with that information, more of us would choose reparability.

Private actors have made major efforts to increase transparency about reparability. For years, iFixit has scored new products on a 1–10 scale on the basis of detailed device tear downs.[65] From smartphones and laptops to game consoles and headphones, iFixit offers interested consumers a clear, accessible assessment of how hard it is to fix a product. Devices that are glued together or require complex disassembly procedures get low scores; those that are easy to open up and come with detailed service manuals earn high scores. As helpful as it is, iFixit's reparability scores aren't perfect. The precise formula used to calculate them isn't publicly available, they turn partly on subjective factors, and they don't fully account for the availability and cost of replacement parts. Those critiques aside, iFixit offers perhaps the most useful tool available for consumers who want to assess the reparability of electronic devices. But unfortunately, most aren't aware of it.

A more effective solution would put reparability information in front of consumers in an easily digestible format at the point of purchase. One option is a certification mark. If you want to communicate that your potatoes are really from Idaho, that your coffee is genuinely organic and fair trade, or that your smoke detectors meet the standards set by Underwriters Laboratories, now simply UL, a certification mark can do the trick. Under US law, certification marks function in much the same way as trademarks, except they don't indicate the source of goods. Instead, they tell consumers that products bearing the mark meet certain criteria.[66] A company like iFixit could allow device makers to include an iFixit Seal of Reparability on the packaging and advertising of qualifying products. Over time, consumers might come to prefer products bearing the seal to those that don't. But certification marks are purely voluntary. Firms are under no obligation to include the mark even if their product qualifies. And they certainly aren't required to disclose that their device fell short of the mark.

Overcoming that problem requires a compulsory labeling system, one that insists on a prominent reparability score for every product, good or bad. Experts have devised standards for measuring and communicating reparability.[67] But none were required by law until France introduced its mandatory labeling system early in 2021. That system looks at five basic criteria: documentation, like manuals, technical bulletins, and self-repair instructions; the disassembly process, including the number of steps, tools required, and types of fasteners used; access to spare parts, delivery times, and availability to independent providers; the price of spare parts; and various considerations specific to the product type.[68] Based on points awarded under each criterion, a final score between 0 and 10 is calculated. That score, reported in a graphic like the one below, must be included on packaging and advertising for a range of products, starting with laptops, lawn mowers, smartphones, televisions, and washing machines. (See Figure 5.)

The French reparability index, while groundbreaking, isn't immune from criticism.[69] Troublingly, scores are calculated by device makers based on self-reported and self-interested assessments of their products. Admittedly, conducting an independent evaluation of every consumer device on the market would be an expensive undertaking. So as a compromise position, manufacturers are required to publish a detailed scoring protocol for each product. Consumers, competitors, and other organizations can then scrutinize their claims.

INDICE DE RÉPARABILITÉ

Figure 5 An example of France's mandatory reparability labeling

A second worry is that, regardless of who does the scoring, the index is too forgiving. Like many grad school courses, it's hard to earn a failing grade. For smartphones and laptops, merely providing information about software updates – whether they are bug fixes, security patches, or upgrades – earns a product a full point on the index. The ability to reset the device's operating system and firmware ups the score by another half point. As a result, scores on the index tend to be closely clustered.

This sort of grade inflation is troubling for at least three reasons. First, it makes it harder for consumers to accurately compare products. If the effective range of the index is narrow, a gap of half a point may look trivial. But with compressed scores, it could represent a significant difference in reparability. Second, inflated numbers might mislead consumers about the reparability of specific devices. Say you're shopping for a new washing machine. You see a reparability score of 6.1 and think, "Not bad. On a scale of 0–10, that's better than most." But in reality, that's the lowest scoring washing machine on the market. That sense of overconfidence is reinforced by the reparability index's color-coding system. Scores of 8–10 earn a dark-green logo; those from 6–7.9 are light green; 4–5.9 are yellow; 2–3.9 are orange, and 0–1.9 are red. So, an iPhone 11, which scores an abysmal 4.6 bears a far-from-alarming yellow label. Finally, this lax standard is at odds with the goal of sparking competition among manufacturers to build more reparable devices. Without clearer distinctions, manufacturers have strong incentives to maintain whatever level of reparability consumers see as "good enough." If a 6.1 earns you a light-green label, why strive for more?

To be fair, the reparability index is new, and it will almost certainly evolve over time. Updating the scoring rubric and tweaking the way scores are presented are relatively straightforward changes that could be implemented in the years to come. At the same time, device makers will be motivated to water down the system, reducing its value to the public. So, consumers and their advocates will need to remain engaged in the push for more rigorous standards.

Another opportunity for reform may come if France's pioneering efforts are subsumed by broader EU-wide measures. As part of its November 2020 right-to-repair resolution, the European Parliament endorsed mandating "clear and easily legible" disclosures about reparability, including information about the price and availability of spare parts. If those recommendations are implemented, the successes and challenges of the French reparability index will offer valuable lessons.

There's one more way that the market could alter incentives for repair. Ultimately, what drives repair restrictions is the desire among firms to sell us more stuff. Devices that work forever or are easy to repair are bad for business. So, firms continue to crank out products with limited lifespans that are inherently hostile to repair. But shifting the costs of short-lived devices from consumers to manufacturers might reverse those incentives. One strategy for doing that is moving away from selling products at all. Over the last two decades, we've seen the ascendency of business models built around access, not ownership.[70] In the business-to-business sector, these arrangements are nothing new. Rolls Royce's Power by the Hour program, which priced jet engines by the time customers spent in the air, dates to the early 1960s.[71] More recently, Philips launched its Pay-per-lux offering. Rather than selling lightbulbs and fixtures, the company offers customers the service of lighting their offices.[72] And the bulk of Amazon's profits comes from selling scalable web services to companies that would rather not purchase their own servers and data centers.[73]

More recently, those trends made their way to the consumer market. Why own a record collection when you can just pay Spotify a few dollars a month? Why buy Photoshop when Adobe offers a subscription plan? And why purchase video games when Microsoft, Sony, Nintendo, Google, and Apple are all happy to provide you a package of downloadable or streaming titles for a low monthly fee? These trends, as I explored with my co-author Jason Schultz in our 2016 book *The End of Ownership*, have profoundly reconfigured our relationship with the products we use every day – in many respects, for the worse. But the appeal of rental and subscription models is easy to understand. They offer flexibility, portability, and variety. And they typically require smaller upfront investments.

So, it's no surprise to see this business model make the leap from digital media to physical products. Clothing subscription services like Rent the Runway and Armoire let you refresh your wardrobe without buying any clothes. Startups like Feather and Fernish offer subscription furniture rental. Even established retailers like Ikea are exploring rental models.[74] And Bosch recently announced its Papillon program, which will put new appliances in the homes of low-income families for about €9 per month.[75]

In theory, this shift from consumer ownership to temporary access could encourage firms to invest in durability and reparability.[76] If your rented couch falls apart or your subscription dishwasher malfunctions, it's up to the manufacturer or rental service to bear that cost – assuming those risks haven't been allocated to the consumer through the terms of service. If producers have to foot the bill for repairs, they may learn to embrace the virtues of long-lasting products that are easy to fix. Think about ski rentals. Resorts have strong incentives to keep their rental skis in good working order for as long as possible. They invest in routine maintenance and repair. And they are more likely to buy skis that are built to last and are relatively easy to repair. But the economics of ski rentals are atypical. Equipment rental is an ancillary consideration for resorts. They aren't in the ski rental business. They sell lodging, dining, and lift tickets. And those services subsidize ski repair. Although this might change as companies like Apple shift towards offering digital services, device makers today are in the business of selling hardware, a goal that remains in tension with repair.

More generally, we ought to be deeply skeptical of the turn towards subscription access for a host of reasons. First, the economic proposition may not be as beneficial to consumers as it appears. Firms are not investing in subscription models out of some principled desire to reduce waste or internalize environmental harms. They are doing it because they think it will be more profitable. Consumers pay a premium for rental. Bosch's Papillon program is pitched as an exercise in "social commitment," but the numbers tell a different story. A new Series 6 Bosch washing machine costs about €599. Over the ten-year rental period envisioned by the Papillon program, the €9 monthly charge adds up to €1,080. And at the end of that decade, having paid nearly twice the retail price, the consumer owns nothing. They either need to buy a new machine or rent another. This arithmetic applies reliably across the new crop of subscription services. Aside from the backing of venture capitalists, better graphic design, and appealing mobile apps, they aren't much different from the predatory rent-to-own vendors familiar from the last century. So, it's no wonder then that the subscription car services announced with much fanfare by Audi, BMW, Cadillac, and Mercedes Benz just a few years ago have all been shuttered.

Second, subscription models leave consumers dependent on producers. Imagine you fill your home with rented appliances – washing machine, dryer, refrigerator, dishwasher, oven, microwave, and coffee machine. You know you're paying a premium, but you decide it's worth it anyway. But what happens if one of those rented appliances breaks? You file a maintenance request with the manufacturer, letting them know your dishwasher won't run. They tell you their technicians are overbooked, and the soonest appointment is in two weeks. You wait patiently. When the tech arrives, they inform you that the part you need is backordered but should arrive in three to four weeks. What choice do you have, but to keep paying your monthly bill? If you don't, the company can simply reclaim their equipment or remotely disable your appliances, as some auto lenders do when customers miss payments.[77] Or what if, a year into the rental, the company decides to increase its monthly rate? Instead of $80 per month, the price jumps to $100. The price hike may be infuriating, but an extra $20 per month is more palatable than spending thousands out of pocket for new appliances.

These risks aren't merely hypothetical. Consider the plight of US libraries. For centuries, libraries bought physical books. Since they owned them, they were free to lend those books out as often as they wanted, with no obligations to pay ongoing royalties to publishers. But that all changed with the introduction of electronic books. Now, instead of buying books, libraries essentially lease them. They pay publishers for the right to lend ebooks a fixed number of times or for a specified duration, often two years. And they pay several times the retail ebook price for the privilege. Once the lease expires, they are expected to pay again. Since they don't own the books outright, they are beholden to publishers. Consumers should think twice before they accept the same sort of terms for their refrigerators.

Third, the benefits of subscription models for durability and reparability are uncertain. If it's profitable to improve their products, firms will. But the results of that calculation are far from obvious. A firm charging a premium for a rental plan – one that exceeds the already-profitable returns it enjoys on a retail sale – may find that it extracts enough profit from a rented television in three or four years. If so, there's no point investing in repair. In fact, the opposite might be true. The low upfront price point of rental models might well increase consumption and speed the upgrade cycle. If the new refrigerator you've had your eye on costs $2,500, you might hesitate to make the purchase until your existing appliance is on its last legs. But if you can rent it for $25 per month, impulse might get the better of you. And if, in two or three years, a new model with an updated look or some new features appeals to you, why not upgrade again? The investments we make in our purchases motivate us to keep them over the long term. We tend to take better care of the things we own. But we're naturally less invested in things we rent. There's a reason rental companies replace their cars after just a year or two.[78] If our devices aren't fixtures in our homes, but just another monthly bill, we may be more inclined to replace them. If so, rental models create incentives for less durable, less reparable products. Even assuming stewardship by device makers did improve durability, consumers would lose out on the knowledge and skills cultivated through repair. They would still be beholden to manufacturers and lack agency with respect to the operation of their devices.

Cheap, temporary access to products is probably not a recipe for durability and repair. What if instead the market shifted in the opposite direction? Companies can establish reputations for durable, high-quality goods and commitments to repair. In the 1960s, the massive popularity of the Volkswagen Beetle was due, in part, to its ease of repair.[79] Today, Patagonia publishes repair guides for many of its clothes, sells inexpensive patches to fix small tears and holes, operates a repair center that mends items for customers, and even tours the United States hosting repair events.[80] Nudie Jeans, based in Sweden, takes a similar approach. It operates denim repair shops in more than a dozen countries, along with mobile repair stations.[81] For the do-it-yourself types, the company will send you a free repair kit with assorted patches, threads, a needle, and instructions. Red Wing repairs its line of boots and shoes by hand, replacing worn heels, gussets, hooks, and eyelets, among other fixes, for a reasonable fee.[82] And Zippo offers free, lifetime repairs on its line of windproof lighters.[83] What these companies have in common, aside from their embrace of repair, are comparatively high price tags. Nudie jeans and Patagonia jackets both start at about $200, a pair of Red Wing shoes will set you back around $300, and a Zippo lighter costs $30. These are, by no means, the most expensive products in their respective markets, but they are far from the cheapest. Repair shouldn't be a luxury reserved for those who can buy high-end goods, but convincing consumers accustomed to cheap, disposable products to invest in more durable ones won't be easy – even if it's the financially wiser choice. Nonetheless, these examples demonstrate that durable, reparable designs can be rewarded in the marketplace.

Changing Design

To enable repair, we need to rethink the way products are built. We've seen how firms embed biases against repair into product design. The difficulty and, in some cases, impossibility of repair is not some inevitable outgrowth of advancing technology. It reflects choices and priorities. In some cases, firms set out to impede repair. In others, they give repair no thought at all. Instead, reparability ought to be a design priority – one on par with aesthetics, size, or energy efficiency.

So, what would products look like if they were designed for repair? In an ideal world, they'd look a lot like the Fairphone. Founded by Bas van Abel in 2013, Amsterdam-based Fairphone has released four iterations of its eponymous smartphone. The company, launched in response to the conflict minerals crisis in Africa, approaches product design with an emphasis on durability and repair. As van Abel explained, "If you use your phone twice as long, you only need to produce half as many phones . . . . So we designed our phone in such a way that we can easily replace parts. The screen, for example. So if you drop the phone and the screen breaks, you can replace it yourself. That goes for all the components of the phone that might break over time."[84]

The Fairphone 3 Plus, released in 2020, retails for a competitive €469, less than half of what you'd pay for a new iPhone. It features a back cover that can be opened by hand, revealing a battery and clearly labeled expandable storage that can likewise be removed and replaced without a single tool. The phone's display can be swapped out with nothing more than a standard Phillips screwdriver, which is helpfully included. Beyond those two most replaced components, the camera, speaker, and USB-C port are all modular, easily snapping into place should you need to replace one. In fact, customers who own the Fairphone 3 can easily swap out their old camera for the upgraded version that comes standard on the 3 Plus, instead of replacing the entire device.[85] And the modules themselves can be easily opened up if you need to replace an internal component. Replacement parts are sold on the company's website at reasonable prices – about €90 for the screen, €50 for the camera, €30 for the battery, and €20 each for the USB module or speaker. It also offers free, step-by-step repair guides to supplement the cues printed inside the phone itself. No wonder then that iFixit gave the Fairphone a perfect score.[86]

The Fairphone, admittedly, doesn't sport the fastest processor, the brightest screen, or the sleekest design.[87] But it is largely indistinguishable from other fully functioning smartphones of recent vintage. All designs entail compromise. A new Apple or Samsung phone might be a few millimeters thinner or load *Among Us* a fraction of a second faster. But the Fairphone's drawbacks are a reasonable sacrifice to make in the name of vastly improved longevity and far lower repair costs.

It might be tempting to dismiss the Fairphone as some sort of gimmick, or more charitably, a proof of concept with no real viability in the marketplace. But Fairphone has sold hundreds of thousands of devices so far, no small feat for a company of its size. It launched its very first product just a few years ago, with no track record or existing infrastructure for designing, manufacturing, and distributing phones. It quickly became one of Europe's fastest-growing startups. Nor is it the only company to pursue the vision of modular, reparable electronics. The German firm Shift offers a range of phones and tablets that reflect similar design philosophies.[88] And Framework announced a modular, reparable laptop in early 2021.[89]

Established technology companies can design reparable products when they put their minds to it. Even Apple sometimes builds devices that are easy to repair. In 2019, its flagship Mac Pro desktop computer garnered an impressive 9 out of 10 score from iFixit.[90] A rotating handle on top of the device allows for one-handed removal of its outer case. RAM can be replaced by hand, and other components, like the I/O board, video card, and power supply, are removable with a just a Phillips screwdriver. For the most part, the machine uses components with standard interfaces, which makes them easy to replace. Helpful graphics and diagrams inside the device guide the user through the process. Apple even offers repair manuals and videos for basic procedures. Other parts, like the CPU, aren't easily accessible, but are among the least likely for end users to repair. Overall, though, the Mac Pro demonstrates that Apple can make a powerful, beautiful machine that's still reparable. Granted, the form factor of the Mac Pro isn't constrained to the same degree a phone or watch is. And its cost, capping out at over $50,000, precludes the annual upgrade business model common for other devices.[91] Nonetheless, other mass-market competitors like HP and Dell have managed to build reliably reparable and affordable portables for years.

Taking a step back from these examples, we can extract some general principles of designing for repair. Unlike the prevalent approach in electronics design – packing everything into as small a space as possible, sealing the shell closed, and hoping for the best – building a product with repair in mind requires making room for the user. The device needs to accommodate, even welcome, intrusions into the formerly sacrosanct interior of the device. Users, and even repair professionals, shouldn't need specialized tools and techniques just to open up a device. Where it makes sense, they should be encouraged to use their hands. And seriously, no glue. Fasteners should be chosen with the understanding and expectation that they will be used to connect and disconnect components more than once. So, if they can't withstand multiple uses, they should be easily replaceable. Likewise, parts should be easy to access, easy to remove, and easy to install. That's especially true for the ones that are most likely to wear out or break, like batteries and screens. Designs should be modular. Swapping out one failed component shouldn't require replacing a board littered with other functioning parts. When parts do need replacing, they ought to be available and affordable. That means, where possible, using standard components available from multiple sources. When designers plan the arrangement of those parts, they should consider the impact on repair. Procedures for removing and replacing components should be intuitive. And the device itself, through its internal layout, text, and diagrams should guide users through the most common repairs. For more complicated or less-common processes, device makers ought to provide manuals and video walkthroughs. Some devices might even be sold unassembled. Kasey Hou, the designer of the Repairable Flatpack Toaster, realized that consumers who put a device together themselves would better understand its operation and grow more confident in their ability to repair it.[92]

No doubt, designing for repair requires a shift in mindset. But new technologies and materials could make it easier than ever. Simply using a stretch-release adhesive, which can be easily removed with a firm pull on an accessible tab, rather than traditional glue improves reparability.[93] Additive manufacturing processes like 3D printing offer even greater advantages.[94] Rather than manufacturing, stocking, and shipping the full complement of replacement parts for every device, manufacturers can print low-cost parts on demand at retail locations. Or if reliable, high-performance home printers become common, consumers could download a file for a new bracket or latch and print it from the comfort of the couch. In the automotive and aerospace industries, 3D printing is already used to make hard-to-source parts. There's no reason the same can't be true for our toasters and vacuum cleaners. Other breakthroughs on the horizon promise self-healing devices. In 2018, researchers from the University of Tokyo developed a new polymer glass that can be mended by hand, simply by applying pressure.[95] More recently, a team at the Korea Institute of Science and Technology announced a new screen, infused with microcapsules of linseed oil, that automatically repairs 95 percent of cracks within just twenty minutes.[96] Around the same time, Apple applied for a patent on a foldable device that incorporates a self-healing screen.[97]

The combination of these advances, growing consumer awareness, and shifts in the market may convince more firms to design for repair. But we can't neglect the role governments can play in shaping design. Device makers would undoubtedly resist any regulatory intervention – or what they would term meddling – in the design process. They would note, accurately, that product design is a complex exercise that requires balancing and prioritizing competing, interdependent considerations. Legal obligations to account for reparability would further complicate that calculus. But durability and reparability are hardly unknown considerations for designers. And there's no shortage of precedent for legal constraints and obligations that shape product design. Firms design around competitors' patents as a matter of course. And US law already intercedes in product design to protect the interests of consumers and the environment. Federal law, for example, has mandated seat belts in motor vehicles since 1968.[98] And beginning in 1975, federal standards have regulated vehicle fuel efficiency.[99] Given the hundreds of billions of dollars US consumers spend on electronics each year and the staggering environmental costs of disposable consumerism, aggressive intervention is justified.[100]

European regulators are taking just such a stance. Rules implementing the Ecodesign Directive outline a number of specific requirements relating to device reparability.[101] For dishwashers, refrigerators, washing machines, and electronic displays, those rules not only mandate the availability of specific spare parts for up to ten years, but they also insist that devices are designed so that those parts can be replaced using common, everyday tools without any permanent damage to the device.[102] Beyond that, they require device makers to provide schematics, diagnostic codes, and other information necessary for repairs. For servers and data storage devices, manufacturers are prohibited from using fasteners or sealing techniques that interfere with repair or replacement of various internal components like memory, processors, motherboards, and power supplies.[103] These design mandates have only recently gone into effect, but the European Commission is actively developing another set of ecodesign rules focusing on the reparability of phones, tablets, and laptops, among other products.[104]

Those regulations could profoundly influence the future of product reparability, not only in Europe but throughout the world. Imagine a rule that insisted firms design laptops and phones with batteries that consumers could replace by hand.[105] This is not some impossible feat of engineering, as the Fairphone illustrates. As late as 2009, Apple sold MacBooks with batteries that could be removed with the press of a switch. Or consider the impact of a rule requiring smartphones with screens that can be replaced easily with everyday tools. The cost savings for consumers would be considerable, as would the environmental impact of longer-lasting devices. Not every part of every device needs to be reparable by the average consumer. There will always be a need for trained repair experts. But even the most skilled would benefit from designs that anticipate repair.

Given the size of the European market, proactive design mandates could set manufacturing standards globally. Firms aren't going to want to build one line of devices with replaceable batteries and screens for Europe and a separate product line for everywhere else. But they aren't going to pull out of Europe altogether either. Nearly two decades ago, the Restriction of Hazardous Substances Directive reshaped the design of electronics by limiting the use of heavy metals.[106] The Ecodesign Directive is poised to do the same for reparability.

Device makers will resist these sorts of rules, objecting that design mandates will impede innovation and interfere with their ability to give customers the devices the market demands. But as Steve Jobs famously said, "People don't know what they want until you show it to them."[107] Apple and its competitors have gotten very good at building ever-smaller and ever-less-reparable devices. And they've gotten just as good at convincing consumers that's what they should value. But that tells us very little about how consumers would respond to new design trends that emphasize repair and durability. These firms employ some of the most talented industrial designers on the planet. We should have confidence in their ability to accommodate reasonable regulatory constraints, and so should their employers. And since these rules will apply to all device makers, they should spur competition to find the most elegant and efficient solutions to enable repair. By giving firms a new basis for distinguishing their products, the rules should spur innovation that benefits us all.

Aside from their repair provisions, the ecodesign regulations also limit energy and water consumption and promote reuse and recycling, where appropriate. In doing so, they reflect a broader effort to incorporate circular design principles in the market for consumer goods. The notion of a circular economy – one that minimizes extractive inputs, pollution, and waste by recovering and reusing materials whenever possible – grows out of decades of work attempting to reconcile economic growth and sustainability.[108] Repair is one key component of a circular economy, slowing the production and consumption cycles.[109] Combined with reuse, recycling, and remanufacturing, it can help us design our way out of the linear paradigm. A model built to extract raw materials, manufacture goods, use them briefly, and then dispose of them as waste is unsustainable. Repair offers another path.

Design can also encourage us to keep the products we already own by leveraging our emotional connections to them. Most of us have held onto a favorite t-shirt or a beat-up bicycle long past the point of rationality. Maybe you see the t-shirt, holes and all, in biographical terms, associating it with the places you wore it, the people you were with, and the experiences you enjoyed. Maybe the bike was a gift, a symbol of the relationship with the person who purchased it. So, you patch the shirt's more conspicuous holes or pour money into the bike's maintenance.[110] These emotional connections can't be engineered, but product design can make them more or less likely. We can build products that facilitate what Johnathan Chapman calls "emotional durability."[111] Some products improve with age. Cowboy boots require breaking in. Cast-iron pans need to be seasoned. And a bronze sculpture develops its distinctive patina over the course of years. Those gradual changes reflect our influence, our effort, our patience. And as a result, we value those objects more.

A design aesthetic that tolerates aging might be more reconcilable with repair and durability than one that strives for sleek, pristine devices. We might see the occasional dent or scuff as character rather than imperfection. Personalization and customization represent another route to emotional connection. The things we own form part of our identity.[112] The more we associate a product with our own identity, the more reticent we will be to discard it. When the smartphone in your pocket is indistinguishable from hundreds of millions of identical models, it becomes a fungible commodity rather than a personal artifact.

Today though, our devices have the power to learn. They can observe our behaviors and extrapolate our preferences. A device that learns and grows with us – a TV that knows you prefer documentaries to buddy comedies – could engender an emotional connection. But in the era of cloud services, the profile generated from those interactions can easily be transferred to a new device. So, your new TV, fresh out of the box, knows you just as well as the one you scrapped after years of use. That shift from owning a device to using a service undermines our sense of psychological ownership.[113] Ownership itself is a kind of emotional attachment between consumers and the devices around them. The less control we have over an object, the less invested we are in it. So, repair, by reasserting our responsibility for the devices we use, helps to develop those emotional investments. Design can make it easier to repair the things we own. It can even raise the emotional stakes of replacing an aging device. But as Fairphone's Bas van Abel emphasizes, "The solution to the whole problem lies with us, the people that buy stuff."[114]

Changing Norms

In the end, repair is a choice we make. Courts and legislatures can remove barriers to repair, markets can be reconfigured to encourage it, and firms can even redesign products to make it easier. But none of those interventions matter if we – individually and collectively – discard our old devices rather than fix them. We can't expect to see meaningful changes in behavior until we shift our attitudes and judgments about repair. How those around us evaluate behavior – whether it is lauded or scorned – has a profound influence on our own assessments and, ultimately, our actions. For better or worse, and usually a fair measure of both, our status as social animals leaves us susceptible to the influence of our fellows. That tendency can steer us down collectively harmful paths, but it can also redirect us towards more constructive alternatives.

Consider the shift in attitudes about littering over the last few decades. Since 1969, roadside litter in the United States has plummeted by 61 percent.[115] During that time, a number of public awareness campaigns tried to reshape the casual acceptance of littering. Generations of children became as familiar with Woodsy Owl and his catchphrase "Give a hoot – don't pollute!" as they were with Scooby Doo or Popeye.[116] A year after Woodsy's 1970 debut, Keep America Beautiful produced a now-famous ad featuring what appeared to be a Native American – actually an Italian actor in Indian garb – shedding a single tear after a passing motorist tosses trash out of a car window.[117] Even the unofficial motto of the Lone Star State, "Don't Mess with Texas," began as an antilitter campaign in 1985.[118] Admittedly, laws penalizing litter played an important role in reducing roadside trash during this period. But disentangling social norms and attitudes from legal sanctions is a tricky task. Once a behavior is deemed unlawful, people are more likely to view it harshly. In a 2012 survey of 1,100 Americans, 59 percent said they would feel "very embarrassed" if someone they admired found out they had thrown trash out of their car window.[119] That was slightly more than those embarrassed about cheating on their taxes, but slightly less than those embarrassed about getting caught drunk driving. So, it's no surprise that the percentage of people who admit to littering dropped from 50 percent in 1968, to 15 percent in 2009.[120]

Similar trends apply to other behaviors. Smoking in the United States has dropped off sharply over the last several decades. In 1953, 47 percent of adults were cigarette smokers.[121] Today, that number has fallen to 14 percent.[122] More accurate information about the health consequences of smoking, tax hikes, and indoor smoking bans no doubt contributed to this decline. But so did changing attitudes about smoking and smokers. In 2001, 39 percent of Americans thought smoking should be illegal in public spaces. By 2019, 62 percent favored a ban.[123] And polling data reveal a steady increase in the number of people who report they have less respect for smokers, from 14 percent in 1994 to 25 percent in 2011.[124] In a sense, smoking is viewed as a moral failing, or at the very least a dirty habit deserving of casual scorn. Some of us may be immune to that sort of social opprobrium, but for most people, it influences our choices. In the same way that our attitudes about littering and smoking helped shift our behavior, buying unrepairable wireless headphones destined for the landfill could become as unseemly as dumping your trash on the sidewalk or exhaling smoke in the face of a stranger.

We've already seen how social pressure and shared commitments can be harnessed to encourage repair. During World War II, with every resource marshaled for military use, citizens on both side of the Atlantic had to get by with less. Repair wasn't merely a fact of life or an economic reality, it was seen as a patriotic duty.[125] Citizens were implored to "Make Do and Mend" or to "Use It Up, Wear It Out, Make It Do." Those government information campaigns were supplemented by private efforts. John Deere, for example, supplied farmers with manuals that offered tips for maintaining and repairing their farm equipment.[126] And everyday citizens encouraged their friends and neighbors to wring every bit of utility they could out of material goods from clothes and food to bicycles and tractors.

Unfortunately, few shared enterprises inspire unity and collective sacrifice quite like war. But armed conflict isn't the only crisis that can catalyze a rethinking of long-held attitudes and routines. The toll of the coronavirus pandemic – in human life, social and psychological wellbeing, and economic loss – was catastrophic. One of the few bright spots to grow out of that global trauma was the renewed appreciation for repair that it sparked in some corners.

In the United States, where too many are fully submerged in the water of disposable consumerism, the pandemic and ensuing lockdown served as reminders of the possibility and necessity of repair. Much the same was true in the UK, Europe, and elsewhere across the world's most developed economies, where the art of repair has withered. Hardware stores saw booming sales as consumers finally had time to get around to long-postponed home repairs.[127] Bikes that sat unused for years or decades were plucked from storage, ready for a tune-up and new tires. Rather than shopping for new jeans and socks, more of us patched, mended, and darned – in some cases to avoid risky trips to the store, in others, just to have something to do. Similarly, iFixit saw a flood of new users looking for information on how to repair laptops, game consoles, and other devices. With repair shops closed, money tight, and people with plenty of time on their hands, the prolonged quarantine gave many of us a chance to rediscover the joys, frustrations, and triumphs of self-repair.[128] As global supply chains for new appliances were disrupted, consumers came to depend more on repair. In many cases, the demand for repair services outstripped supply, demonstrating how our repair infrastructure has been hollowed out by decades of prioritizing replacement.[129]

But what happens next? After World War II, as we know, rampant consumerism was ascendant. Perhaps the post-COVID era will be marked by a similarly exuberant spending spree. There are reasons to resist that prediction. Younger generations – those who didn't experience the post-war economic boom – tend to embrace repair more than their parents and grandparents. A recent study of Londoners found that 85 percent of eighteen- to twenty-four-year-olds and nearly as many in the twenty-five–thirty-four range have repaired clothing, furniture or bikes in the last year. That compares to just 47 per cent of those over fifty-five.[130] We also know that repair preferences are subject to peer pressure. The European Commission found that people are more likely to buy reparable products when they're told that other consumers prefer them.[131] The preference for reparability is self-replicating. And we know that the more consumers understand about the right to repair, the more they support it.[132]

One promising trend is the growing interest in visible mending. Instead of tossing out damaged garments or hiding necessary repairs, more of us are celebrating stitches and patches. Some employ unpolished repair techniques for a homespun charm. Others, inspired by the Japanese *sashiko* technique, mend torn items with elaborate geometric stitching.[133] A raft of how-to books and Instagram hashtags highlight these practices. But visible mending is more than a passing fad. These repairs are "statements of empowerment," explains artist and researcher Bridget Harvey. "Rather than a sign of poverty or neglect," she writes, "a visible repair can signify riches of skills, choice, independence, sharing, and community."[134] Repair speaks to those around us. It draws attention to durability and resilience.[135] And in doing so, it communicates something about what the wearer values – and just as importantly, what they don't.

There's no reason this embrace of repair should be confined to clothing. Our laptops and tractors can proudly bear the marks of repeated repair as well as a treasured pair of well-worn jeans. By normalizing and honoring repair, we express our values and priorities, but we also subtly invite our friends, families, and neighbors to do the same. But encouraging that change on a global scale will take more than individual commitment. It requires building a community.

The Right to Repair Movement

Contemporary culture valorizes innovation. Inventors like Nikola Tesla and Steve Jobs – and fictional counterparts like Doc Brown and Tony Stark – are the subjects of fawning portrayals in major motion pictures. Repair, in contrast, is rarely depicted as heroic. The most notable exception, tellingly, isn't a blockbuster hit. In Terry Gilliam's 1985 dystopian satire *Brazil*, a clerical error leads to the arrest and death of Archibald Buttle.[136] But the authorities are actually after Archibald

Tuttle, a rogue heating and air-conditioning repairman, played memorably by Robert De Niro. In the film, repairs of these temperamental systems can only be lawfully performed by the ominously named Central Services. Tuttle, under cloak of darkness, intercepts service calls and performs illegal repairs as a way of reasserting control over technology and bureaucracy, and partly just for the thrill of it. As he explains, "I came into this game for the action, the excitement. Go anywhere, travel light, get in, get out, wherever there's trouble, a man alone." Unlike in Gilliam's imagined future, unauthorized repair is not a capital offense, at least not yet. And while Tuttle acted as a one-man resistance force, the fight for repair is a collective effort in the real world.

The assault on repair has sparked opposition in communities around the globe. This movement brings together repair professionals, policy advocates, sustainability experts, tinkerers, hobbyists, and everyday people. It includes small businesses repairing consumer electronics, major hospitals fixing medical equipment, and family farmers desperate to keep their equipment operating – cutting across industries, demographics, politics, and geography.[137] Some devote themselves to on-the-ground education and the practice of repair in their local communities. Others build independent parts and service businesses to make repair more affordable and accessible. And still others advocate for broad changes in law and policy. But these roles are by no means exclusive. The right-to-repair movement is characterized by overlapping, collaborative efforts.

Local initiatives to encourage repair have been around for decades in various forms. In 1943 – not coincidentally in the midst of World War II – the Grosse Pointe Rotary Club, in the suburbs of Detroit, launched what is perhaps the first public tool library in an effort to build repair skills.[138] Other cities, like Berkeley, California, and Columbus, Ohio followed suit.[139] These tool libraries prefigured the contemporary repair movement in important ways. They offered material tools, but also knowledge and skills to empower people to take control of the things they own. Bike co-ops – or kitchens as they are sometimes called – perform a similar role for cyclists in hundreds of cities, providing access to expensive tools and a supportive community that shares its collective skills.[140]

This same basic ethos drives the volunteers who operate thousands of repair cafés and other community-based repair projects stretching across six continents. In 2009, Martine Postma started the first repair café in the lobby of an Amsterdam movie theater.[141] Her goal was to create a welcoming, informal environment that encouraged community and collaboration, but also helped people become self-sufficient.[142] Postma's vision, inspired by the artist collective Platform 21, soon energized others.[143] Today there are more than 2,000 repair cafés scattered across thirty-five countries.[144] People bring in their broken items, from sewing machines to laptops, and together with expert volunteers engage in the frustrating but rewarding work of repair.

Around the same time, other groups developed similar programs. The Fixers Collective began holding monthly repair events in Brooklyn in 2008.[145] Peter Mui began holding what he calls Fixit Clinics in Boston in 2009, and his organization now holds events across the United States.[146] The Restart Project, founded by Janet Gunter and Ugo Vallauri, began hosting monthly Restart Parties in London, starting in 2013. Today, its network has expanded to sixty local groups in Africa, Asia, Australia, Europe, and North and South America.[147] Motivated by a shared mission, these groups don't treat each other as competitors, but as collaborators. For those who prefer to build their repair skills from the privacy and comfort of home, YouTube creators like Hugh Jeffreys – who showcases repair tools and techniques – and Richard Benoit – whose channel, Rich Rebuilds, focuses on repairing Teslas and other vehicles – offer opportunities to learn from afar.[148]

While volunteers and nonprofits make crucial contributions to the right-to-repair movement, private businesses are equally integral to the effort. Chief among them is iFixit. Founded in 2003 by Kyle Wiens and Luke Soules, iFixit sells repair tools and replacement parts for everything from laptops and tablets to drones and electric toothbrushes.[149] But calling iFixit a parts supplier drastically undersells its importance to the broader repair movement. In addition to its influential reparability scores, the site hosts a massive repository of free, detailed repair guides that walk users, step-by-step, through tens of thousands of repair procedures. Whether you want to install new headlights on your car, replace the joystick on your Nintendo Switch, or swap out the battery on your Samsung tablet, iFixit can guide you through the process. Many of those guides are generated by iFixit's staff, but others are created by users themselves. The site sees about 10 million unique visitors each month, making it the most active online repair community. Building consumer interest and confidence around repair is certainly good for iFixit's bottom line. But the company's commitment to the principle of repair runs deeper than that. Wiens is a passionate and tireless advocate for repair. A self-described "tinkerer by inclination and fixer by profession," he devotes much of his time to advocating for repair, testifying before various state legislative committees and the US Copyright Office.[150]

Wiens is hardly the only business owner to take on the role of advocate. Jessa Jones, a PhD-trained molecular biologist, began repairing phones and tablets after her toddlers flushed her iPhone down the toilet.[151] She took a sledgehammer to the toilet to retrieve the phone, then turned her attention to salvaging the water-logged device. That incident launched her business, iPad Rehab, which does all manner of repairs, but specializes in data recovery and micro-soldering – services Apple refuses to offer. Because of the challenges her business faces sourcing parts and schematics, Jones too has pushed for legislative reform.[152] Louis Rossmann, who operates the Rossmann Repair Group in New York City, is another prominent voice pushing for repair.[153] In addition to his repair and data recovery business, Rossmann's YouTube channel has 1.5 million subscribers.[154] There he shares walkthroughs of complex repairs – often ones authorized repair providers wouldn't even attempt – as well as his uncompromising perspective on policies that implicate repair. Rossmann too has testified on behalf of repair bills in statehouses across the United States. Increasingly, running a successful independent repair business requires not only some measure of legal expertise, but direct engagement in the legislative process.

Given that landscape, it's no surprise that policy organizations and initiatives dedicated to repair have emerged in recent years. The Repair Association, originally dubbed the Digital Right to Repair Coalition, grew out of the successful push in 2012 for automotive-repair legislation in Massachusetts. The organization, helmed by Gay Gordon-Byrne, represents the interests of individuals, nonprofits, and businesses advocating for repair. Its membership is diverse. It includes individual repair shops and parts providers as well as the Electronic Frontier Foundation, the Natural Resources Defense Council, and the Brooklyn Public Library, among dozens of others.[155] Central to its agenda is a conviction that information, parts, and tools ought to be available to consumers who want to exercise control over the technology they own. The group has lobbied for legislative reform at the state and federal levels, as well as administrative exemptions under the Digital Millennium Copyright Act.

The US Public Interest Research Group (PIRG) is a key partner in those efforts. Since the 1970s the PIRG network has successfully championed a range of environmental and consumer-protection initiatives. Its Right to Repair Campaign, led by Nathan Proctor, has been instrumental in getting dozens of repair bills introduced in state legislatures in recent years. As Proctor has learned, the right-to-repair movement "isn't a bipartisan issue, it's transpartisan."[156] Libertarians are deeply committed to protecting personal property and individual freedom, both of which are at stake in the fight over repair. By the same token, progressives see the issue through the lenses of human rights and environmental justice. In a political climate defined by polarization, repair may be one of the few issues that can achieve consensus.

In Europe, similar coalitions have been constructed. For example, Right to Repair Europe is a collection of organizations that not only informs and connects everyday people but presses for meaningful policy change as well.[157] Efforts like theirs are helping drive the policy reforms that make Europe a leader on legal reforms around repair. Likewise, the nonprofit Halte à l'Obsolescence Programmée has aggressively and successfully sought enforcement of France's planned obsolescence ban and lobbied for the reparability rating the country began implementing in 2021.

Years of community building and policy advocacy are starting to yield measurable progress. Consumers and small businesses are voicing their frustrations, amplified by digital and grassroots organizing. Courts, legislators, and regulators are listening. Faced with the threat of meaningful legal interventions, even device makers are starting to rethink their opposition to repair. In 2018, Motorola became the first major electronics manufacturer to embrace the right-to-repair agenda, partnering with iFixit to sell tool kits and making manuals and other repair information available.[158] And LG recently threw its support behind a right-to-repair framework in Australia.[159] Even Apple may be reconsidering its long-standing opposition to repair. Internal emails released as part of a congressional investigation in 2020 reveal deep divisions within the company about its path forward. As one of those emails concisely posed the question facing the world's most successful device maker, "What is our repair strategy?"[160] The company continues to resist right-to-repair legislation, but at the same time, it's posting service manuals for some products on its website. Perhaps even more tellingly, the company's latest environmental report insists that Apple "take[s] responsibility not only for our direct operations, but for the entire life cycle of our products."[161] As a result, it acknowledges that "making repairs more convenient and reliable is directly aligned with our goal of creating long-lasting products that maximize the resources we use." Apple, it seems, is coming around to what we already know. Our laws, practices, and attitudes about repair are broken. It's time we fix them.

EPILOGUE

In May 2021, the Federal Trade Commission (FTC) issued a report to Congress that was widely hailed by the right-to-repair community. Released after more than two years of study – and coincidentally, a few weeks after I submitted the manuscript for this book – the FTC's *Nixing the Fix* report detailed the Commission's careful analysis of the impact of repair restrictions on consumers and competition in the United States.[1] By recognizing the harms those restrictions impose and balking at the justifications offered by device makers, the FTC endorsed the arguments right-to-repair advocates have been advancing for the better part of a decade. And although the Commission did not announce any sweeping legal reforms or immediate enforcement efforts, the report signaled its willingness, perhaps even eagerness, to tackle repair restrictions head on. And it initiated a brief but promising flurry of federal action around repair.

The FTC acknowledged that, through product design, software locks, and tightly controlled access to parts and manuals, device makers have discouraged repair. Those policies, in the FTC's words, "steered consumers into manufacturers' repair networks or to replace products before the end of their useful lives." As a result, we pay more and wait longer for repairs than we would in a more open, competitive market. The burdens of repair restrictions, as the FTC noted, "fall more heavily on communities of color and lower-income communities." That's true for both consumers, who may lack financial resources and access to alternative devices, as well as the small business owners who serve those communities. Aside from the economic costs of repair restrictions, the FTC recognized their environmental impact. As it noted, "extending the life of consumer products unquestionably delays these products' entry into the waste stream and reduces the amount of energy used to generate replacement products."

In terms of its legal analysis, the Commission highlighted three distinct ways in which repair restrictions might run afoul of US law. First, it reiterated that when firms condition warranty coverage on using a particular brand of parts or service, they violate the Magnuson-Moss Warranty Act – unless those parts or services are free. Second, it suggested that some repair restrictions may amount to unfair practices under § 5 of the FTC Act. Finally, it described how limitations on repair could violate antitrust law, relying on both tying and monopolization theories, but acknowledging the challenges to bringing successful claims.

The Commission largely sidestepped the question of intellectual property (IP) law. Although it cited evidence that makers of vehicles, game consoles, and other devices rely on design patents, trademarks, and anticircumvention rules to limit repair, the report downplayed those barriers, concluding that the "assertion of IP rights does not appear to be a significant impediment to independent repair," noting the temporary and partial exemption to the Digital Millennium Copyright Act granted by the Copyright Office. The FTC's hesitance to fully confront the effects of IP law may reflect an awareness of the limits of its expertise. IP isn't entirely unfamiliar to the Commission, but it is hardly at the core of the FTC's mandate. Rather than wading into the complexities of IP law, the Commission wisely focused its attention on the legal theories it could speak to authoritatively.

Crucially, the FTC expressed palpable skepticism of the litany of justifications device makers and their trade groups routinely offer in defense of repair restrictions. As the report summed things up, "there is scant evidence to support manufacturers' justifications for repair restrictions." The Commission was far from persuaded by device makers' insistence that independent repair poses a threat to consumer safety. Aside from one instance of a cellphone battery combusting in Australia in 2011, device makers "provided no data to support their argument that injuries are tied to repairs performed by consumers or independent repair shops." Nor could they back up their alarmist claims that independent repair providers are less careful or pose a greater threat when they enter consumers' homes. And as the Commission pointed out, if repair presents safety risks, manufacturers are best positioned to mitigate them through design changes.

Likewise, the FTC found manufacturers' assertions that independent repair is a threat to privacy and security without merit. As it concluded, "the record contains no empirical evidence to suggest that independent repair shops are more or less likely than authorized repair shops to compromise or misuse customer data." But to the extent device makers are genuinely worried about consumer privacy and security, the Commission offered a sensible solution: manufacturers could offer independent shops the same parts, tools, and software that their authorized providers use, ensuring consistent levels of security. If you can trust the local Best Buy employee with your data, you can trust the local repair shop too.

Nor could manufacturers substantiate their claim that the quality of independent repair is lower than authorized service. Instead, surveys show that consumers are more satisfied with independent repair. According to the Commission, "the record does not establish that repairs conducted by independent repair shops would be inferior to those conducted by authorized repair shops if independent repair shops were provided with greater access to service manuals, diagnostic software and tools, and replacement parts as appropriate." In other words, even if independent repair were inferior, device makers would be to blame. Without evidence of inferiority, it's no wonder then that the FTC also rebuffed the claims that independent repair threatens the reputations of device makers and exposes them to legal liability.

The FTC's dismissal of these various justifications is telling for at least two reasons. First, they may well preview the Commission's arguments in future antitrust litigation, where device makers will almost certainly offer purportedly pro-competitive rationales for their behavior. Second, by shrugging off these arguments as devoid of any evidentiary basis, the FTC may embolden state legislatures around the country who have been repeatedly entranced by the drumbeat of lobbyists representing firms like Apple and John Deere. The FTC's resistance to those arguments may help inoculate state representatives moving forward.

As a matter of principal, the FTC's *Nixing the Fix* report is a resounding vindication of the right-to-repair movement. By embracing the factual framing of repair advocates and scrutinizing repair restrictions as plausible violations of consumer-protection and antitrust law, the Commission legitimized the movement's critique of device makers. That critique is already widely accepted by the public, but the report marks the first time that an arm of the federal government has offered a clear endorsement of the repair agenda.

What that endorsement amounts to as a practical matter will depend in large part on what concrete steps the FTC takes in the coming years. As the report indicates, the Commission "stands ready to work with legislators, either at the state or federal level, to ensure that consumers and independent repair shops have appropriate access to replacement parts, instructions, and diagnostic software." But of course, the FTC can't introduce bills. And the legislative process, particularly at the federal level, is marked by disfunction. Congress lurches from crisis to crisis, occasionally sneaking a good idea, along with several bad ones, into massive budget reconciliation bills.

But, encouragingly, the *Nixing the Fix* report prefigured three important executive actions, all of which make meaningful federal intervention more likely even in the absence of legislation. First, President Biden named Lina Khan – an outspoken critic of the anticompetitive tactics of technology firms – chair of the FTC.[2] Many interpreted that appointment as the first step towards a more muscular and active Commission.

Then, in July of 2021, President Biden issued an executive order designed to promote competition across the US economy.[3] Two provisions squarely addressed repair. The order instructed the Secretary of Defense to submit a report to the White House outlining a plan to avoid procurement contracts that stand in the way of military personnel repairing equipment in the field. It also encouraged the FTC to use its power to address "unfair anticompetitive restrictions on third-party repair or self-repair," specifically calling out the sorts of "restrictions imposed by powerful manufacturers that prevent farmers from repairing their own equipment."

Less than two weeks later, the FTC – comprised of three Democratic and two Republican appointees – issued a unanimous policy statement outlining its plans to address repair restrictions.[4] That statement was light on details and largely reiterated the prescriptions from the *Nixing the Fix* report. Nonetheless, the FTC officially committed to "prioritize investigations into unlawful repair restrictions" as potential violations of the Magnuson-Moss Warranty Act, antitrust law, and the prohibitions against unfair and deceptive practices. No doubt, the FTC's statement was not as full-throated as repair advocates may have wished. It could have offered greater clarity on the sorts of practices the Commission believes are illegal by calling out particular abuses, for example. That alone may have been enough to force manufacturers to rethink some of their policies and practices. But greater specificity at this stage may have jeopardized the bipartisan unanimity the statement, as crafted, communicated so powerfully.

Moving forward, the Commission will need to bring its considerable expertise and resources to bear by initiating enforcement actions against firms that limit consumer access to repair. Stern warnings are not enough. Until enforcement agencies make the consequences clear, device makers have every incentive to push the legal limits. Beyond that, the FTC needs to establish clear rules that prohibit the most egregious and problematic repair restrictions. Rather than one-off enforcement, it should undertake a broader effort to reshape the market for repair, both to promote competition and to safeguard the interests of consumers.

However promising these developments may seem, we can't expect the FTC – or, for that matter, the European Commission, or any state or national legislature – to serve as some heroic savior of repair. Legislation and regulation are part of the solution, but fixing our culture of repair will demand lasting changes to our behavior as consumers and citizens.

NOTES

1 Introduction

1. Keith Barry, *Profiles in Mileage: Meet the 2.8-Million-Mile Man*, Wired (July 27, 2010), www.wired.com/2010/07/irv-gordon-2–8-million-mile-volvo.
2. Peter Valdes-Dapena, *World's Oldest Car Sells for $4.6 Million*, CNN (Oct. 10, 2011), www.money.cnn.com/2011/10/10/autos/worlds_oldest_car.
3. Matt Litwin, *World's Oldest Operating Motor Vehicle to Highlight RM's Hershey Auction*, Hemmings (Sept. 22, 2011), www.hemmings.com/stories/2011/09/22/worlds-oldest-operating-motor-vehicle-to-highlight-rms-hershey-auction.
4. Parmy Olson, *The World's Oldest Working Clock*, Forbes (Feb. 29, 2008), www.forbes.com/2008/02/28/oldest-work-clock-oped-time08-cx_po_0229salisbury.html.
5. Jason Koebler, *Why American Farmers Are Hacking Their Tractors with Ukrainian Firmware*, Vice (Mar. 21, 2017), www.vice.com/en_us/article/xykkkd/why-american-farmers-are-hacking-their-tractors-with-ukrainian-firmware.
6. Elle Ekman, *Here's One Reason the U.S. Military Can't Fix Its Own Equipment*, New York Times (Nov. 20, 2019), www.nytimes.com/2019/11/20/opinion/military-right-to-repair.html. In recent decades, the number of defense-equipment suppliers has dwindled. Without the ability to repair, the military is increasingly reliant on a handful of private firms, potentially endangering national security. *See, e.g.*, United States Government Accountability Office, *Columbia Class Submarine: Delivery Hinges on Timely and Quality Materials from an Atrophied Supplier Base*, GAO-21–257 (2021), www.gao.gov/assets/gao-21–257.pdf.
7. Jason Koebler, *Hospitals Need to Repair Ventilators. Manufacturers Are Making That Impossible*, Vice (Mar. 18, 2020), www.vice.com/amp/

en_us/article/wxekgx/hospitals-need-to-repair-ventilators-man
ufacturers-are-making-that-impossible; Nathan Proctor &
Kevin O'Reilly, *Hospital Repair Restrictions* (2020), www.uspirg
.org/sites/pirg/files/reports/Hospital_Repair_Restrictions_USPE
F_7.8.20b.pdf.

8. Michael Kan, *Apple: We Actually Lose Money by Offering Repair
   Services*, PC Magazine (Nov. 20, 2019), www.pcmag.com/news/
   apple-we-actually-lose-money-by-offering-repair-services.

9. Shannon Liao, *Apple Says Cheap Battery Replacements Hurt iPhone
   Sales*, Verge (Jan. 2, 2019), www.theverge.com/2019/1/2/
   18165866/apple-iphone-sales-cheap-battery-replacement.

10. Claire Kelloway & Daniel A. Hanley, *Coronavirus Reveals
    Consequences of Restricted Repair*, American Prospect (May 12,
    2020), https://prospect.org/coronavirus/covid-consequences
    -restricted-repair-ventilators/.

11. Amy Feldman, *Meet the Italian Engineers 3D-Printing
    Respirator Parts for Free to Help Keep Coronavirus Patients
    Alive*, Forbes (Mar. 19, 2020), www.forbes.com/sites/amy
    feldman/2020/03/19/talking-with-the-italian-engineers-
    who-3d-printed-respirator-parts-for-hospitals-with-corona
    virus-patients-for-free; Jay Peters, *Volunteers Produce 3D-
    Printed Valves for Life-Saving Coronavirus Treatments*, Verge
    (Mar. 17, 2020), www.theverge.com/2020/3/17/21184308/
    coronavirus-italy-medical-3d-print-valves-treatments.

12. Kellen Browning, *The Digital Divide Starts with a Laptop Shortage*,
    New York Times (Oct. 12, 2020), www.nytimes.com/2020/10/
    12/technology/laptops-schools-digital-divide.html.

13. Sara Morrison, *Lower-Income Students Are Paying the Price for the
    Global Laptop Shortage*, Vox (Aug. 28, 2020), www.vox.com
    /platform/amp/recode/2020/8/28/21403336/laptop-shortage-
    chromebook-tablet-school-reopening.

14. Alex DeBillis, *The Costs of the Digital Divide Are Higher than Ever.
    Repair Can Help*, US PIRG (Apr. 15, 2021), https://uspirg.org
    /blogs/blog/usp/costs-digital-divide-are-higher-ever-repair-can-
    help.

15. Caroline Haskins, *AirPods Are a Tragedy*, Vice (May 6, 2019),
    www.vice.com/en_us/article/neaz3d/airpods-are-a-tragedy.

16. In 2021, Emily Alpert and Emma Stritzinger founded
    Podswap, a company that uses precision robotics to replace
    depleted batteries in AirPods. For $60 the company sends
    customers refurbished earbuds, replaces the batteries in

your old headphones, then passes them on to another customer. Podswap ought to be praised for working around Apple's design, but this elaborate process is not an ideal model for efficient and scalable repair. Kevin Purdy, *Two College Roommates and Some Robots: How Podswap Replaces AirPod Batteries*, iFixit (Mar. 17, 2021), www.ifixit.com/News/49433/two-college-roommates-and-some-robots-how-podswap-replaces-airpod-batteries.

17. Sasha Moss & Aaron Perzanowski, *A Jack of All Trades*, Inside Sources (Oct. 27, 2016), www.insidesources.com/a-jack-of-all-trades.

18. Haskins, *supra* note 15.

19. Geoffrey A. Fowler, *Everyone's AirPods Will Die. We've Got the Trick to Replacing Them*, Washington Post (Oct. 8, 2019), www.washingtonpost.com/technology/2019/10/08/everyones-airpods-will-die-weve-got-trick-replacing-them.

20. Will Oremus, *What Really Happens to AirPods When They Die*, OneZero (May 28, 2019), https://onezero.medium.com/what-really-happens-to-airpods-when-they-die-9ba2fe97b346.

21. Chris Jay Hoofnagle, Aniket Kesari & Aaron Perzanowski, *The Tethered Economy*, 87 George Washington Law Review 783 (2019); Rebecca Crootof, *The Internet of Torts: Expanding Civil Liability Standards to Address Corporate Remote Interference*, 69 Duke Law Journal 583 (2019).

22. Jeffrey Van Camp, *My Jibo Is Dying and It's Breaking My Heart*, Wired (Mar. 8, 2019), www.wired.com/story/jibo-is-dying-eulogy.

23. Natasha Tusikov, *Regulation Through "Bricking": Private Ordering in the "Internet of Things,"* 8 Internet Policy Review no. 2 (June 18, 2019), https://policyreview.info/articles/analysis/regulation-through-bricking-private-ordering-internet-things.

24. Rob Price, *The Smart-Home Device that Google Is Deliberately Disabling Was Sold with a "Lifetime Subscription,"* Business Insider (Apr. 5, 2016), www.businessinsider.com.au/revolv-smart-home-hubs-lifetime-subscription-bricked-nest-google-alphabet-internet-of-things-2016-4.

25. *Id.*; Arlo Gilbert, *The Time That Tony Fadell Sold Me a Container of Hummus*, Medium (Apr. 3, 2016), https://arlogilbert.com/the-time-that-tony-fadell-sold-me-a-container-of-hummus-cb0941c762c1.

26. Louise Matsakis, *Best Buy Made These Smart Home Gadgets Dumb Again*, Wired (Nov. 12, 2019), www.wired.com/story/best-buy-smart-home-dumb.

27. Samsung Electronics Co. v. Apple, Inc., 137 S. Ct. 429 (2016).

28. Jason Koebler, *DHS Seizes Aftermarket iPhone Screens from Prominent Right-to-Repair Advocate* Vice (May 11, 2018), www.vice.com/en_us/article/evk4wk/dhs-seizes-iphone-screens-jessa-jones.

29. Koebler, *supra* note 5.

30. Exemption to Prohibition on Circumvention of Copyright Protection Systems for Access Control Technologies, 80 Fed. Reg. 65944 (Oct. 28, 2015).

31. Exemption to Prohibition on Circumvention of Copyright Protection Systems for Access Control Technologies, 83 Fed. Reg. 54010 (Oct. 28, 2018).

32. *Id.*

33. Adam Belz, *For Tech-Weary Midwest Farmers, 40-Year-Old Tractors Now a Hot Commodity*, Star Tribune (Jan. 5, 2020), www.startribune.com/for-tech-weary-midwest-farmers-40-year-old-tractors-now-a-hot-commodity/566737082.

2 Why Repair Matters

1. Christopher R. Henke, *The Mechanics of Workplace Order: Toward a Sociology of Repair*, 44 Berkeley Journal of Sociology 55 (1999). ("Repair is not at the margins of order, waiting to be deployed if something goes wrong. Instead, it is a practice at the center of social order. Repair work makes workplaces normal.")

2. Elizabeth V. Spelman, Repair: The Impulse to Restore in a Fragile World (2002).

3. Spelman explores the important distinction between repair and restoration. The former is a question of functionality, the latter entails additional consideration of aesthetics, authenticity, and historical accuracy. *Id.*

4. Albert Borgmann, Technology and the Character of Contemporary Life: A Philosophical Inquiry (1984). ("Whenever something is replaced rather than repaired, a piece of history, something that bespeaks and sustains the continuity of life is then surrendered to the garbage heap; and an opportunity to mark and affirm the stages of life is lost.")

5. Małgorzata Oleszkiewicz-Peralba, The Black Madonna in Latin America and Europe: Tradition and Transformation (2009); Katie Edwards, *Beyoncé and the Black Madonna: How Her First Picture with Sir and Rumi Carter Challenges Racial Stereotypes of Motherhood*, Newsweek (July 18, 2017), www.newsweek.com/beyonce-and-black-madonna-how-singers-represents-good-motherhood-first-picture-638170.

6. Martin Filler, *A Scandalous Makeover at Chartres*, New York Review of Books (Dec. 14, 2014), www.nybooks.com/daily/2014/12/14/scandalous-makeover-chartres.

7. *See* Lee Vinsel & Andrew L. Russell, The Innovation Delusion (2020).

8. Eric Griffith, *The $944 Billion Smartphone Market Is Only Half Phones*, PC (Dec. 12, 2019), www.pcmag.com/news/the-944-billion-smartphone-market-is-only-half-phones.

9. Paul Gao, Hans-Werner Kaas, Detlev Mohr & Dominik Wee, *Disruptive Trends that Will Transform the Auto Industry*, McKinsey & Company Report (Jan. 1, 2016), www.mckinsey.com/indus tries/automotive-and-assembly/our-insights/disruptive-trends-that-will-transform-the-auto-industry.

10. Tim Cooper, *The Significance of Product Longevity, in* Longer Lasting Products: Alternatives to the Throwaway Society (Tim Cooper, ed., 2010).

11. *Id.*

12. Harald Wieser, Nina Tröger & Renate Hübner, *The Consumers' Desired and Expected Product Lifetimes*, PLATE (2015), www.plateconference.org/consumers-desired-expected-product-lifetimes; Tim Cooper, *Inadequate Life? Evidence of Consumer Attitudes to Product Obsolescence*, 27 Journal of Consumer Policy 421 (2004).

13. Harald Wieser, *Beyond Planned Obsolescence: Product Lifespans and the Challenges to a Circular Economy*, 25 GAIA Ecological Perspectives for Science and Society 156 (Jan. 1, 2016) (collecting and summarizing studies).

14. Nigel Cassidy, *Getting in a Spin: Why Washing Machines Are No Longer Built to Last*, BBC (May 2, 2014), www.bbc.com/news/business-27253103.

15. *How Long Will Your Appliances Last?*, Consumer Reports (June 20, 2019), www.consumerreports.org/appliances/how-long-will-your-appliances-last.

16. *Id.*

17. Yuliya Kalmykova, João Patrício, Leonardo Rosado & Per E. O. Berg, *Out with the Old, Out with the New: The Effect of Transitions in TVs and Monitors Technology on Consumption and WEEE Generation in Sweden 1996–2014*, 46 Waste Management 511 (2015).
18. Callie W. Babbitt, Ramzy Kahhat, Eric Williams & Gregory A. Babbitt, *Evolution of Product Lifespan and Implications for Environmental Assessment and Management: A Case Study of Personal Computers in Higher Education*, 43 Environmental Science & Technology 5106 (2009).
19. J. Schoenung & Hai-Yong Kang, *End-of-Life Personal Computer Systems in California: Analysis of Emissions and Infrastructure Needed to Recycle in the Future*, Proceedings of the 2006 IEEE International Symposium on Electronics and the Environment 321 (2006).
20. Abigail Ng, *Smartphone Users Are Waiting Longer before Upgrading – Here's Why*, CNBC (May 16, 2019), www.cnbc.com/2019/05/17/smartphone-users-are-waiting-longer-before-upgrading-heres-why.html.
21. Nathan Bomey, *Old Cars Everywhere: Average Vehicle Age Hits All-Time High*, USA Today (June 28, 2019), www.usatoday.com/story/money/cars/2019/06/28/average-vehicle-age-ihs-markit/1593764001; Kyle Hyatt, *The Average Age of Cars on America's Roads Went Up Again, Report Says*, CNET (June 27, 2019), www.cnet.com/roadshow/news/average-vehicle-age-increase-america.
22. Miles Park, *Defying Obsolescence, in* Longer Lasting Products: Alternatives to the Throwaway Society (Tim Cooper, ed., 2010).
23. Joannes Mongardini & Aneta Radzikowski, *Global Smartphone Sales May Have Peaked: What Next?*, International Monetary Fund (May 29, 2020), www.imf.org/~/media/Files/Publications/WP/2020/English/wpiea2020070-print-pdf.ashx.
24. Lauren Thomas, *Resale Market Expected to Be Valued at $64 billion in 5 Years, as Used Clothing Takes Over Closets*, CNBC (June 23, 2020), www.cnbc.com/2020/06/23/thredup-resale-market-expected-to-be-valued-at-64-billion-in-5-years.html.
25. US Department of Energy, *Used Vehicle Sales Are More than Double the Number of New Vehicle Sales* (July 15, 2019), www.energy.gov/eere/vehicles/articles/fotw-1090-july-15–2019-used-vehicle-sales-are-more-double-number-new-vehicle.
26. Cooper, *supra* note 10.

27. John McCollough, *The Effect of Income Growth on the Mix of Purchases Between Disposable Goods and Reusable Goods,* 31 International Journal of Consumer Studies 213 (2007).

28. Adam Minter, Secondhand (2019).

29. Alex DeBellis & Nathan Proctor, *Repair Saves Families Big,* US PIRG (2021).

30. Jared Gilmour, *Americans Break Two Smartphone Screens Each Second, Costing $3.4 Billion a Year, Report Says,* Miami Herald (Nov. 21, 2018), www.miamiherald.com/news/nation-world /national/article222040170.html; *Mobile Myths Cost Consumers Dearly, as Americans Report Spending $3.4 Billion Replacing Millions of Smartphone Screens Last Year,* PR Newswire (Nov. 20, 2018), www.prnewswire.com/news-releases/mobile-myths-cost-con sumers-dearly-as-americans-report-spending-3-4-billion-replacing-millions-of-smartphone-screens-last-year-30075341 9.html.

31. Jim Gorzelany, *Soaring Cost of Parts Means Your Car Is More Likely to Be Totaled in an Accident,* Forbes (Feb. 15, 2018), www .forbes.com/sites/jimgorzelany/2018/02/15/the-sum-not-the-whole-is-greater-when-it-comes-to-the-skyrocketing-cost-of-car-parts.

32. Melissa Burden, *Parts, Service and Accessories Boost Ford, FCA, GM Revenue,* Detroit News (Mar. 23, 2017), www .detroitnews.com/story/business/autos/general-motors /2017/03/23/parts-accessories-boost-ford-fca-gm-revenue /99562692.

33. *Where Does the Car Dealer Make Money?,* Edmunds (June 13, 2019), www.edmunds.com/car-buying/where-does-the-car-dealer-make-money.html.

34. Daniel Hanley, Claire Kelloway & Sandeep Vaheesan, *Fixing America: Breaking Manufacturers' Aftermarket Monopoly and Restoring Consumers' Right to Repair,* Open Markets Institute Report (2020); Claire Bushey, *Why Deere and Cat Don't Want Customers to Do it Themselves,* Crain's Chicago Business (May 10, 2019), www.chicagobusiness.com/man ufacturing/why-deere-and-cat-dont-want-customers-do-it-themselves.

35. Michael Kan, *Apple: We Actually Lose Money by Offering Repair Services,* PC Magazine (Nov. 20, 2019), www.pcmag.com/news/ apple-we-actually-lose-money-by-offering-repair-services.

36. Gordon Kelly, *Apple's Absurd iPhone Repair Charges Inadvertently Exposed By Samsung*, Forbes (Apr. 11, 2019), www.forbes.com /sites/gordonkelly/2019/04/11/apple-iphone-xs-max-xr-repair-charges.

37. Sophie Curtis, *Apple Spent $10,000 Repairing MacBook Pro Only to Discover a Really Simple Fix*, Mirror (June 13, 2019), www .mirror.co.uk/tech/apple-spent-10000-repairing-macbook -16511936.

38. Derek Thompson, *How Hollywood Accounting Can Make a $450 Million Movie "Unprofitable*," Atlantic (Sept. 14, 2011), www .theatlantic.com/business/archive/2011/09/how-hollywood-accounting-can-make-a-450-million-movie-unprofitable /245134. *Tolkien Heirs Sue Lord of the Rings Studio for $150m*, The Guardian (Feb. 12, 2008), www.theguardian.com/film/2008/ feb/12/lordoftherings.jrrtolkien.

39. Tim Cooper, *Slower Consumption: Reflections on Product Life Spans and the "Throwaway Society*," 9 Journal of Industrial Ecology 51 (2005).

40. Cooper, *supra* note 10.

41. John McCollough, *Consumer Discount Rates and the Decision to Repair or Replace a Durable Product: A Sustainable Consumption Issue*, 44 Journal of Economic Issues 183 (2010); US Bureau of Labor Statistics, *Employment by Detailed Occupation*, www .bls.gov/emp/tables/emp-by-detailed-occupation.htm; United States Census Bureau, *A Look at the 1940 Census*, www .census.gov/newsroom/cspan/1940census/CSPAN_1940slides .pdf.

42. Nathan Proctor, *Americans Toss 151 Million Phones a Year. What If We Could Repair Them Instead?*, WBUR (Dec. 11, 2018), www .wbur.org/cognoscenti/2018/12/11/right-to-repair-nathan-proctor.

43. Vanessa Forti, Cornelis Peter Baldé, Ruediger Kuehr & Garam Bel, *Global E-waste Monitor 2020*, www.itu.int/en/ITU-D/Environment/Documents/Toolbox/GEM_2020_def.pdf. Per capita, the most electronic waste is generated in Europe (16.2 kg), Oceania (16.1 kg), and the Americas (13.3 kg).

44. Brook Larmer, *E-Waste Offers an Economic Opportunity as Well as Toxicity*, New York Times (July 5, 2018), www.nytimes.com/ 2018/07/05/magazine/e-waste-offers-an-economic-opportu nity-as-well-as-toxicity.html.

45. Forti, Baldé, Kuehr & Bel, *supra* note 43.

46. *Id.*
47. Aimin Chen, Kim N. Dietrich, Xia Huo & Shuk-mei Ho, *Developmental Neurotoxicants in E-waste: An Emerging Health Concern*, 119 Environmental Health Perspectives 431 (Apr. 2011).
48. Alexandra Ossola, *Where Do Recycled Electronics Go?*, Popular Science (Dec. 23, 2014), www.popsci.com/where-do-recycled-electronics-go. In the United States, only 19 of the 50 states have laws against tossing electronics out with household trash. Alana Semuels, *The World Has an E-waste Problem*, Time (June 3, 2019), https://time.com/5594380/world-electronic-waste-problem/.
49. Rashmi Makkar Panwar & Sirajuddin Ahmed, *Assessment of Contamination of Soil and Groundwater Due to E-waste Handling*, 114 Current Science 166 (2018), www.currentscience.ac.in /cs/Volumes/114/01/0166.pdf.
50. Devin N. Perkins, Marie-Noel Brune Drisse, Tapiwa Nxele & Peter D. Sly, *E-Waste: A Global Hazard*, 80 Annals of Global Health 286 (July 2014), www.sciencedirect.com/science/arti cle/pii/S2214999614003208; Kristen Grant, Fiona C. Goldizen, Peter D. Sly, Marie-Noel Brune, Maria Neira, Martin van den Berg & Rosana E. Norman, *Health Consequences of Exposure to E-waste: A Systematic Review*, 1 Lancet Global Health 350 (Dec. 2013), www.thelancet.com /journals/langlo/article/PIIS2214-109X(13)70101–3/fulltext.
51. After accepting the bulk of the world's e-waste for years, China began banning imports in 2018. Larmer, *supra* note 44.
52. Basel Convention, www.basel.int/TheConvention/ Overview/TextoftheConvention/tabid/1275/Default.aspx; *Frequent Questions on International Agreements on Transboundary Shipments of Waste*, United States Environmental Protection Agency, www.epa.gov/hwgenerators/frequent-questions-international-agreements-transboundary-shipments -waste#basel.
53. Zhaohua Wang, Bin Zhang & Dabo Guan, *Take Responsibility for Electronic-Waste Disposal*, Nature (Aug. 3, 2016), www.nature .com/news/take-responsibility-for-electronic-waste-disposal-1.20345#/b6.
54. In many cases, used electronics shipped overseas are intended for reuse and repair. Those secondary markets should be supported and celebrated. At the same time,

given the tendency of developed economies to foist their junk on the rest of the world. some skepticism is warranted. Larmer, *supra* note 44; Minter, *supra* note 28.

55. Paul Mohai & Robin Saha, *Which Came First, People or Pollution? Assessing the Disparate Siting and Post-Siting Demographic Change Hypotheses of Environmental Injustice*, IOP Science (Nov. 18, 2015), https://iopscience.iop.org/article/10.1088/1748-9326/10/11/115008/meta; Bryce Covert, *Race Best Predicts Whether You Live Near Pollution*, Nation (Feb. 18, 2016), www.thenation.com/article/archive/race-best-predicts-whether-you-live-near-pollution.

56. European Automobile Manufacturers' Association, *World Motor Vehicle Production*, www.acea.be/statistics/tag/category/world-production; Jon Chavez, *Huge Whirlpool Plant Runs Heart of Clyde*, Toledo Blade (Mar. 19, 2017), www.toledoblade.com/business/2017/03/19/Huge-Whirlpool-plant-runs-heart-of-Clyde.html.

57. Matthew Humphries, *Human Life Requires 26 Essential Elements, an iPhone Requires 75*, PC Magazine (Nov. 30, 2016), www.pcmag.com/news/human-life-requires-26-essential-elements-an-iphone-requires-75.

58. Brian Merchant, The One Device: The Secret History of the iPhone (2017); Brian Merchant, *Everything That's Inside Your iPhone*, Vice (Aug. 15, 2017), www.vice.com/en/article/433wyq/everything-thats-inside-your-iphone.

59. Sam Costello, *How Many iPhones Have Been Sold Worldwide?*, Lifewire (Dec. 27, 2019), www.lifewire.com/how-many-iphones-have-been-sold-1999500.

60. The raw materials necessary to produce an iPhone vary between models, so this figure represents a rough estimate. It also doesn't account for Apple's small but growing recycling efforts.

61. Sophia Chen, *Mercury Pollution Is Way Up. One Huge Culprit? Gold Mines*, Wired (Nov. 29, 2018), www.wired.com/story/mercury-poisoning-gold-mines.

62. Jules Morgan, *Mining and Tuberculosis: We Need to Dig Deeper*, Lancet Respiratory Medicine (Oct. 2014), www.cdc.gov/niosh/mining/topics/respiratorydiseases.html.

63. Merchant, *Everything That's Inside Your iPhone*, *supra* note 58.

64. Livia Albeck-Ripka, *Abandoned Rio Tinto Mine Is Blamed for Poisoned Bougainville Rivers*, New York Times (Sept. 30,

2020), www.nytimes.com/2020/09/30/world/australia/rio-tinto-abandoned-mine-poison-rivers.html.

65. Sam Ro, *Here's How Many Tons of Rock You Have to Mine Just for an Ounce of Gold*, Business Insider (Apr. 24, 2013), www.businessin sider.com/tons-of-rock-for-an-ounce-of-gold-2013-4.

66. Lewis Gordon, *The Environmental Impact of a Playstation 4*, Verge (Dec. 5, 2019), www.theverge.com/2019/12/5/20985330/ps4-sony-playstation-environmental-impact-carbon-footprint-manufacturing-25-anniversary.

67. Kiera Butler, *Your Smartphone's Dirty, Radioactive Secret*, Mother Jones (Nov. 2012), www.motherjones.com/environ ment/2012/11/rare-earth-elements-iphone-malaysia.

68. Marla Cone, *Desert Lands Contaminated by Toxic Spills*, Los Angeles Times (Apr. 24, 1997), www.latimes.com/archives/la-xpm-1997-04-24-mn-51903-story.html.

69. Yao-Hua Law, *Radioactive Waste Standoff Could Slash High Tech's Supply of Rare Earth Elements*, Science (Apr. 1, 2019), www.scien cemag.org/news/2019/04/radioactive-waste-standoff-could-slash-high-tech-s-supply-rare-earth-elements.

70. Tim Maughan, *The Dystopian Lake Filled by the World's Tech Lust*, BBC (Apr. 2, 2015), www.bbc.com/future/article/20150402-the-worst-place-on-earth.

71. Butler, *supra* note 67.

72. Cécile Bontron, *Rare-Earth Mining in China Comes at a Heavy Cost for Local Villages*, The Guardian (Aug. 7, 2012), www.theguar dian.com/environment/2012/aug/07/china-rare-earth-village-pollution.

73. *Id.*

74. Butler, *supra* note 67.

75. Xinkai Fu, Danielle N. Beatty, Gabrielle G. Gaustad, Gerbrand Ceder, Richard Roth, Randolph E. Kirchain, Michele Bustamante, Callie Babbitt & Elsa A. Olivetti, *Perspectives on Cobalt Supply through 2030 in the Face of Changing Demand*, 54 Environmental Science & Technology 2985 (2020).

76. Siddharth Kara, *Is Your Phone Tainted by the Misery of the 35,000 Children in Congo's Mines?*, The Guardian (Oct. 12, 2018), www.theguardian.com/global-development/2018/oct/12/phone-misery-children-congo-cobalt-mines-drc.

77. Omar Akhtar, *Tantalum: A Metal for Bond Villains*, Fortune (Oct. 9, 2012), https://fortune.com/2012/10/09/tantalum-a-metal-for-bond-villains/.

78. Lynnley Browning, *Where Apple Gets the Tantalum for Your iPhone*, Newsweek (Feb. 4, 2015), www.newsweek.com/2015/02/13/where-apple-gets-tantalum-your-iphone-304351.html.

79. Noah Shachtman, *Inside Africa's "PlayStation War,"* Wired (July 15, 2008), www.wired.com/2008/07/the-playstation-2.

80. In 2012, the US Securities and Exchange Commission adopted a rule that requires companies to disclose whether their products contained conflict minerals that originated in the DRC or neighboring countries. In addition, the rule demanded firms provide a report describing the measures it took to investigate the source of those minerals that and identify any of its products that are not "conflict free." Those disclosures, under the rule, were to be made available to the public on the firm's website. 17 CFR 240.13p-1. After the National Association of Manufacturers, a trade group representing device makers sued, the D.C. Circuit Court of Appeals held the regulations violated the First Amendment because they compelled firms to classify their products as not "conflict free." Nat'l Ass'n of Manufacturers v. S.E.C., 800 F.3d 518 (D.C. Cir. 2015).

81. International Labor Organization, *Sectoral Survey of Child Labour in Informal Tin Mining in Kepulauan Bangka Belitung Province, Indonesia* 2014 (2015), www.ilo.org/ipec/Informationresources/WCMS_IPEC_PUB_27535/lang–en/index.htm; Cam Simpson, *The Deadly Tin Inside Your Smartphone*, Bloomberg (Aug. 23, 2012), www.bloomberg.com/news/articles/2012–08–23/the-deadly-tin-inside-your-smartphone.

82. Merchant, *Everything That's Inside Your iPhone*, *supra* note 58.

83. *Id.* Kate Hodal, *Samsung Admits Its Phones May Contain Tin from Area Mined by Children*, The Guardian (Apr. 25, 2013), www.theguardian.com/environment/2013/apr/25/samsung-tin-mines-indonesia-child-labour.

84. Gordon, *supra* note 66.

85. *Id.*

86. Joanie Faletto, *The Stupidly Dangerous Chemical Chlorine Trifluoride Can Make Anything Burst Into Flames on Contact*, Discovery (Aug. 1, 2019), www.discovery.com/science/Dangerous-Chemical-Chlorine-Trifluoride.

87. *Semiconductor Industry*, United States Environmental Protection Agency, www.epa.gov/f-gas-partnership-programs/semiconductor-industry.

88. Gordon, *supra* note 66.
89. Lotfi Belkhir & Ahmed Elmeligi, *Assessing ICT Global Emissions Footprint: Trends to 2040 & Recommendations*, 177 Journal of Cleaner Production 448 (2018).
90. Gordon, *supra* note 66.
91. This figure is based on an iPhone 11 with 256GB of storage. According to Apple, the total carbon footprint for this model is 89 kg, roughly 80% of which is attributable to production. The bulk of the remainder comes from energy required to charge the device over its useful life. Apple, *Product Environmental Report: iPhone 11* (Sept. 10, 2019), www.apple.com/environ ment/pdf/products/iphone/iPhone_11_PER_sept2019.pdf.
92. Apple, *Apple Commits to Be 100 Percent Carbon Neutral for Its Supply Chain and Products by 2030* (July 21, 2020), www.apple.com/ newsroom/2020/07/apple-commits-to-be-100-percent-carbon-neutral-for-its-supply-chain-and-products-by-2030; Sony, *Road to Zero*, www.sony.net/SonyInfo/csr/eco/RoadToZero/gm_en .html.
93. Jessica F. Green, *Why Do We Need New Rules on Shipping Emissions? Well, 90 Percent of Global Trade Depends on Ships*, Washington Post (Apr. 17, 2018), www.washingtonpost.com/news/monkey-cage/wp/2018/04/17/why-do-we-need-new-rules-on-shipping-emissions-well-90-of-global-trade-depends-on-ships.
94. Oceana, *Shipping Pollution*, https://europe.oceana.org/en/ship ping-pollution-1.
95. Miguel Jaller, *Evaluating the Environmental Impacts of Online Shopping: A Behavioral and Transportation Approach*, 80 Transportation Research Part D: Transport and Environment, 102223 (March 2020), www.sciencedirect.com/science/article/ abs/pii/S1361920919302639?via%3Dihub.
96. Irina Ivanova, *How Free One-Day Shipping Is Heating Up the Planet*, CBS (May 24, 2019), www.cbsnews.com/news/amazon-prime-day-one-day-shipping-has-a-huge-carbon-footprint.
97. Amazon, *All In: Staying the Course on Our Commitment to Sustainability* (2020), https://sustainability.aboutamazon .com/december_2020_report.pdf.
98. Apple, *Environmental Progress Report* (2020), www.apple.com/ environment/pdf/Apple_Environmental_Progress_Report_20 20.pdf.
99. Justine Calma, *Tesla to Make EV Battery Cathodes without Cobalt*, Verge (Sept. 22, 2020), www.theverge.com/2020/9/22/

21451670/tesla-cobalt-free-cathodes-mining-battery-nickel-ev-cost.

100. Max Opray, *Nickel Mining: The Hidden Environmental Cost of Electric Cars*, The Guardian (Aug. 24, 2017), www.theguardian.com/sustainable-business/2017/aug/24/nickel-mining-hidden-environmental-cost-electric-cars-batteries; Alec Luhn, *Where the River Runs Red: Can Norilsk, Russia's Most Polluted City, Come Clean?*, The Guardian (Sept. 15, 2016), www.theguardian.com/cities/2016/sep/15/norilsk-red-river-russias-most-polluted-city-clean.

101. Radina Gigova, *Russian River Turned Red by Metallurgical Waste, Norilsk Nickel Says*, CNN (Sept. 13, 2016), www.cnn.com/2016/09/12/world/russia-red-river-siberia/index.html; *Arctic River Turns Red Again – Two Years after "Pollution Problem" Supposedly Fixed*, Siberian Times (June 14, 2018), https://siberiantimes.com/ecology/others/news/arctic-river-turns-red-again-two-years-after-pollution-problem-supposedly-fixed/; Mary Ilyushina, *The Russian Whistleblower Risking It All to Expose the Scale of an Arctic Oil Spill Catastrophe*, CNN (July 10, 2020), www.cnn.com/2020/07/10/europe/arctic-oil-spill-russia-whistleblower-intl/index.html.

102. Maddie Stone, *Russian Indigenous Communities Are Begging Tesla Not to Get Its Nickel from this Major Polluter*, Grist (Sept. 21, 2020), https://grist.org/justice/russian-indigenous-communities-are-begging-tesla-not-to-get-its-nickel-from-this-major-polluter/.

103. Forti, Baldé, Kuehr & Bel, *supra* note 43.

104. US Environmental Protection Agency, *Frequent Questions about the Sustainable Materials Management (SMM) Electronics Challenge*, www.epa.gov/smm-electronics/frequent-questions-about-sustainable-materials-management-smm-electronics-challenge.

105. Steve McCaskill, *Raw Materials Needed for Mobile Phones Could Run Out without More Recycling*, Techradar (Aug. 21, 2019), www.techradar.com/news/raw-materials-needed-for-mobile-phones-could-run-out-without-more-recycling.

106. Taptic engines account for only 25% of the rare earth metals used in new iPhones, however. Apple, *supra* note 98.

107. Microsoft, *End-of-Life Management and Recycling*, www.microsoft.com/en-us/legal/compliance/recycling.

108. Tesla, *Impact Report* (2019), www.tesla.com/ns_videos/2019-tesla-impact-report.pdf.

109. Apple, *Environmental Responsibility Report* (2019), www
     .apple.com/environment/pdf/Apple_Environmental_Respon
     sibility_Report_2019.pdf. The company's latest robot, Dave,
     is designed specifically to recover rare-earth elements from
     taptic engines. *Id.*

110. Apple, *Apple Expands Global Recycling Programs* (Apr. 18,
     2019), www.apple.com/newsroom/2019/04/apple-expands-
     global-recycling-programs.

111. *Id.*

112. Larmer, *supra* note 44.

113. Homer, of course, was referring to alcohol. *The Simpsons*,
     Season 8, Episode 18 (1997).

114. Forti, Baldé, Kuehr & Bel, *supra* note 43.

115. *Id.*

116. *Id.*

117. Diana Maria Ceballos & Zhao Dong, *The Formal Electronic
     Recycling Industry: Challenges and Opportunities in Occupational
     and Environmental Health Research*, 96 Environment
     International 157 (2016).

118. Kun Wang, Junxi Qian & Lixiong Liu, *Understanding
     Environmental Pollutions of Informal E-Waste Clustering in
     Global South via Multi-Scalar Regulatory Frameworks: A Case
     Study of Guiyu Town, China*, 17 International Journal of
     Environmental Research and Public Health 2802 (2020).

119. Perkins et al., *supra* note 50.

120. *Id.*; Wang et al., *supra* note 118.

121. *Id.*; Anthony Boardman, Jeff Geng & Bruno Lam, *The Social
     Cost of Informal Electronic Waste Processing in Southern China*,
     10 Administrative Sciences 1 (2020).

122. Basel Action Network, *Scam Recycling: e-Dumping on Asia by
     US Recyclers* (2016), https://wiki.ban.org/images/1/12/
     ScamRecyclingReport-web.pdf.

123. FDA, *Firmware Update to Address Cybersecurity Vulnerabilities
     Identified in Abbott's (formerly St. Jude Medical's) Implantable
     Cardiac Pacemakers* (Aug. 29, 2017), https://web.archive.org
     /web/20170830080601/www.fda.gov/medicaldevices/
     safety/alertsandnotices/ucm573669.htm.

124. Peter Loftus, *Hacking Is a Risk for Pacemakers. So Is the Fix*,
     Wall Street Journal (Oct. 20, 2017), www.wsj.com/arti
     cles/hacking-is-a-risk-for-pacemakers-so-is-the-fix-
     1508491802.

125. Matthew Gault, *Colorado Denied Its Citizens the Right-to-Repair after Riveting Testimony*, Vice, 5 Apr. 2021.
126. Adam Minter, *Don't Drop Your iPhone Now: Repairing It Is a Problem*, Bloomberg (Mar. 28, 2020), www.bloomberg.com/opinion/articles/2020–03–28/apple-s-rules-make-iphone-repairs-hard-to-get-amid-coronavirus.
127. Henke, *supra* note 1.
128. Lara Houston, Steven J. Jackson, Daniela K. Rosner, Syed Ishtiaque Ahmed, Meg Young & Laewoo Kang, *Values in Repair*, Proceedings of the 2016 CHI Conference on Human Factors in Computing Systems 1403 (2016).
129. Amir-Homayoun Javadi, Beatrix Emo, Lorelei R. Howard, Fiona E. Zisch, Yichao Yu, Rebecca Knight, Joao Pinelo Silva & Hugo J. Spiers, *Hippocampal and Prefrontal Processing of Network Topology to Simulate the Future*, 8 Nature Communications (2017), www.nature.com/articles/ncomms14652.
130. Douglas Harper, Working Knowledge: Skill and Community in a Small Shop 62 (1987).
131. Katherine White, *What if Bicycles Held the Secret to Human Flight?*, Henry Ford Museum, www.thehenryford.org/explore/stories-of-innovation/what-if/wright-brothers; Brittany McCrigler, *The Wright Way: Repair Teaches Engineering*, iFixit (Mar. 21, 2013), www.ifixit.com/News/4404/the-wright-way-to-teach-engineering.
132. Kathleen Franz, Tinkering: Consumers Reinvent the Early Automobile (2011).
133. Guy Keulemans, *The Geo-cultural Conditions of Kintsugi*, 9 The Journal of Modern Craft 15 (2016).
134. Sophia Smith, *The Japanese Art of Recognizing Beauty in Broken Things*, Make (Aug. 17, 2015), https://makezine.com/2015/08/17/kintsugi-japanese-art-recognizing-beauty-broken-things/. As an aside for Star Wars fans, kintsugi inspired the design of Kylo Ren's rebuilt helmet in The Rise of Skywalker. Dom Nero, *J.J. Abrams Has Confirmed a Big Kylo Ren Fan Theory about Star Wars: The Rise of Skywalker*, Esquire (Oct. 1, 2019), www.esquire.com/entertainment/movies/a29318997/kylo-ren-star-wars-the-rise-of-skywalker-fan-theory-confirmed-jj-abrams.
135. Keulemans, *supra* note 133.
136. Julian E. Orr, Talking about Machines: An Ethnography of a Modern Job (1996).

137. Christophe Lejeune, *Interruptions, Lunch Talks, and Support Circles: An Ethnography of Collective Repair in Steam Locomotive Restoration*, in Repair Work Ethnographies: Revisiting Breakdown, Relocating Materiality (Ignaz Strebel, Alain Bovet & Philippe Sormani, eds., 2019).
138. Syed Ishtiaque Ahmed, Stephen J. Jackson & Md. Rashidujjaman Rifat, *Learning to Fix: Knowledge, Collaboration and Mobile Phone Repair in Dhaka, Bangladesh*, Proceedings of the Seventh International Conference on Information and Communication Technologies and Development 1 (2015).
139. Daniela K. Rosner, *Making Citizens, Reassembling Devices: On Gender and the Development of Contemporary Public Sites of Repair in Northern California*, 26 Public Culture 51 (2014).
140. Volkswagen, *Electric Vehicles with Lowest CO2 Emissions* (Apr. 24, 2019), www.volkswagen-newsroom.com/en/press-releases/electric-vehicles-with-lowest-co2-emissions-4886; Tesla, *supra* note 108.
141. C. Britt Bousman, *Coping with Risk: Later Stone Age Technological Strategies at Blydefontein Rock Shelter, South Africa*, 24 Journal of Anthropological Archaeology 193 (Sept. 2005).

3 The History of Repair

1. Ron Shimelmitz, Michael Bisson, Mina Weinstein-Evron & Steven L. Kuhn, *Handaxe Manufacture and Re-Sharpening throughout the Lower Paleolithic Sequence of Tabun Cave*, 428 Quaternary International 118 (2017).
2. Talía Lazuén, *European Neanderthal Stone Hunting Weapons Reveal Complex Behaviour Long before the Appearance of Modern Humans*, 39 Journal of Archaeological Science 2304 (2012); Paola Villa, Paolo Boscato, Filomena Ranaldo & Annamaria Ronchitelli, *Stone Tools for the Hunt: Points with Impact Scars from a Middle Paleolithic Site in Southern Italy*, 36 Journal of Archaeological Science 850 (2009).
3. Fiona Coward, Robert Hosfield, Matt Pope & Francis Wenban-Smith, *To See a World in a Hafted Tool: Birch Pitch Composite Technology, Cognition and Memory*, in Settlement, Society and Cognition in Human Evolution: Landscapes in the Mind (Fiona Coward, Robert Hosfield, Matt Pope & Francis Wenban-Smith, eds., 2015); Nick Walker, *The Late Stone Age of Botswana: Some Recent Excavations*, 26 Botswana Notes and Records 1 (1994);

Steven L. Kuhn, *On Planning and Curated Technologies in the Middle Paleolithic*, 48 Journal of Anthropological Research 185 (1992).

4. Sindya N. Bhanoo, *Oldest Known Pottery Found in China*, New York Times (June 28, 2012), www.nytimes.com/2012/07/03/science/oldest-known-pottery-found-in-china.html.

5. Pia Guldager Bilde & Søren Handberg, *Ancient Repairs on Pottery from Olbia Pontica*, 116 American Journal of Archaeology 461 (2012). In fact, this technique was used to repair stone vessels that predated the invention of pottery. Renske Dooijes & Olivier Peter Nieuwenhuyse, *Ancient Repairs in Archaeological Research: A Near Eastern Perspective*, in Holding It All Together: Ancient and Modern Approaches to Joining, Repair and Consolidation (Janet Ambers, Catherine Higgitt & Lynne Harrison, eds., 2009).

6. *Id.*

7. Renske Dooijes & Olivier Peter Nieuwenhuyse, *Ancient Repairs: Techniques and Social Meaning*, in Konservieren Oder Restaurieren: Die Restaurierung Griechischer Vasen von der Antike bis Heute (Martin Bentz & Ursula Kästner, eds., 2007).

8. Renske Dooijes, *Ancient Repairs of Bronze Objects*, Exarc (2012), https://exarc.net/issue-2012-3/ea/ancient-repairs-bronze-objects.

9. Peter Clark, *Shipwrights, Sailors and Society in the Middle Bronze Age of NW Europe*, 5 Journal of Wetland Archaeology 87 (2005).

10. Joanna Brück, *Houses, Lifecycles and Deposition on Middle Bronze Age Settlements in Southern England*, 65 Proceedings of the Prehistoric Society 145 (1999).

11. L. Richardson, Jr., A New Topographical Dictionary of Ancient Rome (1992).

12. Jody Joy, *"Fire Burn and Cauldron Bubble": Iron Age and Early Roman Cauldrons of Britain and Ireland*, 80 Proceedings of the Prehistoric Society 327 (2014).

13. Kristian Kristiansen, *The Tale of the Sword: Swords and Swordfighters in Bronze Age Europe*, 21 Oxford Journal of Archaeology 319 (2002).

14. Chris Gosden, *Social Ontologies*, 363 Philosophical Transactions of the Royal Society B: Biological Sciences 2003 (2008).

15. Helen Chittock, *Iron Age Antiques: Assessing the Functions of Old Objects in Britain from 400 bc to ad 100*, in Objects of the Past in the Past: Investigating the Significance of Earlier Artefacts

in Later Contexts (Matthew G. Knight, Dot Boughton & Rachel E. Wilkinson, eds., 2019).

16. *Id.*

17. Arnold Hugh Martin Jones, The Later Roman Empire, 284–602: A Social Economic and Administrative Survey 695 (1986); James W. Ermatinger, The Roman Empire: A Historical Encyclopedia 84 (2018).

18. Eric Poehler, Juliana van Roggen & Benjamin M. Crowther, *The Iron Streets of Pompeii*, 123 American Journal of Archaeology 237 (2019).

19. Kelly Robert DeVries & Robert Douglas Smith, Medieval Military Technology 55 (2012).

20. Heather Swanson, Building Craftsmen in Late Medieval York 11 (1983).

21. Ruth A. Johnston, All Things Medieval: An Encyclopedia of the Medieval World 707 (2011).

22. Jennifer M. Sheppard, *"Make Do and Mend": Evidence of Early Repairs and the Re-use of Materials in Early Bindings in a Cambridge College Library, in* Care and Conservation of Manuscripts 6 (Gillian Fellows-Jensen & Peter Spingborg, eds., 2002).

23. Clifford J. Rogers, The Oxford Encyclopedia of Medieval Warfare and Military Technology 22 (2010); David Featherstone Harrison, The Bridges of Medieval England: Transport and Society, 400–1800 (2004).

24. Anglo-Saxon brooches from the fifth and sixth centuries CE help illustrate the distinction. Toby Martin, *Riveting Biographies: The Theoretical Implications of Early Anglo-Saxon Brooch Repair, Customisation and Use-Adaptation, in* Make-do and Mend: Archaeologies of Compromise, Repair and Reuse (Ben Jervis & Alison Kyle, eds., 2012). These brooches, used to fasten garments, were frequent objects of repair. In some cases, repair served an aesthetic purpose, like when a decorative element was reattached. And given the importance of brooches in burial rights, repairs took on additional symbolic meaning.

25. Shelton A. Gunaratne, *Paper, Printing and the Printing Press: A Horizontally Integrative Macrohistory Analysis*, 63 Gazette 459 (2001).

26. Leonard Dudley, The Singularity of Western Innovation 172 (2017).

27. *Id.*

28. Ken Alder, *Innovation and Amnesia: Engineering Rationality and the Fate of Interchangeable Parts Manufacturing in France*, 38 Technology and Culture 273 (1997); David A. Hounshell, From the American System to Mass Production, 1800–1932: The Development of Manufacturing Technology in the United States (1984).

29. Dudley, *supra* note 26.

30. Alder, *supra* note 28.

31. Dudley, *supra* note 26.

32. *Id.*

33. Thomas Coulson, *The Origin of Interchangeable Parts*, 238 Journal of the Franklin Institute 335 (1944).

34. R.A. Church, *Nineteenth-Century Clock Technology in Britain, the United States, and Switzerland*, 28 The Economic History Review 616 (1975).

35. *Id.*

36. *Id.*

37. Joel Mokyr, *The Second Industrial Revolution, 1870–1914, in* Storia dell'economia Mondiale (Valerio Castronovo, ed., 1999); Alder, *supra* note 28; Coulson, *supra* note 33; Hounshell, *supra* note 28.

38. John Paxton, *Taylor's Unsung Contribution: Making Interchangeable Parts Practical*, 17 Journal of Business and Management 75 (2011).

39. Office of Technology Assessment, Global Standards: Building Blocks for the Future (1992); Harold C. Livesay, American Made: Shaping the American Economy (2016).

40. Alfred D. Chandler, Jr., The Visible Hand: The Managerial Revolution in American Business (1977).

41. James P. Womack, Daniel T. Jones & Daniel Roos, The Machine that Changed the World (1990); Royce Peterson, *The 1911 Model T Ford Tool Kit*, Model T Ford Fix (Jan. 14, 2018), https://modeltfordfix.com/the-1911-model-t-ford-tool-kit/.

42. Henry Ford & Samuel Crowther, My Life and Work (1922).

43. Daniel Hanley, Claire Kelloway & Sandeep Vaheesan, *Fixing America: Breaking Manufacturers' Aftermarket Monopoly and Restoring Consumers' Right to Repair*, Open Markets Institute Report (2020).

44. This strategy obviously benefits monopolists, since they can capture all replacement sales. But oligopolists, those

competing in concentrated markets stand to benefit from this strategy as well since consumers have few options. Jeremy Bulow, *An Economic Theory of Planned Obsolescence*, 101 Quarterly Journal of Economics 729 (1986).

45. Kamila Pope, Understanding Planned Obsolescence: Unsustainability Through Production, Consumption and Waste Generation (2017).

46. Bernard London, Ending the Depression Through Planned Obsolescence (1932).

47. Giles Slade, Made to Break: Technology and Obsolescence in America (2006).

48. Ford & Crowther, *supra* note 42.

49. J. George Frederick, *Is Progressive Obsolescence the Path toward Increased Consumption?*, 10 Advertising and Selling 11 (1928).

50. Susan Strasser, Waste and Want (1999).

51. *Id.*

52. Slade, *supra* note 47.

53. Daniel Joseph Boorstin, The Americans: The Democratic Experience (1974).

54. Slade, *supra* note 47.

55. Hanley et al., *supra* note 43.

56. Brian Burns, *Re-evaluating Obsolescence and Planning for It, in* Longer Lasting Products: Alternatives to the Throwaway Society (Tim Cooper, ed., 2010).

57. *Id.*

58. Frequency Service Allocations to Non-Government Fixed & Mobile Services in the Band 42–44 Mc, 39 F.C.C. 252 (1946).

59. Slade, *supra* note 47.

60. Dan Piepenbring, *Planned Obsolescence*, Paris Review (Oct. 7, 2014), www.theparisreview.org/blog/2014/10/07/planned-obsolescence.

61. Markus Krajewski, *The Great Lightbulb Conspiracy*, IEEE Spectrum (Sept. 24, 2014), https://spectrum.ieee.org/tech-history/dawn-of-electronics/the-great-lightbulb-conspiracy.

62. Letter from L.C. Porter to M.I. Sloan, Nov. 1, 1932. U.S. v. G.E. Civil Action No. 1364, 82 F. Supp. 753 Ex. 1860-G.

63. Krajewski, *supra* note 61.

64. United States v. General Electric Co., 82 F. Supp. 753 (D.N.J. 1949).

65. Strasser, *supra* note 50.

66. Jacqueline Morley, Make Do and Mend: A Very Peculiar History (2015).
67. *Make-Do and Mend Says Mrs. Sew-and-Sew*, Imperial War Museum, www.iwm.org.uk/collections/item/object/32395.
68. *Keep the Wheels Turning!: Repair Work Is Vital to the War Effort*, University of North Texas Digital Library, https://digital.library.unt.edu/ark:/67531/metadc394/.
69. *Use It Up – Wear It Out – Make It Do!*, New Hampshire State Library, www.nh.gov/nhsl/ww2/ww15.html.
70. Slade, *supra* note 47.
71. Bjoern Bartels, Ulrich Ermel, Peter Sandborn & Michael G. Pecht, Strategies to the Prediction, Mitigation and Management of Product Obsolescence (2012).
72. Slade, *supra* note 47.
73. Alan Philips, *Why the Things You Buy Don't Last*, Maclean's, Dec. 17, 1960.
74. Christian Dior, Christian Dior and I (1957).
75. Philips, *supra* note 73.
76. *Id.*
77. Vance Packard, The Waste Makers (1960).
78. *Id.* (quoting Victor Lebow, *Price Competition in 1955*, The Journal of Retailing 7 (1955).
79. Dwight D. Eisenhower, *The President's News Conference* (Apr. 9, 1958), www.presidency.ucsb.edu/documents/the-presidents-news-conference-261.
80. Packard, *supra* note 77.
81. Slade, *supra* note 47.
82. Packard, *supra* note 77.
83. *Id.*
84. Nokia Bell Labs, *1956 Nobel Prize in Physics*, www.bell-labs.com/about/recognition/1956-transistor.
85. Jason Cross, *Inside Apple's A13 Bionic System-on-Chip*, Macworld (Oct. 2, 2019), www.macworld.com/article/3442716/inside-apples-a13-bionic-system-on-chip.html.
86. Slade, *supra* note 47.
87. *Id.*
88. Instructables, *How to Repair and Revive an American Made Zenith Transistor Radio*, www.instructables.com/id/How-to-repair-and-revive-an-american-made-Zenith-t.
89. United States Census Bureau, *Population and Housing Unit Counts* (2012), www.census.gov/prod/cen2010/cph-2–1.pdf.

90. *See* Isabel Wilkerson, The Warmth of Other Suns (2010).
91. University of Virginia Library, *The Hillbilly Highway*, www .arcgis.com/apps/Cascade/index.html?appid=b44 f93ec18844109b1d26979d541b426.
92. Javins v. First Nat. Realty Corp., 428 F.2d 1071, 1077 (D.C. Cir. 1970).
93. *Id.* at footnote 30.
94. Michael J. Davis & Phillip E. DeLaTorre, *A Fresh Look at Premises Liability As Affected by the Warranty of Habitability*, 59 Washington Law Review 141, 143 (1984).
95. Michael A. Brower, *The "Backlash" of the Implied Warranty of Habitability: Theory vs. Analysis*, 60 DePaul Law Review 849, 854 (2011).
96. Francis H. Bohlen, *Landlord and Tenant*, 35 Harvard Law Review 633, 636 (1922).
97. Davis & DeLaTorre, *supra* note 94.
98. One question was whether such laws created private rights that allowed tenants to sue or to assert the failure to repair as a defense or if, instead, repair obligations could only be asserted by local housing officials.
99. Richard H. Chused, *Saunders (a.k.a. Javins) v. First National Realty Corporation 10th Anniversary Symposium Issue: Empowering the Poor and Disenfranchised: Making a Difference through Community, Advocacy, and Policy*, 11 Georgetown Journal on Poverty Law and Policy 191 (2004).
100. *Javins*, 428 F.2d at 1078.
101. Reste Realty Corp. v. Cooper, 53 N.J. 444, 452 (1969).
102. *Javins*, 428 F.2d at 1080.
103. Joshua Fairfield has drawn a more explicit connection between feudal landowners and modern day device makers. As he argues, if consumers cannot control the devices they purchase – including the ability to repair them – then we no more own our smartphones and cars than feudal tenants owned the land they worked for the benefit of their local lord. Joshua A.T. Fairfield, Owned (2017).

4 Breaking Repair

1. Matthias Gafni, *Has BART's Cutting-Edge 1972 Technology Design Come Back to Haunt It?*, Mercury News (Mar. 25, 2016), www

.mercurynews.com/2016/03/25/has-barts-cutting-edge-1972-
technology-design-come-back-to-haunt-it.

2. Peter Hartlaub, *The Shiny, Futuristic BART that Wowed President
Nixon*, San Francisco Chronicle (Mar. 25, 2016), www
.sfchronicle.com/oursf/article/Nixon-s-futuristic-BART-ride-
It-does-look-7025172.php.

3. An Act for Regulating the Gauge of Railways 1846, www
.railwaysarchive.co.uk/documents/HMG_Act_Reg1846
.pdf.

4. Aaron Mak, *An Interview with the Guy Behind That Viral Railroad-
Gauge Tweet Thread*, Slate (Oct. 2, 2019), www.slate.com/tech
nology/2019/10/bill-holohan-viral-railroad-gauge-twitter-
interview.html.

5. Angela Johnston, *Hey Area: How the Width of BART Tracks Affects
Your Commute*, KALW (July 5, 2016), www.kalw.org/post/hey-
area-how-width-bart-tracks-affects-your-commute.

6. San Francisco Bay Area Rapid Transit District, *2005 Annual
Report*, https://web.archive.org/web/20060922203544/www
.bart.gov/docs/AR2005.pdf.

7. Alix Martichoux, *BART Upgrading 47-Year-Old Equipment in Big
Step Toward Trains Every 2 Minutes*, Chron (Jan. 10, 2020), www
.chron.com/public-transportation/article/BART-new-train-
control-system-capacity-frequency-14965556.php.

8. Darrell Etherington, *Amazon Echo Is a $199 Connected
Speaker Packing an Always-On Siri-Style Assistant*, Tech
Crunch (Nov. 6, 2014), https://techcrunch.com/2014/11/
06/amazon-echo/.

9. Kyle Wiggers, *Canalys: 200 Million Smart Speakers Will Be Sold
before Year-End*, Venture Beat (Apr. 14, 2019), www.venture
beat.com/2019/04/14/canalys-200-million-smart-speakers-
will-be-sold-by-2019/.

10. *General Motors Reports Record Sales Of New Disposable Car*, The
Onion (Mar. 4, 2001), www.theonion.com/general-motors-
reports-record-sales-of-new-disposable-c-1819565961.

11. Tim Moynihan, *Samsung Finally Reveals Why the Note 7 Kept
Exploding*, Wired (Jan. 22, 2017), www.wired.com/2017/01/
why-the-samsung-galaxy-note-7-kept-exploding.

12. Shannon Liao, *Apple Says Cheap Battery Replacements Hurt
iPhone Sales*, Verge (Jan. 2, 2019), www.theverge.com/2019/
1/2/18165866/apple-iphone-sales-cheap-battery-replace
ment; Rajesh Kumar Singh, *Deere Bets on Cost Cuts, Services*

Push to Boost Profits, Reuters (Jan. 8, 2020), www
.reuters.com/article/us-deere-strategy/deere-bets-on-cost-
cuts-services-push-to-boost-profits-idUSKBN1Z72TA.

13. Sarah Emerson, *Documents Reveal Apple's Struggle to Define Its
Stance on Right to Repair*, OneZero (July 30, 2020), https://
onezero.medium.com/documents-reveal-apples-struggle-to
-define-its-stance-on-right-to-repair-15a757103261.

14. Lawrence Lessig, *The New Chicago School*, 27 Journal of Legal
Studies 661 (1998).

15. As Veblen noted at the end of the nineteenth century, some
luxury goods do not follow this rule. As their prices increase,
so does demand. For goods meant to communicate the
wealth and status of their owner, a higher price makes
them more desirable. Thorstein Veblen, The Theory of the
Leisure Class (1899).

16. *Microsoft Surface Laptop Teardown*, iFixit (June 15, 2017), www
.ifixit.com/Teardown/Microsoft+Surface+Laptop+Teardown/
92915.

17. This tweet thread from Cory Doctorow explores the details.
Cory Doctorow, *Caveat Emptor!*, Thread Reader (Apr. 9,
2021), https://threadreaderapp.com/thread/1380554358824
136706.html.

18. *Motorola Razr Teardown*, iFixit (Feb. 13, 2020), www.ifixit.com
/Teardown/Motorola+Razr+Teardown/130414.

19. Kelsea Weber, *Bit History: The Spanner*, iFixit (Apr. 22, 2018),
www.ifixit.com/News/9907/bit-history-the-spanner.

20. Bryce Security Fastener, *Tamperproof Screws Are History ... The
Age of High Security Screws Has Begun* (Jan. 31, 2012), www
.brycefastener.com/bryce-security-blog.html/2012/01/31/tam
perproof-screws-are-history-the-age-of-high-security-screws-
has-begun/#:~:text=The%20Age%20Of%20High%20Security%
20Screws%20Has%20Begun,-Jan%2031%2C%202012&text=
The%20tamperproof%20fastener%20industry%20has,public%
20restroom%20fixtures%20even%20today.

21. Matthew Shaer, *The Pentalobe Screws Saga: How Apple Locked
Up Your iPhone 4*, Christian Science Monitor (Jan. 21, 2011),
www.csmonitor.com/Technology/Horizons/2011/0121/
The-Pentalobe-screws-saga-How-Apple-locked-up-your-
iPhone-4.

22. Retro Consoles Wiki, *Proprietary Screw Drives*, https://retro
consoles.fandom.com/wiki/Proprietary_Screw_Drives.

23. Vivienne Pearson, *Is It Better to Repair or Replace Broken Washing Machines?*, Australian Broadcasting Corporation (Sept. 19, 2017), www.abc.net.au/news/2017–09–20/repair-or-replace-broken-washing-machines/8957918.

24. Kimberley Mok, *Lawsuit over Front-Load Washers May Drive Consumers Back to Energy-Wasting Models*, Treehugger (Oct. 3, 2019), www.treehugger.com/lawsuit-mold-problem-front-load-washing-machine-4858336.

25. Terri Williams, *What Causes a Basket Spider to Break on a Front-Load Washer?*, Hunker, www.hunker.com/12003231/what-causes-a-basket-spider-to-break-on-a-front-load-washer; *The Washer Suffered from Planned Obsolescence*, Design News (Nov. 5, 2014), www.designnews.com/materials-assembly/washer-suffered-planned-obsolescence.

26. Douglas Adams, The Ultimate Hitchhiker's Guide, Complete and Unabridged (1997).

27. Joe Santoson, *The Audi S4 Model You Should Never Buy*, Motor Biscuit (Feb. 28, 2020), www.motorbiscuit.com/the-audi-s4-model-you-should-never-buy.

28. Chris Jay Hoofnagle, Aniket Kesari & Aaron Perzanowski, *The Tethered Economy*, 87 George Washington Law Review 783 (2019).

29. Matthew Panzarino, *Apple Apologizes and Updates iOS to Restore iPhones Disabled by Error 53*, Techcrunch (Feb. 18, 2016), https://techcrunch.com/2016/02/18/apple-apologizes-and-updates-ios-to-restore-iphones-disabled-by-error-53/; Miles Brignall, *"Error 53" Fury Mounts as Apple Software Update Threatens to Kill Your iPhone 6*, The Guardian (Feb. 5, 2016), www.theguardian.com/money/2016/feb/05/error-53-apple-iphone-software-update-handset-worthless-third-party-repair.

30. Jennifer Bisset, *Apple Fined $6.6M in Australia after Error 53 Controversy*, Cnet (June 18, 2018), www.cnet.com/news/apple-bricked-our-phones-with-error-53-now-it-owes-6-8-million-in-australia.

31. Adi Robertson, *Apple Agrees to $500 Million Settlement for Throttling Older iPhones*, Verge (Mar. 2, 2020), www.theverge.com/2020/3/2/21161271/apple-settlement-500-million-throttling-battery-gate-class-action-lawsuit.

32. Jason Koebler, *Tim Cook to Investors: People Bought Fewer New iPhones Because They Repaired Their Old Ones*, Vice (Jan. 2, 2019), www.vice.com/en_us/article/zmd9a5/tim-cook-to-investors-

people-bought-fewer-new-iphones-because-they-repaired-their-old-ones.

33. Jason Koebler, *Apple's New Proprietary Software Locks Will Kill Independent Repair on New MacBook Pros*, Vice (Oct. 4, 2018), www.vice.com/en_us/article/yw9qk7/macbook-pro-soft ware-locks-prevent-independent-repair.

34. Matthew Gault, *Apple's T2 Security Chip Has Created a Nightmare for MacBook Refurbishers*, Vice (May 4, 2020), www .vice.com/en_us/article/akw558/apples-t2-security-chip-has-created-a-nightmare-for-macbook-refurbishers.

35. Allison Conwell & Nathan Proctor, *Locked Out: The Unintended Consequences of Phone Activation Locks and How We Can Fix It* (2019), https://copirg.org/sites/pirg/files/reports/Locked%20Out.pdf.

36. Brian X. Chen, *Smartphones Embracing "Kill Switches" as Theft Defense*, New York Times (June 19, 2014), https://bits .blogs.nytimes.com/2014/06/19/antitheft-technology-led-to -a-dip-in-iphone-thefts-in-some-cities-police-say/.

37. Conwell & Proctor, *supra* note 35.

38. Jason Koebler, *Why Tens of Thousands of Perfectly Good, Donated iPhones Are Shredded Every Year*, Vice (Apr. 12, 2020), www.vice .com/amp/en_us/article/43jywd/why-tens-of-thousands-of-perfectly-good-donated-iphones-are-shredded-every-year.

39. Chris Welch, *Apple's iPhone 11 and 11 Pro Will Show a Warning on Your Lock Screen If They Can't Verify a Replaced Screen*, Verge (Sept. 25, 2019), www.theverge.com/2019/9/25/20884287/ apple-iphone-11-pro-max-display-screen-replacement-verifi cation-warning.

40. Kevin Purdy, *The New "Important" iPhone Camera Message Is Another Bad Omen*, iFixit (Jan. 27, 2021), www.ifixit.com /News/48768/the-new-important-iphone-camera-message-is -another-bad-omen.

41. Kevin Purdy, *Is This the End of the Repairable iPhone?*, iFixit (Oct. 29, 2020), www.ifixit.com/News/45921/is-this-the-end-of-the-repairable-iphone.

42. Hugh Jeffreys, *Samsung Starts Blocking 3rd Party Repairs? – Galaxy A51 Teardown and Repair Assessment*, YouTube (Jan. 16, 2021), www.youtube.com/watch?v=zGLQ9ZRntZo.

43. Kyle Wiens, *Copyright Law Is Bricking Your Game Console. Time to Fix That*, Wired (Dec. 11, 2020), www.wired.com/story/ copyright-law-is-bricking-your-game-console-time-to-fix-that.

44. Kyle Wiens, *You Gotta Fight for Your Right to Repair Your Car*, Atlantic (Feb. 13, 2014), www.theatlantic.com/technology/archive/2014/02/you-gotta-fight-for-your-right-to-repair-your-car/283791. Europe has its own framework for regulating the availability of automotive parts. *See* Commission Regulation (EU) No. 461/2010 of May 27, 2010.

45. Angus Loten, *Mechanics Seek Out "Right to Repair,"* Wall Street Journal (Feb. 10, 2011), www.wsj.com/articles/SB10001424052 748703555804576102272750344178.

46. Jason Koebler, *Why American Farmers Are Hacking Their Tractors with Ukrainian Firmware*, Vice (Mar. 21, 2017), www .vice.com/en_us/article/xykkkd/why-american-farmers-are-hacking-their-tractors-with-ukrainian-firmware.

47. Jason Koebler & Matthew Gault, *John Deere Promised Farmers It Would Make Tractors Easy to Repair. It Lied*, Vice (Feb. 18, 2021), www.vice.com/amp/en/article/v7m8mx/john-deere-promised-farmers-it-would-make-tractors-easy-to-repair-it-lied.

48. Leo Schwartz & Devi Lockwood, *Why It's So Hard for a Hospital in Tanzania to Fix Broken Incubators*, Rest of World, www.restof world.org/2021/why-its-so-hard-for-a-hospital-in-tanzania-to-fix-broken-baby-incubators.

49. Jason Koebler, *Why Repair Techs Are Hacking Ventilators with DIY Dongles from Poland*, Vice (July 9, 2020), www.vice.com /en/article/3azv9b/why-repair-techs-are-hacking-ventilators -with-diy-dongles-from-poland.

50. Jason Koebler, *Hacker Bypasses GE's Ridiculous Refrigerator DRM*, Vice (June 12, 2020), www.vice.com/en_us/article/ jgxpjy/hacker-bypasses-ges-ridiculous-refrigerator-drm.

51. This shift also amplifies concerns around privacy and security, among others. Hoofnagle, Kesari & Perzanowski, *supra* note 28.

52. Eventually, a company acquired the patents and other assets associated with Jibo, offering owners new hope. But this development only underscores that ownership of physical devices is insufficient to maintain or restore their functionality. Ashley Carman, *Jibo, the Social Robot that Was Supposed to Die, Is Getting a Second Life*, Verge (July 23, 2020), www.theverge.com/2020/7/23/21325644/jibo-social-robot-ntt-disruptionfunding.

53. Samsung, *Samsung-Authorized Galaxy Repair Services*, www .samsung.com/us/support/repair/pricing.

54. Luke Tully, *Apple Tries to Charge as Much as a New MacBook Pro for a Screen Replacement* (Sept. 14, 2020), https://luke tully.ca/macbook-screen-replacement-costs-as-much-as-a-brand-new-model/; Rob Beschizza, *Fix a Laptop Screen? That'll Cost More than a New Laptop*, Boing Boing (Sept. 15, 2020), www.boingboing.net/2020/09/15/fix-a-laptop-screen-thatll.html.

55. Rajesh Kumar Singh, *Deere Bets on Cost Cuts, Services Push to Boost Profits*, Reuters (Jan. 8, 2020), www.reuters.com/arti cle/us-deere-strategy/deere-bets-on-cost-cuts-services-push-to-boost-profits-idUSKBN1Z72TA; Claire Bushey, *Why Deere and Cat Don't Want Customers to Do it Themselves*, Crain's Chicago Business (May 10, 2019), www.chicagobu siness.com/manufacturing/why-deere-and-cat-dont-want-customers-do-it-themselves; *Where Does the Car Dealer Make Money?*, Edmunds (June 13, 2019), www.edmunds.com/car-buying/where-does-the-car-dealer-make-money.html.

56. Jeffrey Jablansky, *Why Your Replacement Headlight Cost $2,000*, Men's Journal, www.mensjournal.com/gear/most-expensive-car-parts-why-replacement-headlights-cost-2000-w434026/headlights-w434028.

57. *Mirror – BMW (51–16–7–352–368)*, https://parts.bmwofsoutha tlanta.com/oem-parts/bmw-mirror-51167352368.

58. *10851200 Handle for fridge doors*, www.mieleusa.com/e/han dle-handle-stainless-steel-look-10851200-p.

59. *Washer Control Knob 137314627*, www.searspartsdirect.com /product/33vrmtmhqq-0026–417/id-137314627.

60. *DG94-02738C*, www.samsungparts.com/Products/ Parts_and_Accessories/PID-DG94-02738C.aspx.

61. Koebler, *supra* note 46.

62. Elizabeth Chamberlain, *How Nikon Is Killing Camera Repair*, iFixit (Feb. 14, 2012), www.ifixit.com/News/1349/how-nikon -is-killing-camera-repair.

63. Maddie Stone, *How Apple Decides Which Products Are "Vintage" and "Obsolete,"* OneZero (May 26, 2020), https://onezero .medium.com/how-apple-decides-which-products-are-vintage-and-obsolete-6055d0bda422.

64. Matthew Gault, *After 18 Years of Telling You Not to Fix It Yourself, Sony Will Stop Repairing the PlayStation 2*, Vice (Sept. 4, 2018), www.vice.com/en_us/article/ev8yyn/sony-playstation-2-sup port-ending.

65. Earnest Cavalli, *Microsoft Ends Repair Service for Original Xbox*, Wired (Mar. 2, 2009), www.wired.com/2009/03/microsoft-ends.

66. Apple, *Vintage and Obsolete Products*, https://support.apple.com/en-gb/HT201624.

67. California Civil Code § 1793.03.

68. Vintage and Obsolete Products, *supra* note 66.

69. Chaim Gartenberg, *Apple's Most Expensive Mac Pro Costs $53,799*, Verge (Dec. 10, 2019), www.theverge.com/circuit breaker/2019/12/10/21003636/apple-mac-pro-price-most-expensive-processor-ram-gpu.

70. Apple, *iPad Service and Repair*, https://support.apple.com/ipad/repair/service.

71. Kate Conger, *California Sues Uber and Lyft, Claiming Workers Are Misclassified*, New York Times (May 5, 2020), www.nytimes.com/2020/05/05/technology/california-uber-lyft-lawsuit.html.

72. Yaël Eisenstat, *I Worked on Political Ads at Facebook. They Profit by Manipulating Us*, Washington Post (Nov. 4, 2019), www.washingtonpost.com/outlook/2019/11/04/i-worked-politi cal-ads-facebook-they-profit-by-manipulating-us.

73. David Roberts, *Fossil Fuel Companies Impose More in Climate Costs than They Make in Profits*, Vox (June 20, 2016), www.vox.com/2015/7/24/9035803/fossil-fuel-companies-cost-of-carbon.

74. Kevin Purdy, *Here Are the Secret Repair Tools Apple Won't Let You Have*, iFixit (Oct. 28, 2019), www.ifixit.com/News/33593/heres-the-secret-repair-tool-apple-wont-let-you-have.

75. Jason Koebler, *Do You Know Anything about Apple's "Authorized Service Provider" Program?*, Vice (Mar. 16, 2017), www.vice.com/en_us/article/ypkqxw/do-you-know-anything-about-apples-authorized-service-provider-program.

76. *Apple Authorised Service Provider Program*, www.apple.com/support/assets/docs/products/programs/aasp/aasp_applicatio n_au_2013.pdf.

77. One independent repair shop owner estimated that becoming an AASP would cost him 75% of his business. Koebler, *supra* note 75.

78. Apple, *Apple Partners with Best Buy for Expanded Repair Service* (June 19, 2019), www.apple.com/newsroom/2019/06/apple-partners-with-best-buy-for-expanded-repair-service; Apple, *Apple Expands iPhone Repair Services to Hundreds of New Locations Across the US* (July 8, 2020), www.apple.com/news

room/2020/07/apple-expands-iphone-repair-services-to-hun
dreds-of-new-locations-across-the-us.
79. *Id.*
80. Ashley Carman, *Apple's Independent Repair Program Expands to Macs*, Verge (Aug. 17, 2020, www.theverge.com/2020/8/17/21372022/apple-independent-repair-program-mac-fix.
81. Maddie Stone, *Apple's Independent Repair Program Is Invasive to Shops and Their Customers, Contract Shows*, Vice (Feb. 6, 2020), www.vice.com/en_us/article/qjdjnv/apples-independent-repair-program-is-invasive-to-shops-and-their-customers-con tract-shows.
82. Daisuke Wakabayashi, *Apple Legal Fees in Samsung Patent Case Topped $60 Million*, Wall Street Journal (Dec. 6, 2013), www .wsj.com/articles/apple-legal-fees-in-samsung-patent-case-topped-60-million-1386360450.
83. Kevin Purdy, *Nikon Is Killing Its Authorized Repair Program*, iFixit (Dec. 9, 2019), www.ifixit.com/News/34241/nikon-is-killing-its-authorized-repair-program.
84. Nikon, *Nikon Professional Services*, www.nikonpro.com /MemberLevels.aspx.
85. Nikon, *NPS Membership Qualifying Equipment*, www .nikonpro.com/ProductList.aspx.
86. Yossy Mendelovich, *Nikon Is Suspending Equipment Repairs Due to COVID-19*, Y.M. Cinema Magazine (Mar. 23, 2020), http:// ymcinema.com/2020/03/23/nikon-is-suspending-equipment-repairs-due-to-impact-of-covid-19/.
87. Mike Moffitt, *The Thing About Owning a Tesla No One Talks About – Nightmarish Repair Delays*, SF Gate (May 1, 2019), www.sfgate .com/cars/article/tesla-repair-wait-time-complaints-electric-car-13796037.php; https://carbuzz.com/news/tesla-model -3-production-has-been-sorted-but-not-service-centers1; *Tesla's Hell Moves from the Production Line to the Repair Shop*, Bloomberg (Oct. 31, 2019), www.bloomberg.com/graphics/2019-tesla-model-3-survey/customer-service-battery.html.
88. Priya Anand, *What's Amazon's Share of Retail? Depends Who You Ask*, Information (June 13, 2019), www.theinformation.com/ articles/whats-amazons-share-of-retail-depends-who-you-ask; Daniel Keyes, *3rd-Party Sellers Are Thriving on Amazon*, Business Insider (May 13, 2019), www.businessinsider .com/amazon-third-party-sellers-record-high-sales-2019-5? r=US&IR=T.

89. Sarah Perez, *Amazon Sues Online Influencers Engaged in a Counterfeit Scheme*, Techcrunch (Nov. 12, 2020), https:// techcrunch.com/2020/11/12/amazon-sues-online-influencers -engaged-in-a-counterfeit-scheme/.

90. Nick Statt, *Amazon Will Start Selling Nike Shoes Directly for the First Time*, Verge (June 21, 2017), www.theverge.com/2017/6/ 21/15847700/amazon-nike-shoes-deal-e-commerce-zappos.

91. Jason Koebler, *Amazon Is Kicking All Unauthorized Apple Refurbishers Off Amazon Marketplace*, Vice (Nov. 9, 2018), www.vice.com/en_us/article/bjexb5/amazon-is-kicking-all-unauthorized-apple-refurbishers-off-the-site.

92. Nick Statt, *Apple and Amazon Cut a Deal that Upended the Mac Resale Market*, Vergem (May 21, 2019), www.theverge.com/ 2019/5/21/18624846/amazon-marketplace-apple-deal-iphones-mac-third-party-sellers-john-bumstead.

93. Reed Albergotti, Apple Says It Never "Recycles" Old Devices If They Can Still Be Used. Its Lawsuit against a Canadian Recycler Suggests Otherwise, Washington Post (Oct. 7, 2020), www.washingtonpost.com/technol ogy/2020/10/07/apple-geep-iphone-recycle-shred.

94. Lauren Feiner, *Google U.S. Ad Revenue Will Drop for the First Time this Year, eMarketer says*, CNBC (June 22, 2020), www .cnbc.com/2020/06/22/google-ad-revenue-will-drop-this-year-emarketer-says.html.

95. Michael Kan, *Google Ad Policy Change Leaves Third-Party Repair Industry in a Lurch*, PC (Aug. 8, 2019), www.pcmag.com/news/ google-ad-policy-change-leaves-third-party-repair-industry-in-a-lurch.

96. Google, *Other Restricted Businesses*, www.support.google .com/adspolicy/answer/6368711?hl=en.

97. Samarth Bansal & Rob Barry, *Tech-Support Scams Prompt Google to Act*, Wall Street Journal (Aug. 31, 2018), www.wsj .com/articles/tech-support-scams-on-google-trigger-crack down-1535755023.

98. Kan, *supra* note 95.

99. David Graff, *Restricting Ads in Third-Party Tech Support Services*, Google Ads & Commerce Blog (Aug. 31, 2018), www.blog .google/products/ads/restricting-ads-third-party-tech-sup port-services.

100. Google, *Get Your Pixel Phone Repaired*, www.support.google .com/store/answer/9004345.

101. Karl Bode & Matthew Gault, *Sonos Makes It Clear: You No Longer Own the Things You Buy*, Vice (Jan. 22, 2020), www.vice.com/en_us/article/3a8dpn/sonos-makes-it-clear-you-no-longer-own-the-things-you-buy.

102. Chris Welch, *Sonos Explains Why It Bricks Old Devices with "Recycle Mode,"* Verge (Dec. 30, 2019), www.theverge.com/2019/12/30/21042871/sonos-recycle-mode-trade-up-program-controversy.

103. Allen St. John, *Sonos Ends "Recycling" Program that Disabled Older Devices*, Consumer Reports (Mar. 6, 2020), www.consumerreports.org/speakers/sonos-ends-recycling-program-that-disabled-older-devices.

104. Chris Welch, *Sonos Will Release a New App and Operating System for Its Speakers in June*, Verge (May 17, 2020), www.theverge.com/2020/3/17/21182164/sonos-s2-announced-app-operating-system-high-res-audio-dolby-atmos.

105. Apple, *Apple Trade In*, www.apple.com/shop/trade-in.

106. Electronics recycling, while far preferable to disposing of devices in landfills, has its own downsides. In many instances, devices are shredded and the metal components are shipped to polluting smelters. Other times, devices are simply shipped to scrapyards in developing economies where they contribute to environmental harms and health risks. Peter Holgate, *The Model for Recycling Our Old Smartphones Is Actually Causing Massive Pollution*, Vox (Nov. 8, 2017), www.vox.com/2017/11/8/16621512/where-does-my-smartphone-iphone-8-x-go-recycling-afterlife-toxic-waste-environment. To their credit, companies like Apple have invested in improving this process. But they still recycle only a tiny fraction of the devices distributed into the global ecosystem.

107. Adam Minter, Secondhand 192–99 (2019).

108. The Global Baby Car Seat Market Is Expected to Grow from USD 5,050.17 Million in 2019 to USD 7,624.36 Million by the End of 2025 at a Compound Annual Growth Rate (CAGR) of 7.10%, Yahoo Finance (July 10, 2020), www.finance.yahoo.com/news/global-baby-car-seat-market-183754146.html.

109. Graco, *Car Seat Expiration*, www.gracobaby.com/carseatexpirationpage.html.

110. Minter, *supra* note 107. The current version of the website uses the passive voice to avoid attributing this advice to anyone in particular. "It is also advised not to purchase

a car seat secondhand." Target, *Car Seat Guide*, www
.target.com/c/car-seat-guide/-/N-4rqwe.

111. James Calvin Davis & Charles Mathewes, *Saving Grace and
Moral Striving: Thrift in Puritan Theology*, in Thrift and Thriving
in America: Capitalism and Moral Order from the Puritans to
the Present (Joshua Yates & James Davison Hunter, eds.,
2011).

112. Bruce H. Yenawine, Benjamin Franklin and the Invention
of Microfinance (2015); Andrew L. Yarrow, Thrift: The
History of an American Cultural Movement (2014).

113. Yarrow, *supra* note 112.

114. Marianne Bertrand & Emir Kamenica, *Coming Apart?
Cultural Distances in the United States over Time*, NBER
Working Paper Series (2018), www.nber.org/system/files/
working_papers/w24771/w24771.pdf.

115. Match, *Singles in America: Match Releases Largest Study on U.S.
Single Population* (Feb. 6, 2017), https://ir.mtch.com/news-
and-events/press-releases/press-release-details/2017/
Singles-in-America-Match-Releases-Largest-Study-on-US-
Single-Population/default.aspx.

116. It's not just the age of the device that can be stigmatized,
but the brand as well. C. Scott Brown, *Dear iPhone Users:
Please Don't Forget that a Green Bubble Is a Person*, Android
Authority (Aug. 24, 2019), www.androidauthority.com
/green-bubble-phenomenon-1021350.

117. Jayne Cox, Sarah Griffith, Sara Giorgi & Geoff King,
Consumer Understanding of Product Lifetimes, 79 Resources,
Conservation and Recycling 21–29 (2013).

118. *See, e.g.*, Apple, *Apple iMac (Retina 5K, 27-inch, Mid 2015) –
Important Product Information Guide*, www.yumpu.com/en/docu
ment/view/55992267/apple-imac-retina-5k-27-inch-mid-2015-
important-product-information-guide-imac-retina-5k-27-
inch-mid-2015-important-product-information-guide; Apple,
Mac mini Important Product Information Guide, https://manuals
.info.apple.com/MANUALS/1000/MA1630/en_US/mac_mini-
late-2012-important_product_info.pdf.

119. Apple, *iMac Essentials*, https://books.apple.com/us/book/
imac-essentials/id1041601527.

120. Apple, *Important safety information for iPhone*, www.support
.apple.com/guide/iphone/important-safety-information-
iph301fc905.

5 Repair and Intellectual Property

1. William W. Fisher III, *Property and Contract on the Internet*, 73 Chicago-Kent Law Review 1203, 1249 (1998) (arguing copyright should "give creators enough entitlements to induce them to produce the works from which we all benefit but no more"); Glynn S. Lunney, Jr., *Patent Law, the Federal Circuit, and the Supreme Court: A Quiet Revolution*, 11 Supreme Court Economics Review 1, 5 (2003) (suggesting patent protection should be conferred only to the "precise extent[] necessary to secure each individual innovation's *ex ante* expected profitability").

2. Anne Sraders, *Markets Rally for a Second Day, Pushing Apple's Market Cap Back Above $1 Trillion*, Forbes (Mar. 25, 2020), https://fortune.com/2020/03/25/aapl-apple-stock-market-cap-dow-jones-sp-500-today-news-rally/; Jessica Bursztynsky, *Apple Now has $193.82 Billion in Cash on Hand*, CNBC (July 30, 2020), www.cnbc.com/2020/07/30/apple-q3-cash-hoard-heres-how-much-apple-has-on-hand.html.

3. Aaron Perzanowski & Kate Darling, Creativity without Law (2017).

4. Glynn Lunney, Copyright's Excess (2018).

5. Feist Publications, Inc. v. Rural Telephone Service Co., 499 U.S. 340 (1991).

6. Dan MacGuill, *Did Samuel Beckett Drive a Young André the Giant to School?*, Snopes (Apr. 18, 2018), www.snopes.com/fact-check/andre-the-giant-samuel-beckett.

7. 17 U.S.C. § 102(b); Baker v. Selden, 101 U.S. 99 (1880).

8. 17 U.S.C. § 101.

9. *See* Star Athletica v. Varsity Brands, 137 S. Ct. 1002 (2017). European law is even more forgiving of copyright claims on functional designs. *See* Case C-833/18, SI and Brompton Bicycle Ltd. v. Chedech/Get2Get.

10. Campbell v. Acuff-Rose Music, Inc., 510 U.S. 569 (1994); Swatch Grp. Mgmt. Servs. Ltd. v. Bloomberg L.P., 742 F.3d 17 (2d Cir. 2014); Sega Enterprises Ltd. v. Accolade, Inc., 977 F.2d 1510 (9th Cir. 1992); Authors Guild, Inc. v. Google, Inc., 804 F.3d 202 (2d Cir. 2015).

11. Doan v. American Book Co., 105 F. 772 (7th Cir. 1901).

12. Toro Co. v. R & R Prod. Co., 787 F.2d 1208, 1213 (8th Cir. 1986).

13. ATC Distribution Grp., Inc. v. Whatever It Takes Transmissions & Parts, Inc., 402 F.3d 700, 703 (6th Cir. 2005).
14. Southco, Inc. v. Kanebridge Corp., 258 F.3d 148 (3d Cir. 2001).
15. *Works Not Protected by Copyright*, US Copyright Office Circular 33 (2020), www.copyright.gov/circs/circ33.pdf.
16. Future Proof, *Tim's Laptop Service Manuals*, www.tim.id.au/bl og/tims-laptop-service-manuals/#toc-toshiba; Mike Masnick, *Toshiba: You Can't Have Repair Manuals Because They're Copyrighted And You're Too Dumb To Fix A Computer*, Techdirt (Nov. 12, 2012), www.techdirt.com/articles/20121110/ 22403121007/toshiba-you-cant-have-repair-manuals-because-theyre-copyrighted-youre-too-dumb-to-fix-computer.shtml.
17. Kyle Wiens, *Introducing the World's Largest Medical Repair Database, Free for Everyone*, iFixit (May 19, 2020), www.ifixit .com/News/41440/introducing-the-worlds-largest-medical-repair-database-free-for-everyone.
18. Frank's Hospital Workshop, www.frankshospitalwork shop.com.
19. Letter from Steris to iFixit (May 26, 2020), www.eff.org/docu ment/letter-steris-ifixit-5-16-2020.
20. *Maintenance Manual: Harmony LA Surgical Lighting and Visualization System*, iFixit, www.ifixit.com/Document/ IDkC64cSlRNYhqYc/Steris+Harmony+LA+Surgical +Lighting+Maintenance+Manual.pdf.
21. Morrissey v. Proctor & Gamble Co., 379 F.2d 675 (1st Cir. 1967).
22. *Maint Manual Reliance Synergy Washer/Disinfector*, Steris, http:// shop.steris.com/en/us/parts/maint-manual-reliance-syngery -washer-disinfector-p764330664.
23. American Intellectual Property Law Association, *Report of the Economic Survey* (2019), www.aipla.org/docs/default-source/ student-and-public-resources/publications/aipla-2019-report-of-the-economic-survey-final-online.pdf.
24. Letter from EFF to Steris on behalf of iFixit (June 10, 2020), www.eff.org/document/letter-eff-steris-behalf-ifixit-5-26-2020.
25. MAI Systems Corp. v. Peak Computer, Inc., 991 F.2d 511 (9th Cir. 1993).
26. Aaron Perzanowski, *Fixing Ram Copies*, 104 Northwestern University Law Review 1067 (2010).
27. 17 U.S.C. § 101.

28. Cartoon Network, LP v. CSC Holdings, Inc., 536 F.3d 121 (2d Cir. 2008).
29. The statute defines "maintenance" as "the servicing of the machine in order to make it work in accordance with its original specifications and any changes to those specifications authorized for that machine" and "repair" as "the restoring of the machine to the state of working in accordance with its original specifications and any changes to those specifications authorized for that machine." 17 U.S.C. § 117(d).
30. Apple relies on a similar strategy to discourage independent replacement of faulty batteries. Jason Koebler, *Apple Is Locking Batteries to Specific iPhones, a Nightmare for DIY Repair*, Vice (Aug. 8, 2019), www.vice.com/en_us/article/59nz3k/apple-is-locking-batteries-to-specific-iphones-a-nightmare-for-diy-repair.
31. Jason Koebler, *Why American Farmers Are Hacking Their Tractors with Ukrainian Firmware*, Vice (Mar. 21, 2017), www.vice.com/en_us/article/xykkkd/why-american-farmers-are-hacking-their-tractors-with-ukrainian-firmware.
32. License Agreement for John Deere Embedded Software, www.deere.com/privacy_and_data/docs/agreement_pdfs/english/2016–10–28-Embedded-Software-EULA.pdf.
33. MDY Indus. v. Blizzard Entm't., 629 F.3d 928, 941 (9th Cir. 2010).
34. For decades, Deere has used the tagline "Nothing runs like a Deere." *Nothing Runs Like A Deere*, John Deere Journal (Dec. 13, 2019), https://johndeerejournal.com/2019/12/snowmobiles-and-helmets-the-story-of-a-famous-tagline. John Deere told the US Copyright Office that farmers obtain an implied license to run the code that operates their tractors. Lily Hay Newman, *Who Owns the Software in the Car You Bought?*, Slate (May 2, 2015), www.slate.com/blogs/futuretense/2015/05/22/gmandjohndeeresaytheystillownthesoftwareincarscustomersbuy.html.
35. Newman, *supra* note 34.
36. 17 U.S.C. § 1201.
37. *Id.*
38. Brian T. Yeh, *The Digital Millennium Copyright Act: Exemptions to the Prohibitions to the Prohibition of Circumvention*, Congressional Research Service (2008).

39. Chamberlain Group, Inc. v. Skylink Technologies, Inc., 381 F.3d 1178 (Fed. Cir. 2004), Lexmark International, Inc. v. Static Control Components, Inc., 387 F.3d 522 (6th Cir. 2004).

40. Storage Tech. Corp. v. Custom Hardware Eng'g & Consulting, Inc., 421 F.3d 1307 (Fed. Cir. 2005).

41. Chamberlain, 381 F.3d 1178.

42. MDY Industries, LLC v. Blizzard Entertainment, Inc., 629 F.3d 928 (9th Cir. 2010).

43. 17 U.S.C. § 1201(a)(1)(C).

44. Exemption to Prohibition on Circumvention of Copyright Protection Systems for Access Control Technologies, 80 Fed. Reg. 208, 65954 (Oct. 28, 2015).

45. Exemption to Prohibition on Circumvention of Copyright Protection Systems for Access Control Technologies, 83 Fed. Reg. 208, 54023 (Oct. 26, 2018).

46. In 2018, the Office moved away from its prior practice of renewing each exemption proposal de novo and adopted a process of presumptive renewal in the absence of "meaningful opposition." US Copyright Office, *Transcript of Informational Video on Rulemaking*, Streamlined Petitions for Renewed Exemptions (2018), www.copyright.gov/1201/ 1201_streamlined_renewal_transcript.pdf. How long this new streamlined system will remain in effect is an open question.

47. 17 U.S.C. § 1201.

48. Office of the United States Trade Representative, *Free Trade Agreements*, https://ustr.gov/trade-agreements/free-trade-agreements. Similar provisions were included in the Trans-Pacific Partnership before the United States abruptly pulled out of the agreement under President Trump for unrelated reasons.

49. Council Directive 2001/29 on the Harmonization of Certain Aspects of Copyrights and Related Rights in the Information Society, art. 6. At the time, the Software Directive already prohibited the circulation and possession of tools that facilitate the circumvention of technical devices that protect computer programs. Directive 91/250. For a careful analysis of these parallel anticircumvention regimes and their implications for repair, see Anthony D. Rosborough, *Unscrewing the Future: The Right to Repair and the Circumvention*

of Software TPMs in the EU, 11 Journal of Intellectual Property, Information Technology and Electronic Commerce Law 26 (2020).

50. Thiru Balasubramaniam, *2020: USTR Takes Aim at South Africa over Copyright Limitations and Exceptions*, Knowledge Ecology International (Apr. 22, 2020), www.keionline.org /32804.

51. Diamond v. Diehr, 450 U.S. 175, 185 (1981) ("Excluded from such patent protection are laws of nature, natural phenomena, and abstract ideas.").

52. 35 U.S.C. § 102.

53. *Id*. § 103.

54. *Id*. § 101; Brenner v. Manson, 383 U.S. 519 (1966).

55. European Patent Convention, arts. 54–57.

56. *Id*. art. 63; 35 U.S.C. § 153.

57. 35 U.S.C. § 271(a).

58. Bowman v. Monsanto, 569 U.S. 278 (2013) ("And by 'exhaust[ing] the [patentee's] monopoly' in that item, the sale confers on the purchaser, or any subsequent owner, 'the right to use [or] sell' the thing as he sees fit.").

59. Bloomer v. McQuewan, 55 U.S. (14 How.) 539 (1852).

60. Adams v. Burke, 84 U.S. 453, 455 (1873).

61. Impression Prods. v. Lexmark Int'l, 137 S. Ct. 1523 (2017).

62. Bowman, 569 U.S. 278.

63. 50 U.S. (9 How.) 109 (1850).

64. 365 U.S. 336 (1961).

65. Goodyear Shoe Mach. Co. v. Jackson, 112 F. 146, 150 (1st Cir. 1901).

66. Sage Prods., Inc. v. Devon Indus., Inc., 45 F.3d 1575, 1578 (Fed. Cir. 1995).

67. Dana Corp. v. American Precision Co., 827 F.2d 755 (Fed. Cir. 1987).

68. Wilbur–Ellis Co. v. Kuther, 377 U.S. 422 (1964).

69. Jazz Photo Corp. v. Int'l Trade Comm'n, 264 F.3d 1094, 1098 (Fed. Cir. 2001).

70. Mark D. Janis, *A Tale of the Apocryphal Axe: Repair, Reconstruction and the Implied License in Intellectual Property Law*, 58 Maryland Law Review 423, 425 (1999); *see also* Aktiebolag v. E.J. Co., 121 F.3d 669, 673 (Fed. Cir. 1997).

71. Goodyear Shoe Mach. Co. v. Jackson, 112 F. 146, 150 (1st Cir. 1901).

72. Dunlop Pneumatic Tyre Co. v. Holborn Tyre [1901] R.P.D. & T.M. 222; *see also* FMC Corp. v. Up-Right, Inc., 21 F.3d 1703. (Fed. Cir. 1994).
73. Plutarch, *Theseus* 23.1.
74. Janis, *supra* note 70.
75. *Id.*
76. Supreme Court of Japan, Nov. 8, 2007, Canon Ink Tank, 39 IIC 39 (2008).
77. *Id.*; Mineko Mohri, *Repair and Recycle as Direct Patent Infringement?*, *in* Spares, Repairs and Intellectual Property Rights (Christopher Heath & Anselm Kamperman Sanders, eds., 2009).
78. X ZR 97/11 – Palettenbehälter II; X ZR 55/16 – Trommeleinheit (where members of the trade would have no clear expectation about the replacement of a part, and that part does not embody the inventive contribution of the patented device, replacement was considered noninfringing repair).
79. Solar Thomson Engineering Co. v. Barton [1977] R.P.C. 537 (C.A.); *see also* Sirdar Rubber Co. Ltd. v. Wallington Weston & Co. (1907), 24 R.P.C. 539 (U.K. H.L. (Eng.)) at 543 ("you may prolong the life of a licensed article but you must not make a new one under the cover of repair.").
80. Schutz (UK) Ltd. v. Werit (UK) Ltd. [2013] UKSC 16; *see also* Julia Powles, *Replacement of Part and Patent Infringement*, 72 Cambridge Law Journal 518 (2013).
81. Calidad Pty Ltd. v. Seiko Epson Corporation [2020] HCA 41.
82. MacLennan v. Produits Gilbert, Inc., 2008 FCA 35.
83. Tesh W. Dagne & Gosia Piasecka, *The Right to Repair Doctrine and the Use of 3D Printing Technology in Canadian Patent Law*, 14 Canadian Journal of Law and Technology 263 (2106).
84. *MacLennan*, 2008 FCA 35.
85. [1998] 2 SCR 129.
86. 2004 SCC 34.
87. *See, e.g.*, *MacLennan*, 2008 FCA 35; Rucker Co. v. Gavel's Vulcanizing Ltd. [1985] F.C.J. No. 1031 (Fed. T.D.).
88. Jay Peters, *Volunteers Produce 3D-Printed Valves for Life-Saving Coronavirus Treatments*, Verge (May 17, 2020), www .theverge.com/2020/3/17/21184308/coronavirus-italy-medical -3d-print-valves-treatments.

89. *See Aro*, 365 U.S. at 336–7 ("No element, not itself separately patented, that constitutes one of the elements of a combination patent is entitled to patent monopoly … "); *Jazz Photo*, 264 F.3d at 1107 (noting that "the remanufacturing processes simply reuse the original components, such that there is no issue of replacing parts that were separately patented").

90. Act of Aug. 29, 1842, ch. 263, § 3, 5 Stat. 543, 543–44.

91. 35 U.S.C. § 171(a).

92. *Id.* § 171(a) & (b).

93. Sarah Burstein, *The "Article of Manufacture" in 1887*, 32 Berkeley Technology Law Journal 1 (2017).

94. 35 U.S.C. § 271(a).

95. Egyptian Goddess, Inc. v. Swisa, Inc., 543 F.3d 665, 682 (Fed. Cir. 2008).

96. US Patent Statistics Chart Calendar Years 1963–2019, US Patent and Trademark Office, www.uspto.gov/web/offices/ac/ido/oeip/taf/us_stat.htm.

97. *Id.*

98. Dennis David Crouch, *A Trademark Justification for Design Patent Rights* (Univ. of Mo. Sch. of Law Legal Studies, Research Paper No. 2010–17, 2010), https://papers.ssrn.com/sol3/papers.cfm?abstract_id=1656590.

99. Reuters, *Jury Awards Apple $539 Million in Samsung Patent Case*, New York Times (May 24, 2018), www.nytimes.com/2018/05/24/business/apple-samsung-patent-trial.html.

100. Auto. Body Parts Ass'n v. Ford Glob. Techs., LLC, 930 F.3d 1314 (Fed. Cir. 2019).

101. *Id.*

102. Autocare Association, *Total U.S. Aftermarket Forecast to Decline 8.8% But Expected to Rebound in 2021*, www.autocare.org/news/latest-news/details/2020/06/05/Total-U-S-Aftermarket-Forecast-to-Decline-8-8-But-Expected-to-Rebound-in-2021-6219.

103. Joshua D. Sarnoff, *White Paper on Protecting the Consumer Patent Law Right of Repair and the Aftermarket for Exterior Motor Vehicle Repair Parts: The Parts Act, S. 812; H.R. 1879, 115th Congress* (2017), https://papers.ssrn.com/sol3/papers.cfm?abstract_id=3082289.

104. *Id.*

105. *Id.*

106. 35 U.S.C. § 171.
107. Samsung Electronics Co. v. Apple, Inc., 137 S. Ct. 429 (2016).
108. Burstein, *supra* note 93.
109. 35 U.S.C. §§ 101 and 171.
110. Burstein, *supra* note 93; *Ex parte* Adams, 1898 Dec. Comm'r Pat. 115; *Ex parte* Steck, 1902 Dec. Comm'r Pat. 9.
111. *In re* Koehring, 37 F.2d 421 (CCPA 1930).
112. Pelouze Scale & Mfg. Co. v. Am. Cutlery Co., 102 F. 916, 918 (7th Cir. 1900); *see also* Gorham Co. v. White, 81 U.S. 511 (1871); Sarah Burstein, *How Design Patent Law Lost Its Shape*, 41 Cardozo Law Review 555, 594 (2019).
113. *Ex parte* Northup, 24 USPQ 63 (Pat. Off. Bd. App. 1932).
114. Application of Zahn, 617 F.2d 261 (C.C.P.A. 1980).
115. *Id.*
116. Burstein, *supra* note 112.
117. *Id.*
118. Sarah Burstein, *Costly Designs*, 77 Ohio State Law Journal 107, 124 (2016) (noting $5,000 estimate); Crouch, *supra* note 98 (noting allowance rate over 90%).
119. Sarah Burstein, *Is Design Patent Examination Too Lax?*, 33 Berkeley Technology Law Journal 607, 608 (2018).
120. High Point Design LLC v. Buyer's Direct, Inc., 621 F. App'x 632, 638 (Fed. Cir. 2015).
121. *Id.* (noting minor variations in the sole and fuzzy trim on shoe designs).
122. MRC Innovations, Inc. v. Hunter Mfg., 747 F.3d 1326, 1331 (Fed. Cir. 2014).
123. Burstein, *supra* note 119.
124. Christopher Buccafusco, Mark A. Lemley & Jonathan S. Masur, *Intelligent Design*, 68 Duke Law Journal 75 (2018).
125. Best Lock Corp. v. Ilco Unican Corp., 94 F.3d 1563, 1567 (Fed. Cir. 1996).
126. *Id.*; Ethicon Endo-Surgery, Inc. v. Covidien, Inc., 796 F.3d 1312, 1329 (Fed. Cir. 2015); *see also* Burstein, *supra* note 119.
127. Burstein, *supra* note 119.
128. Buccafusco, Lemley & Masur, *supra* note 124.
129. Apple, Inc. v. Samsung Elecs. Co., 786 F.3d 983 (Fed. Cir. 2015).
130. Richardson v. Stanley Works, Inc., 597 F.3d 1288 (Fed. Cir. 2010).

131. Burstein, *supra* note 119.
132. *In re* Webb, 916 F.2d 1553, 1557 (Fed. Cir. 1990).
133. Directive 98/71/EC.
134. If instead you dented your ship or airplane, so long as it was registered in another country, you'd be entitled to make, import, buy, or use any necessary parts. *Id.* art. 13(2).
135. *Id.* art. 7.
136. Jason J. DuMont and Mark D. Janis, *Functionality in Design Protection Systems*, 19 Journal of Intellectual Property Law 261, 293 (2012).
137. Case C-395/16, DOCERAM GmbH v. CeramTec GmbH, ECLI: EU:C:2017:779 (Opinion of Advocate General Saugsmandsgaard Øe), para. 31.
138. Jens Schovsbo & Graeme B. Dinwoodie, *Design Protection for Products that Are "Dictated by Function,"* in The EU Design Approach: A Global Appraisal (Annette Kur, Marianne Levin & Jens Schovsbo, eds., 2018).
139. Directive 98/71/EC, art. 7. An exception to this rule allows protection for "a design serving the purpose of allowing multiple assembly or connection of mutually interchangeable products within a modular system." *Id.* This so-called "LEGO-exception" reportedly resulted from intense lobbying by the Danish toy maker. Schovsbo & Dinwoodie, *supra* note 138.
140. Procter & Gamble Co. v. Reckitt Benckiser (UK) Ltd. [2007] EWCA Civ 936 at [27].
141. Commission Staff Working Document Evaluation of EU Legislation on Design Protection, SWD (2020) 264 final.
142. Directive 98/71/EC, art. 14.
143. Council Regulation (EC) No. 6/2002, art. 110.
144. *Id.* recital 13.
145. *See, e.g.*, Bayerische Motoren Werke Aktiengesellschaft v. Round and Metal Ltd. [2012] EWHC 2099 (Pat) (July 27, 2012); Audi AG v. Acacia & Pneusgardia, Milan, Nov. 27, 2014; Audi, IP Court of Milan decision 2271/2015 of Feb. 19, 2015; OLG Stuttgart, 2 U 46/14, Sept. 11, 2014, GRUR 2015, 380 Tz 34; LG Hamburg, 09.18.2015 – 308 O 143/14; LG Dusseldorf, 30.04.2015 – 14c O 183/13; Porsche v. Acacia, LG Düsseldorf 14c O 304/12 28-11-2013.
146. Joined Cases C-397/16 and C-435/16, Acacia v. Pneusgarda, Audi and Porsche, ECLI:EU:C:2017:992, para. 54.

147. Designs Act of 2003 § 72.
148. GM Global Technology Operations LLC v. S.S.S. Auto Parts Pty Ltd. [2019] FCA 97.
149. Registered Designs Act 1949 § 1C(2).
150. *Id.* § 7A(5) ("The right in a registered design of a component part which may be used for the purpose of the repair of a complex product so as to restore its original appearance is not infringed by the use for that purpose of any design protected by the registration.").
151. Copyright, Designs and Patents Act 1988 § 213(3).
152. Dyson Limited v. Qualtex (UK) Limited [2006] EWCA Civ 166.
153. Bosch, *The Armature in a Circle* (Oct. 25, 2018), www.bosch.com/stories/creation-of-the-bosch-logo.
154. *See* Kellogg Co. v. Nat'l Biscuit Co., 305 U.S. 111 (1938); USPTO v. Booking.com, 140 S. Ct. 2298, 2301 (2020).
155. Whitson Gordon, *How a Brand Name Becomes Generic*, New York Times (June 24, 2019), www.nytimes.com/2019/06/24/smarter-living/how-a-brand-name-becomes-generic.html.
156. Abercrombie & Fitch Co. v. Hunting World, Inc., 537 F.2d 4, 9 (2d Cir. 1976).
157. Jason Kilar, *What's in a Name?*, Hulu (May 13, 2008), https://web.archive.org/web/20181031160852/http://blog.hulu.com/2008/05/13/meaning-of-hulu/.
158. *Abercrombie*, 537 F.2d at 10.
159. Wal-Mart Stores, Inc. v. Samara Bros., 529 U.S. 205, 212 (2000). According to the Supreme Court, unlike product design, product packaging may sometimes be inherently distinctive.
160. Koninklijke Philips Electronics NV v. Remington Consumer Products Ltd., 2002 E.C.R. I-05475; Joined Cases C-53–55/01, Linde AG, Judgment, 2003 E.C.R. I-3177; Joined Cases C-456–57/01 P, Henkel KGaA v. OHIM, Judgment, 2004 E.C.R. I-5115. *See also* César J Ramírez-Montes, *The Elusive Distinctiveness of Trade Dress in EU Trademark Law*, 34 Emory International Law Review 277 (2020).
161. C-417/16, August Storck KG v. EUIPO, ECLI:EU:C:2017:340 (2017).
162. TrafFix Devices, Inc. v. Marketing Displays, Inc., 532 U.S. 23 (2001).
163. Directive (EU) 2015/2436, art. 4(1); Regulation (EU) 2017/1001, art. 7(1).

164. The mark consists of a configuration of a vehicle grille, Registration No. 3,453,754 (Ford Motor Company registration for the design of an automobile grille); The mark consists of a configuration of a vehicle taillight design, Registration No. 3,440,628 (Volvo Car Corporation registration for the design of car taillights); Leah Chan Grinvald & Ofer Tur-Sinai, *Intellectual Property Law and the Right to Repair*, 88 Fordham Law Review 63 (2019).

165. Gen. Motors Corp. v. Lanard Toys, Inc., 468 F.3d 405, 420 (6th Cir. 2006).

166. Chrysler Corp. v. Vanzant, 44 F. Supp. 2d 1062, 1071–72 (C. D. Cal. 1999).

167. Apple, Inc. v. Samsung Electronics Co., Ltd., 786 F.3d 983 (2015).

168. 15 U.S.C. § 1114.

169. Volkswagenwerk Aktiengesellschaft v. Church, 411 F.2d 350, 351 (9th Cir. 1969).

170. *See also* Hypertherm, Inc. v. Precision Products, Inc., 832 F. 2d 697 (1st Cir. 1987) ("In the absence of false representations or palming off, the sale of unpatented replacement parts by one other than the manufacturer of the original equipment is neither unlawful nor actionable.").

171. Under Article 12 of the Trade Mark Directive and Article 14 of the Regulation, a trade mark "shall not entitle the proprietor to prohibit a third party from using in the course of trade: ... indications concerning the kind, quality, quantity, intended purpose, value, geographical origin, the time of production of the goods or of rendering of the service, or other characteristics of the goods or service; [or] the trade mark where it is necessary to indicate the intended purpose of a product or service, in particular as accessories or spare parts, provided he uses them in accordance with honest practices in industrial or commercial matters." Council Directive 2015/2436; Council Regulation 2017/1001.

172. Case C-63/97, Bayerische Motorenwerke AG and another v. Deenik [1999] ETMR 339.

173. Bayerische Motoren Weke AG v. Technosport London Ltd. [2017] EWCA Civ 779, No. A3 2016 1801.

174. Sebastian Int'l, Inc. v. Longs Drug Stores Corp., 53 F.3d 1073, 1074 (9th Cir. 1995) (the right "to control distribution of its trademarked product does not extend beyond the first sale of the product").

175. Zino Davidoff SA v. CVS Corp., 571 F.3d 238, 243 (2d Cir. 2009).

176. Yvette Joy Liebesman & Benjamin Wilson, *The Mark of a Resold Good*, 20 George Mason Law Review 157 (2012).

177. Chanel, Inc. v. RealReal, Inc., 449 F. Supp. 3d 422 (S.D.N.Y. 2020).

178. Champion Spark Plug Co. v. Sanders, 331 U.S. 125 (1947).

179. Nitro Leisure Prod., L.L.C. v. Acushnet Co., 341 F.3d 1356, 1357 (Fed. Cir. 2003).

180. *See* Societe Des Produits Nestle, S.A. v. Casa Helvetia, Inc., 982 F.2d 633, 635 (1st Cir. 1992).

181. Bourdeau Bros. v. Int'l Trade Comm'n, 444 F.3d 1317 (Fed. Cir. 2006). On occasion, courts have applied a similar rule to purely domestic sales when the reseller fails to comply with the trademark owner's quality control measures. *See* Warner-Lambert Co. v. Northside Dev. Corp., 86 F.3d 3, 6 (2d Cir. 1996) (determining that the sale of cough drops past their expiration date was infringing).

182. *Bourdeau Bros.*, 444 F.3d at 1323–24.

183. *Id.*

184. Gamut Trading Co. v. U.S. Int'l Trade Comm'n, 200 F.3d 775, 781 (Fed. Cir. 1999). The court reached a similar result in a case about imported mushrooms, but there, in addition to the languages on the labels, the US mushrooms were certified organic, but the Japanese variety were not. Hokto Kinoko Co. v. Concord Farms, Inc., 738 F.3d 1085, 1094 (9th Cir. 2013).

185. Davidoff & CIE, S.A. v. PLD Int'l Corp., 263 F.3d 1297, 1302 (11th Cir. 2001).

186. Bose Corp. v. Ejaz, No. CIV.A. 11–10629-DJC, 2012 WL 4052861, at *8 (D. Mass. Sept. 13, 2012), aff'd, 732 F.3d 17 (1st Cir. 2013).

187. Ultimately, the court held that since the trademark holder failed to make those services available to all customers, it could not prove that substantially all imported goods were materially different. SKF USA, Inc. v. Int'l Trade Comm'n, 423 F.3d 1307, 1308 (Fed. Cir. 2005); *see also* Heraeus Kulzer LLC

v. Omni Dental Supply, No. 12–11099-RGS, 2013 U.S. Dist. LEXIS 91949, at *17–18 (D. Mass. July 1, 2013) (finding material difference due to variations in customer support and warranty coverage between foreign and domestic products).

188. Irene Calboli, Market Integration and (the Limits of) the First Sale Rule in North American and European Trademark Law, 51 Santa Clara Law Review 1241 (2011).
189. Dupont of Canada Ltd. v. Nomad Trading Co. (1968), 55 C.P.R. 97 (Can. Que. S.C.).
190. TM Directive (Art. 7) and the CTM Trademark Regulation (art. 13).
191. *See* Joined Cases C-427, C-429, and C-436/93, Bristol-Myers Squibb v. Paranova A/S, 1996 E.C.R. 1–3457, 1–3536–45; Case C-379/97, Pharmacia & Upjohn SA v. Paranova A/S, 1999 E.C.R. 1–6927; Irene Calboli, *Market Integration and (the Limits of) the First Sale Rule in North American and European Trademark Law*, 51 Santa Clara Law Review 1241 (2011).
192. *Id.*
193. Case C-59/08, Copad SA v. Christian Dior Couture SA; *see also* Irene Calboli, *Reviewing the (Shrinking) Principle of Trademark Exhaustion in the European Union (Ten Years Later)*, 16 Marquette Intellectual Property Law Review 257 (2012).
194. Brealey v. Nomination De Antonio E Paolo Gensini SNC [2020] EWCA Civ 103.
195. Jason Koebler, *Apple Sued an Independent iPhone Repair Shop Owner and Lost*, Vice (Apr. 13, 2018), www.vice.com/en_us/article/a3yadk/apple-sued-an-independent-iphone-repair-shop-owner-and-lost.
196. Jason Koebler, *DHS Seizes Aftermarket iPhone Screens from Prominent Right-to-Repair Advocate*, Vice (May 11, 2018), www.vice.com/en_us/article/evk4wk/dhs-seizes-iphone-screens-jessa-jones.
197. *Id.*; *iPhone XS and XS Max Teardown*, iFixit (Sept. 21, 2018), www.ifixit.com/Teardown/iPhone+XS+and+XS+Max+Teardown/113021.
198. Koebler, *supra* note 196.
199. Matthew Gault & Jason Koebler, *DHS Seized Aftermarket Apple Laptop Batteries from Independent Repair Expert Louis Rossmann*, Vice (Oct. 19, 2018), www.vice.com/en_us/arti

cle/a3ppvj/dhs-seized-aftermarket-apple-laptop-batteries-from-independent-repair-expert-louis-rossman.

200. Huseby v. Apple, Inc., HR-2020–1142-A (sak nr. 19-141420SIV-HRET).

201. New York and North Carolina are the remaining holdouts. Uniform Law Commission, *Trade Secrets Act*, www.uniform laws.org/committees/community-home?community key=3a2538fb-e030-4e2d-a9e2-90373dc05792&tab=groupde tails.

202. 18 U.S.C. § 1836, et seq.

203. Directive (EU) 2016/943.

204. *Id.*; 18 U.S.C. § 1839; Uniform Trade Secrets Act § 1.

205. *Id.*

206. Toshiba insists its repair manuals are available only to authorized parties under strict confidentiality agreements. *See* Letter from John Ryan to Tim Hicks (July 31, 2012), www.wired.com/wp-content/uploads/blogs/opinion/wp-content/uploads/2012/11/toshiba_timhicks_ta kedownletter.jpeg.

207. Koebler, *supra* note 196.

208. *See* Leah Chan Grinvald & Ofer Tur-Sinai, *Smart Cars, Telematics and Repair*, 54 University of Michigan Journal of Law Reform (2021).

209. Kewanee Oil Co. v. Bicron Corp., 416 U.S. 470 (1974) ("discovery by fair and honest means, such as by independent invention, accidental disclosure, or by so-called reverse engineering").

210. *See* Chicago Lock Co. v. Fanberg, 676 F.2d 400 (9th Cir. 1981).

211. Uniform Trade Secrets Act § 1.

212. DVD Copy Control Assn., Inc. v. Bunner, 116 Cal. App. 4th 241, 251, 10 Cal. Rptr. 3d 185, 193 (2004).

213. Religious Technology Center. v. Lerma, 897 F. Supp. 260, 266 (E.D. Va. 1995).

214. Deepa Varadarajan, *Trade Secret Fair Use*, 83 Fordham Law Review 1401 (2014); Deepa Varadarajan, *The Uses of IP Misuse*, 68 Emory Law Journal 739 (2019).

215. Annemarie Bridy, *Trade Secret Prices and High-Tech Devices: How Medical Device Manufacturers Are Seeking to Sustain Profits by Propertizing Prices*, 17 Texas Intellectual Property Law Journal 187 (2009); David S. Levine, *Secrecy and Unaccountability: Trade Secrets in Our Public Infrastructure*, 59

Florida Law Review 135 (2007); Mary L. Lyndon, *Secrecy and Access in an Innovation Intensive Economy: Reordering Information Privileges in Environmental, Health, and Safety Law*, 78 University of Colorado Law Review 465 (2007).

216. 18 U.S.C. § 1833(b)(1)(A).
217. Restatement (Third) of Unfair Competition § 40 cmt. c (1995).
218. Directive (EU) 2016/943.
219. Pamela Samuelson, *First Amendment Defenses in Trade Secrecy Cases, in* The Law and Theory of Trade Secrecy (Rochelle C. Dreyfuss & Katherine J. Strandburg, eds., 2010).
220. CBS, Inc. v. Davis, 510 U.S. 1315, 1318 (1994).
221. Ford Motor Co. v. Lane, 67 F. Supp. 2d 745 (E.D. Mich. 1999).
222. O'Grady v. Superior Court, 139 Cal. App. 4th 1423, 1475 (6th Dist. 2006).
223. Grinvald & Tur-Sinai, *supra* note 164.
224. *See* 26 U.S.C. § 6033; Guidance under Section 6033 Regarding the Reporting Requirements of Exempt Organizations, 85 Federal Register 31959 (May 28, 2020).
225. Nutrition Labeling and Education Act of 1990 (Public Law 101–535).
226. US Constitution, art. 1, § 8, cl. 8.
227. 35 U.S.C. § 287(c).
228. US Patent No. 9,547,842 (issued Jan. 17, 2017).
229. US Patent No. 10,385,360 (issued Aug. 20, 2019).
230. Ben Beaumont-Thomas, *Waxahatchee: Saint Cloud Review – The Best Album of the Year So Far*, The Guardian (Mar. 27, 2020), www.theguardian.com/music/2020/mar/27/waxa hatchee-saint-cloud-review.
231. Herbert J. Hovenkamp, *Schumpeterian Competition and Antitrust*, 4 Competition Policy International 1 (2008).
232. Grinvald & Tur-Sinai, *supra* note 164.
233. Kewanee Oil Co. v. Bicron Corp., 416 U.S. 470, 480 (1974).
234. Twentieth Century Music Corp. v. Aiken, 422 U.S. 151, 156 (1975).
235. Margaret Chon, *Postmodern "Progress": Reconsidering the Copyright and Patent Power*, 43 DePaul Law Review 97 (1993).

6 Repair and Competition

1. Majority Staff of Subcommittee on Antitrust, Commercial & Administrative Law, House Committee on the Judiciary

116th Congress, Investigation of Competition in Digital Markets, 337 (2020) (noting that "the Committee sought information and continues to investigate competition and conduct in the resale and repair markets for Apple products.").

2. Letter from US House of Representatives, Committee on the Judiciary to Tim Cook (Sept. 13, 2019).

3. *Apple Korea, Under Antitrust Probe, Proposes $84 Million to Support Small Businesses*, Reuters (Aug. 23, 2020), www.reuters.com/article/us-apple-southkorea-antitrust/apple-korea-under-anti trust-probe-proposes-84-million-to-support-small-businesses-idUSKBN25K09X.

4. European Commission, *Antitrust: Statement on Apple's iPhone Policy Changes* (Sept. 25, 2010), https://ec.europa.eu/commis sion/presscorner/detail/en/IP_10_1175.

5. Lina Khan, *The Ideological Roots of America's Market Power Problem*, 127 Yale Law Journal Forum 960 (2018).

6. Northern Pacific R. Co. v. United States, 356 U.S. 1, 4 (1958).

7. 15 U.S.C. § 1.

8. United States v. Grinnell Corp., 384 U.S. 563, 57071 (1966).

9. Standard Oil Co. of New Jersey v. United States, 221 U.S. 1 (1911).

10. Richard M. Steuer, *Exclusive Dealing in Distribution*, 69 Cornell Law Review 101, 104 (1983).

11. 15 U.S.C. § 18.

12. *Id.* § 14.

13. *Id.* § 13.

14. 221 U.S. 1.

15. *See* United States v. American Tel. and Tel. Co., 552 F. Supp. 131 (D.D.C. 1983).

16. United States v. Microsoft Corp., 97 F. Supp. 2d 59 (D.D.C. 2000).

17. United States v. Microsoft Corp., 253 F.3d 34 (D.C. Cir. 2001).

18. Complaint, United States v. Google LLC, Case 1:20-cv-03010 (D.D.C. Oct. 20, 2020); Federal Trade Commission v. Facebook, Inc., Case No.: 1:20-cv-03590 (D.D.C. Jan. 13, 2021).

19. IBM Corp. v. United States, 298 U.S. 131 (1936).

20. International Salt Co. v. United States, 332 U.S. 392 (1947).

21. United States v. IBM Corp., 1956 Trade Cas. (CCH) P68,245 (S.D.N.Y. 1956). The consent decree was finally terminated

nearly four decades later. United States v. IBM Corp., 163 F.3d 737 (2d Cir. 1998).

22. See Joseph P. Bauer, *Antitrust Implications of Aftermarkets*, 45 Antitrust Bulletin 31 (2007).

23. *Id.*

24. Eastman Kodak Co. v. Image Technical Services, Inc., 504 U.S. 451 (1992); *see also* Daniel Cadia, *Fix Me: Copyright, Antitrust, and the Restriction on Independent Repairs*, 52 U.C. Davis Law Review 1701 (2019).

25. Joseph Farrell & Paul Klemperer, *Coordination and Lock-In: Competition with Switching Costs and Network Effects*, *in* Handbook of Industrial Organization (Mark Armstrong & Robert H. Porter, eds., 2007).

26. *See* Severin Borenstein, Jeffrey K. MacKie-Mason & Janet Netz, *Antitrust Policy in Aftermarkets*, 63 Antitrust Law Journal 455, 459 (1995).

27. Free-riding, it should be noted, is often used as a pejorative. But there is nothing inherently harmful, immoral, or illegal about free-riding. And in fact, it is central to a competitive economy. *See* Mark Lemley, *Property, Intellectual Property, and Free Riding*, 83 Texas Law Review 1031 (2005).

28. Image Technical Services, Inc. v. Eastman Kodak, 125 F.3d 1195 (9th Cir. 1997).

29. United States v. Westinghouse Electric Corp., 648 F.2d 642, 646 (9th Cir. 1981).

30. *In re* Independent Service Organizations Antitrust Litigation, 203 F.3d 1322 (Fed. Cir. 2000); *see also* Schor v. Abbott Labs., 457 F.3d 608, 613 (7th Cir. 2006) (describing the *Kodak* decision as adopting "an undisciplined monopoly-leveraging principle").

31. 203 F.3d at 1326.

32. *See also* Service & Training, Inc. v. Data General Corp., 963 F.2d 680, 686 (4th Cir. 1992); Data General Corp. v. Grumman Systems Support Corp., 36 F.3d 1147 (1st Cir. 1994).

33. F.T.C. v. Actavis, Inc., 570 U.S. 136 (2013).

34. *See* Daniel Hanley, Claire Kelloway & Sandeep Vaheesan, *Fixing America: Breaking Manufacturers' Aftermarket Monopoly and Restoring Consumers' Right to Repair*, Open Markets Institute Report (2020).

35. Northern Pacific R. Co. v. United States, 356 U.S. 1, 5–6 (1958).

36. Jefferson Parish Hosp. Dist. No. 2 v. Hyde, 466 U.S. 2, 12 (1984).

37. *Id.* Although the Supreme Court has characterized this as a modified *per se* rule against tying, some lower courts have applied the more forgiving rule of reason framework in tying cases.

38. Illinois Tool Works, Inc. v. Independent Ink, Inc., 547 U.S. 28 (2006).

39. Brokerage Concepts, Inc. v. U.S. Healthcare, Inc., 140 R3d 494, 517 (3d Cir. 1998); Suture Express, Inc. v. Owens & Minor Distribution, Inc., 851 F.3d 1029, 1042 (10th Cir. 2017).

40. Bauer, *supra* note 22.

41. 356 U.S. at 11.

42. Luther Ray Abel, *A Computer-Repair Expert Takes on Big Tech*, National Review (July 1, 2020), www.nationalre view.com/2020/07/a-computer-repair-expert-takes-on-big-tech. As Louis Rossmann described, "With the newest MacBook, there's one particular charging chip that I cannot get anywhere ... Now what I need to do, because [Apple] told Intersil, 'Don't sell to anybody but us,' is I have to buy a $120 wireless-charging, extended-battery case thing for the iPhone XR, rip that chip off of it, and then put it into the Macbook."

43. Cadia, *supra* note 24.

44. Craig Lloyd, *Apple Is Locking iPhone Batteries to Discourage Repair*, iFixit (Aug. 7, 2019), www.ifixit.com/News/32343/apple-is-locking-batteries-to-iphones-now.

45. United States v. Colgate & Co., 250 U.S. 300 (1919).

46. Aspen Skiing Co. v. Aspen Highlands Skiing Corp., 472 U.S. 585 (1985).

47. Verizon Communications, Inc. v. Law Offices of Curtis V. Trinko, LLP, 540 U.S. 398, 407 (2003).

48. Bacchus Indus., Inc. v. Arvin Indus., Inc., 939 F.2d 887, 894 (10th Cir. 1991); Phillip E. Areeda & Herbert Hovenkamp, Antitrust Law, ¶ 801, at 382 (2008); William M. Landes & Richard A. Posner, *Market Power in Antitrust Cases*, 94 Harvard Law Review 937, 937 (1981) (defining monopoly power as "a high degree of market power").

49. 472 U.S. 585.

50. 540 U.S. at 409.

51. The sacrifice of short-term profits is neither necessary nor sufficient to establish that conduct is predatory. Viamedia, Inc. v. Comcast Corp., 951 F.3d 429, 462 (7th Cir. 2020); Novell, Inc. v. Microsoft Corp., 731 F.3d 1064, 1075 (10th Cir. 2013).

52. Elizabeth Chamberlain, *How Nikon Is Killing Camera Repair*, iFixit (Feb. 14, 2012), www.ifixit.com/News/1349/how-nikon -is-killing-camera-repair.

53. Kevin Purdy, *Nikon Is Killing Its Authorized Repair Program*, iFixit (Dec. 9, 2019), www.ifixit.com/News/34241/nikon-is-killing-its-authorized-repair-program.

54. 125 F.3d 1195.

55. 203 F.3d 1322.

56. See Joseph P. Bauer, *Refusals to Deal with Competitors by Owners of Patents and Copyrights: Reflections on the Image Technical and Xerox Decisions*, 55 DePaul Law Review 1211 (2006).

57. *Id.*

58. The Ninth Circuit itself recently accepted a patent owner's justification for refusing to license its technology. Federal Trade Commission v. Qualcomm, Inc., 969 F.3d 974, 994 (9th Cir. 2020).

59. ZF Meritor, LLC v. Eaton Corp., 696 F.3d 254, 270 (3d Cir. 2012) ("[T]he law is clear that an express exclusivity requirement is not necessary because de facto exclusive dealing may be unlawful.").

60. Courts have applied somewhat different standards depending on the statutory basis of the claims. For example, some say § 3 Clayton Act and § 1 Sherman Act claims require equal degrees of foreclosure. *See, e.g.,* Roland Mach. Co. v. Dresser Indus., Inc., 749 F.2d 380, 393 (7th Cir. 1984). But other courts disagree, requiring a higher measure of foreclosure under the Sherman Act. *See, e.g.,* Barr Labs. v. Abbott Labs., 978 F.2d 98, 110 (3d Cir. 1992).

61. Interface Group, Inc. v. Mass. Port Auth., 816 F.2d 9, 11 (1st Cir. 1987)

62. *See, e.g.,* Stop & Shop Supermarket Co. v. Blue Cross & Blue Shield of R.I., 373 F.3d 57, 68 (1st Cir. 2004); Minnesota Mining & Manufacturing Co. v. Appleton Papers, Inc., 35 F. Supp. 2d 1138, 1143 (D. Minn. 1999); McWane, Inc. v. FTC, 783 F.3d 814, 837 (11th Cir. 2015).

63. United States v. Microsoft Corp., 253 F.3d 34, 64 (D.C. Cir. 2001) (en banc).
64. Louis Rossmann, *Written Testimony in Support of Bills SB0723 & HB1124* (Mar. 11, 2020), https://mgaleg.maryland.gov/cmte_testimony/2020/ecm/3981_03112020_103037-492.pdf.
65. Daniel A. Hanley, *The First Thing a Biden FTC Should Tackle*, Slate (Nov. 18, 2020), https://slate.com/technology/2020/11/biden-ftc-right-repair-exclusive-contracts.html.
66. *See* Hanley, Kelloway & Vaheesan, *supra* note 34.
67. Tomi Kilgore, *Amazon's Stock Surge to Boost Market Cap Past Microsoft to Be the 2nd-Most Valuable Company*, Market Watch (July 31, 2020), www.marketwatch.com/story/amazons-stock-surge-to-boost-market-cap-past-microsoft-to-be-the-2nd-most-valuable-company-2020–07–31.
68. Koebler, *supra*, Chapter 5 note 196.
69. Abbott Labs. v. Teva Pharm. USA, Inc., 432 F. Supp. 2d 408, 421 (D. Del. 2006) ("a court faces a difficult task when trying to distinguish harm that results from anticompetitive conduct from harm that results from innovative competition.").
70. *Microsoft*, 253 F.3d 34.
71. C.R. Bard, Inc. v. M3 Sys., Inc., 157 F.3d 1340, 1382 (Fed. Cir. 1998); New York ex rel. Schneiderman v. Actavis PLC, 787 F.3d 638, 659 (2d Cir. 2015); Abbott Laboratories v. Teva Pharmaceuticals USA, 432 F. Supp. 2d 408; Intel Corp., 61 F. T.C 247 (2010).
72. Jonathan Jacobson, Scott Sher & Edward Holman, *Predatory Innovation: An Analysis of Allied Orthopedic v. Tyco in the Context 35 of Section 2 Jurisprudence*, 23 Loyola Consumer Law Review 1 (2010); *see also* Allied Orthopedic Appliances, Inc. v. Tyco Health Care Grp. LP, 592 F.3d 991, 998–99 (9th Cir. 2010) ("a design change that improves a product by providing a new benefit to consumers does not violate Section 2 absent some associated anticompetitive conduct").
73. Kevin Purdy, *Is This the End of the Repairable iPhone?*, iFixit (Oct. 29, 2020), www.ifixit.com/News/45921/is-this-the-end-of-the-repairable-iphone.
74. Nicholas O. Stephanopoulos & Eric M. McGhee, *Partisan Gerrymandering and the Efficiency Gap*, 82 University of Chicago Law Review 831 (2015).

75. Nathaniel Friedman, *What Should the NBA Do When Nobody Can Touch the Superteams?*, GQ (May 23, 2017), www.gq.com /story/nba-superteams-2017.

76. Jennifer Medina, Katie Benner & Kate Taylor, *Actresses, Business Leaders and Other Wealthy Parents Charged in U.S. College Entry Fraud*, New York Times (Mar. 12, 2019), www .nytimes.com/2019/03/12/us/college-admissions-cheating-scandal.html.

77. Nicolás Rivero, *The Acquisitions that Made Google a Search Monopoly*, Quartz (Oct. 20, 2020), https://qz.com/ 1920334/the-acquisitions-that-built-googles-monopoly-on-search/; Casey Newton, *How Facebook's Past Acquisitions Could Haunt Its Purchase of Giphy*, Verge (May 19, 2020), www.theverge.com/interface/2020/5/19/21262451/face book-giphy-acquisition-gif-instagram-whatsapp.

78. Michael Goldstein, *Will US Airlines Like United, American And Delta Lose Market Share after Coronavirus?*, Forbes (Apr. 16, 2020), www.forbes.com/sites/michaelgoldstein/2020/04/16/ will-us-airlines-like-united-american-and-delta-lose-market-share-after-coronavirus; Ben Sisario, *Senators Ask for Antitrust Probe in Concert Ticketing*, New York Times (Aug. 28, 2019), www.nytimes.com/2019/08/28/arts/live-nation-tickets-regula tion.html; Daisuke Wakabayashi, *Google Dominates Thanks to an Unrivaled View of the Web*, New York Times (Dec. 14, 2020), www.nytimes.com/2020/12/14/technology/how-google-domi nates.html; Open Markets Institute, *Washer & Dryer Manufacturing*, America's Concentration Crisis, https://concen trationcrisis.openmarketsinstitute.org/industry/washer-dryer-manufacturing/.

79. For a concise treatment, see Tim Wu, The Curse of Bigness: Antitrust in the New Gilded Age (2018).

80. *Id.*

81. Robert H. Bork, The Antitrust Paradox (1978).

82. Khan, *supra* note 5.

83. *See* John J. Flynn, *The Reagan Administration's Antitrust Policy, "Original Intent" and the Legislative History of the Sherman Act*, 33 Antitrust Bulletin 259 (1988); Eleanor M. Fox, *The Modernization of Antitrust: A New Equilibrium*, 66 Cornell Law Review 1140 (1981); Robert H. Lande, *Wealth Transfers as the Original and Primary Concern of Antitrust: The Efficiency Interpretation Challenged*, 34 Hastings Law Journal 65 (1982).

84. Reiter v. Sonotone Corp., 442 U.S. 330, 343 (1979) ("Congress designed the Sherman Act as a 'consumer welfare prescription.'") (quoting Bork's *The Antitrust Paradox*).
85. Marshall Steinbaum & Maurice E. Stucke, *The Effective Competition Standard: A New Standard for Antitrust*, 87 University of Chicago Law Review 595 (2020).
86. *Trinko*, 540 U.S. 398.
87. Khan, *supra* note 5; Steinbaum & Stucke, *supra* note 85.
88. *Id.*
89. Khan, *supra* note 5.
90. Rebecca Allensworth, *Adversarial Economics in Antitrust Litigation*, 106 Northwestern University Law Review 1261, 1273 (2012).
91. Maurice Stucke, *Does the Rule of Reason Violate the Rule of Law?*, 42 U.C. Davis Law Review 1375, 1427 (2009).
92. Michael A. Carrier, *The Rule of Reason: An Empirical Update for the 21st Century*, 16 George Mason Law Review 827, 828–30 (2009).
93. Steinbaum & Stucke, *supra* note 85.
94. United States v. Microsoft Corp., 87 F. Supp. 2d 30, 35 (D.D.C. 2000), affd in part, rev'd in part, 253 F. 3d 34, 118–19 (D.C. Cir. 2001).
95. A few key examples of this work include: Lina M. Khan, *Amazon's Antitrust Paradox*, 126 Yale Law Journal 710 (2017); Wu, *supra* note 79; Zephyr Teachout, Break 'Em Up: Recovering Our Freedom from Big Ag, Big Tech, and Big Money (2020); John Kwoka, Controlling Mergers and Market Power: A Program for Reviving Antitrust in America (2020).
96. Tim Wu, *The Utah Statement: Reviving Antimonopoly Traditions for the Era of Big Tech*, Medium (Nov. 18, 2019), https://one zero.medium.com/the-utah-statement-reviving-antimono poly-traditions-for-the-era-of-big-tech-e6be198012d7.
97. Lina Khan, *The End of Antitrust History Revisited*, 133 Harvard Law Review 1655 (2020).
98. Elizabeth Warren, *Reigniting Competition in the American Economy* (June 29, 2016), www.warren.senate.gov/newsroom/press-releases/senator-elizabeth-warren-delivers-remarks-on-reignit ing-competition-in-the-american-economy; Investigation of Competition in Digital Markets, *supra* note 1; Ken Buck, *The Third Way*, House Judiciary Committee Subcommittee on Antitrust, Commercial, and Administrative Law (2020),

https://buck.house.gov/sites/buck.house.gov/files/wysiwyg_u ploaded/Buck%20Report.pdf; Robert McMillan, *Lawmakers on Both Sides Call for Antitrust Action Against Big Tech*, Wall Street Journal (Oct. 19, 2020), www.wsj.com/articles/lawmakers-on-both-sides-call-for-antitrust-action-against-big-tech-11603130044. Admittedly, some supporters of antitrust reform appear eager to target large technology firms, like Facebook and Amazon, but appear to have little interest in pursuing broader market reforms. *See, e.g., Senator Hawley Statement on DOJ Antitrust Lawsuit Against Google* (Oct. 20, 2020), www.hawley.senate.gov/senator-hawley-statement-doj-antitrust-lawsuit-against-google. And some antitrust efforts are nakedly political. David Dayen, *Is Trump's Justice Department Trying to Discredit All Antitrust?*, American Prospect (Sept. 11, 2019), https://prospect.org/justice/trump-s-justice-department-trying-discredit-antitrust/.

99. John Kwoka, Mergers, Merger Control, and Remedies (2014).
100. Andrew S. Oldham, *Sherman's March (In)to the Sea*, 74 Tennessee Law Review 319 (2007).
101. See Daniel A. Crane, *Antitrust Antitextualism*, 96 Notre Dame Law Review 1205, 1206 (2020); Sanjukta Paul, *Reconsidering Judicial Supremacy in Antitrust*, 131 Yale Law Journal (forthcoming).
102. Treaty on the Functioning of the European Union, art. 101.
103. Directive (EU) 2019/1.
104. European Commission, *Antitrust: Commission Fines Google €2.42 Billion for Abusing Dominance as Search Engine by Giving Illegal Advantage to Own Comparison Shopping Service*, Press Release (June 27, 2017), https://ec.europa.eu/commission/presscorner/detail/en/IP_17_1784.
105. European Commission, *Antitrust: Commission Fines Google €4.34 Billion for Illegal Practices Regarding Android Mobile Devices to Strengthen Dominance of Google's Search Engine*, Press Release (July 18, 2018), https://ec.europa.eu/commission/presscorner/detail/en/IP_18_4581.
106. European Commission, *Antitrust: Commission Fines Google €1.49 Billion for Abusive Practices in Online Advertising*, Press Release (Mar. 20, 2019), https://ec.europa.eu/commission/presscorner/detail/en/IP_19_1770.
107. Sam Schechner, Emily Glazer & Valentina Pop, *EU Deepens Antitrust Inquiry Into Facebook's Data Practices*, Wall Street

Journal (Feb. 6, 2020), www.wsj.com/articles/eu-deepens-antitrust-inquiry-into-facebooks-data-practices-11580994001.

108. European Commission, *Antitrust: Commission Opens Investigation into Possible Anti-competitive Conduct of Amazon*, Press Release (July 17, 2019), https://ec.europa.eu/commission/presscorner/detail/en/IP_19_4291. To be clear, there's nothing inherently wrong with copying a competitors product, much less the idea for a product. The concern is that Amazon has unique access to information about third-party products that is unavailable to other competing sellers.

109. Adam Satariano & Jack Nicas, *Apple's App Store Draws Antitrust Scrutiny in European Union*, New York Times (June 16, 2020), www.nytimes.com/2020/06/16/business/apple-app-store-european-union-antitrust.html. The Commission is also investigating Apple Pay and the restrictions around access to devices' near field communication capability. *Id.*

110. Karin Matussek, *Amazon, Apple Probed by Germany over Online Sales Curbs*, Bloomberg (Oct. 29, 2020), www.bloomberg.com/news/articles/2020–10–29/amazon-apple-probed-by-germany-over-online-sales-curbs.

111. Anu Bradford, Adam Chilton, Katerina Linos & Alexander Weaver, *The Global Dominance of European Competition Law over American Antitrust Law*, 16 Journal of Empirical Legal Studies 731 (2019).

112. *Id.*

113. *See* Hugin Cash Registers v. Commission [1979] E.C.R. 1869.

114. Case No. V/34.330, Pelikan/Kyocera (1995); Case No. IV/E 2/36.431, Info-Lab/Ricoh (1999).

115. Commission's XXVIIth Report on Competition Policy (1997).

116. Case COMP/C-3/39692, IBM Maintenance Services (2011); Stephen Castle, *I.B.M. Settles Antitrust Case with E.U.*, New York Times (Dec. 14, 2011), www.nytimes.com/2011/12/15/technology/ibm-settles-antitrust-case-with-eu.html.

117. 203 F.3d at 1327. ("In the absence of any indication of illegal tying, fraud in the Patent and Trademark Office, or sham litigation, the patent holder may enforce the statutory right to exclude others from making, using, or selling the claimed invention free from liability under the antitrust laws.")

118. Case C-238/87, AB Volvo v. Erik Veng (UK) Ltd., ECLI:EU: C:1988:332; *see also* Case C-53/87, Consorzio italiano della componentistica di ricambio per autoveicoli and Maxicar v. Régie nationale des usines Renault, ECLI:EU:C:1988:472.
119. Case C-418/01, IMS Health GmbH & Co. OHG v. NDC Health GmbH & Co. KG, ECLI:EU:C:2004:257, para. 38; *see also* Joined Cases C-241–42/91 P, RTE and ITP v. Commission ('Magill') [1995] E.C.R. I-743.
120. Robert O'Donoghue & Jorge Padilla, The Law and Economics of Article 102 TFEU (2013).
121. Jens Schovsbo & Graeme B. Dinwoodie, *Design Protection for Products that Are "Dictated by Function,"* in The EU Design Approach: A Global Appraisal (Annette Kur, Marianne Levin & Jens Schovsbo, eds., 2018).
122. *IMS* cites *Volvo* approvingly on this point, as does the more recent *Huawei* decision. Case C-170/13, Huawei Technologies Co. Ltd. v. ZTE Corp. (2015).
123. Schovsbo & Dinwoodie, *supra* note 121.
124. Bradford, Chilton, Linos & Weaver, *supra* note 111.
125. *See* Aaron S. Edlin, *Stopping Above-Cost Predatory Pricing*, 111 Yale Law Journal 941, 991 (2002) (citing Joseph R. Conlin, The Morrow Book of Quotations in American History 48 (1984)). *But see* Peter S. Campbell, *Democracy v. Concentrated Wealth: In Search of a Louis D. Brandeis Quote*, 16 Green Bag 2d 251, 256 (2013) (concluding after exhaustive research that "[w]hile there is no positive proof Brandeis ever said these exact words, he expressed a similar sentiment numerous times. If it is not a Brandeis quote, it is at least a Brandeisian one").

7 Repair and Consumer Protection

1. 15 U.S.C. §§ 41 et seq.
2. 15 U.S.C. § 1692.
3. *See, e.g.*, Directive (EU) 2011/83/; Directive (EU) 2019/2161; Directive (EU) 2019/770; Directive (EU) 2019/771.
4. Aaron Perzanowski, *Consumer Perceptions of the Right to Repair*, 96 Indiana Law Journal 361 (2021).
5. These devices were chosen for several reasons. First, they reflect a range of prices from less than a hundred to thousands of dollars. Second, some are nearly ubiquitous, while others are relatively uncommon. Third, they are all

devices consumers experience difficulty repairing to some degree.

6. The remaining 24% were neutral, unclear, or nonresponsive. Positive responses tended to express confidence that manufacturers have greater expertise and can ensure high-quality repairs. Others expressed the mistaken view that restrictions on repair were necessary to maintain warranty protections.

7. European Commission, *Behavioural Study on Consumers' Engagement in the Circular Economy* (Oct. 2018), https://ec.europa.eu/info/sites/default/files/ec_circular_economy_final_report_0.pdf.

8. The stronger influence of durability information may suggest that it was presented in a more memorable way. The researchers noted that 71% of respondents correctly recalled claims about durability, while only 42% did for reparability information. *Id.*

9. Willingness to pay was measured using choice modeling. By varying the prices, reparability, and durability of products, statistical analysis revealed the price premium for durability and repair. *Id.*

10. 15 U.S.C. § 45.

11. *See* Chris Jay Hoofnagle, Federal Trade Commission Privacy Law and Policy (2016).

12. Federal Trade Commission, *Nixing the Fix: A Workshop on Repair Restrictions*, www.ftc.gov/news-events/events-calendar/nixing-fix-workshop-repair-restrictions.

13. *See* Federal Trade Commission, FTC Policy Statement on Unfairness, Opinion Letter (Dec. 17, 1980).

14. *See* US Food & Drug Administration, *FDA Report on the Quality, Safety, and Effectiveness of Servicing of Medical Devices* (2018), www.fda.gov/media/113431/download.

15. *See* Chris Jay Hoofnagle, Aniket Kesari & Aaron Perzanowski, *The Tethered Economy*, 87 George Washington Law Review 783 (2019).

16. Federal Trade Commission, FTC Policy Statement on Deception, Opinion Letter (Oct. 14, 1983).

17. *See* Aaron Perzanowski & Chris Jay Hoofnagle, *What We Buy When We Buy Now*, 165 University of Pennsylvania Law Review 315, 343 (2017).

18. *Groupe SEB's Commitment to Repairability*, www.groupeseb.com /en/node/442.
19. *See, e.g.*, Market Development Corp., 95 F.T.C. 100, 212 (1980) (failing to disclose extra charges or conditions imposed on use of vacation certificates); Peacock Buick, Inc., 86 F.T.C. 1532, 1557–58 (1975) (failing to disclose handling and service fees), aff'd, 553 F.2d 97 (4th Cir. 1977).
20. Patricia P. Bailey & Michael Pertschuk, *The Law of Deception: The Past as Prologue*, 33 American University Law Review 849, 879–80 (1984).
21. *See* Novartis Consumer Health, Inc. v. Johnson & Johnson-Merck Consumer Pharmaceuticals Co., 290 F.3d 578, 594 (3d Cir. 2002) ("[W]e believe that survey evidence demonstrating that 15% of the respondents were misled ... is sufficient to establish ... [a] claim for false or misleading advertising ... ."); Firestone Tire & Rubber Co. v. FTC, 481 F.2d 246, 249 (6th Cir. 1973) (affirming the FTC's finding of deception when an ad "misled 15% (or 10%) of the buying public").
22. FTC Policy Statement on Deception, *supra* note 16.
23. Charles of the Ritz Distribs. Corp. v. FTC, 143 F.2d 676, 679 (2d Cir. 1944); *see also* Giant Food, Inc. v. FTC, 322 F.2d 977, 982 (D.C. Cir. 1963) ("The Act was not intended to protect 'sophisticates.'").
24. *See, e.g.*, Carlson v. Coca-Cola Co., 483 F.2d 279, 280 (9th Cir. 1973) ("The protection against unfair trade practices afforded by the [FTCA] vests initial remedial power solely in the Federal Trade Commission."). The Lanham Act, the federal trademark statute, also prohibits the use of "any ... false or misleading description of fact ... in commercial advertising or promotion [that] misrepresents the nature, characteristics, qualities, or geographic origin" of goods or services. 15 U.S.C. § 1125. However, courts have consistently ruled that the Lanham Act does not grant consumers standing to bring false advertising claims. Competitors who lose market share can sue, but not consumers who were duped by false claims. Lexmark International, Inc. v. Static Control Components, Inc., 572 U.S. 118, 132 (2014). In some cases, a competitor might be motivated to sue a firm that falsely claims its products are

reparable. But there's hardly a guarantee that a competitor will vindicate consumer interests.

25. *See* FTC v. Winsted Hosiery Co., 258 U.S. 483, 493 (1922) ("The fact that misrepresentation and misdescription have become so common in [the market] ... does not prevent their use being an unfair method of competition."); Johnson Prods. Co. v. FTC, 549 F.2d 35, 41 (7th Cir. 1977); Ger-Ro-Mar, Inc. v. FTC, 518 F.2d 33, 35 (2d Cir. 1975) ("the Commission is under no obligation to start simultaneous suits against all alleged offenders").

26. *See* Federal Trade Commission, *A Brief Overview of the Federal Trade Commission's Investigative and Law Enforcement Authority* (2008), www.ftc.gov/about-ftc/what-we-do/enforcement-authority.

27. National Consumer Law Center, *Unfair and Deceptive Acts and Practices*, https://library.nclc.org/udap/0101.

28. California Business & Professional Code § 17200.

29. *Id.* § 17500.

30. California Civil Code § 1770.

31. Directive 2005/29/EC.

32. Guidance on the implementation/application of Directive 2005/29/EC on Unfair Commercial Practices, SWD/2016/0163 final.

33. Directive 2005/29/EC, art. 6.

34. *Id.*

35. *Id.* art. 7.

36. *Id.*

37. Guidance, *supra* note 32.

38. *Id.*

39. Directive 2005/29/EC, Annex I.

40. Henry Gabriel, *The Revision of the Uniform Commercial Code-How Successful Has It Been?*, 52 Hastings Law Journal 653 (2001).

41. Uniform Commercial Code § 2–312.

42. *Id.* § 2–314. Where the seller knows the goods are meant for some specific purpose and the buyer relies on the seller's expertise in selecting them, there is an implied warranty that the goods are fit for that particular purpose. *Id.* § 2–315.

43. California Civil Code § 1790 et seq.

44. These provisions only apply to products with express warranties. *Id.* § 1793.2. Other jurisdictions also directly regulate the availability of repair. New Zealand's Consumer

Guarantees Act, for example, provides "a guarantee that the manufacturer will take reasonable action to ensure that facilities for repair of the goods and supply of parts for the goods are reasonably available for a reasonable period after the goods are so supplied." Consumer Guarantees Act 1993 § 12. *See also* Christian Twigg-Flesner, *The Law on Guarantees and Repair Work, in* Longer Lasting Products (Tim Cooper, ed., 2010).

45. California Civil Code § 1793.03.
46. *Id.* Regardless of price, device makers are required to maintain service and repair facilities in California – either their own or under contract with third-party providers. *Id.* § 1793.2.
47. If it were an independent nation, California would be the fifth-largest economy on the planet. *California Is Now the World's Fifth-Largest Economy, Surpassing United Kingdom*, Los Angeles Times (May 4, 2018), www.latimes.com/business/la-fi-california-economy-gdp-20180504-story.html.
48. Bahr v. Canon U.S.A., Inc., 656 F. App'x 276, 277 (9th Cir. 2016).
49. California Civil Code § 1793.2.
50. *Id.* § 1793.03. The statute defines "independent repair or service facility" and "independent service dealer" as "any individual, partnership, corporation, association, or other legal entity, not an employee or subsidiary of a manufacturer or distributor, that engages in the business of servicing and repairing consumer goods." *Id.* § 1791; *see also* Bronson v. Samsung Elecs. Am., Inc., No. 3:18-CV-02300-WHA, 2019 WL 2299754 (N.D. Cal. May 30, 2019).
51. Directive (EU) 2019/771, art. 7.
52. *Id.* art. 10.
53. Norwegian Consumer Sales Act, nr. 34, § 27 (2002). *See also* Eléonore Maitre-Ekern & Carl Dalhammar, *A Scandinavian Perspective on the Role of Consumers in the Circular Economy, in* Consumer Protection in a Circular Economy (Bert Keirsbilck & Evelyne Terryn, eds., 2019).
54. Sale of Goods and Supply of Services Act (1980).
55. Directive (EU) 2019/771, art. 10.
56. *Id.* art 13.
57. Stefan Wrbka & Larry A. DiMatteo, *Comparative Warranty Law: Case of Planned Obsolescence*, 21 University of Pennsylvania Journal of Business Law 907 (2019).

58. Uniform Commercial Code § 2–313.
59. 15 U.S.C. § 2302.
60. This provision applies to products that cost more than $10. *Id.* § 2303.
61. *Id.* § 2304.
62. *Id.* § 2302. The FTC has promulgated rules relating to the disclosure of warranty terms, their presale availability, and the use of informal dispute resolution procedures. *See* 16 C.F.R. Parts 701–3.
63. Directive (EU) 2019/771, art. 17.
64. *Id.*
65. 15 U.S.C. § 2302(c).
66. Prohibited Tying, 16 C.F.R. § 700.10 (2015).
67. Nathan Proctor & David Peters, Warranties in the Void (2018).
68. Matthew Gault, *FTC Gives Sony, Microsoft, and Nintendo 30 Days to Get Rid of Illegal Warranty-Void-If-Removed Stickers*, Vice (May 1, 2018), www.vice.com/en_us/article/xw7b3z/war ranty-void-if-removed-stickers-sony-microsoft-nintendo-ftc-letters.
69. Proctor & Peters, *supra* note 67.
70. Mike Cherney, *Apple Fined as Customers Win a Right-to-Repair Fight*, Wall Street Journal (June 19, 2018), www.wsj.com/arti cles/apple-fined-as-customers-win-a-right-to-repair-fight -1529399713.
71. *See* Evelyne Terryn, *A Right to Repair? Towards Sustainable Remedies in Consumer Law*, *in* Consumer Protection in a Circular Economy (Bert Keirsbilck & Evelyne Terryn, eds., 2019).
72. *Id.*
73. Larry A. DiMatteo & Stefan Wrbka, *Planned Obsolescence and Consumer Protection: The Unregulated Extended Warranty and Service Contract Industry*, 28 Cornell Journal of Law & Public Policy 483 (2019).
74. *Id.*
75. 15 U.S.C. § 2301.
76. *Id.* § 2306.
77. DiMatteo & Wrbka, *supra* note 73.
78. *Id.*
79. Directive (EU) 2019/771, art. 2.
80. DiMatteo & Wrbka, *supra* note 73.

81. Tatum v. Chrysler Grp. LLC., 2011 WL 1253847 (D.N.J. Mar. 28, 2011).

82. Proposition de résolution en vue de lutter contre l'obsolescence programmée des produits liés à l'énergie, 5–1251/1, Senat de Belgique (2011); Regierungsentwurf, Deutscher Bundestag: Drucksachen [BT] 17/13917; Disposizioni per il contrasto dell'obsolescenza programmata dei beni di consumo, Open Parlamento (2015).

83. Code de la Consommation L441-2.

84. *Id.* L454-6.

85. Patrick Nelson, *France Goes after Companies for Deliberately Shortening Life of Hardware*, Network World (Jan. 5, 2018), www.networkworld.com/article/3245765/france-goes-after-companies-for-deliberately-shortening-life-of-hardware.html.

86. Chris Morris, *Apple Hit with $27 Million Fine for Slowing Down French iPhones*, Fortune (Feb. 7, 2020), https://fortune.com/2020/02/07/apple-iphone-slowdown-update-fine-france/.

87. Cecilia D'Anastasio, *A Literal Child and His Mom Sue Nintendo over "Joy-Con Drift,"* Wired (Oct. 5, 2020), www.wired.com/story/nintendo-joy-con-lawsuit.

8 Rebuilding Repair

1. Australian Productivity Commission, *Right to Repair Issues Paper* (2020).

2. Aaron Perzanowski, *Consumer Perceptions of the Right to Repair*, 96 Indiana Law Journal 361 (2021).

3. *Id.*

4. *Should You Repair or Replace that Product? How to Save Money on Appliances, Electronics, and Lawn and Yard Gear*, Consumer Reports (Jan. 2014), www.consumerreports.org/cro/magazine/2014/02/repair-or-replace/index.htm.

5. H.R. 2735, 107th Cong. (2001).

6. H.R. 1449, 112th Cong. § 3 (2011).

7. S. 812, 115th Cong. (2017); H.R. 1879, 115th Cong. (2017).

8. S. 812; H.R. 1879.

9. S. 4473, 116th Cong. (2020), H.R. 7956, 116th Cong. (2020).

10. L441-3. The law allows for limited exceptions to this prohibition, defined by regulation, where there is

evidence of safety concerns or other legitimate reasons to limit repair. *Id.*

11. L441-4.
12. L454-6.
13. L441-5.
14. European Parliament, *Towards a More Sustainable Single Market for Business and Consumers* (2020), www.europarl.europa.eu/doceo/document/TA-9–2020–0318_EN.html.
15. H. 4362, 187th Gen. Ct. (Mass. 2012).
16. *Id.*
17. *2012 – Statewide – Question 1, Mass. Election Statistics*, https://electionstats.state.ma.us/ballot_questions/view/6811. To reconcile disparities between the ballot initiative and the House bill, another bill was passed in 2013. H. 3757, 188th Gen. Ct. (Mass. 2013).
18. *Memorandum of Understanding Among Kathleen Schmatz, President & CEO, Auto. Aftermarket Indus. Ass'n, Ray Pohlman, President, Coal. for Auto Repair Equal., Mitch Bainwol, President & CEO, All. Auto. Mfrs., and Michael Stanton, President & CEO, Ass'n Glob. Automakers* (Jan. 15, 2014), www.nastf.org/files/public/OtherReference/MOU_SIGNED_1_15_14.pdf. In exchange for their promise to abide by the substantive terms of the law, carmakers extracted a promise from repair providers to withdraw support and funding for similar bills in other states. *Id.* Notably, Tesla is not a signatory.
19. *Id. See also* Adrian Ma, *Your Car Talks to the Manufacturer. Advocates Want It to Talk to You, Too*, WBUR (Aug. 6, 2019), www.wbur.org/bostonomix/2019/08/06/right-to-repair-ballot-measure.
20. *See* Leah Chan Grinvald & Ofer Tur-Sinai, *Smart Cars, Telematics and Repair*, 54 University of Michigan Journal of Law Reform (2021); Maddie Stone, *Want to Fix Your Own Tesla? Massachusetts Just Made It Easier*, Grist (Nov. 23, 2020), https://grist.org/politics/tesla-want-to-fix-your-own-massachusetts-just-made-it-easier/.
21. Callum Borchers, *Mass. Voters Say "Yes" On Question 1, Expanding Access to Car Repair Data*, WBUR (Nov. 3, 2020), www.wbur.org/news/2020/11/03/ballot-question-1-right-to-repair-passes.
22. Matthew Gault, *Auto Industry Has Spent $25 Million Lobbying against Right to Repair Ballot Measure*, Vice (Sept. 29, 2020),

www.vice.com/en/article/z3ead3/auto-industry-has-spent-dollar25-million-lobbying-against-right-to-repair-ballot-measure; Matthew Gault, *Auto Industry TV Ads Claim Right to Repair Benefits "Sexual Predators,"* Vice (Sept. 1, 2020), www.vice.com/en/article/qj4ayw/auto-industry-tv-ads-claim-right-to-repair-benefits-sexual-predators.

23. Kathryn Rattigan, *Massachusetts Ballot Question 1 Still on the Forefront as Automakers Sue to Block Its Implementation*, National Law Review (Nov. 25, 2020), www.natlawreview.com/article/massachusetts-ballot-question-1-still-forefront-automakers-sue-to-block-its.

24. S.B. 136, 2014 Legis. Assemb., 89th Sess. (S.D. 2014).

25. Those states included: California, Delaware, Florida, Georgia, Hawaii, Illinois, Indiana, Massachusetts, Maryland, Minnesota, Missouri, Montana, Nebraska, North Dakota, Nevada, New Hampshire, New Jersey, New York, Oklahoma, Oregon, Pennsylvania, South Carolina, South Dakota, Vermont, Virginia, Washington, and West Virginia. *California Becomes 20th State in 2019 to Consider Right to Repair Bill*, US PIRG (Mar. 18, 2019), https://uspirg.org/news/usp/california-becomes-20th-state-2019-consider-right-repair-bill; Kevin Purdy, *Right to Repair Is Gaining Ground in 2020*, iFixit (Feb. 14, 2020), www.ifixit.com/News/35606/right-to-repair-is-gaining-ground-in-2020.

26. *We Are the Repair Industry*, Repair Association, www.repair.org/aboutus.

27. Repair Association, *Model State Right-to-Repair Law* (Jan. 22, 2020), www.repair.org/s/2021-Model-R2R-Bill-3.docx.

28. *Id.*

29. *Id.*

30. California Civil Code § 1793.03(b) (requiring manufacturers of electronics and appliances with wholesale prices of $100 or more with express warranties to "make available to service and repair facilities sufficient service literature and functional parts"). Such a requirement undoubtedly increases costs for device makers, some of which may be passed onto consumers indirectly. To the extent such price increases internalize the costs of device production and disposal, they should be celebrated. The costs of legacy support may also slow the introduction of new products, but a reduction in the frequency of minor, incremental improvements meant to

drive product upgrade cycles may be a reasonable tradeoff for achieving a corresponding reduction in the environmental harm of digital consumerism.

31. Kevin O'Reilly, *American Farm Bureau Reaffirms Support for Right to Repair*, US PIRG (Jan. 22, 2020), https://uspirg.org/ blogs/blog/usp/american-farm-bureau-reaffirms-support-right-repair.

32. Agam Shah, *Who Has a Right to Repair Your Farm or Medical Tools?*, ASME (Apr. 16, 2019), www.asme.org/topics-resources/content/has-right-repair-farm-medical-tools.

33. New York Times Editorial Board, *It's Your iPhone. Why Can't You Fix It Yourself?*, New York Times (Apr. 6, 2019), www .nytimes.com/2019/04/06/opinion/sunday/right-to-repair-eli zabeth-warren-antitrust.html.

34. Napoleon Linarthatos, *Apple's Quiet War on Independent Repairmen*, American Conservative (Apr. 10, 2021), www .theamericanconservative.com/articles/david-vs-goliath-and-the-right-to-repair.

35. Matthew Gault, *Bernie Sanders Calls for a National Right-to-Repair Law for Farmers*, Vice (May 5, 2019), www.vice.com/ en_us/article/8xzqmp/bernie-sanders-calls-for-a-national-right-to-repair-law-for-farmers.

36. Team Warren, *Leveling the Playing Field for America's Family Farmers*, Medium (Mar. 27, 2019), https://medium.com/ @teamwarren/leveling-the-playing-field-for-americas-family-farmers-823d1994f067.

37. *See* Jason Koebler, *The Right to Repair Battle Has Come to Silicon Valley*, Vice (Mar. 7, 2018), www.vice.com/en_us/ article/8xdp94/right-to-repair-california-bill; Jason Koebler, *Hospitals Need to Repair Ventilators. Manufacturers Are Making That Impossible*, Vice (Mar. 18, 2020), www.vice.com/amp/ en_us/article/wxekgx/hospitals-need-to-repair-ventilators-manufacturers-are-making-that-impossible; Jason Koebler, *Appliance Companies Are Lobbying to Protect Their DRM-Fueled Repair Monopolies*, Vice (Apr. 25, 2018), www.vice.com/en_us/ article/vbxk3b/appliance-companies-are-lobbying-against-right-to-repair; Jason Koebler, *Apple Is Lobbying against Your Right to Repair iPhones, New York State Records Confirm*, Vice (May 18, 2017), www.vice.com/en/article/nz85y7/apple-is-lobbying-against-your-right-to-repair-iphones-new-york-state-records-confirm; Olivia Solon, *A Right to Repair: Why*

Nebraska Farmers Are Taking on John Deere and Apple, The Guardian (Mar. 6, 2017), www.theguardian.com/environ ment/2017/mar/06/nebraska-farmers-right-to-repair-john-deere-apple.

38. Gault, *supra* note 35; Koebler, *Hospitals Need to Repair Ventilators, supra* note 37.
39. Michael Hiltzik, *How Apple and Other Manufacturers Attack Your Right to Repair Their Products*, L.A. Times (Nov. 16, 2018), www.latimes.com/business/hiltzik/la-fi-hiltzik-right-repair-20181116-story.html.
40. Jason Koebler, *Apple Is Telling Lawmakers People Will Hurt Themselves if They Try to Fix iPhones*, Vice (Apr. 30, 2019), www.vice.com/en_us/article/wjvdb4/apple-is-telling-law makers-people-will-hurt-themselves-if-they-try-to-fix-iphones.
41. Koebler, *Appliance Companies, supra* note 37.
42. Sam Metz, *Big Tech and Independent Shops Clash over "Right to Repair,"* Associated Press (Mar. 29, 2021), www.apnews.com/ article/legislature-nevada-coronavirus-pandemic-laws-5ade405a7befdf16e9f0107b7e142be3.
43. *Statement of Principles*, Securepairs, www.securepairs.org/ statement-of-principles.
44. Dennis Slater, *The "Right to Repair" Is a Complicated Issue*, Wall Street Journal (Apr. 5, 2021), www.wsj.com/articles/the-right-to-repair-is-a-complicated-issue-11617643453.
45. Paul Roberts, *How Big Ag Weaponizes the Clean Air Act to Keep Its Repair Monopoly*, Fight to Repair (Feb. 19, 2021), https://fight torepair.substack.com/p/how-big-ag-weaponizes-the-clean-air.
46. Kevin O'Reilly, *Deere in the Headlights*, US PIRG Education Fund (2021), https://uspirg.org/sites/pirg/files/reports/ DeereInTheHeadlights/WEB_USP_Deere-in-the-Headlights_ V3.pdf.
47. Koebler, *Hospitals Need to Repair Ventilators, supra* note 37.
48. *Id.*
49. US Food & Drug Administration, *FDA Report on the Quality, Safety, and Effectiveness of Servicing of Medical Devices* (2018), www.fda.gov/media/113431/download.
50. *Id.*
51. *Two-Thirds of Surveyed Medical Equipment Repair People Say They Have Fixed Machinery the Manufacturer Could Not*, US PIRG (Oct. 8, 2020), https://uspirg.org/news/usp/two-thirds-sur

veyed-medical-equipment-repair-people-say-they-have-fixed-machinery.

52. Samantha Masunaga, *California Companies Jump in to Supply Ventilators Needed in Coronavirus Fight*, L.A. Times (Mar. 23, 2020), www.latimes.com/business/story/2020–03–23/coro navirus-california-companies-medical-supplies.

53. Perzanowski, *supra* note 2.

54. Michael S. Sharbaugh, Andrew D. Althouse, Floyd W. Thoma, Joon S. Lee, Vincent M. Figueredo & Suresh R. Mulukutla, *Impact of Cigarette Taxes on Smoking Prevalence from 2001–2015: A Report Using the Behavioral and Risk Factor Surveillance Survey (BRFSS)*, PLoS ONE (2018), www.ncbi.nlm .nih.gov/pmc/articles/PMC6147505/.

55. S. Gouchoe, V. Everette & R. Haynes, *Case Studies on the Effectiveness of State Financial Incentives for Renewable Energy*, National Renewable Energy Laboratory, NREL/SR-620–32819 (2002), www.nrel.gov/docs/fy02osti/32819.pdf.

56. Alexander Starritt, *Sweden Is Paying People to Fix their Belongings Instead of Throwing Them Away*, World Economic Forum (Oct. 27, 2016), www.weforum.org/agenda/2016/10/ sweden-is-tackling-its-throwaway-culture-with-tax-breaks-on-repairs-will-it-work.

57. Markus Piringer & Irene Schanda, *Austria Makes Repair More Affordable*, Right to Repair (Sept. 22, 2020), https://repair.eu/ news/austria-makes-repair-more-affordable/.

58. Raphaella Stavrinou, *France Offers Bike Repair Subsidies to Boost Cycling Post-Lockdown*, New Europe (May 1, 2020), www.new europe.eu/article/france-offers-bike-repair-subsidies-to-boost-cycling-post-lockdown.

59. Department of Housing and Urban Development, *Home Investment Partnership Program*, https://www.hud.gov/progra m_offices/comm_planning/home; Department of Housing and Urban Development, *Income Limits*, https://www .hudexchange.info/programs/home/home-income-limits; Federal Transit Administration, *Job Access and Reverse Commute Program*, www.transit.dot.gov/funding/grants/grant-programs/ job-access-and-reverse-commute-program-5316; Department of Consumer Affairs, *Consumer Assistance Program*, www.bar.ca .gov/Consumer/Consumer_Assistance_Program.

60. James Ellsmoor, *United States Spend Ten Times More on Fossil Fuel Subsidies than Education*, Forbes (June 15, 2019), www

.forbes.com/sites/jamesellsmoor/2019/06/15/united-states-spend-ten-times-more-on-fossil-fuel-subsidies-than-educa tion/?sh=7e21ef974473.

61. Dan Charles, *Farmers Got Billions from Taxpayers in 2019, and Hardly Anyone Objected*, NPR (Dec. 31, 2019), www.npr.org/sec tions/thesalt/2019/12/31/790261705/farmers-got-billions-from-taxpayers-in-2019-and-hardly-anyone-objected.
62. National Telecommunications and Information Administration, *NTIA Welcomes Congressional Action on DTV Delay as Opportunity for More Americans to Prepare for the End of the Digital TV Transition* (Feb. 5, 2009), www.ntia.doc.gov/press-release/2009/commerces-ntia-welcomes-congressional-action-dtv-delay-opportunity-more-americans.
63. Canada has embraced some aspects of extended producer responsibility as well. Government of Canada, *Overview of Extended Producer Responsibility in Canada*, www.canada.ca/en/environment-climate-change/services/managing-redu cing-waste/overview-extended-producer-responsibility.html. In the United States, the concept has been recognized, to varying degrees, by a handful of states, but has yet to catch on more broadly. *See* Emily G. Brown, *Time to Pull the Plug? Empowering Consumers to Make End-of-Life Decisions for Electronic Devices through Eco-Labels and Right to Repair*, 2020 University of Illinois Journal of Law Technology & Policy 227 (2020).
64. Directive (EU) 2018/852; Directive 2000/53/EC; Directive 2012/19/EU.
65. *Smartphone Repairability Scores*, iFixit, www.ifixit.com/smart phone-repairability.
66. 15 U.S.C. § 1064. The certifying entity is required to maintain exclusive control over the mark and certify any goods that meet its established criteria. And it has to refrain from selling any goods of its own.
67. *See, e.g.*, Mauro Cordella, Felice Alfieri & Javier Sanfelix, *Analysis and Development of a Scoring System for Repair and Upgrade of Products*, European Commission, Joint Research Centre (2019).
68. Ministère de la Transition Écologique, *Instructions Manual for the Calculation of the Repairability Index of Electrical and Electronic Equipments* (2021).

69. Adéle Chasson, *French Repairability Index: What to Expect in January?*, Right to Repair (Nov. 3, 2020), http://repair.eu/news/french-repairability-index-what-to-expect-in-january/.
70. Aaron Perzanowski & Jason Schultz, The End of Ownership (2016).
71. Rolls-Royce, *Rolls-Royce Celebrates 50th Anniversary of Power-by-the-Hour* (Oct. 30, 2012), www.rolls-royce.com/media/press-releases-archive/yr-2012/121030-the-hour.aspx.
72. Ellen MacArthur Foundation, *Selling Light as a Service*, www.ellenmacarthurfoundation.org/case-studies/selling-light-as-a-service.
73. Jordan Novet, *Amazon's Cloud Division Reports 28% Revenue Growth; AWS Head Andy Jassy to Succeed Bezos as Amazon CEO*, CNBC (Feb. 2, 2021), www.cnbc.com/2021/02/02/aws-earnings-q4-2020.html.
74. Sapna Maheshwari, *They See It. They Like It. They Want It. They Rent It.*, New York Times (June 8, 2019), www.nytimes.com/2019/06/08/style/rent-subscription-clothing-furniture.html; Sarah Butler, *Kitchen for Rent? Ikea to Trial Leasing of Furniture*, The Guardian (Feb. 4, 2019), www.theguardian.com/business/2019/feb/04/kitchen-for-rent-ikea-to-trial-leasing-of-furniture.
75. Bosch, *Papillon Project*, www.bosch.com/stories/papillon-project.
76. Bert Keirsbilck & Sandra Rousseau, *The Marketing Stage: Fostering Sustainable Consumption Choices in a "Circular" and "Functional" Economy*, in Consumer Protection in a Circular Economy (Bert Keirsbilck & Evelyne Terryn, eds., 2019).
77. Michael Corkery & Jessica Silver-Greenberg, *Miss a Payment? Good Luck Moving that Car*, New York Times (Sept. 24, 2014), https://dealbook.nytimes.com/2014/09/24/miss-a-payment-good-luck-moving-that-car/.
78. Scott McCartney, *Rental Cars with Higher Mileage Populate Lots*, Wall Street Journal (Aug. 28, 2013), www.wsj.com/articles/SB10001424127887324463604579040870991145200.
79. Daniela K. Rosner & Morgan Ames, *Designing for Repair? Infrastructures and Materialities of Breakdown*, Proceedings of Seventeenth ACM Conference on Computer-Supported Cooperative Work and Social Computing 319 (2014).
80. Patagonia, *Worn Wear*, https://wornwear.patagonia.com/repairs.

81. Nudie Jeans, *Repair Spots*, www.nudiejeans.com/repair-spots.

82. Red Wing Shoes, *Repairs*, www.redwingshoes.com/custo mer-service-contact-us/repairs.html.

83. Zippo, *Repairs: Windproof Lighter*, www.zippo.com/pages/ repairs-windproof-lighter.

84. Manuela Kasper-Claridge, *Bas van Abel: "We're Suffering from Electronic Anorexia,"* DW (Sept. 26, 2018), www.dw.com/en/ bas-van-abel-were-suffering-from-electronic-anorexia /a-45649263.

85. Jon Porter, *You Can Buy Fairphone's New Handset or Just Its Cameras as an Upgrade*, The Verge (Aug. 27, 2020), www .theverge.com/2020/8/27/21375326/fairphone-3-plus-release-date-news-features-cameras-ethical-sustainable.

86. *Fairphone 3 Teardown*, iFixit (Sept. 11, 2019), www.ifixit.com /Teardown/Fairphone+3+Teardown/125573#.

87. Samuel Gibbs, *Fairphone 3 Review: The Most Ethical and Repairable Phone You Can Buy*, The Guardian (Sept. 18, 2019), www.theguardian.com/technology/2019/sep/18/fairphone-3-review-ethical-phone.

88. *Shiftphones*, www.shiftphones.com/en/.

89. D. Cooper, *Startup Designs a Modular, Repairable Laptop*, Engadget (Feb. 25, 2021), www.engadget.com/framework-laptop-modular-repairable-swappable-right-to-repair -150022495.html.

90. *Mac Pro 2019 Teardown*, iFixit (Dec. 17, 2019), www.ifixit.com /Teardown/Mac+Pro+2019+Teardown/128922.

91. Chaim Gartenberg, *Apple's Most Expensive Mac Pro costs $53,799*, The Verge (Dec. 10, 2019), www.theverge.com/cir cuitbreaker/2019/12/10/21003636/apple-mac-pro-price-most-expensive-processor-ram-gpu.

92. Kasey Hou, *Repairable Flatpack Toaster*, www.kaseyhou.com /repairable-flatpack-toaster.

93. Kevin Purdy, *What Is Stretch Release Adhesive (and Why Do We Love It)?*, iFixit (Oct. 28, 2020), www.ifixit.com/News/45779/ask-ifixit-what-is-stretch-release-adhesive-and-why-do-we-love-it.

94. Miles Park, *Print to Repair: Opportunities and Constraints of 3D Printing Replacement Parts*, Product Lifetimes and the Environment (2015), www.plateconference.org/print-repair-opportunities-constraints-3d-printing-replacement-parts; Serena Cangiano & Zoe Romano, *Ease of Repair as a Design Ideal: A Reflection on How Open Source Models Can*

Support Longer Lasting Ownership of, and Care for, Technology, 19 Ephemera 441 (May 2019); Matthew Rimmer, *3D Printing, the Maker Movement, IP Litigation and Legal Reform*, WIPO Magazine (Oct. 2019), www.wipo.int/wipo_magazine/en/2019/05/article_0007.html.

95. Yu Yanagisawa, Yiling Nan, Kou Okuro & Takuzo Aida, *Mechanically Robust, Readily Repairable Polymers Via Tailored Noncovalent Cross-Linking*, Science (Jan. 5, 2018), https://science.sciencemag.org/content/359/6371/72.full.

96. Youngnam Kim, Ki-Ho Nam, Yong Chae Jung & Haksoo Han, *Interfacial Adhesion And Self-Healing Kinetics of Multi-Stimuli Responsive Colorless Polymer Bilayers*, 203 Composites Part B: Engineering (2020).

97. US Patent Application No. 16/774948 (Oct. 1, 2020).

98. *See* 49 U.S.C. §§ 30101–12.

99. Energy Policy and Conservation Act of 1975, Pub. L. No. 94–163, 89 Stat. 871.

100. Associated Press, *Consumer Tech U.S. Sales to Reach Record $422 Billion in 2020; Streaming Services Spending Soars, Says CTA*, Press Release (Jan. 6, 2020), https://apnews.com/press-release/pr-businesswire/712622c00b204d8c96316abeca61d41e. The environmental externalities of some products, like plastic lollipop handles with glowing LEDs that sell for a few cents at wholesale, outweigh their utility and ought to be banned entirely.

101. Directive 2009/125/EC. Despite Brexit, the United Kingdom is implementing these rules as well. Roger Harrabin, *"Right to Repair" Law to Come in This Summer*, BBC (Mar. 10, 2021), www.bbc.com/news/amp/business-56340077.

102. Annexes to the Commission Regulation Laying Down Ecodesign Requirements for Refrigerating Appliances, SEC (2019) 333 final, Oct. 1, 2019; Annexes to the Commission Regulation Laying Down Ecodesign Requirements for Electronic Displays, SEC (2019) 339 final, Oct. 1, 2019; Annexes to the Commission Regulation Laying Down Ecodesign Requirements for Household Dishwashers, SEC (2019) 348 final, Oct. 1, 2019; Annexes to the Commission Regulation Laying Down Ecodesgin Requirements for Household Washing Machines and Household Washer-Dryers, SEC (2019) 337 final, Oct. 1, 2019.

103. Commission Regulation 2019/424, Laying Down Ecodesign Requirements for Servers and Data Storage Products, Mar. 15, 2019.

104. European Commission, *Questions and Answers: A New Circular Economy Action Plan for a Cleaner and More Competitive Europe* (Mar. 11, 2020), https://ec.europa.eu/com mission/presscorner/detail/en/qanda_20_419; European Commission, *Designing Mobile Phones and Tablets to Be Sustainable*, https://ec.europa.eu/info/law/better-regulation /have-your-say/initiatives/12797-Designing-mobile-phones -and-tablets-to-be-sustainable-ecodesign_en.

105. Charlie Wood & Sophia Ankel, *Europe May Force Makers of Smartphones, Tablets and Wireless Earphones to Install Easily Replaceable Batteries*, Business Insider (Feb. 27, 2020), www.businessinsider.com/europe-smartphone-tablet-wireless-earphone-makers-replaceable-batteries-propo sal-2020-2.

106. Anu Bradford, *The Brussels Effect*, 107 Northwestern University Law Review 1 (2012).

107. Walter Isaacson, Steve Jobs (2011).

108. Michael Braungart & William McDonough, Cradle to Cradle: Remaking the Way We Make Things (2002); Ken Webster, The Circular Economy: A Wealth of Flows (2015).

109. Sahra Svensson-Hoglund, Jennifer D. Russell, Jessika Luth Richter & Carl Dalhammar, *A Future of Fixing: Upscaled Repair Activities Envisioned Using a Circular Economy Repair Society System Framework*, Electronics Goes Green, International Congress Proceedings, 434 (2020), https:// online.electronicsgoesgreen.org/wp-content/uploads/ 2020/10/Proceedings_EGG2020_v2.pdf.

110. Lisa S. McNeill, Robert P. Hamlin, Rachel H. McQueen, Lauren Degenstein, Tony C. Garrett, Linda Dunn & Sarah Wakes, *Fashion Sensitive Young Consumers and Fashion Garment Repair: Emotional Connections to Garments as a Sustainability Strategy*, 44 International Journal of Consumer Studies 361 (2020); Alex Lobos & Callie W. Babbitt, *Integrating Emotional Attachment and Sustainability in Electronic Product Design*, 4 Challenges 19 (2013).

111. Jonathan Chapman, *Design for (Emotional) Durability*, 25 Design Issues 29 (Autumn 2009).

112. Russell W. Belk, *Possessions and the Extended Self*, 15 Journal of Consumer Research 139 (1988).
113. Carey K. Morewedge, Ashwani Monga, Robert W. Palmatier, Suzanne B. Shu & Deborah A. Small, *Evolution of Consumption: A Psychological Ownership Framework*, 85 Journal of Marketing 196 (2021).
114. Dennis de Vries, *Fairphone Founder Bas van Abel About Turning a Bunch of Rocks into a Smartphone*, Silicon Anals (Sept. 3, 2020), https://siliconcanals.com/news/fairphone-3-plus-bas-van-abel-interview/.
115. Keep America Beautiful, *Litter in America*, https://kab.org/wp-content/uploads/2019/11/LitterinAmerica_FactSheet_CostsofLittering.pdf.
116. Harald Fuller-Bennett & Iris Velez, *Woody at 40*, Forest History Today 22 (Spring 2012).
117. Keep America Beautiful was created and funded by the US packaging industry. Whatever good its ad campaign achieved for environmental awareness, it was designed in part to deflect responsibility and minimize corporate responsibility. Finis Dunaway, *The "Crying Indian" Ad that Fooled the Environmental Movement*, Chicago Tribune (Nov. 21, 2017), www.chicagotribune.com/opinion/commentary/ct-perspec-indian-crying-environment-ads-pollution-1123–20171113-story.html.
118. Katie Nodjimbadem, *The Trashy Beginnings of "Don't Mess with Texas": A True Story of the Defining Phrase of the Lone Star State*, Smithsonian Magazine (March 10, 2017), www.smithsonianmag.com/history/trashy-beginnings-dont-mess-texas-180962490/.
119. *Survey: Getting Caught Throwing Trash Out Window More Embarrassing than Cheating on Taxes*, Business Wire (Mar. 29, 2012), www.businesswire.com/news/home/20120329005123/en/Survey-Getting-Caught-Throwing-Trash-Out-Window-More-Embarrassing-Than-Cheating-on-Taxes.
120. Keep America Beautiful, *Littering Behavior in America* (2009), https://kab.org/wp-content/uploads/2019/10/NewsInfo_Research_LitteringBehaviorinAmerica_2009Report_Final.pdf.
121. K. Michael Cummings & Robert N. Proctor, *The Changing Public Image of Smoking in the United States: 1964–2014*, 23 Cancer Epidemiology, Biomarkers & Prevention 32 (2014).

122. Centers for Disease Control and Prevention, *Current Cigarette Smoking Among Adults in the United States*, www .cdc.gov/tobacco/data_statistics/fact_sheets/adult_data/ cig_smoking/index.htm.

123. Gallup, *Tobacco and Smoking*, https://news.gallup.com/poll/ 1717/tobacco-smoking.aspx .

124. *Id.*

125. Katherine Wilson, Tinkering: Australians Reinvent DIY Culture (2017). Since the burden of repair fell largely on women, it was a uniquely gendered variety of patriotism. Phil Goodman, *"Patriotic Femininity": Women's Morals and Men's Morale During the Second World War*, 10 Gender & History 278 (July 1998).

126. Adam Minter, *Don't Drop Your iPhone Now: Repairing It Is a Problem*, Bloomberg Quint (Mar. 28, 2020), www .bloombergquint.com/business/apple-s-rules-make-iphone -repairs-hard-to-get-amid-coronavirus.

127. Peter Chapman, *Mend and Make New – How the Pandemic Reignited a Repairs Revival*, Financial Times (Jan. 30, 2021), www.ft.com/content/d3c30d12-5cde-4f29-b800-1ec015 1a2b9a.

128. Shira Ovide, *The Joys of Fixing Your Own Stuff*, New York Times (May 14, 2020), www.nytimes.com/2020/05/14/tech nology/fixing-gadgets-diy.html.

129. Soo Youn, *Ovens, Dishwashers and Washing Machines Are Breaking Down Like Never Before. But There's Nobody to Fix Them*, Washington Post (Oct. 22, 2020), www.washing tonpost.com/road-to-recovery/2020/10/22/appliance-repair -services-pandemic.

130. Darrel Moore, *Gen Z Londoners Lead the Way in Repair Culture*, Circular (Oct. 8, 2020), www.circularonline.co.uk/news/ gen-z-londoners-lead-the-way-in-repair-culture.

131. European Commission, *Behavioural Study on Consumers' Engagement in the Circular Economy* (Oct. 2018), https://ec .europa.eu/info/sites/default/files/ec_circular_economy_fi nal_report_0.pdf.

132. Perzanowski, *supra* note 2.

133. Meghan Racklin, *Instead of Hiding Rips and Tears, the Visible Mending Movement Turns Them into Art*, Vox (Mar. 25, 2019), www.vox.com/the-goods/2019/3/25/18274743/visible- mending-sashiko-mending-fast-fashion-movement.

134. Bridget Harvey, *Repair-Making: Craft, Narratives, Activism*, PhD thesis, University of the Arts London (2019), https:// bridgetharvey.co.uk/wp-content/uploads/2020/10/bridget-harvey-pHd-thesis-repair-making-2020.pdf.

135. Steven Kurutz, *Now Is When We All Learn to Darn Our Socks Again*, New York Times (Mar. 12, 2020), www.nytimes.com/2020/03/12/style/visible-mending.html.

136. Although somewhat less memorable, the 2005 animated film *Robots* centers on a young robot named Rodney who thwarts the plans of the evil Bigweld Industries. In a bid to sell expensive upgrades, Bigweld refuses to provide robots the spare parts they need to survive, instead melting them down for raw materials.

137. Leah Chan Grinvald & Ofer Tur-Sinai, *The Right to Repair: Perspectives from the United States*, 31 Australian Intellectual Property Journal 98 (2020).

138. Grosse Pointe Public Library, *Tool Collection*, https://grosse pointelibrary.org/special-collections.

139. Berkeley Public Library, *Tool Lending Library – a Brief History*, www.berkeleypubliclibrary.org/locations/tool-lending-library/tool-lending-library-brief-history; Kevin Williams, *The First Ever Tool Library Was Started in Columbus in 1976 and It's Still a Life-Changing Service Today*, Columbus Navigator, www.columbusnavigator.com/franklin-county-tool-library.

140. Bike Collectives Wiki, *Community Bicycle Organizations*, www.bikecollectives.org/wiki/Community_Bicycle_Organ izations; Sam Bliss, *This Co-op Bike Shop Will Teach You to Fix Your Own Damn Bike (and that Matters)*, Grist (Mar. 11, 2015), https://grist.org/cities/this-co-op-bike-shop-will-teach-you-to-fix-your-own-damn-bike-and-that-matters/.

141. Elizabeth Knight & John Wackman, Repair Revolution: How Fixers Are Transforming Our Throwaway Culture (2020).

142. Tara Bahrampour, *Have Old Broken Stuff? These People will Fix It for You – For Free*, Washington Post (Jan. 15, 2019), www .washingtonpost.com/lifestyle/2019/01/15/dont-throw-out-that-old-clock-these-folks-want-keep-it-ticking.

143. Platform 21, *Repair Manifesto*, www.platform21.nl/down load/4375.

144. Repair Cafe, *Visit a Repair Cafe*, www.repaircafe.org/en/visit.

145. Knight & Wackman, *supra* note 141.
146. PBS News Hour, *The Clinic that Brings Your Broken Toaster Back to Life* (June 19, 2017), www.pbs.org/newshour/show/clinic-brings-broken-toaster-back-life.
147. Restart Project, *The Restart Network*, www.therestartproject.org/groups.
148. Hugh Jeffreys, YouTube, www.youtube.com/channel/ UCQDhxkSxZA6lxdeXE19aoRA; Jon Christian, *The Rogue Tesla Mechanic Resurrecting Salvaged Cars*, Vice (July 27, 2018), www.vice.com/en/article/qvm3z5/rich-rebuilds-tesla-repair-and-salvage.
149. David Whitford, *Meet the $21 Million Company That Thinks a New iPhone Is a Total Waste of Money*, Inc. (Apr. 2017), www.inc.com/magazine/201704/david-whitford/ifixit-repair-men.html.
150. Kyle Wiens, *Why We Fix: A DIY Manifesto*, Popular Mechanics (May 31, 2014), www.popularmechanics.com/home/how-to/a10652/why-we-fix-a-diy-manifesto-16846653.
151. Alex Shprintsen, *"Apple Can't Help": How a Molecular Biologist Trained Stay-at-Home Moms to Recover Lost iPhone Photos*, CBC (Apr. 6, 2019), www.cbc.ca/news/apple-can-t-help-how-a-molecular-biologist-trained-stay-at-home-moms-to-recover-lost-iphone-photos-1.5079639.
152. Testimony of Jessa Jones, www.mgaleg.maryland.gov/ cmte_testimony/2020/ecm/3981_03112020_102826–562.pdf.
153. Luther Ray Abel, *A Computer-Repair Expert Takes on Big Tech*, National Review (July 1, 2020), www.nationalreview.com /2020/07/a-computer-repair-expert-takes-on-big-tech.
154. Louis Rossmann, YouTube, www.youtube.com/channel/ UCl2mFZoRqjw_ELax4Yisf6w.
155. Repair Association, *We Are the Repair Industry*, www .repair.org/members.
156. Brianna Baker, *He's Fighting for Your Right to Repair*, Grist (Dec. 3, 2020), www.grist.org/fix/hes-fighting-for-your-right-to-repair.
157. Right to Repair, *Who We Are*, www.repair.eu/about.
158. Sam Blum, *Motorola Backs the Right to Repair with Kits for Your Phone*, Popular Mechanics (Oct. 24, 2018), www.popularme chanics.com/technology/a24170768/motorola-repair-kits-ifixit.

159. Aimee Chanthadavong, *LG Electronics Calls for Australia to Develop a Right to Repair Framework*, ZDNet (Feb. 8, 2021), www.zdnet.com/google-amp/article/lg-electronics-calls-for-australia-to-develop-a-right-to-repair-framework.

160. Ashley Carman, *Apple Was Conflicted over Right-to-Repair Stance, Emails Show*, Verge (July 30, 2020), www.theverge.com/2020/7/30/21348240/apple-right-to-repair-legislation-antitrust-investigation-policy.

161. Apple, *Environmental Progress Report* (2020), www.apple.com/vn/environment/pdf/Apple_Environmental_Progress_Report_2020.pdf. The company also highlighted a 42% increase in refurbished devices, totaling more than 11 million in 2019.

Epilogue

1. Federal Trade Commission, *Nixing the Fix: An FTC Report to Congress on Repair Restrictions* (May, 2021), www.ftc.gov/system/files/documents/reports/nixing-fix-ftc-report-congress-repair-restrictions/nixing_the_fix_report_final_5521_630pm-508_002.pdf.

2. Federal Trade Commission, *Lina Khan Sworn in as Chair of the FTC* (June 15, 2021), www.ftc.gov/news-events/press-releases/2021/06/lina-khan-sworn-chair-ftc.

3. Exec. Order 14,036, 86 Fed. Reg. 36987 (July 9, 2021).

4. Policy Statement of the Federal Trade Commission on Repair Restrictions Imposed by Manufacturers and Sellers (July 21, 2021), www.ftc.gov/system/files/documents/public_statements/1592330/p194400repairrestrictionspolicystatement.pdf.

Index

3D-printing, 132, 249

Abbott pacemakers, 42
ABPA. *See* Automotive Body Parts
    Association (ABPA)
activation locks, 88
Adams, Douglas, 86
Adams, John, 53
AdvaMed, 232, 234
Advertising and Selling, 57
aftermarket competition, 171–77
air pollution, 36
Alliance for Automotive
    Innovation, 231
allocative efficiency, 191
Amazon, 35, 188, 195, 219
    Apple agreement, 100
    Echo, 75
American Book Company, 113
American Conservative, 232
American Farm Bureau, 232
anticircumvention, 123, 124, 264
antitrust law, 12, 167, 199
    hurdles to, 190–94
    US foundations, 168–71
Apple, 2, 23, 25, 95, 157, 189
    AirPods, 4–6, 77
    Amazon agreement, 100
    Authorized Service Provider
        (AASP) program, 96, 179, 185
    butterfly keyboards, 85
    Daisy robot, 38
    design patent, 139
    Error 53, 87
    iMac, 107, 108

Independent Repair Provider
    (IRP) program, 97, 98, 99, 159,
    179, 185
iPhone, 2, 22, 30, 87, 96, 108,
    158
Mac Pro, 247
MacBooks, 84, 251
    pentalobe screws in, 84
    reconsideration of repair, 262
    recycling program, 37
    restrictions on third-party
        repairs, 167
    software restrictions, 86–93
    software updates, 221
    trade-in incentives, 104
    unlawfully tying parts, 178
Apple
Apple v. Samsung case, 149
architecture, in shaping behavior,
    79
*Aro Manufacturing v. Convertible Top
    Company* case, 127, 129
articles of manufacture, 136, 137
Asia, e-waste recycling, 39
Aspen Skiing v. Aspen Highlands Skiing
    case, 182
assembly line production, 66
AT&T, 169
ATC v. Whatever It Takes case, 114
Audi S4, 86
Australian Productivity
    Commission, 223
authorized repair, 3, 96–100
Automotive Body Parts Association
    (ABPA), 134

Baogang Steel and Rare Earth mine, 32
Baotou, China, 32
Bardeen, John, 65
BART. *See* Bay Area Rapid Transit (BART)
Basel Convention, 29
battery recycling, 38
Bay Area Rapid Transit (BART), 72
Beckett, Samuel, 112
Behr, 115
Bell telephone monopoly, 169
Benoit, Richard, 259
Best Buy, 97, 103, 233
Bingham Canyon copper mine, 31,
bitumen, 50
Black Madonna, 15
Blanc, Honoré, 53, 55
Bloom Energy, 234
BMWs, 151
Bork, Robert, 190
Bosch, 145
    Papillon program, 242, 243
Bougainville, 31
Boussac, Marcel, 63
Brandeis, Louis, 198
Brattain, Walter Houser, 65
Brazil, 257
Bronze Age, 50
Brown & Sharpe, 54
Bryce Fastener, 83
Bumstead, John, 101, 153
Bunner, Andrew, 161
Bureau of Labor Statistics, 23
butterfly keyboards, 85

Calidad, 131
California
    Consumer Legal Remedies Act, 211
    False Advertising Law, 211
    Song-Beverly Act, 214, 232
    Unfair Competition Law, 211
California Farm Bureau, 91
Car Allowance Rebate System, 59
carbon dioxide (CO_2) emission, 34
carbon footprints, of consumer devices, 34
carbon-neutrality goals, 27

Casa Romuli, 50
cash for clunkers program, 59
Caterpillar, 232
cerium, 31
Cerro Rico, 33
Champion, 153
Chanel, 152
Chapman, Johnathan, 252
Chartres Cathedral, restoration of, 15
Chiari, Italy, hospital repair in, 4
child labor, 33,
Chrysler, 148, 221
Church, Douglas, 150
circular economy, 252
circumvention, 119–24
Clarke, Yvette, 228
Clayton Act, 169, 186, 194
climate change, 27, 166
cobalt, 32
    free batteries, 36
coltan, 33
commercial guarantees, 216–19
    paid-for, 219–20
competition law, 167
    in Europe, 194–98
consumer
    behavior, 20, 64, 87, 93, 212, 235, 237
    norms, 104–9
    repair decisions of, 224–27
    welfare, 191, 195
Consumer Financial Protection Bureau, 200
consumer law, 12, 218
    Norway, 215
consumer protection, and repair, 199–200
    perceptions of consumers, 200–6
    unfairness and deception, 206–13
Cook, Tim, 3, 88
Copad v. Dior case, 156
Copyright Act, 120, 121
Copyright Office, 9
copyrights, 9, 111–24, 166
COVID-19 pandemic, 2, 43
    mask wearing, 78
    necessity of repair, 255
Craigslist, 20

Critical Medical Infrastructure
    Right-to-Repair Act, 228
cyanide leaching, 31

Daisy robot, 38
de Dion, Jules-Albert, 1
dead batteries, replacing, 5
death dating, 63
DeCSS program, 161
Defend Trade Secrets Act (DTSA),
    159, 162
Democratic Republic of Congo
    (DRC), 32, 33, 36,
Dennison, Aaron, 54
Department of Justice, 60, 169, 193,
    194
design patents, 133–40
design rights, 140–44
designing barriers, to repair, 81–93
Digital Equipment Corporation
    (DEC), 196
Digital Millennium Copyright Act
    (DMCA), 9, 122, 227
Digital Right to Repair Coalition,
    261
digital rights management (DRM)
    technology, 122, 123, 228
Dior, Christian, 63, 156
distinctiveness, of trademarks,
    145–47
DMCA. *See* Digital Millennium
    Copyright Act (DMCA)
Doan v. American Book Company case,
    113
Doan, George, 113
DTSA. *See* Defend Trade Secrets Act
    (DTSA)
DVD Copy Control Association, 161
Dyson, 143, 232
dysprosium, 31

Easterbrook, Frank, 190
Eastman Kodak, 196
    and aftermarket competition,
    171–77
    monopoly power of, 174
    tying arrangement, 172, 174, 177
eBay
    refurbished devices, 20

Ecodesign Directive, 250, 251
economic benefits, of repair, 11, 18
    cost savings, 22–24
    extending product lifespans,
    18–20
    potential costs, 24–27
    supplying secondary markets,
    20–22
Eisenhower, Dwight, 63
Electronic Frontier Foundation, 119
electronic waste (e-waste), 3, 27–29
    raw materials from, 37
    recycling, 37–41
electronics
    recycling rates, 39
Eli Lilly v Novopharm case, 132
emotional durability, 252
End of Ownership, The, 242
Enlightenment, 52
Entertainment Software
    Association, 232
entropy, 14, 17
environmental benefits, of repair,
    11, 27
    curbing electronic waste, 27–29
    recycling, 37–41
    reducing extraction and produc-
    tion, 30–37
environmental harms, 27
Environmental Protection Agency,
    34, 233
EPR program. *See* extended
    producer responsibility (EPR)
    program
Epson, 131
Equipment Dealers Association,
    232
Europe
    competition law in, 194–98
    e-waste recycling, 39
European Commission
    Behavioural Study on
    Consumers' Engagement in the
    Circular Economy, 205, 225
europium, 31
exclusive dealing, 186–88
exhaustion, 113, 125, 126, 131
    of trademarks, 152–59
express warranties, 216–19

extended producer responsibility
    (EPR) program, 237
extended warranties, 219–20
externalities, 36, 237
extraction and production, 30–37

Facebook, 96, 195
Fair Debt Collection Practices Act,
    200
Fairphone, 246,
false advertising law, 210
FDA. *See* Food and Drug
    Administration (FDA)
Federal Communications
    Commission, 59
Federal Trade Commission, 194
Federal Trade Commission (FTC),
    200, 206
    Nixing the Fix report, 263, 266
Federal Trade Commission Act, 199
first sale doctrine. *See* exhaustion
Fixers Collective, 259
Fixit Clinics, 11
Food and Drug Administration
    (FDA), 234
Ford, 55, 56, 134
    Model T, 45, 55, 95
Ford, Henry, 55
formal recycling, 40
Fowler, Geoffrey, 5
Framework, 247
France, 63
    against planned obsolescence,
        222
    Hamon Law, 221, 222, 229
Frank's Hospital Workshop, 116
Franklin, Benjamin, 106
Franz, Kathleen, 45
Frederick, Christine, 57
Frederick, J. George, 57
free-riding, 175
freeze-plus clause, 142
French repairability index, 239, 241
Friedman, Milton, 190
front-loading washing machines, 85
FTC. *See* Federal Trade Commission
    (FTC)
FTC v. Actavis case, 177
Fuji, 128

functionality, of trademarks,
    147–49
Future Proof, 116

gadolinium, 31
Gauge Act, 73
GE Healthcare, 232
GEEP, 102
General Electric, 60, 92
General Motors, 23, 121, 148
German Federal Cartel Authority,
    195
Gilliam, Terry, 257
gold mines, 31
Goodwill, 21
Google
    AdSense service, 195
    manipulating search results to
        own services, 195
Gordon, Irv, 1
Gordon-Byrne, Gay, 261
Graco, 105
Gravity's Rainbow (novel), 59
Great Depression, 56, 61
Great Migration, 66
greenwashing, 212
grey-market goods, 154, 157
Grinvald, Leah Chan, 165
Grosse Pointe Rotary Club, 258
guarantees, 213–20
    commercial, 216–19
    legal, 213–16
    paid-for commercial, 219–20
Guiyu, China, 40
Gunter, Janet, 259

Halte á l'Obseolescence
    Programmée, 221, 262
Hamon Law, 221, 222, 229
Harper, Douglas, 45
Harvey, Bridget, 257
Hicks, Tim, 116
Hillbilly Highway, 66
Hollywood accounting, 24
Homo neanderthalensis, 50
Homo sapiens, 50
Hou, Kasey, 249
House Judiciary Committee,
    167

Houston, Lara, 44
Huseby, Henrik, 158

IBM, 196
    antitrust law, 170,
iFixit, 11, 80, 118, 160, 238, 256, 259
    Medical Device Repair Database,
        116
    Seal of Reparability, 239
Ikea, 242
Illinois Health and Hospital
    Association, 232
implied warranties, 213–16
implied warranty of habitability, 68
incompatibility, 7
Independent Repair Provider (IRP)
    program, 97, 179
independent service organizations
    (ISOs), 171
industrialization, 49, 52–55, 67
informal recycling, 39, 40
innovation, 16
    repair and, 44
Insignia, 92
intellectual property (IP) laws, 8, 12,
    110, 185
    copyrights, 111–24
    design patents, 133–40
    design rights, 140–44
    trade secrets, 159–64
    trademarks, 144–59
    utility patents, 124–32
interchangeability, 52–55
Internal Revenue Code, 236
International Salt, 170
Internet of Things, 6
Intersil, 187
inventions, 16, 125
IP laws. *See* intellectual property (IP)
    laws
iPad Rehab, 260
Iron Age, 50
ISOs. *See* independent service
    organizations (ISOs)

Javins v. First National Realty Corp case,
    68
Jazz Photo, 128
Jefferson, Thomas, 53,

Jeffreys, Hugh, 259
Jibo, 7, 92
Jobs, Steve, 251, 257
Johansen, Jon, 161
John Deere, 232
John Deere tractors, 9–10, 23, 91,
    154, 189, 233, 255
    tying arrangement, 180
    unauthorized software for,
        121
Jones, Jessa, 158, 260
JSC Jewelry, 156

Kanebridge, 115
Keep America Beautiful, 254
Kelley, Leon, 61
Khan, Lina, 191
Kimberly Clark, 59
kintsugi, 46
Kirkburn sword, 50
Kodak. *See* Eastman Kodak
Kubota tractors, 154

La Marquise, 1
landlords, and law of repair, 66–71
laptop shortage, 4
Lebow, Victor, 63
legal guarantees, 213–16
Leland, Henry, 55
lemon law, 214
Lessig, Lawrence, 78
Lexmark, 126, 131, 232
LG, 232, 262
libraries, 244
lifecycle pricing, 173, 196
littering, 254
London, Bernard, 56, 59, 61
LOX drivers, 83

MacBook Pro, 23, 187
Made to Break, 57
Maestas, Kenny, 42
Magill and *IMS* cases, 197
Magnuson-Moss Warranty Act, 217,
    218, 220, 264, 267
MAI v. Peak case, 120
maintenance, 15, 61
manuals, 113–19
market restrictions, 93–104

Massachusetts repair law, 90, 230, 235
material differences, 154, 155
Maudslay, Henry, 52
Medical Device Repair Database, 116, 118
medical devices, 42, 170, 189, 234
Medtronic, 232
Merchant, Brian, 30
mercury pollution, 31
merger doctrine, 118
Microsoft, 189, 232
    recycling program, 38
    Surface Pro Laptop, 82
Middle Ages, 51
Minter, Adam, 105
misappropriation, 160
monopolization, 168, 174, 181, 191, 192
Monsanto v. Schmeiser case, 132
Moore, Tim, 1
Mortorq drivers, 83
Motor Vehicle Owners Right to Repair Act, 227
Motorola, 262
    Razr, 82
Mui, Peter, 259
must-fit parts, 141

negative externalities, 3
neodymium, 31
Neolithic humans, 50
Nest, 7, 103
New York Times, 232
nickel, 36
Nikon, 99
    Professional Services program, 99
    refusal to deal, 184
    shifting policies, 183
Nintendo, 222
    gamebits, 84
Nitro Leisure v. Acushnet case, 153
nitrogen trifluoride, 34
Nixon, Richard, 73
Nomination, 156
nominative fair uses, 150, 151
nonobviousness, 138, 140
North, Simeon, 54
Norwegian Consumer Law, 215

Notre Dame de Pilar (Black Madonna), 15
Nudie Jeans, 245

obsolescence, 58
    planned, 49, 57, 61, 66, 75, 212, 219, 220–22
    post-war, 62, 63
    progressive, 57
    psychological, 64
    technological, 58
obsolete products, 95
Office of War Information, 62
omissions, of material information, 212
open-pit mines, 31
ornamental design, 20, 133, 139
Orr, Julian, 46
Oscar Mayer Wienermobile, 62

Packard, Vance, 64
paid-for commercial guarantees, 219–20
Paleolithic humans, 50
part numbers, 113–19
PARTS Act. *See* Promoting Automotive Repair, Trade, and Sales (PARTS) Act
Patagonia, 245
Patent And Trademark Office, 134
patents, 111
    design, 133–40
    utility, 124–32
Peak Computing, 119
pentalobe screws, 84,
perfluorocarbons, 34
Philips
    Pay-per-lux offering, 241
Philips screwdrivers, 83
Philips, Anton, 60
Phoebus cartel, 60, 61
PIRG. *See* Public Interest Research Group (PIRG)
planned obsolescence, 49, 57, 61, 66, 75, 212, 219, 220–22
Posner, Richard, 190
Postma, Martine, 259
post-war obsolescence, 62, 63
potential costs, of repair, 24–27

pottery, 50
Pozidriv drivers, 83
praseodymium, 31
predatory product design, 189–90
Printers' Ink, 61
problem-solving skills, 43
Proctor, Nathan, 261
product lifespans, 19, 20, 22, 29, 59, 60, 219, 221
product lifespans, extending, 18–20
progressive obsolescence, 57
Promoting Automotive Repair, Trade, and Sales (PARTS) Act, 227
psychological obsolescence, 64
psychological ownership, 253
Public Interest Research Group (PIRG), 261
Pynchon, Thomas, 59

Qualtex, 143

R&R Products, 114
radioactive waste, 32
rare-earth mining, 31
raw materials
    extraction of, 30
    from e-waste, 37
RDKL, Inc., 101, 153
RealReal, 152
rebuilding repair, 223
    changing design, 246–53
    changing law, 227–35
    changing markets, 235–46
    changing norms, 253–57
    repair decisions of consumers, 224–27
reconstruction, and repair, 128
recycling, 27, 37–41
Red Wing, 245
referential use, of trademarks, 149–52
refurbished goods, 4, 20, 153, 188
refusals to deal, 181–85
Registered Design Act, 143
Renaissance, 52
rental services, 242
repair
    defined, 14

economic benefits. *See* economic benefits, of repair
environmental benefits. *See* environmental benefits, of repair
    innovation and, 44
    maintenance and, 15, 61
    reconstruction and, 128
    restoration and, 15
    social benefits. *See* social benefits, of repair
    subsidizing, 236
repair history, 49
    industrialization and interchangeability, 52–55
    inventing obsolescence, 56–66
    landlords and law of repair, 66–71
    origins, 50–52
repair markets, antitrust theories for, 177
    exclusive dealing, 186–88
    predatory product design, 189–90
    refusals to deal, 181–85
    tying, 177–81
repair restrictions
    authorized repair, 96–100
    consumer norms, 104–9
    designing barriers, 81–93
    limiting resale markets, 100–2
    market restrictions, 93–104
    price and availability, 93–96
    regulating behavior, 78–81
    reparability as design choice, 72–78
    restricting advertising, 102–3
    trade-in programs, 103–4
Repairable Flatpack Toaster, 249
reparability, 6, 238
    as design choice, 72–78
resale markets, limited, 100–2
Restart Parties, 11, 259
restoration, 15
Restriction of Hazardous Substances Directive, 251
Revolv, 7, 92
Right to Repair movement, 257–62
Robertson drivers, 83
Robinson, T.R., 1
Robinson-Patman Act, 169

Rolls Royce
    Power by the Hour program, 241
Roman Empire, 51
Rossmann, Louis, 158, 260

Salisbury Cathedral clock, 1
Samsung, 25
    Galaxy 9, 22
    Galaxy Note, 77, 151
Sanders v Champion case, 153
Sanders, Bernie, 232
sashiko technique, 257
Schultz, Jason, 242
Schütz v Werit case, 130
SEB manufacturer, 208
secondary markets, 20–22, 27
Secondhand, 105
secondhand goods, 21, 105, 152
Securepairs, 233
security screws, 83
self-healing devices, 249
Sherman Act, 168, 172, 186, 194
Sherwin Williams, 115
Shift, 247
Shockley, William Bradford, 65
Simpson, Homer, 38
single-use products, 59
Slade, Giles, 57
Slater, Dennis, 233
Sloan, Alfred, 58
smart devices, 6, 7, 8, 92, 124
smart speakers, 75
smartphones
    breakage of, 2
    outsourcing mental processes to,
        42
Smith of Derby Group, 1
smoking, 254
social benefits, of repair, 11, 41–48
social norms, in shaping behavior,
    79
software design, 86–93
software, and circumvention,
    119–24
Song-Beverly Act, 214, 232
Sonos, and recycle mode, 103
Sony
    PlayStation CO_2 emission, 34
Sotheby's auctions, 21

Soules, Luke, 259
Southco v. Kanebridge case, 115
spanners, 83
Spotify, 195
Stafford, E.S., 63
Standard Oil, 169
Steris, 117, 118
Stevens, Brooks, 62
Stigler, George, 190
Stone Age hunter-gatherers, 48
*Storage Tech. v. Custom Hardware
    Engineering* case, 123
stretch-release adhesive, 249
subscriptions, 242, 243,
    durability and reparability,
        244
Sweitzer, Walter, 91

T2 chip, 88
tantalum, 33
Tatum v. Chrysler case, 221
Taylor, Frederick Winslow, 54
TechNet, 232
Technosport, 152
terbium, 31
Terry, Eli, 54
Tesla, 36
    recycling program, 38
Tesla, Nikola, 257
Theseus, 129
third-party repairs, 167, 175,
    234
thorium, 32
Thrift Weeks (YMCA), 106
Titleist, 153
tool libraries, 258
Toro v. R&R Products case, 114
Torx screws, 83, 84
Toshiba, 116, 160
toxic waste, 3, 28
Toyota, 153, 232
trade dress, 147
    infringement, 148
trade secrets, 111, 159–64
trade-in programs, 8, 93, 103–4, 224
trademarks, 144–59, 264
    distinctiveness, 145–47
    exhaustion and importation,
        152–59

functionality, 147–49
referential use, 149–52
transistor radios, 65
Treaty on the Functioning of the
European Union, 194
Tur-Sinai, Ofer, 165
tying arrangement, 177–81
of Kodak, 172, 174, 177

Uber, 96
Unfair Commercial Practices
Directive, 211
Unfair Competition Law, 211
unfairness and deception, 206–13
Uniform Commercial Code (UCC),
213
Uniform Trade Secrets Act, 159
uranium, 32
urbanization, 66
utility patents, 124–32

Vallauri, Ugo, 259
value-added tax (VAT), for repairs,
236
van Abel, Bas, 246, 253
Varadarajan, Deepa, 162
Verizon, 232
vintage products, 95
visible mending, 257
Volkswagen, 150

Beetle, 245
Volvo, 196

Wahl, 82, 232,
warranties, 213–20
express, 216–19
extended, 219–20
implied, 213–16
repairs, 24, 167
Warren, Elizabeth, 232
washing machines, 85
Waste Makers, The, 64
Wheatley, Russell, 117
Whitney, Eli, 53, 55
Wiens, Kyle, 259
Wilson v. Simpson case, 126
Wireless Alliance, 88
Woodsy Owl, 254
Wright, Orville, 45
Wright, Wilbur, 45
Wyden, Ron, 228

Xerox, 46, 176

Young Men's Christian Association
(YMCA), 106
yttrium, 31

Zenith, 65
Zippo lighters, 245